READING THE POETRY OF FIRST ISAIAH

For Tom Trimble,
With deep gratitude for
all that you have taught
me.

[signature]
1/24/17

Reading the Poetry of First Isaiah

The Most Perfect Model of the Prophetic Poetry

J. BLAKE COUEY

OXFORD
UNIVERSITY PRESS

OXFORD
UNIVERSITY PRESS

Great Clarendon Street, Oxford, OX2 6DP,
United Kingdom

Oxford University Press is a department of the University of Oxford.
It furthers the University's objective of excellence in research, scholarship,
and education by publishing worldwide. Oxford is a registered trade mark of
Oxford University Press in the UK and in certain other countries

© J. Blake Couey 2015

The moral rights of the author have been asserted

First Edition published in 2015

Impression: 1

All rights reserved. No part of this publication may be reproduced, stored in
a retrieval system, or transmitted, in any form or by any means, without the
prior permission in writing of Oxford University Press, or as expressly permitted
by law, by licence or under terms agreed with the appropriate reprographics
rights organization. Enquiries concerning reproduction outside the scope of the
above should be sent to the Rights Department, Oxford University Press, at the
address above

You must not circulate this work in any other form
and you must impose this same condition on any acquirer

Published in the United States of America by Oxford University Press
198 Madison Avenue, New York, NY 10016, United States of America

British Library Cataloguing in Publication Data
Data available

Library of Congress Control Number: 2014957418

ISBN 978-0-19-874355-2

Printed and bound by
CPI Group (UK) Ltd, Croydon, CR0 4YY

Links to third party websites are provided by Oxford in good faith and
for information only. Oxford disclaims any responsibility for the materials
contained in any third party website referenced in this work.

In memory of Bobby R. Couey
1933–2009

Preface

This work is a substantially revised version of my doctoral dissertation, which I completed in 2009 at Princeton Theological Seminary. Portions of Chapters 2 and 3 appeared in two previous publications: "The Disabled Body Politic in Isaiah 3:1, 8," *Journal of Biblical Literature* 133 (2014): 95–109; and "Evoking and Evading: The Poetic Presentation of the Moabite Catastrophe in Isaiah 15–16," in *Concerning the Nations: Essays on the Oracles Against the Nations in Isaiah, Jeremiah, and Ezekiel* (eds. Andrew Mein, Else K. Holt, and Hyun Chul Paul Kim. Library of Hebrew Bible/Old Testament Studies 612; New York: Bloomsbury T&T Clark, 2015), 19–31. I am grateful to the Society of Biblical Literature and Bloomsbury Publishing for allowing me to reuse this material.

The process of writing and revising this book has provided an occasion for reflection on the literary (to use the term very loosely) characteristics of scholarly monographs. A section of acknowledgments such as this one is a standard feature of that genre. The generic character of the following remarks, however, in no way means that the gratitude expressed in them is any less sincere or heartfelt. First and foremost, I must acknowledge my substantial debt to my dissertation advisor, F. W. Dobbs-Allsopp, who has both expertly taught me how to interpret biblical poetry and enthusiastically modeled how to delight in it. He consistently pushed me to be more rigorous in my analysis and more precise in my description. He remains for me the model of a careful and gracious biblical scholar, and my work is infinitely better for his guidance and friendship. I am also deeply grateful for the perceptive critique and unflagging support of my other committee members, Jacqueline Lapsley and J. J. M. Roberts. I especially thank Professor Roberts for his willingness to remain on my committee beyond his retirement from Princeton Theological Seminary. All of them greatly impacted the direction of my scholarship even before I began work on my dissertation; my dual interests in biblical poetry and First Isaiah stem from M.Div. courses with Professors Dobbs-Allsopp and Roberts in 2001, while Professor Lapsley introduced me to critical literary methods and theory in my first Ph.D. seminar in 2002.

At various stages along the way, a number of teachers, colleagues, and friends have provided feedback on this project, including Peter Altmann, James Charlesworth, Casey Elledge, Jeremy Hutton, Tod Linafelt, Dennis Olson, Katharine Doob Sakenfeld, Jeremy Schipper, Leong Seow, Brent Strawn, and the anonymous reviewers who read the manuscript for Oxford University Press. Their suggestions have greatly improved this book; any remaining errors or infelicities are, of course, my own responsibility.

Additional thanks go to the many teachers in high school and college who fostered my love for poetry of all kinds; to Karen Raith and Tom Perridge of Oxford University Press for their patient and perceptive editorial assistance; and to my colleagues at Millsaps College and Gustavus Adolphus College for their encouragement and support through the later stages of this project. The John S. Kendall Center for Engaged Learning at Gustavus Adolphus College regularly sponsors writing retreats for faculty, which were immensely helpful as I was revising this book.

My dissertation was dedicated to my grandfather, Bobby R. Couey, a longtime Sunday School teacher at the church in which I grew up. Over the years, he and I had many delightful conversations about biblical texts, and his commitment to the study of the Bible remains an inspiration to me. Sadly, "Big Daddy" died in August 2009, but he lived long enough to see my completed dissertation and read the dedication. I now dedicate this work to his memory.

Finally, but certainly not least, I thank my parents Steve and Vanessa Couey for their continued love and support, and my partner Jonathan Henke for the many kinds of poetry that he has brought into my life over the past seven years.

J. Blake Couey

St. Peter, Minnesota, USA
January 2015

Contents

Sigla and Abbreviations	xi
Introduction: "The Most Perfect Model of the Prophetic Poetry"	1
Isaiah and the Study of Biblical Poetry	4
Poetry and History	14
Plan of this Study	18
1. The Line in First Isaiah	21
The Problem of Lineation in Biblical Hebrew Verse	22
Markers of Lineation	27
Reading of Isaiah 22:1b–14	54
2. Structure and Movement	68
The Couplet	69
Triplets, Quatrains, Larger Groups, and Single Lines	95
From Line Groups to Poems	108
Reading of Isaiah 3:1–15	127
3. Imagery and Metaphor	139
Theory and Method	140
Agricultural Imagery	147
Animal Imagery	165
Reading of Isaiah 1:2–20	186
Conclusion: "More or Less Happy Misunderstandings"	201
Bibliography	209
Index of Selected Authors	233
Index of Biblical and other Ancient Texts	236
Index of Subjects	244

Sigla and Abbreviations

*	hypothetical or unattested form
√	root
1 Kgs	First Kings
1 Sam	First Samuel
1QIsa^a	Qumran Cave 1, Isaiah Scroll A (Great Isaiah Scroll)
2 Chr	Second Chronicles
2 Kgs	Second Kings
2 Sam	Second Samuel
AB	Anchor Bible
ABD	Anchor Bible Dictionary
ACEBT	*Amsterdamse Cahiers voor Exegese en bijbelse Theologie*
Akk.	Akkadian
ANEP	*The Ancient Near East in Pictures.* J. B. Pritchard. 2nd ed. Princeton, 1969
Aq.	Aquila
Arab.	Arabic
Aram.	Aramaic
ARM	Archives royales de Mari
ASOR	American Schools of Oriental Research
Bauer-Leander	Bauer, H. and P. Leander. *Historische Grammatik der hebräischen Sprache des Alten Testamentes*
BDB	Brown, F., S. R. Driver, and C. A. Briggs. *A Hebrew and English Lexicon of the Old Testament.* Oxford, 1907
*BH*³	*Biblical Hebraica.* Edited by R. Kittel. 3rd ed. Stuttgart, 1937
BHS	*Biblia Hebraica Stuttgartensia.* Edited by K. Elliger and W. Rudolph. Stuttgart, 1983
Bib	*Biblica*
Bibl. Heb.	Biblical Hebrew
BibOr	*Biblica et Orientalia*
BRev	*Bible Review*
BZAW	Beihefte zur Zeitschrift für die alttestamentliche Wissenchaft
CAD	*The Assyrian Dictionary of the Oriental Institute of the University of Chicago.* Chicago, 1956–
CBQ	*Catholic Biblical Quarterly*
CC	Continental Commentary

xii   Sigla and Abbreviations

CHP	Classical Hebrew Poetry. W. G. Watson. Journal for the Study of the Old Testament: Supplement Series 26. Sheffield, 1986
CR:BS	Currents in Research: Biblical Studies
Dan	Daniel
Deut	Deuteronomy
DNWSI	Dictionary of the North-West Semitic Inscriptions. J. Hoftijzer and K. Jongeling. 2 vols. Leiden, 1995
Eng.	English
Esth	Esther
Exod	Exodus
Ezek	Ezekiel
fig(s).	figure(s)
Gen	Genesis
GBS	Guides to Biblical Scholarship
GKC	Gesenius' Hebrew Grammar. Edited by E. Kautsch. Translated by A. E. Cowley. 2nd ed. Oxford, 1910
Hab	Habakkuk
Hag	Haggai
HALOT	The Hebrew and Aramaic Lexicon of the Old Testament. L. Koehler, W. Baumgartner, and J. J. Stamm. Translated and edited under the supervision of M. E. J. Richardson. 4 vols. Leiden, 1994–1999
HAR	Hebrew Annual Review
HB	Hebrew Bible
HO	Handbuch der Orientalistik
Hos	Hosea
HSM	Harvard Semitic Monographs
HTKAT	Herders Theologischer Kommentar zum Alten Testament
HTR	Harvard Theological Review
HVS	Hebrew Verse Structure. M. O'Connor. 2nd ed. Winona Lake, Ind., 1997
ICC	International Critical Commentary
IBHS	An Introduction to Biblical Hebrew Syntax. B. K. Waltke and M. O'Connor. Winona Lake, Ind., 1990
Isa	Isaiah
JAOS	Journal of the American Oriental Society
JBL	Journal of Biblical Literature
Jer	Jeremiah
JNSL	Journal of Northwest Semitic Languages
Josh	Joshua
Joüon	Joüon, P. A Grammar of Biblical Hebrew. Translated and revised by T. Muraoka. 2 vols. Subsidia biblica 14/1–2. Rome, 1991

Sigla and Abbreviations

JQR	*Jewish Quarterly Review*
JSOT	*Journal for the Study of the Old Testament*
JSOTSup	*Journal for the Study of the Old Testament*: Supplement Series
JSS	*Journal of Semitic Studies*
JTS	*Journal of Theological Studies*
Judg	Judges
K	Kethib
KAI	*Kanaanäische und aramäische Inschriften.* H. Donner and W. Röllig. Wiesbaden, 1962–64
KJV	King James Version
KTU²	*The Cuneiform Alphabetic Texts from Ugarit, Ras Ibn Hani, and Other Places.* Edited by M. Dietrich, O. Loretz, and J. Sanmartín. 2nd ed. Abhandlungen zur Literatur Alt-Syren-Palästinas und Mesopotamiens 8. Münster, 1995
Lam	Lamentations
Lev	Leviticus
LHBOTS	Library of Hebrew Bible/Old Testament Studies
LXX	Septuagint
LXX^L	Septuagint, Lucianic recension
Mal	Malachi
Matt	Matthew
Mic	Micah
Mid. Heb.	Middle Hebrew
ms(s).	manuscript(s)
MT	Masoretic Text
MT^A	Codex Aleppo
MT^L	Codex Leningrad
NAB	New American Bible
Nah	Nahum
NASB	New American Standard Bible
NEB	New English Bible
Neh	Nehemiah
NIB	*New Interpreter's Bible*
NIDB	*New Interpreter's Dictionary of the Bible*
NIV	New International Version
NJB	New Jerusalem Bible
NJPS	*Tanakh: The Holy Scriptures: The New JPS Translation according to the Traditional Hebrew Text*
NRSV	New Revised Standard Version
NS	New Series
Num	Numbers
OBO	Orbis Biblicus et Orientalis

	Sigla and Abbreviations
OTL	Old Testament Library
OtSt	*Oudtestamentische Studiën*
Prov	Proverbs
Ps(s)	Psalm(s)
Q	Qere
Qoh	Qoheleth (Ecclesiastes)
REB	Revised English Bible
SBLDS	Society of Biblical Literature Dissertation Series
SBLMS	Society of Biblical Literature Monograph Series
SBLRBS	Society for Biblical Literature Resources for Biblical Study
SBLSP	Society of Biblical Literature Seminar Papers
SBLSymS	Society of Biblical Literature Symposium Series
SemSt	Semeia Studies
SJOT	*Scandinavian Journal of the Old Testament*
Sym.	Symmachus
Syr.	Syriac; the Syriac Peshitta
Tg.	Targum
Theod.	Theodotion
TNPEPP	*The New Princeton Encyclopedia of Poetry and Poetics.* Edited by Alex Preminger and T. V. F. Brogan. Princeton, 1993
UF	*Ugarit-Forschungen*
Ug.	Ugaritic
VT	*Vetus Testamentum*
VTSup	Supplements to *Vetus Testamentum*
ZAW	*Zeitschrift für die alttestamentliche Wissenschaft*
Zech	Zechariah
Zeph	Zephaniah

Introduction

"The Most Perfect Model of the Prophetic Poetry"

Poetry is notoriously difficult to define, in part because no single definition fits all literary works commonly identified as poems. It is easier—and often adequate—simply to say, "I know it when I see it," as United States Supreme Court Justice Potter Stewart reportedly said of pornography. At the same time, certain recurring features appear in most poems, including those in the Hebrew Bible. A partial list of these features can be assembled by comparing the definitions of poetry by literary critics T. V. F. Brogan, Terry Eagleton, and Burton Raffel.[1] All three definitions include the word "verbal," highlighting that poems are made of words. They claim respectively that poetry uses language in "heightened," "inventive," or "disciplined" ways, which differ from everyday uses of language. Poems exploit a wider range of features of words, such as their sounds, subtle nuances, multivalences, and the like. While this may also be true of prose literary language, it happens to a greater degree in poetry, which is all the more striking because most poems are noticeably shorter than other kinds of literature. Samuel Taylor Coleridge captures something of this difference in his dictum, "Prose = words in their best order; poetry = the *best* words in the best order."[2] Brogan and Eagleton further note that poetry is written in lines. This arrangement makes it clear that poems are artificial linguistic constructions, especially when

---

[1] T. V. F. Brogan, "Poetry," *TNPEPP*, 938; Terry Eagleton, *How to Read a Poem* (Oxford: Blackwell, 2007), 25; Burton Raffel, *How to Read a Poem* (New York: Meridian, 1984), 1.

[2] Samuel Taylor Coleridge, *Specimens of the Table Talk of the Late Samuel Taylor Coleridge* (2 vols; New York: Harper & Brothers, 1835), 1:76.

line divisions are achieved through atypical syntactic structures. Finally, poems generally display some kind of patterning or structure, whether of sounds, syntactic structures, or tropes or images. All speech is patterned to some degree, but the patterns of poetic speech usually seem more perceptible and more meaningful.

Although more could be said by way of description, one may at least conclude that a close, even indissolvable relationship exists between form and content in poetry. Cleanth Brooks makes this point forcibly in his aptly titled essay, "The Heresy of Paraphrase."[3] More recently, Eagleton has argued, "It is not as though the language [of a poem] is a kind of disposable cellophane in which the ideas come ready-wrapped. On the contrary, the language of a poem is *constitutive* of its ideas."[4] Form and content mutually reinforce each other in literary prose as well, but Eagleton has in mind the distinctively poetic manipulations of language and form that are integral to the ways that poems achieve meaning. The poetic medium is not simply an ornamental container for some formless message that could be communicated equally well by other means. To put the problem in terms of the texts explored in this book, an adequate understanding of Isaiah's prophetic proclamation is impossible without sufficient attention to his linguistic artistry, to the formal and thematic features that make his words poetry.

In view of this necessity, this book aims to provide a broad account of the poetic style of First Isaiah through close reading of selected texts. By the designation "First Isaiah," I mean either the eighth-century BCE prophet Isaiah of Jerusalem or the prophetic speeches in Isa 1–39 that most probably represent his work, not Isa 1–39 as a discrete literary unit, as the appellative is sometimes used in scholarly literature.[5] Any treatment of poetic style must proceed from

---

[3] Cleanth Brooks, "The Heresy of Paraphrase," in *The Well-Wrought Urn: Studies in the Structure of Poetry* (New York: Harcourt, Brace, Jovanovich, 1975), 67–79.

[4] Eagleton, *How to Read a Poem*, 2, emphasis original; see also Brogan, "Poetry," 939.

[5] Although there likely existed some pre-exilic collection of speeches attributed to Isaiah, it seems unlikely that Isa 1–39 in its present form was ever an independent work. For proposals concerning the redaction history of these chapters, see, among others, Hermann Barth, *Die Jesaja-Worte in der Josiazeit* (Wissenschaftliche Monographien zum Alten und Neuen Testament 48; Neukirchen-Vluyn: Neukirchener Verlag, 1977); Ronald E. Clements, "The Prophecies of Isaiah and the Fall of Jerusalem in 587 B.C.," *VT* 3 (1980): 421–36; Matthijs J. de Jong, *Isaiah Among the Ancient Near Eastern Prophets: A Comparative Study of the Earliest Stages of the Isaiah Tradition and the Neo-Assyrian Prophecies* (VTSup 117; Leiden: Brill, 2007); Marvin A. Sweeney,

Introduction: "The Most Perfect Model of the Prophetic Poetry" 3

the attentive explication of poems; consequently, the project has two additional goals—first, to describe an approach to reading Biblical Hebrew poetry, in particular prophetic texts, that I have found to be fruitful; and, second, to offer readings of particular Isaianic poems. These readings, I hope, will show how greater attention to Isaiah's style yields increased clarity of insight into his thought, thereby demonstrating that interpreters of these texts do well to attend carefully to questions of poetry, regardless of their interpretative goals or whether or not they style themselves "literary critics." To date, I am aware of no full-length scholarly work that offers anything close to a comprehensive overview of Isaiah's poetry.[6] This project seeks to remedy this gap in biblical scholarship, although the subject is much too extensive and rich for anyone to claim to have filled it.

Despite the absence of such a treatment, Isaianic poetry has been the object of critical study for over three centuries, during which time there have been many insightful studies of this corpus on which the present work builds. Indeed, the Book of Isaiah has long held a prominent place in scholarship on the poetry of the Hebrew Bible. It is surely no accident that the authors of the two most important studies of biblical poetry prior to the late 1970s, Robert Lowth and George Buchanan Gray, also wrote commentaries on Isaiah. The last thirty-five years have seen an explosion of fresh approaches to the study of biblical poetry and to literary work on the Book of Isaiah, energized by a number of new methodologies in biblical studies. The following survey of scholarship, while selective, situates my work generally in this history of inquiry. I then describe my own method

---

Isaiah 1–4 and the Post-Exilic Understanding of the Isaianic Tradition (BZAW 171; Berlin: Walter de Gruyter, 1988); Marvin A. Sweeney, *Isaiah 1–39, with an Introduction to Prophetic Literature* (Forms of the Old Testament Literature 16; Grand Rapids: Eerdmans, 1996); H. G. M. Williamson, *The Book Called Isaiah: Deutero-Isaiah's Role in Composition and Redaction* (Oxford: Oxford University Press, 1994); Jacques Vermeylen, *Du prophète Isaïe à l'apocalyptique* (2 vols; Etudes bibliques; Paris: Gabalda, 1977–78).

[6] Note the following short treatments: Luis Alonso Schökel, "Isaiah," in *The Literary Guide to the Bible* (eds. Robert Alter and Frank Kermode; Cambridge, Mass.: The Belknap Press of Harvard University Press, 1987), 165–83, especially 166–74; Willem A. M. Beuken, *Jesaja 1–12* (trans. Ulrich Berges; HTKAT; Freiburg: Herder, 2003), 39–45; John J. Schmitt, *Isaiah and his Interpreters* (New York: Paulist, 1986), 37–48; Theodore L. Steinberg, "Isaiah the Poet," in *Mappings of the Biblical Terrain: The Bible as Text* (eds. Vincent L. Tollers and John R. Maier; Bucknell Review 33:2; Lewisburg, Pa.: Bucknell University Press, 1990), 299–310; Hans Wildberger, *Isaiah 28–39* (CC; trans. Thomas H. Trapp; Minneapolis: Fortress, 2002), 666–93.

and clarify its relationship to other approaches, before finally outlining the plan for this study.

ISAIAH AND THE STUDY OF BIBLICAL POETRY

For all practical purposes, the study of Isaianic poetry—like the modern study of Biblical Hebrew poetry itself—began nearly three hundred years ago with the work of Robert Lowth (1710–1787), a bishop in the Church of England and Professor of Poetry at the University of Oxford. Lowth applied his expertise in classical literature to the study of biblical poetry in a series of lectures in 1741. These lectures were first published in 1753 as *Praelectiones Academicae de Sacra Poesi Hebraeorum* and then translated into English as *Lectures on the Sacred Poetry of the Hebrews* in 1787.[7] The impact of this work for the direction of subsequent research can hardly be overstated. Lowth assumed that the poetry of the Hebrew Bible should be studied in conjunction with and in the same way as other corpora of poetry.[8] His best-known contribution remains his identification of parallelism as the most accessible stylistic feature of biblical poetry, but his lectures covered an expansive range of topics, including meter, diction, and imagery. He devoted special attention to describing the different poetic styles of the Bible, including the elegy, the ode, didactic poetry, and perhaps most significantly, prophetic poetry. Against traditional, theologically motivated views in Christian and Jewish scholarship, Lowth insisted that the prophetic books are

---

[7] Robert Lowth, *Lectures on the Sacred Poetry of the Hebrews* (ed. Calvin E. Stowe; trans. G. Gregory; new ed.; Boston: Crocker & Brewster, 1829).

[8] Anna Cullhed, "Original Poetry: Robert Lowth and Eighteenth-Century Poetics," in *Sacred Conjectures: The Context and Legacy of Robert Lowth and Jean Astruc* (ed. John Jarick; LHBOTS 457; New York: T&T Clark, 2007), 35–7; George Buchanan Gray, *The Forms of Hebrew Poetry* (London: Hodder & Stoughton, 1915; repr., New York: Ktav Publishing House, 1972), 5; Patricia K. Tull, "What's New in Lowth? Synchronic Reading in the Eighteenth and Twenty-first Centuries," *Society of Biblical Literature Seminar Papers 2000* (SBLSP 39: Atlanta: Society of Biblical Literature, 2000), 198. Nonetheless, religious concerns remained crucial to Lowth's work, as argued by Cullhed, "Original Poetry," 34, 40–2; Robert P. Gordon, "The Legacy of Lowth: Robert Lowth and the Book of Isaiah in Particular," in *Biblical Hebrews, Biblical Texts: Essays in Memory of Michael P. Weitzman* (eds. Ada Rapoport-Albert and Gillian Greenberg; JSOTSup 333/Hebrew Bible and its Versions 2; Sheffield: Sheffield Academic Press, 2001), 59.

Introduction: "The Most Perfect Model of the Prophetic Poetry"   5

comprised in large measure of poetry, based on their considerable similarity to more conventionally acknowledged poetic texts such as the Psalms.[9] The now-common recognition of the poetic character of biblical prophecy owes itself almost entirely to his work.

In Lecture XXI, "The Peculiar Character of Each of the Prophets," Lowth turned to the Book of Isaiah:

> Isaiah, the first of the prophets, both in order and dignity, abounds in such transcendant excellencies, that he may be properly said to afford the most perfect model of the prophetic poetry. He is at once elegant and sublime, forceful and ornamented; he unites energy with copiousness, and dignity with variety. In his sentiments there is uncommon elevation and majesty; in his imagery the utmost propriety, elegance, dignity, and diversity; in his language uncommon beauty and energy; and, notwithstanding the obscurity of his subjects, a surprising degree of clearness and simplicity. To these we may add, there is such sweetness in the poetical composition of his sentences, whether it proceed from art or genius, that if the Hebrew poetry at present is possessed of any remains of its native grace and harmony, we shall find them chiefly in the writings of Isaiah.[10]

Even with allowances for Lowth's typically hyperbolic style, his esteem for the poetry of Isaiah is obvious, and this book takes as a guiding principle the sentiment, if not always the substance, of his assessment. One caveat, however, is in order. Although Lowth regarded the entire Book of Isaiah as the work of the eighth-century BCE prophet, he recognized the very different style of Isa 40–66 and made clear that his high praise had these chapters especially in view.[11] Modern interpreters apparently share his preference, as Isa 40–66 has attracted far more attention than Isa 1–39 since the recent rise of literary approaches in biblical studies.[12] Against this tendency, the present study attempts to make the case that, granted their very

---

[9] Lowth, *Lectures*, 145–75.   [10] Lowth, *Lectures*, 176.

[11] Lowth, *Lectures*, 177. The majority of Lowth's worked examples from Isaiah, in both the *Lectures* and the "Preliminary Dissertation" to his Isaiah commentary, come from Isa 40–66.

[12] To cite one telling example, James Muilenburg's article "Form Criticism and Beyond," which is generally credited with the rise of literary approaches in recent biblical scholarship, focused extensively on Isa 40–55 ("Form Criticism and Beyond," *JBL* 88 [1969]: 1–18). For an overview of scholarship on the poetry of Second Isaiah, see Katie M. Heffelfinger, *I am Large, I Contain Multitudes: Lyric Cohesion and Conflict in Second Isaiah* (Biblical Interpretation Series 105; Leiden: Brill, 2011), 3–21.

different styles, First Isaiah ought to be regarded as the literary equal of his later counterpart.

Lowth also published a commentary on Isaiah in 1778, consisting of three parts: a "Preliminary Dissertation," an abbreviated and supplemented recapitulation of his understanding of biblical poetry; a "New Translation" of the Book of Isaiah, one of the first in the English language to be based on substantial text-critical analysis; and a section of "Notes, Critical, Philological, and Explanatory," which focused primarily on text-critical, historical, and theological issues.[13] The most enduring contribution of Lowth's commentary has been his translation, especially his decision to present the poetic sections of Isaiah in lineated format. Stansell explains, "If Isaiah was a poet, then in Lowth's view his prophecies must be presented visually to the reader in verse form, with each line or stichos of a verse printed in parallel. The result was a poetic appearance without either rhyme or meter, a common sight today in both ancient and modern poetry, but highly unusual in the eighteenth century."[14] This novel arrangement of lines, for which Lowth had no precedent in available biblical manuscripts, generally followed his practice in the *Praelectiones*, where he presented both lineated Hebrew texts as well as lineated translations, although only the latter appear in Gregory's English translation. The visual impression of poetry conveyed by the format of his translation powerfully reinforced the assertion of the poetic nature of Isaiah's speech, and the continuation of this practice in biblical text editions, translations, and commentaries today—even though it did not catch on immediately—is one of Lowth's enduring legacies.[15]

---

[13] Robert Lowth, *Isaiah: A New Translation; With a Preliminary Dissertation, and Notes, Critical, Philological, and Explanatory* (10th ed.; Cambridge, Mass.: James Munroe and Company, 1834). For dissenting appraisals of Lowth's text-critical work, see Gordon, "Legacy of Lowth," 59–72, 76; Gary Stansell, "The Poet's Prophet: Bishop Robert Lowth's Eighteenth-Century Commentary on Isaiah," in *"As Those who are Taught": The Interpretation of Isaiah from the LXX to the SBL* (eds. Claire Mathews McGinnis and Patricia K. Tull; SBLSymS 27; Atlanta: Society of Biblical Literature, 2006), 231–2; Tull, "What's New in Lowth," 200–1.

[14] Stansell, "The Poet's Prophet," 229. One should remember that, only a century earlier, the appearance of printed lines of unrhymed poetry in the first edition of Milton's *Paradise Lost* had so scandalized readers that the second edition included a defense of the versification in 1674.

[15] Stansell, "The Poet's Prophet," 232; Tull, "What's New in Lowth," 203–7.

Introduction: "The Most Perfect Model of the Prophetic Poetry" 7

While not nearly as famous nowadays as the *Lectures*, Lowth's commentary was well received by his contemporaries, although late eighteenth- and nineteenth-century German critics took up his text- and historical-critical insights more than his literary ones, particularly as they had been augmented by J. B. Koppe's notes in the German translation of the commentary.[16] The hallmark of German Isaiah scholarship in this period was the isolation of different historical layers in the Book of Isaiah, culminating in Bernhard Duhm's distinction among First, Second, and Third Isaiah in his 1892 commentary.[17] Duhm readily acknowledged that the majority of all three sections of Isaiah are poetic; indeed, he viewed prophecy and poetry as practically inseparable. His interest in the personalities of the prophets drove his literary analysis, which he saw as the key to uncovering their original words.[18] To this end, he relied extensively on meter—a feature of biblical poetry that Lowth believed could not be recovered[19]—as a criterion for distinguishing the "authentic" prophetic words from later additions and glosses, frequently emending and sometimes extensively rearranging texts to arrive at poems with consistent metrical and strophic patterns. The heyday of this tradition of *metri causa* emendation would last well into the twentieth century.

After Lowth, perhaps the most important figure in the study of Biblical Hebrew poetry was another British scholar affiliated with Oxford, George Buchanan Gray (1865–1922), who published both a commentary on Isaiah in 1912 and a treatise on biblical poetry in 1915.[20] In the latter, titled *The Forms of Hebrew Poetry*, Gray

---

[16] Stansell, "The Poet's Prophet," 237–9. Perhaps not coincidentally, German literary scholars in this period no longer assigned biblical poetry a preeminent place in the historical canon of world poetry, as they had immediately following the publication of Lowth's *Lectures* (Cullhed, "Original Poetry," 45–7).

[17] Bernhard Duhm, *Das Buch Jesaia übersetzt und erklärt* (5th ed.; Göttingen: Vandenhoeck & Ruprecht, 1968); on Lowth's influence on Duhm, see Stansell, "The Poet's Prophet," 239.

[18] Kemper Fullerton, "The Book of Isaiah: Critical Problems and a New Commentary," *HTR* 6 (1913): 489–90; Henning Graf Reventlow, *From the Enlightenment to the Twentieth Century* (vol. 4 of *History of Biblical Interpretation*; trans. Leo G. Perdue; SBLRBS 63; Atlanta: Society of Biblical Literature, 2010), 333; Winfried Thiel, "Duhm, Bernhard Lauardus (1847–1928)," in *Dictionary of Biblical Interpretation* (ed. John H. Hayes; 2 vols; Nashville: Abingdon, 1999), 1:310–11.

[19] Lowth, *Lectures*, 31–6.

[20] George Buchanan Gray, *A Critical and Exegetical Commentary on the Book of Isaiah I–XXVII* (ICC; Edinburgh: T. & T. Clark, 1912); George Buchanan Gray, *Forms*. On Gray's contribution to the "standard description" of Biblical Hebrew

advanced Lowth's work in several ways. He refined the categories of parallelism along lines that anticipated more recent linguistic approaches, critiqued then-current solutions to the problem of meter, including Duhm's, and treated more fully the question of poetic structure at levels beyond parallelistic line groups, such as the stanza or verse paragraph and the whole poem. Whereas Lowth had drawn primarily on his expertise in Greek and Latin verse, Gray was able to situate biblical poetry in a larger literary context that included poetry in other Semitic languages, such as classical Arabic and Akkadian texts. This important contribution seems even more remarkable given that he died in 1922, seven years before the discovery of the first Ugaritic tablets and twenty-five years before the discovery of the Dead Sea Scrolls, which would greatly advance the comparative study of biblical and other ancient Near Eastern poetries. Gray's Isaiah commentary, not surprisingly, feels dated at many points today, yet it remains exemplary for its literary sensitivity. The introduction included a section on the basic features of prophetic poetry, and the comments throughout gave frequent and consistent attention to stylistic matters. He did sometimes resort to radical emendations, as in his extensive rearrangement of the admittedly difficult Isa 2:6–22, but he did so with much more restraint than Duhm, whom he criticized for his more extreme liberties with the text.[21] Unfortunately, Gray's commentary only covers Isa 1–27, as a planned second volume was never completed.

For the twentieth century, the definitive commentary on Isa 1–39 is Hans Wildberger's magisterial three-volume work, first published in German in 1972–82 and then translated into English in 1991–2002.[22] Wildberger never lost sight of the fact that most of these chapters contain poetry, even if that awareness did not always affect his exegesis as much as one would like. The introduction to the commentary, which only appeared at the end of the third volume, included a brief sketch titled "Language and Forms of Speech for Isaiah and his 'Successors,'" treating rhythm and poetic structure,

---

poetry, see Michael P. O'Connor, *Hebrew Verse Structure* (2nd ed.; Winona Lake, Ind.: Eisenbrauns, 1997), 32–3.

[21] Gray, *Isa I–XXVII*, 212; see also Gray, *Forms*, 203, 225–36.

[22] Hans Wildberger, *Isaiah 1–39: A Commentary* (trans. Thomas H. Trapp; 3 vols; CC; Minneapolis: Fortress, 1991–2002); trans. of *Jesaja* (3 vols; Biblischer Kommentar, Altes Testament 10/1-3; Neukirchen-Vluyn: Neukirchener Verlag, 1972–82).

Introduction: "The Most Perfect Model of the Prophetic Poetry" 9

diction and imagery, the use of quotations, and genre, among other topics.[23] His discussion of rhythm was especially instructive and slightly ahead of its time in its recognition that Isaiah's poems lack metrical regularity and its disavowal of *metri causa* emendation. Following the principles laid out in this section, each section of the commentary included a prosodic analysis of the passage under consideration. Wildberger also displayed an especially keen ear for soundplay and an eye for imagery in his comments on particular texts. The aspect of his work that most shows signs of datedness is his form-critical analysis. Following traditional approaches championed by Duhm and others, he consistently divided the text into short units that he believed to represent originally independent speeches by Isaiah of Jerusalem.[24] While this trend persists in some corners, at least some recent scholarly work on prophetic literature has allowed for the compositional integrity of larger textual units.

Commentaries since Wildberger's have continued to acknowledge the poetic character of Isaiah and occasionally comment on such matters as parallelism or imagery, but by and large their exegesis is not substantially informed by attention to poetic artistry.[25] In some cases, this absence may be attributed to the constraints of the particular commentary series, but overall it appears to be symptomatic of recent research in Isaiah. Representing an extreme position, Joseph Blenkinsopp questions the very existence of poetry in Isa 1–39 in his commentary. His remarks on Isa 1 are typical: "Like most of the Isaianic material printed as verse in MT [the Masoretic Text] and modern translations, this composition approximates more closely a kind of heavily accented *recitative* or high rhetorical prose than

---

[23] Wildberger, *Isa 28–39*, 666–93.

[24] See Marvin A. Sweeney, "Reevaluating Isaiah 1–39 in Recent Critical Research," *CR:BS* 4 (1996): 88–9. For a critique of this long-standing tendency in prophetic scholarship, see Brian C. Jones, *Howling over Moab: Irony and Rhetoric in Isaiah 15–16* (SBLDS 157; Atlanta: Scholars Press, 1996), 76–83.

[25] For example, Joseph Blenkinsopp, *Isaiah 1–39: A New Translation with Introduction and Commentary* (AB 19; New York: Doubleday, 2000); Brevard S. Childs, *Isaiah* (OTL; Louisville: Westminster John Knox, 2001); Ronald E. Clements, *Isaiah 1–39* (New Century Bible; Grand Rapids: Eerdmans, 1980); John H. Hayes and Stuart A. Irvine, *Isaiah the Eighth Century Prophet: His Times and his Preaching* (Nashville: Abingdon, 1987); Otto Kaiser, *Isaiah 1–12: A Commentary* (trans. John Bowden; 2nd ed.; OTL; Philadelphia: Westminster, 1983); Otto Kaiser, *Isaiah 13–39: A Commentary* (trans. R. A. Wilson; OTL; Philadelphia: Westminster, 1974); Christopher R. Seitz, *Isaiah 1–39* (Interpretation; Louisville: Westminster John Knox, 1993); Sweeney, *Isa 1–39*.

poetry as generally understood, though we will with some license nevertheless call it a poem."[26] Notwithstanding the acknowledged influence of James Kugel on this statement, Blenkinsopp and other recent commentators generally interact minimally with numerous studies of Biblical Hebrew poetry since the late 1970s. These studies, however, have considerably advanced our knowledge of the workings of biblical poetry, particularly in the area of linguistics, which had previously moved little beyond the work of Lowth and Gray.[27]

Two recent commentaries stand out as exceptions to this general trend. The first volume of H. G. M. Williamson's projected three-volume commentary on Isa 1–27 appeared in 2005, covering the first five chapters of the book.[28] Although his most significant contributions lie in the areas of composition history and redaction history, Williamson interacts with the latest studies of Biblical Hebrew poetry and deftly addresses matters of style throughout his comments. In particular, he stands out among commentators in his attention to the problem of lineation in Isaiah's verse, as for example in his comments on Isa 3:2–4 and 5:29. Williamson's literary sensitivity makes his work a worthy successor to that of Gray in the International Critical Commentary series. Even more recently, Patricia K. Tull published her commentary on Isa 1–39 in 2010 in the Smyth & Helwys Bible Commentary series, for which she will also publish a volume on Isa 40–66.[29] Surprisingly, the introduction does not contain a section on Hebrew poetry, as many far less stylistically sensitive commentaries do, but Tull is consistently attentive to literary style and offers some of the most perceptive readings of chapters from Isa 1–39 that I have found. Her attention to imagery, rhythm, and sound are particularly

---

[26] Blenkinsopp, *Isa 1–39*, 181; see also 79–80, 303. Presumably, he means *BHS* by "MT," since Hebrew mss. of Isaiah are typically not lineated. Blenkinsopp's skepticism follows that of James L. Kugel in *The Idea of Biblical Poetry* (New Haven: Yale University Press, 1981; repr., Baltimore: Johns Hopkins University Press, 1998).

[27] For overviews of these studies and their contributions, see J. Kenneth Kuntz, "Biblical Hebrew Poetry in Recent Research, Part I," *CR:BS* 6 (1998): 31–64; J. Kenneth Kuntz, "Biblical Hebrew Poetry in Recent Research, Part II," *CR:BS* 7 (1999): 35–79; Wilfred G. E. Watson, "The Study of Biblical Hebrew Poetry: Past—Present—Future," in *Sacred Conjectures: The Context and Legacy of Robert Lowth and Jean Astruc* (ed. John Jarick; LHBOTS 457; New York: T&T Clark, 2007), 124–54.

[28] H. G. M. Williamson, *A Critical and Exegetical Commentary on Isaiah 1–5* (ICC; London: T&T Clark, 2006).

[29] Patricia K. Tull, *Isaiah 1–39* (Smyth & Helwys Bible Commentary 14A; Macon, Ga.: Smyth & Helwys, 2010).

Introduction: "The Most Perfect Model of the Prophetic Poetry" 11

notable. Due to the limitations of the commentary genre, of course, the work of both Williamson and Tull falls short of a comprehensive account of the poetics of this corpus.

In a 1980 review article, A. Graeme Auld called for greater attention to the poetic character of Isaianic texts, decrying the distinction between form and content that had marked much previous interpretation.[30] With the concurrent rise of literary approaches in biblical studies, many monographs and articles over the last thirty-five years have addressed literary style in First Isaiah.[31] These studies are generally narrow in scope, focusing on particular texts or stylistic features, and reflect a variety of methodologies. Nonetheless, many have made significant contributions to the study of Isaianic poetry. Overall, though, poetic questions have not been at the fore of recent research on Isaiah, as Blenkinsopp observes: "The most recent phase of scholarship on the book has ... concentrated much more on the structuring and organization of the material, in its internal interconnections and intertextual links, than on the more traditional subject matter of literary criticism (poetics, imagery, etc.)."[32] Blenkinsopp refers to the growing tendency to seek structural coherence or even a unified message in the final form of the Book of Isaiah as a whole, which began seriously to emerge in biblical studies in the 1980s.[33] In

---

[30] A. Graeme Auld, "Poetry, Prophecy, Hermeneutic: Recent Studies in Isaiah," *Scottish Journal of Theology* 33 (1980): 577–81.
[31] For example, Robert Alter, *The Art of Biblical Poetry* (New York: Basic Books, 1985), 137–62; Andrew H. Bartelt, *The Book around Immanuel: Style and Structure* (Biblical and Judaic Studies 4; Winona Lake, Ind.: Eisenbrauns, 1996); Katheryn Pfisterer Darr, *Isaiah's Vision and the Family of God* (Literary Currents in Biblical Interpretation; Louisville: Westminster John Knox, 1994); J. Cheryl Exum, "Of Broken Pots, Fluttering Birds, and Visions of the Night: Extended Simile and Poetic Technique in Isaiah," *CBQ* 43 (1981): 331–52; A. Joseph Everson and Hyun Chul Paul Kim (eds.), *The Desert Will Bloom: Poetic Visions in Isaiah* (Society of Biblical Literature: Ancient Israel and its Literature 4; Atlanta: Society of Biblical Literature, 2009); Jones, *Howling over Moab*; R. Reed Lessing, *Interpreting Discontinuity: Isaiah's Tyre Oracle* (Winona Lake, Ind.: Eisenbrauns, 2004); Peter D. Miscall, *Isaiah* (Readings; Sheffield: JSOT Press, 1993); Peter D. Miscall, "Isaiah: The Labyrinth of Images," *Semeia* 54 (1992): 103–21; Kirsten Nielsen, *There is Hope for a Tree: The Tree as Metaphor in First Isaiah* (JSOTSup 65; Sheffield: JSOT Press, 1989); Peter D. Quinn-Miscall, *Reading Isaiah: Poetry and Vision* (Louisville: Westminster John Knox, 2001); J. J. M. Roberts, "Double Entendre in First Isaiah," *CBQ* 54 (1992): 39–48; Gary Roye Williams, "Frustrated Expectations in Isaiah v 1–7: A Literary Interpretation," *VT* 35 (1985): 459–65.
[32] Blenkinsopp, *Isa 1–39*, 181.
[33] On this approach, see Edgar W. Conrad, *Reading Isaiah* (Overtures to Biblical Theology; Minneapolis: Fortress, 1991), 3–33; Roy F. Melugin, "The Book of Isaiah

some examples of this approach, the unity of Isaiah is understood as a strictly linear progression and discussed in terms of plot or drama, which seem ill-suited to a book comprised almost entirely of non-narrative poetry.[34] It is unclear how these discussions would differ greatly if the work in question were a collection of prose writings. Other final form treatments take greater account of the poetic character of Isaiah but are more interested in recurring images or themes across the book than in close readings of the poems themselves.[35]

In some tension with recent approaches, my study treats individual poems in Isa 1–39 largely in isolation, with minimal attention to their arrangement or connections to other parts of the book. It is not self-evident that an ancient work such as Isaiah was meant to be read sequentially from beginning to end, as many final form treatments insist. John Barton points out that this assumption privileges the

and the Construction of Meaning," in vol. 1 of *Writing and Reading the Scroll of Isaiah: Studies of an Interpretive Tradition* (2 vols; eds. Craig C. Broyles and Craig A. Evans; VTSup 70; Formation and Interpretation of Old Testament Literature 1–2; Leiden: Brill, 1997), 39–55; Marvin A. Sweeney, "The Book of Isaiah in Recent Research," *CR:BS* 1 (1993): 141–62; Marvin E. Tate, "The Book of Isaiah in Recent Study," in *Forming Prophetic Literature: Essays on Isaiah and the Twelve in Honor of John D. W. Watts* (eds. James W. Watts and Paul R. House; JSOTSup 235; Sheffield: Sheffield Academic Press, 1996), 22–5, 43–50; Patricia K. Tull, "One Book, Many Voices: Conceiving of Isaiah's Polyphonic Message," in *"As Those who are Taught": The Interpretation of Isaiah from the LXX to the SBL* (eds. Claire Mathews McGinnis and Patricia K. Tull; SBLSymS 27; Atlanta: Society of Biblical Literature, 2006), 279–314. The question has been a particular focus of the Formation of the Book of Isaiah Seminar of the Society of Biblical Literature from 1990 to the present.

[34] For example, Christopher R. Seitz, "Isaiah 1–66: Making Sense of the Whole," in *Reading and Preaching the Book of Isaiah* (ed. Christopher R. Seitz; Philadelphia: Fortress, 1988), 105–26; John D. W. Watts, *Isaiah* (2 vols; rev. ed.; Word Biblical Commentary, 24–5; Waco, Tex.: Word Books, 2005), lxxxii–cxxi. Note how Seitz repeatedly appeals to the "story" of Isaiah, compares it to novels such as *Moby Dick*, and refers to God and Zion as "characters." For a critique of attempts to find narrative-like unity in other biblical texts or the Bible as a whole, see J. Cheryl Exum, *Song of Songs: A Commentary* (OTL; Louisville: Westminster John Knox, 2005), 42–5; Brent A. Strawn, "Lyric Poetry," in *Dictionary of the Old Testament: Wisdom, Poetry & Writings* (eds. Tremper Longman III and Peter Enns; Downers Grove, IL: InterVarsity Press, 2008), 443–4.

[35] For example, Everson and Kim, *The Desert Will Bloom*; Darr, *Isaiah's Vision*; Miscall, *Isaiah*; Robert H. O'Connell, *Concentricity and Continuity: The Literary Structure of Isaiah* (JSOTSup 188; Sheffield: Sheffield Academic Press, 1994). The essays in Everson and Kim, published under the auspices of the Formation of the Book of Isaiah Seminar of the Society of Biblical Literature, represent a welcome advancement in the study of Isaiah's poetry, but the focus is limited largely to imagery. In fact, in the programmatic first essay of the collection, Roy Melugin uses the terms "figurative language" and "poetic vision" interchangeably.

modern novel as its model.³⁶ In their emphasis on unity, many final form readings risk leveling the rich complexity of the diverse traditions of the book, which resist easy synthesis.³⁷ Given this complexity, perhaps one may better designate the Book of Isaiah in its final form as a collection or anthology.³⁸ This assessment is hardly an indictment of the literary quality of the text but simply a judgment about its genre. Writing well before critical distinctions among different sections of Isaiah became current, Lowth—whom no one would accuse of lacking literary sensitivity—maintained that the poems in the book "are often improperly connected, without any marks of discrimination, which injudicious arrangement, on some occasions, creates almost insuperable difficulties."³⁹ A literary reading of Isaiah, then, need not be a final form reading. Even if poems in Isa 1–39 take on additional meanings in their larger context within the book, the appreciation of the whole can only benefit from a more thorough analysis of the parts on their own terms. Gary Stansell, himself an advocate of final form readings, offers this cautionary word: "We need from Lowth a reminder that Hebrew prophecy will not be grasped in a way that is most appropriate to its nature if we over-emphasize the prophetic BOOK at the expense of the individual poem."⁴⁰ The need for a study such as this one thus remains, despite the current proliferation of literary treatments of Isaiah.

---

[36] John Barton, "Historical Criticism and Literary Interpretation: Is There Any Common Ground?" in *Crossing the Boundaries: Essays in Biblical Interpretation in Honour of Michael D. Goulder* (eds. Stanley E. Porter et al.; Biblical Interpretation Series 8; Leiden: Brill, 1994), 12–15.

[37] David Carr, "Reaching for Unity in Isaiah," *JSOT* 57 (1993): 71; Tull, "One Book," 311–14.

[38] Carr, "Reaching for Unity," 78–9; J. J. M. Roberts, "Historical-Critical Method, Theology, and Contemporary Exegesis," in *The Bible and the Ancient Near East* (Winona Lake, Ind.: Eisenbrauns, 2002), 399; repr. from *Biblical Theology: Problems and Perspectives in Honor of J. Christian Beker* (eds. S. J. Kraftchick et al.; Nashville, Abingdon: 1995); Benjamin D. Sommer, "The Scroll of Isaiah as Jewish Scripture, or, Why Jews Don't Read Books," in *SBL Seminar Papers, 1996* (SBLSP 35; Chico, Calif.: Scholars Press, 1996), 230–3, 238–9; Karel van der Toorn, *Scribal Culture and the Making of the Hebrew Bible* (Cambridge, Mass.: Harvard University Press, 2007), 16, 123, 177. Throughout the history of interpretation, Jewish and Christian readers have tended to focus not on whole biblical books but on individual verses or pericopes, as Roberts and Sommer observe.

[39] Lowth, *Lectures*, 177.

[40] Gary Stansell, "Lowth's Isaiah Commentary and Romanticism," in *SBL Seminar Papers 2000* (SBLSP 39; Atlanta: Society of Biblical Literature, 2000), 178, emphasis original.

POETRY AND HISTORY

A central presupposition of this book, articulated already in the discussion of Lowth's work, is that biblical poems should be read in much the same way as other poems. Certainly, a particular constellation of features distinguishes biblical poetry, but almost all of these features are attested individually in other world poetries, and the constellation itself is largely characteristic of ancient Near Eastern poetry more generally.[41] As a result, the study of Biblical Hebrew poetry has much to gain from engagement with literary studies of poetry from all times and places. My approach may be described as formalist or stylistic, insofar as it depends on attentiveness to philology, syntax, and other linguistic features of poems in the service of reading them holistically as literary works.[42] The necessity of attending to such matters arises from the "verbally inventive" quality of poetry, to borrow Eagleton's description.[43] At the same time, I draw freely from a wide range of methodologies to the degree that they illumine some aspect of Isaiah's poetry.

While its topic is obviously literary by nature, this project has a decidedly historical component, as its focus on *First* Isaiah suggests. Many studies of Biblical Hebrew poems lack attention to their historical contexts.[44] The first wave of literary readings of biblical texts in the 1970s and 1980s was hugely influenced by the literary school of New Criticism and its disavowal of authorial intention.[45] Many of

---

[41] For accessible discussions of these features, see Adele Berlin, "Introduction to Hebrew Poetry," *NIB* 4:301-15; F. W. Dobbs-Allsopp, "Poetry, Hebrew," *NIDB* 4:550-8; Patrick D. Miller, "The Theological Significance of Biblical Poetry," in *Language, Theology, and the Bible: Essays in Honour of James Barr* (eds. Samuel E. Balantine and John Barton; Oxford: Clarendon Press, 1994), 215-25.

[42] See Peter Barry, *Beginning Theory: An Introduction to Literary and Cultural Theory* (2nd ed.; Manchester: Manchester University Press, 2002), 203-21, for an overview of stylistics.

[43] Eagleton, *How to Read a Poem*, 41-7.

[44] David L. Petersen and Kent Harold Richards, *Interpreting Hebrew Poetry* (GBS; Minneapolis: Fortress, 1992), 18. Muilenburg anticipated and already criticized this tendency, particularly as it pertained to the study of prophetic literature, in his 1969 study ("Form Criticism and Beyond," 5-6).

[45] See W. K. Wimsatt and Monroe C. Beardsley, "The Intentional Fallacy," in *The Verbal Icon: Studies in the Meaning of Poetry* (Lexington, Ky.: University Press of Kentucky, 1954), 3-19; note Exum's appeal to Wimsatt and Beardsley in "Broken Pots," 331, n. 1. My critique of this aspect of New Criticism should not be taken as a wholesale dismissal of the approach, as I have been greatly influenced by its emphasis on close reading.

Introduction: "The Most Perfect Model of the Prophetic Poetry" 15

these studies explicitly, at times polemically, presented themselves as alternatives to traditional historical-critical approaches. Some more recent theoretical approaches within literary studies value historical inquiry more highly, and these have exercised growing influence on biblical scholarship over the last fifteen years.[46] Nevertheless, the ahistoricist impulse remains entrenched among some literary practitioners in the field. For Isaiah, in particular, the emphasis on the final form still represents in many cases a backlash against the traditional threefold division of the book, regarded as a hallmark of historical criticism.

Ahistorical approaches, however, prove myopic for ancient poems that force the interpreter to take account of the significant linguistic differences of a dead language and the alien literary conventions and sensibilities of a past culture.[47] Indeed, many prophetic texts of the Hebrew Bible revel in their historical particularity, with frequent references to contemporary persons, places, and events. Knowledge of these poems' historical settings imparts depth to one's reading of them, just as knowledge of the assassination of United States President Abraham Lincoln enriches the experience of Walt Whitman's poem "When Lilacs Last in the Door-Yard Bloomed," even if one would never confuse the poem with a journalistic report of the event. The argumentative or rhetorical character of Isaiah's poems—that is, the fact that the prophet sought to create specific religious and sociopolitical changes through them—is especially significant for their interpretation.[48] A key concern in treating these texts, consequently,

---

[46] Barry, *Beginning Theory*, 172–91; for the impact of such approaches in biblical studies, see F. W. Dobbs-Allsopp, "Rethinking Historical Criticism," *Biblical Interpretation* 7 (1999): 236–7; Gina Hens-Piazza, *New Historicism* (GBS; Minneapolis: Fortress, 2002).

[47] Jeremy A. Black, *Reading Sumerian Poetry* (London: Athlone Press, 1998), 20–47; O'Connor, *HVS*, 6. Black takes special note of the inadequacy of New Criticism's ahistorical stance, noting that its practitioners typically work with poetry from cultural contexts similar to their own (*Reading Sumerian Poetry*, 6).

[48] Yehoshua Gitay has refined a rhetorical approach to prophetic texts in numerous works, including "The Effectiveness of Isaiah's Speech," *JQR* 75 (1984): 162–72; *Isaiah and His Audience: The Structure and Meaning of Isaiah 1–12* (Studia Semitica Neerlandica; Assen: Van Gorcum, 1991); "Oratorical Rhetoric: The Question of Prophetic Language with Special Attention to Isaiah," *ACEBT* 10 (1989): 72–83; see also Jones, *Howling over Moab*, 217–71. These studies are sensitive to questions of style but often use the categories of rhetorical analysis that were designed for prose texts, rather than poetic analysis. On the complicated relationship between these approaches, see Gerald Morris, *Prophecy, Poetry and Hosea* (JSOTSup 219; Sheffield:

should be their reception by their first readers or hearers.[49] An appreciation for the otherness of the real, if never completely recoverable, persons who first composed, heard, and read ancient poems is finally a matter of ethical sensitivity for contemporary readers who wish to avoid cultural appropriation of these texts.[50]

Even interpreters who value historical inquiry, however, have increasingly begun to challenge the practice of interpreting texts from First Isaiah against a putative eighth-century BCE setting. Darr identifies the first readers of Isaiah as members of Israel's intelligentsia during the fourth century BCE, who she argues would have read all sixty-six chapters from beginning to end.[51] While appreciative of her attempt to imagine sympathetically an original audience for Isaiah's poetry, I do not find Darr's reconstruction especially convincing. Besides the problems already noted for sequential, final form approaches, the centuries during which the Book of Isaiah might have reached its final form are not well attested historically, making it difficult to identify socio-cultural factors that would have shaped a reader's reception of the book. A different case obtains for a number of texts in Isa 1–39 that historically oriented scholars typically identify as the work of an eighth-century BCE prophet. For these texts, a greater number of contemporary historical sources provides a much stronger foundation for imagining an audience, namely the citizens of Jerusalem between roughly 735–700 BCE at the height of Neo-Assyrian expansion into the Levant. This putative audience seems at least as compelling and helpful a construct as Darr's. Of course, no reconstruction of an ancient audience can be regarded as objectively certain, and twenty-first-century CE interpreters cannot magically transform themselves into eighth-century BCE audiences. Subjectivity, however, is a necessary condition of historical inquiry, and it does not

---

Sheffield Academic Press, 1996), 18–47; Thomas A. Sloane, "Rhetoric and Poetry," *TNPEPP*, 1045–52.

[49] Katheryn Pfisterer Darr, "Literary Perspectives on Prophetic Literature," in *Old Testament Interpretation: Past, Present, and Future: Essays in Honor of Gene M. Tucker* (eds. James Luther Mays et al.; Nashville: Abingdon, 1995), 141.

[50] Dobbs-Allsopp, "Rethinking Historical Criticism," 265–8.

[51] Darr, *Isaiah's Vision*, 30; see further Edgar W. Conrad, "Prophet, Redactor and Audience: Reforming the Notion of Isaiah's Formation," in *New Visions of Isaiah* (eds. Roy F. Melugin and Marvin A. Sweeney; JSOTSup 214; Sheffield: Sheffield Academic Press, 1996), 323–4; Miscall, *Isaiah*, 18–20.

Introduction: "The Most Perfect Model of the Prophetic Poetry" 17

negate the usefulness of a reconstructed audience as at least a heuristic device for reading Isaianic poetry.[52]

Obviously, this task requires the selection of material within Isa 1-39 that likely dates to the eighth century BCE and may therefore be reasonably attributed to Isaiah of Jerusalem.[53] The recovery of the *ipsissima verba* of Isaiah—the prophet's actual, spoken words—was an obsession of earlier scholarship, but most scholars now rightly acknowledge the impossibility of the task, which among other problems raises the unanswerable question of the correspondence of Isaiah's oral proclamation to its written representation.[54] Nonetheless, with the appropriate caveats, the identification of texts that may approximate the words of the historical prophet remains a reasonable goal, and the available comparative material, especially Neo-Assyrian sources, provides some measure of control for this task.[55] In the end, this process is ultimately no more speculative than the attempt to imagine how a Persian-period audience might have read the book. After all, the oldest complete manuscript of Isaiah, the Great Isaiah Scroll from Qumran (1QIsa^a), dates to the late second century BCE;[56] consequently, one can be no more certain of the content of the

---

[52] Black, *Reading Sumerian Poetry*, 47-9; Dobbs-Allsopp, "Rethinking Historical Criticism," 253-4.

[53] On this question, see Antoon Schoors, "Historical Information in Isaiah 1-39," in *Studies in the Book of Isaiah: Festschrift Willem A. M. Beuken* (eds. J. van Reuiten and M. Vervenne; Bibliotheca Ephemeridum theologicarum Lovaniensium 132; Leuven: Leuven University Press/Uitgeverij Peeters, 1997), 75-93; de Jong, *Isaiah Among the Ancient Near Eastern Prophets*, 13-24, 191-249, 345-51; H. G. M. Williamson, "In Search of the Pre-Exilic Isaiah," in *In Search of Pre-Exilic Israel: Proceedings of the Oxford Old Testament Seminar* (ed. John Day; JSOTSup 406; London: T&T Clark, 2004), 181-206.

[54] On the process by which biblical traditions were committed to writing, see David M. Carr, *Writing on the Tablet of the Heart: Origins of Scripture and Literature* (Oxford: Oxford University Press, 2005); William M. Schniedewind, *How the Bible Became a Book: The Textualization of Ancient Israel* (Cambridge: Cambridge University Press, 2004); van der Toorn, *Scribal Culture*. For prophetic literature, in particular, note the essays in Ehud Ben Zvi and Michael H. Floyd (eds.), *Writings and Speech in Israelite and Ancient Near Eastern Prophecy* (SBLSymS 10; Atlanta: Society of Biblical Literature, 2000); Martti Nissinen, "How Prophecy Became Literature," *SJOT* 19 (2005): 153-72.

[55] Peter Machinist has modeled such comparative analysis in "Assyria and its Image in the First Isaiah," *JAOS* 103 (1983): 719-37.

[56] Eugene Ulrich and Peter W. Flint, *Introductions, Commentary, and Textual Variants* (vol. 2 of *Qumran Cave 1 II: The Isaiah Scrolls*; Discoveries in the Judaean Desert 32; Oxford: Clarendon Press, 2010), 61.

fourth-century BCE Book of Isaiah than of the eighth-century BCE speeches of Isaiah.

In this study, I work with the following group of texts that consist largely of poetry and contain material attributable to Isaiah of Jerusalem: Isa 1:1–31; 2:5–22; 3:1–4:1; 5:1–29; 8:9–22; 8:23–9:20 (Eng. 9:1–21); 10:1–34; 11:1–10; 14:4b–32; 15:1–16:12; 17:1–14; 18:1–6; 19:1–15; 22:1–23; 23:1–14; 28:1–29; 29:1–16; 30:1–17, 27–33; 31:1–9. Although this is a larger corpus than many recent commentators are willing to date to the eighth century BCE, at least a plurality if not a majority of commentators have traditionally assigned most of these texts to the historical prophet. As needed throughout the book, I discuss the dating of individual passages for which there is less critical consensus. Working with these texts necessarily entails emendation, to make sense of textual problems and identify probable later material. To keep my work grounded in textual *realia* as much as possible, I propose emendations with hesitance, especially when lacking manuscript support, and explain my rationale as clearly as possible when they seem necessary. The stylistic implications of these decisions are sometimes an important factor in making them—an admittedly circular logic, yet one that seems appropriate for this study.

PLAN OF THIS STUDY

Each of the following chapters explores a different aspect of First Isaiah's poetic style. Although successive chapters assume the conclusions of earlier ones, they stand more or less on their own. Chapter 1 addresses the question of the line in Isaiah's poetry. Guided by the assumption that lineation is a constitutive feature of poetry, I outline principles for discerning line breaks in Biblical Hebrew poems and consider the meaningfulness of line formation in First Isaiah. In Chapter 2, I explore the issue of poetic structure, conceived broadly as the movement from single lines to whole poems. This movement is discussed at two levels: smaller groups of lines—mostly couplets and triplets—and larger units composed of couplets and triplets that in turn comprise the whole poems. The structures of Isaianic poems involve many different formal and thematic devices and thus exhibit huge variety, with the result that this chapter is the

Introduction: "The Most Perfect Model of the Prophetic Poetry" 19

longest of the three. The topic of Chapter 3 is poetic imagery and metaphor. While noting the striking variety of Isaiah's imagery, the chapter examines in depth two recurring complexes in this corpus—agricultural and animal images—before offering general observations about the use of images in Isaiah's poetry. These are not the only possible topics that one could explore within these poems, of course, and other features such as soundplay receive at least passing attention in each chapter. A broad description of Isaiah's poetic style may be found in the Conclusion to this volume.

In keeping with the larger goal of demonstrating the exegetical payoff of attention to poetry, each chapter closes with a close reading of a complete poem from Isaiah (Isa 22:1b–14; Isa 3:1–15; Isa 1:2–20), highlighting the stylistic feature under discussion in the chapter without ignoring other relevant interpretive issues. These longer readings balance the smaller examples analyzed in less detail throughout the book. Attention to literary style is not an end in itself; its product should always be richer, more compelling readings of poems. Thus, while these readings are intended to bolster the arguments of their respective chapters, they are as important in their own right as any of the broader claims of this study. It should be noted that I treat each of these texts as a literary unity, at least in its present form. In terms of their composition histories, the vast majority of scholars argue that they are composite texts, assembled from smaller, once independent units that include both the work of the historical prophet and later additions. These arguments often assume that shifts in theme or style indicate originally separate compositions. Such shifts occur frequently in poetry, however, and they are especially at home in a poetic corpus that prefers loose, decentralized structures, as is the case for Biblical Hebrew poetry. As a result, I hesitate to dismiss the possibility of considerable, if not total, original unity in these poems, especially Isa 22:1–14 and 3:1–15. At the same time, I recognize the validity of arguments for their composite character, especially when evidence besides perceived stylistic incongruities can be adduced, and I readily admit that the literary sophistication of these poems could be the result of skilled scribal activity. My readings of these texts as poems do not finally demand a particular view of their composition.

Unless otherwise indicated, all translations of ancient texts are my own. My translations of Isaiah stick closely—at times even woodenly—to the Hebrew. One could well argue that higher literary quality in the target language does greater justice to the poetic character of the original language, despite the necessary sacrifice of literalness required to achieve it. Instead, although I attempt when possible to recreate in English certain poetic features of the Hebrew, I have erred on the side of literalness so that my translations might better serve my description and analysis.[57]

---

[57] Compare Robert Alter's reflections on translating Biblical Hebrew poetry in the Psalms: *The Book of Psalms: A Translation with Commentary* (New York: Norton, 2009), xxviii–xxxi.

1

The Line in First Isaiah

All poetry is written in verse, and lineation is the basic feature that distinguishes verse from prose.[1] The poet Mary Kinzie, for instance, describes the line as "the medium of expression poetry has and prose lacks."[2] This division into lines impacts the reader or listener's experience of verse in significant ways. Lines slow the movement of a poem, as a slight pause accompanies the end of each line. In this way, they set limits on the length of thought units, creating the impression of a more measured form of discourse, in contrast to the unrestricted syntax that characterizes prose. The pauses afford the reader or hearer an opportunity to process the preceding line and form both an impression of its meaning and expectations for the meaning of subsequent lines.[3] The more consistent the lengths of the lines, obviously, the more regularly these pauses occur. Even when they do not occur with predictable regularity, their greater frequency in comparison to prose nonetheless conditions the reader or hearer to expect them at certain junctures. Stephen Geller discusses these issues in terms of Biblical Hebrew verse:

---

[1] On the difference between poetry and verse, see T. V. F. Brogan, "Verse and Prose," *TNPEPP*, 1346–51; John Hollander, *Rhyme's Reason* (3rd ed.; New Haven: Yale University Press, 2000), 1; Charles Hartman, *Free Verse: An Essay on Prosody* (Princeton: Princeton University Press, 1980; repr., Evanston, Ill.: Northwestern University Press, 1996), 11.

[2] Mary Kinzie, *A Poet's Guide to Poetry* (Chicago Guides to Writing, Editing, and Publishing; Chicago: University of Chicago Press, 1999), 433; see also Brogan, "Verse and Prose," 1348.

[3] Edward L. Greenstein, "How Does Parallelism Mean?" in *A Sense of Text: The Art of Language in the Study of Biblical Literature* (ed. L. Nemoy; JQR Supplement; Winona Lake, Ind.: Eisenbrauns, 1983), 51–2; Barbara Herrnstein Smith, *Poetic Closure: A Study of How Poems End* (Chicago: University of Chicago Press, 1968), 10–14.

An essential empirical fact is the general symmetry in clause length displayed in most passages which, on other grounds, might reasonably be termed "poetic."... It is reasonable to suppose that passages with such symmetry form an expectation in the reader's mind that after a certain number of words a caesura or line break will occur. The specific phonetic, and therefore prosodic, aspect is the silence, real or potential, awaited at the limit of explanation, which usually corresponds to clause closure. The unit so delimited is the line.[4]

Others similarly acknowledge the determinative character of the line for biblical poetry.[5]

Given the importance of lineation, my treatment of the poetry of First Isaiah begins with a discussion of the identification and interpretive significance of lines in Isaianic poems. The first section of this chapter deals with the nearly complete lack of lineated manuscripts of Isaiah from antiquity; although this poses no small challenge, it does not finally make it impossible to talk about the line in this corpus. It does, however, require explicit arguments for the location of line breaks. The next section proposes criteria for determining these breaks, treating in turn questions of style, rhythm, and syntax. Finally, I summarize some significant tendencies in line formation in First Isaiah and their poetic effects, and I then undertake a close reading of Isa 22:1b–14, a poem that relies heavily on lineation for its creation of meaning.

THE PROBLEM OF LINEATION IN BIBLICAL HEBREW VERSE

The absence of ancient traditions concerning lineation, especially lineated manuscripts, poses no small problem for the study of verse in the prophetic books. Many Biblical Hebrew poetic texts—including

---

[4] Stephen A. Geller, "Hebrew Prosody and Poetics: I. Biblical," *TNPEPP*, 509-10.
[5] For example, Walter Theophilus Woldemar Cloete, *Versification and Syntax in Jeremiah 2-25: Syntactical Constraints in Hebrew Colometry* (SBLDS 117; Atlanta: Scholars Press, 1989), 5-6; Terrence Collins, *Line-Forms in Hebrew Poetry: A Grammatical Approach to the Stylistic Study of the Hebrew Prophets*, (Studia Pohl: Series Maior 7; Rome: Pontifical Biblical Institute, 1978), 276; F. W. Dobbs-Allsopp, "The Enjambing Line in Lamentations: A Taxonomy (Part I)," *ZAW* 113 (2001), 221-2; Gray, *Forms*, 54-5; Lowth, *Isaiah*, xl-xli; O'Connor, *HVS*, 297; Wilfred G. E. Watson, *Classical Hebrew Poetry: A Guide to its Techniques* (*CHP*) (JSOTSup 26; Sheffield: JSOT Press, 1986; repr., London, T&T Clark, 2005), 46.

Psalms, Job, Proverbs, Lamentations, Sirach, and certain poems embedded in narratives (Exod 15; Deut 32; Judg 5; 2 Sam 22)—are visually arranged by line in some Qumran and later Masoretic manuscripts, and a few Talmudic and rabbinic texts attempt to codify these practices (for example, Babylonian Talmud, tractate *Megillah* 16b).[6] Not insignificantly, this fact offers decisive evidence for the recognition of poetry among Biblical Hebrew texts in antiquity.[7] Prophetic texts, however, are never so treated. It is uncertain whether this fact means that ancient scribes did not view these texts as poetry or whether other, unknown factors might have been in play.[8] A partial outlier is Isa 61:10–62:9 in 1QIsa^a L, 8–22, where added spacing in the continuous text clearly divides lines, but without clean, graphic line breaks as in the texts noted earlier.[9] No other section in 1QIsa^a is treated this way, and no other ancient or medieval Hebrew manuscript treats these verses in this way, making it difficult to account for this idiosyncratic example. Compared to Hebrew manuscripts, early codices of the Septuagint graphically represent a much larger corpus of the Hebrew Bible as verse, but they, too, do not use this distinctive format for prophetic books.[10] Punctuation systems in

---

[6] Kugel, *Idea*, 119–25; O'Connor, *HVS*, 29–30; Emmanuel Tov, *Scribal Practices and Approaches Reflected in the Texts Found in the Judean Desert* (Studies on the Texts of the Desert of Judah 54; Leiden: Brill, 2004), 166–78; James L. Kugel, *Textual Criticism of the Hebrew Bible* (2nd ed.; Minneapolis: Fortress, 2001), 212; Tull, "What's New in Lowth," 188–91.

[7] F. W. Dobbs-Allsopp, "Space, Line, and the Written Biblical Poem in Texts from the Judean Desert," in *Puzzling Out the Past: Studies in Northwest Semitic Languages and Literatures in Honor of Bruce Zuckerman* (eds. Marilyn J. Lundberg, Steven Fine, and Wayne T. Pitard; Culture and History of the Ancient Near East 55; Leiden: Brill, 2012), 19–61; O'Connor, *HVS*, 29–31; Tov, *Scribal Practices*, 167.

[8] O'Connor suggests that ancient scribes did not recognize prophetic poems because they only distinguished between poetry and prose at the level of whole books (O'Connor, *HVS*, 30, 634). Similarly, Tov suggests that the mixture of poetry and prose in prophetic books explains the lack of lined formatting in these books, although it is possible that scribes might have been aware of the existence of poetry in them (Tov, *Scribal Practices*, 166). While not implausible, these proposals leave open the question of why poems such as Deut 32 or Judg 5 in otherwise prose books did receive special formatting.

[9] For an image of the ms., see Dobbs-Allsopp, "Space, Line, and the Written Biblical Poem," 58, fig. 30. Note also the digital images of 1QIsa^a online at <http://dss.collections.imj.org.il/isaiah> (accessed 6 November 2014).

[10] Thomas S. Pattie, "The Creation of the Great Codices," in *The Bible as Book: The Manuscript Tradition* (eds. John L. Sharpe III and Kimberly van Kampen; London/New Castle, Del.: British Library/Oak Knoll Press, 1998), 63, cited in Tull, "What's New in Lowth," 191–3. Digital images of Isaiah from Codex Sinaiticus can be seen

various manuscript traditions, such as the accents in the Masoretic Text or dots in the Septuagint, may sometimes mark divisions at the level of poetic lines in Isaiah, but there is great variation among these systems.[11] At any rate, this evidence is far less useful than ancient lineated manuscripts would be. Jerome's Latin translation of Isaiah is divided into lines; however, he clearly states in the preface to his translation that he does so for rhetorical purposes, not because he regards biblical prophetic literature as poetic.[12] Insofar as his decisions concerning line breaks seem to be original to him, they are evidence for early literary interpretation of Isaiah, but they do not move us closer to an ancient tradition concerning its lineation.

This absence of lineated manuscripts hardly suggests that texts in Isaiah should not be considered verse, however, as if lineation were merely a typographical phenomenon, or poetry itself merely a textual art. Robert Pinsky has suggested that poetry is inherently something that one hears, and that the appearance of poetry in writing merely approximates that experience—not unlike the difference between a musical performance and musical score.[13] Brogan takes a slightly different position, regarding poems as abstractions that may be realized either aurally through hearing or visually through reading, much like language itself.[14] Both views presuppose that a poem exists separately from its appearance in writing and thereby establish the validity of poetry as an aural phenomenon experienced through performance. Most likely, that is how Isaiah's original audience would have encountered his poems, sidestepping the thorny and probably undecidable question of whether they were originally

online at <http://codexsinaiticus.org/en/manuscript.aspx> (accessed 6 November 2014).

[11] E. Ulrich, "Sense Divisions in Ancient Manuscripts of Isaiah," in *Unit Delimitation in Biblical Hebrew and Northwest Semitic Literature* (eds. Marjo C. A. Korpel and Josef M. Oesch, *Pericope: Scripture as Written and Read in Antiquity 4*. Assen: Koninklijke Van Gorcum, 2003), 297–301.

[12] See "Incipit Prologus Hieronymi in Isaia Propheta," in *Biblia Sacra Vulgata: Iuxta Vulgatum Versionem* (ed. Robert Weber; 2 vols, 4th ed.; Stuttgart: Württembergische Bibelanstalt, 1994), 2:1096. Lowth already refers to these statements by Jerome in the "Preliminary Dissertation" to his Isaiah commentary, and, as Tull notes, they have been cited in "nearly every modern discussion of biblical poetry or biblical page layout" (Lowth, *Isaiah*, ii–iii; Tull, "What's New in Lowth," 192, n. 18).

[13] Robert Pinsky, *The Sounds of Poetry: A Brief Guide* (New York: Farrar, Straus, & Giroux, 1998), 43.

[14] Brogan, "Poetry," 940–1.

composed orally or in writing.[15] If poems exist apart from their written representations, then, and lineation is a necessary feature of poetry, it follows that lineation as a phenomenon is separable from graphic conventions for marking line breaks.[16] This possibility holds true even for much non-metrical poetry, or free verse—the category to which Biblical Hebrew verse belongs, as will be argued later in this chapter.[17]

The issue, then, is not the presence of lines in Biblical Hebrew verse but the discernment of their boundaries. Although various features may mark line breaks with relative clarity, they are hardly self-evident, and the onus falls on the interpreter to justify proposed divisions. W. T. W. Cloete confidently affirms the existence of a "correct" lineation of Hebrew verse.[18] While he does not specify the nature of this "correct" lineation, his positivistic language suggests that he regards it as something inherent in the text. By contrast, Ruth Finnegan argues that lineation must be regarded as a relative phenomenon, especially in poetry intended for performance.[19] Certainly, there are poetic segments in First Isaiah for which multiple line divisions seem equally defensible, such as the two couplets in Isa 15:1b.[20] It is even possible that line breaks in some poems could have varied among different ancient performances. Pinsky goes so far as to

---

[15] In Isa 5:1, the poem opens with the cohortative verb 'āšîrâ-nā' ("let me sing"), suggesting an oral, sung performance (see Ezek 33:32), and the prophet imagines his opponents mocking the sounds of his speech in Isa 28:9–10. On the oral or performative qualities of biblical prophetic poetry more generally, see Yehoshua Gitay, "Deutero-Isaiah: Oral or Written?" *JBL* 99 (1980): 185–97, especially 194–5; Susan Niditch, *Oral World and Written Word: Ancient Israelite Literature* (Library of Ancient Israel; Louisville: Westminster John Knox, 1996), 117–20. Van der Toorn has argued that the main function of all writing in ancient Israel was to aid oral performances (*Scribal Culture*, 11–14).

[16] Cloete, *Versification and Syntax*, 6; O'Connor, *HVS*, 30; Pinsky, *Sounds of Poetry*, 35.

[17] Smith, *Poetic Closure*, 88. There remain, of course, poems in which the lineation cannot be discerned without recourse to visual conventions. The existence of such poems qualifies but does not invalidate my argument.

[18] Cloete, *Versification and Syntax*, 15–16.

[19] Ruth Finnegan, *Oral Poetry: Its Nature, Significance, and Social Context* (Cambridge: Cambridge University Press, 1977; repr. Bloomington, Ind.: Indiana University Press, 1992), 106, 130.

[20] Each couplet contains five words, and it is unclear whether they should be divided into two- and three-word lines, or vice versa. Contrast, for example, BH^3; BHS; NAB; NIV; Blenkinsopp, *Isa 1–39*, 293; Wildberger, *Isa 13–27*, 104 (all 2:3) with Gray, *Isa I-XXVII*, 273; Lowth, *Isaiah*, 225; NRSV; REB (all 3:2). See further the discussion in Jones, *Howling over Moab*, 164–75.

suggest that one should not uncritically accept the lineation of any poem—even one supported by an "authoritative" tradition of lineated texts—as a given:

> If it can't be demonstrated why the author's version is better, the question should be open. Such demonstration requires thinking about what the poem means. By asking what, precisely, it is about, one can begin to form a judgment about how it should sound, and therefore about what arrangement in lines best brings out those vocal rhythms for the reader.[21]

If versification remains a potentially unsettled issue even for poems with a tradition of clear lineation, the question is certainly open for poems that have no such tradition. For Pinsky, the "correct" lineation reinforces the poem's meaning. Any proposal for lineation, consequently, should proceed in process with the interpretation of the poem, rather than as a preliminary step, and the persuasiveness of any proposal will depend on the persuasiveness of the reading into which it is integrated.[22]

The definitiveness of lineation for poetry, on the one hand, and potential questions about the lineation of prophetic poems in the Hebrew Bible, on the other, make this a vital interpretive question. Surprisingly, it has received little explicit attention. Cloete blames this state of affairs on the "authoritative" status of standard texts of the Hebrew Bible that graphically mark line breaks in biblical poems, which leads scholars to assume that the matter is settled.[23] Both BH^3 and BHS take for their base text Codex Leningrad, which does not graphically represent lineation in Isaiah. Their arrangement of poetic texts—such as the decision to regard certain texts as poetry in the first place—is a modern scholarly proposal, the rationale for which is

---

[21] Pinsky, *Sounds of Poetry*, 46. Pinsky raises this possibility to illustrate the relationship among lineation, sound, and meaning in a Robert Frost poem, and he concludes that the standard lineation in published versions of the poem does, in fact, best bring out its meaning. Thus, he is not—and neither am I—advocating the rampant relineation of classic poems!

[22] For persuasiveness as a criterion for evaluating critical arguments, see Dobbs-Allsopp, "Rethinking Historical Criticism," 260-1. One might criticize the circularity of Pinsky's view, objecting that the interpreter has created the text. Much contemporary theory, however, holds that this fluid situation obtains to some degree for all texts, in which case the question of lineation foregrounds for biblical prophetic poetry a phenomenon common to all literature.

[23] Cloete, *Versification and Syntax*, 13; see also Petersen and Richards, *Interpreting Hebrew Poetry*, 4-5; Tull, "What's New in Lowth," 185-6.

never made explicit.[24] Often, commentaries or translations simply follow the lineation of one of these editions, and even scholarly treatments of Hebrew poetry do not always justify their division of poetic lines. In an effort to avoid this shortcoming, this chapter grounds my treatment of Isaianic poetry in a discussion of lineation, identifying potential indicators of line breaks in selected textual examples. In the process, I also discuss more generally the character and effects of lineation in First Isaiah. The discussion does not attempt to be exhaustive, but it suggests in detail the considerations that will inform my proposed line divisions of poetic texts throughout this study. Arguments for these divisions will be provided as necessary in subsequent chapters.

MARKERS OF LINEATION

Persuasive arguments for the lineation of biblical poems must account for a number of factors. The most conclusive marker of line breaks is the alphabetic acrostic, which provided the linchpin for Lowth's identification of verse in biblical texts.[25] First Isaiah, however, contains no examples of this form.[26] Among other features of style, the most consistently reliable one is parallelism, which among other functions often marks the limits of lines in which it occurs, particularly in oral poetry.[27] While it is not universal in biblical poetry, despite occasional claims to that effect, parallelism establishes the sense of the line in enough cases to provide some expectations for the shape of non-parallel lines, for which other stylistic features may give additional confirmation. Enjambed verse, the primary alternative to parallelistic verse in the Hebrew Bible, has its own distinctive linear tendencies that permit description. Rhythm is another consideration. Lines of Biblical

---

[24] Tull, "What's New in Lowth," 186.
[25] Lowth, *Isaiah*, iv; Lowth, *Lectures*, 32; see further David Noel Freedman, "Acrostics and Metrics," in *Poetry, Pottery, and Prophecy: Studies in Early Hebrew Poetry* (Winona Lake, Ind.: Eisenbrauns, 1980), 51–2; repr. from *HTR* 65 (1972).
[26] With the exception of the partial acrostic in Nah 1:2–8, acrostic poems do not occur in the prophetic corpus, as noted by Lowth, *Lectures*, 148.
[27] Finnegan, *Oral Poetry*, 107. This relationship between stylistic devices and lineation corroborates Pinsky's insistence that questions of lineation belong to the larger process of interpretation.

Hebrew verse show a variability of length associated with non-metrical, free verse poetry, but within approximately quantifiable limits. These limits offer a helpful check for decisions about lineation and can eliminate possibilities when other factors prove inconclusive. Similarly, syntactic analyses of Biblical Hebrew verse suggest that certain constraints restrict the number and combination of syntactic elements within a line. These constraints provide another set of criteria for describing hypothetical limits to the line and thus identifying potential line breaks. Finally, sense divisions suggested by the punctuation in ancient manuscripts provide some clues to lineation.[28] As noted earlier, these divisions may not always correspond to poetic divisions, but they do so often enough to merit consideration in uncertain cases. Moreover, they represent ancient interpretive traditions that may reflect cultural memories of poetic performances no longer accessible to modern readers.[29]

Stylistic Features

As is well known, parallelism has been regarded as a distinctive feature of Biblical Hebrew poetry since the work of Lowth, who famously defined the phenomenon as "a certain equality, resemblance, or parallelism, between the members of each period; so that in two lines (or members of the same period) things for the most part shall answer to things, and words to words, as if fitted to each other by a kind of rule or measure."[30] The present discussion is primarily concerned with the function of parallelism to mark line breaks in biblical poems; its other poetic effects will be treated in the following chapter. Parallelism provides a reliable guide to lineation because parallel lines are typically end-stopped—that is, the ends of lines generally correspond to the boundaries of clauses—because most if not all of the syntactic units in a given line have matching terms in the

---

[28] As recognized already by Lowth, *Isaiah*, xx–xxi.
[29] For the growing body of literature on this topic, see Raymond de Hoop, "The Colometry of Hebrew Verse and the Masoretic Accents: A Recent Approach," pts. 1 and 2, *JNSL* 26, no. 1 (2000): 47–73; *JNSL* 26, no. 2 (2000): 61–100; Marjo C. A. Korpel and Josef M. Oesch (eds.), *Delimitation Criticism: A New Tool in Biblical Scholarship* (*Pericope: Scripture as Written and Read in Antiquity 1*. Assen: Koninklijke Van Gorcum, 2000), with subsequent vols in the series; Watson, "Study of Biblical Hebrew Poetry," 134–5, 141.
[30] Lowth, *Lectures*, 157; see also Lowth, *Isaiah*, ix.

next.[31] In parallelistic verse, the reader or hearer comes to expect recurring pauses between sentences with approximately matching syntactic shapes, which often coincide in semantic content. Barbara Herrnstein Smith, commenting on a poem by Whitman, describes this effect as "patterns of intonational cadence which... recur frequently enough to have rhythmic effects."[32] Parallelism thus calls attention to the structures that it repeats and consequently to the lines that they delimit. To be sure, end-stopped lines are not the exclusive line form in Biblical Hebrew verse, nor is parallelism the exclusive trope.[33] Nonetheless, where it does occur, parallelism is probably the most reliable indicator of lineation in Biblical Hebrew verse—including the majority of poems in First Isaiah. In the introduction to his Isaiah commentary, for instance, Gray appeals largely to parallelism for justification of the lineation of his translations of poetic texts.[34]

Parallelism delimits not only individual poetic units but also groups, usually pairs, of such units. Traditionally, discussions of biblical poetry have taken these pairs, typically referred to as "bicola," as the basic unit of Biblical Hebrew verse—in other words, as the poetic line. The primary reason for this identification is the less pronounced stop within the bicolon as compared to the more pronounced stop at the end of it. For Luis Alonso Schökel, this difference corresponds to "the obvious difference between pauses and caesuras."[35] This difference, however, is not so obvious as he would claim.[36] Moreover, several factors strongly suggest that the colon be identified as the line, notably the existence of mono- and tricola, and acrostics that operate on the level of the colon in Psalms 111 and 112.[37] Following most recent interpreters of biblical poetry, then, I assume the

---

[31] Cloete, *Hebrew Versification*, 28, 47; Gray, *Forms*, 127; Greenstein, "How Does Parallelism Mean?" 50; Lowth, *Lectures*, 33–5; O'Connor, *HVS*, 67–8.
[32] Smith, *Poetic Closure*, 90; see also Gray, *Forms*, 126.
[33] Collins, *Line-Forms*, 8–9; Dobbs-Allsopp, "Enjambing Line," 221–3.
[34] Gray, *Isa I–XXVII*, lx; see also Gray, *Forms*, 163.
[35] Luis Alonso Schökel, *A Manual of Hebrew Poetics* (Subsidia Biblica 11; Rome: Pontifical Biblical Institute, 1988), 46; see further Kugel, *Idea*, 51, 54–7.
[36] For instance, as Dobbs-Allsopp observes, the stop within an enjambed bicolon is "perceptually weaker" than that within a parallel bicolon ("Enjambing Line," 222–3). By labeling the stop within the bicolon as "caesura," Alonso Schökel also fails to recognize the possibility of caesura within the colon, created, for instance, by internal parallelism.
[37] Dobbs-Alsopp, "Poetry, Hebrew," 551.

30 Reading the Poetry of First Isaiah

colon as the basic unit of biblical verse.[38] In this study, however, I will generally use the terms "line," "couplet," and "triplet," which are more widely used in literary criticism, instead of "colon," "bicolon," and "tricolon." The first half of the royal poem in Isa 11 nicely illustrates the role of parallelism in establishing line boundaries in biblical verse. One finds substantial agreement among different critical editions, translations, and commentaries concerning the lineation of these verses, which suggests that the line breaks are practically intuitive as a result of the parallelism. Nonetheless, a closer examination of how parallelism delimits these lines will prove instructive:

[1] wĕyāṣā' ḥōṭer miggēzaʿ yīšāy
    wĕnēṣer miššārāšāyw yipreh
[2] wĕnāḥâ ʿālāyw rûaḥ yhwh
    rûaḥ ḥokmâ ûbînâ
    rûaḥ ʿēṣâ ûgĕbûrâ
    rûaḥ daʿat wĕyirʾat yhwh[39]
[3] wĕlōʾ lĕmarʾēh ʿênāyw yišpôṭ
    wĕlōʾ lĕmišmaʿ ʾoznāyw yôkîaḥ
[4] wĕšāpaṭ bĕṣedeq dallîm
    wĕhôkîaḥ bĕmîšôr lĕʿanwê ʾāreṣ
    wĕhikkâ ʾereṣ[40] bĕšēbeṭ pîw
    ûbĕrûaḥ śĕpātāyw yāmît rāšāʿ
[5] wĕhāyâ ṣedeq ʾēzôr motnāyw
    wĕhāʾĕmûnâ ʾēzôr ḥălāṣāyw

---

[38] For example, Cloete, *Versification and Syntax*, 84; Dobbs-Allsopp, "Enjambing Line," 221-2; O'Connor, *HVS*, 52-4, 134-5; Petersen and Richards, *Interpreting Hebrew Poetry*, 23-4; Watson, *CHP*, 12. Exceptions include Alter, *Art of Biblical Poetry*, 9 and J. P. Fokkelman *Reading Biblical Poetry: An Introductory Guide* (trans. Ineke Smit; Louisville: Westminster John Knox, 2001), 38.

[39] MT has an additional line waḥărîḥô bĕyirʾat yhwh ("and his scent by the fear of YHWH") at the beginning of v. 3. Although the line is attested in all of the versions, its difficult sense and close similarity to the preceding verse suggest that it is a dittograph (for example, Blenkinsopp, *Isa 1-39*, 263; Gray, *Isa I-XXVII*, 221; Hans Wildberger, *Isaiah 1-12* [trans. Thomas H. Trapp; CC; Minneapolis: Fortress, 1991], 461).

[40] Many commentators emend MT ʾereṣ ("earth") to ʿārîṣ ("violent"), arguing that it provides a better parallel for rāšāʿ ("wicked"); see Blenkinsopp, *Isa 1-39*, 263; Gray, *Isa I-XXVII*, 218; Wildberger, *Isa 1-12*, 461; etc. The phonetic interchange of ʾ and ʿ has precedent (Tov, *Textual Criticism*, 251), and the occurrence of ʾereṣ in the preceding line could have influenced the change. On the other hand, in light of the prominent repetition in the poem, this detail could also support MT. As the text stands, the parallelism effectively joins a general statement with a more nuanced statement.

[1] There will come forth a shoot from the stump of Jesse,
   and the sprout from his roots will bear fruit.
[2] And there will rest upon him the spirit of Yhwh:
   the spirit of wisdom and of perception;
   the spirit of counsel and of strength;
   the spirit of knowledge and of the fear of Yhwh.
[3] And he will not judge according to the sight of his eyes,
   nor reprove according to the report of his ears.
[4] And he will judge with righteousness the poor,
   and reprove with equity for the humble of the earth.
And he will strike the earth with the rod of his mouth,
   and with the breath of his lips slay the wicked.
[5] And righteousness will be the belt around his loins,
   and steadfastness the belt around his waist. (Isa 11:1–5)[41]

The lines exhibit considerable variety of shape, which prevents the poetry from becoming rote and predictable, but this variety does not overcome the pervasive sense of symmetry effected by the parallelism. Reflecting the end-stopped character of the lines, every line in this poetic segment begins with the *w-* conjunction, except for the three lines of v. 2b.[42] Moreover, each line break corresponds to a major disjunctive accent in the Masoretic Text—either the 'atnāḥ or zāqēp qāṭôn in most cases—again a function of the correspondence of line breaks with syntactic boundaries.

The parallelism seems most apparent in vv. 3 and 4a, where corresponding syntactic and semantic units occupy the same position in each line. This arrangement highlights the outer limits of the lines, since parallel terms mark their beginnings and especially their ends. One does see subtle variations between matching terms, such as the parallel single noun and construct chain in v. 4a, but these variations do not obscure the parallelism. By contrast, vv. 1 and 4b are partially

---

[41] For biblical quotations that contain more than one couplet, triplet, or the like, I follow the convention of most recent Eng. Bible translations and use indention to mark the lines that belong to each group, both in my Hebrew text and translation. Although the appearance is admittedly untidy, the brief moment that it takes for the reader's eye to return from the indented line to the left margin somewhat approximates the emphatic pause that accompanies the end of a line group. Blank lines divide larger sections of the poem, as in the reading of Isa 22:1b–14 at the end of this chapter.

[42] Some interpreters, however, regard the *w-* conjunction at the beginning of poetic lines as secondary in many cases: for example, Frank Moore Cross Jr. and David Noel Freedman, *Studies in Ancient Yahwistic Poetry* (SBLDS 21; Missoula, Mont.: Scholars Press, 1975; repr. Biblical Resource Series; Grand Rapids: Eerdmans, 1997), 20, 83–4.

chiastic, like many lines in Biblical Hebrew verse.[43] While the repetition of grammatical structures establishes the common shapes of the parallel lines, the inversion of that structure in the second line of each couplet underscores the line break, as the first line ends and the second begins with parallel grammatical units: the subject with prepositional phrase in v. 1 and the prepositional phrase in v. 4b. In v. 5, the verb wĕhāyâ ("and will be") in the A-line has no parallel in the B-line, although it must still be assumed to govern the object in that line. Such omission of repeated or parallel syntactic units—a linguistic phenomenon variously known as "deletion," "ellipsis," or "gapping"— occurs frequently in biblical poetry but rarely in prose.[44] It poses no problem for discerning lineation, since the presence of a word at the beginning of v. 5b (hā'ĕmûnâ, "faithfulness") parallel to a term from v. 5a (ṣedeq, "righteousness") clearly signals the beginning of the second parallel line, as does the waw-conjunction.[45]

A similar case obtains for the quatrain in v. 2. The first two words in v. 2a (wĕnāḥâ 'ālāyw, "and there will rest upon him") have no parallel in the following lines.[46] Once again, the line break can be discerned on the basis of the parallelism, the ellipsis notwithstanding. Moreover, the opening word of the next line (v. 2bα) is not merely a synonym of a word from the previous line; the word itself (rûaḥ, "spirit") is repeated, and its repetition opens the following lines of the quatrain as well. The heightened parallelism resulting from the initial

---

[43] Watson, *CHP*, 201–2. Verse 1, as he notes, fits his category of "split-member chiasmus... where the /a/ and /b/ components are themselves split into yet smaller elements" (a-bc/b'c'-a'); other examples include Ps 22:13 (Eng. 22:12); Prov 7:21. The pattern in v. 4b (a-b-cd/cd'-a'-b') is another possibility for this kind of chiasm, as in Isa 33:4; Job 3:6; etc.

[44] Gray, *Forms*, 59, 72–83; Greenstein, "How Does Parallelism Mean?" 46–53; Cynthia L. Miller, "A Linguistic Approach to Ellipsis in Biblical Poetry (Or, What to Do When Exegesis of What is There Depends on What Isn't)," *Bulletin for Biblical Research* 13 (2003): 251–70; O'Connor, *HVS*, 122–9, 401–7.

[45] Cynthia L. Miller observes that the w- conjunction always joins poetic lines in which the verb *hāyâ* ("to be") has been deleted ("The Relation of Coordination to Verb Gapping in Biblical Poetry," *JSOT* 32 [2007]: 53–4).

[46] Alternatively, one could take the following three lines as a series of phrases in apposition to the final phrase of v. 2a, *rûaḥ yhwh* ("the spirit of Yhwh"). This explanation might best account for the absence of the conjunctive w-, which otherwise marks the beginnings of lines in vv. 1–5. In cases like this, however, it is difficult to determine whether one is dealing with verbal ellipsis or apposition (Dobbs-Allsopp, "Enjambing Line," 228; Greenstein, "How Does Parallelism Mean?" 52). The poetic effect remains largely the same; the question is how one describes the syntax that produces it.

repetition strengthens the sense of line breaks, which offsets the fact that these lines consist of phrases instead of whole clauses, as one more commonly finds with parallel lines in Biblical Hebrew verse. Such repetition of a word or phrase at the beginning of each of a series of syntactic units is known as anaphora. In contrast to parallelism, which establishes the ends of lines in biblical verse through its end-stopped character, anaphora marks the beginnings of lines. It should, nonetheless, be regarded as a species of parallelism, since repetition is the strongest form of parallelism.[47]

Because of its characteristic repetition, anaphora can be an especially obvious marker of lineation.[48] This principle holds true even in the following example, where the repeated phrases alternate between one line and the next, demonstrating the flexibility with which Isaiah uses basic poetic devices:

[7] *wattimmālē' 'arṣô kesep wĕzāhāb*
wĕ'ên qēṣeh lĕ'ōṣĕrōtāyw
wattimmālē' 'arṣô sûsîm
wĕ'ên qēṣeh lĕmarkĕbōtāyw
[8] *wattimmālē' 'arṣô 'ĕlîlîm*
lĕma'ăśēh yādāwy yištaḥăwû
la'ăšer 'āśû 'eṣbĕ'ōtāyw

[7] And their land is filled with silver and gold,
and there is no limit to their treasuries.
[8] And their land is filled with horses,
and there is no limit to their chariots.
And their land is filled with "gods"[49]—
to the work of their hands they bow down,
to that which their fingers made. (Isa 2:7–8)

---

[47] Adele Berlin, *The Dynamics of Biblical Parallelism* (Bloomington, Ind.: Indiana University Press, 1985), 131; Finnegan, *Oral Poetry*, 102; O'Connor, *HVS*, 87–8; Dennis Pardee, *Ugaritic and Hebrew Poetic Parallelism: A Trial Cut ('nt I and Proverbs 2)* (VTSup 39; Leiden: Brill, 1988), 169–70, 200–1; *contra* Kugel, *Idea*, 56.
[48] Kinzie, *Poet's Guide*, 393.
[49] The substantive adjective *'ĕlîlîm* is used in First Isaiah as a pejorative designation for deities other than Yнwн (for example, Isa 2:20; 10:10–11; 19:1, 3; cf. Lev 19:4; Ps 96:5; Hab 2:18). The basic sense of the adjective is "worthless, empty" (see Jer 14:14; Job 13:4), but its use with reference to false deities likely plays on the similar sounding word *'ĕlōhîm* ("God"). My translation "gods," with scare quotes, attempts to capture this connotation.

In this sequence, anaphora delimits lines of three to four words. Despite being introduced by the same opening phrase (*wattimmālē' 'arṣô*, "their land is filled"), the first and third lines in v. 7 are not uniform in length, as the pair of singular words *kesep wĕzāhāb* ("silver and gold") in v. 7a matches the single plural term *sûsîm* ("horses") in v. 7b—an interesting variation of expressions of multiplicity. This verse suggests, then, that a stylistic device can secure the boundaries of poetic lines even when they vary in length. The final two lines in the sequence break the pattern because they do not begin with the expected tag *wĕ'ên qēṣeh l-* ("and there is no limit to").[50] Both lines open with the preposition *l-*, however, so the expectation of anaphora is not totally frustrated, even as the departure from the established pattern clearly marks the conclusion of the sequence.[51]

Not all cases are so simple, even when the parallelism is straightforward, because the units isolated by parallelism do not always coincide with lines of verse. Parallelism may also occur at both smaller and larger levels of the poem—that is, within lines and between whole couplets.[52] The first category, lines with internal parallelism, occurs frequently in Isaianic poetry with distinctive poetic effects. Consider the following cluster of such lines in Isa 8:9–10:

[9] *rĕ'û*[53] *'ammîm wāḥōttû*
 wĕha'ăzînû kōl merḥaqqê-'āreṣ

---

[50] A number of commentators propose that a line beginning *wĕ'ên qēṣeh l-* has in fact dropped out here (Blenkinsopp, *Isa 1–39*, 192–3; Duhm, *Jesaia*, 40–1; Gray, *Isa I–XXVII*, 49; Wildberger, *Isa 1–12*, 100–1). Although the proposal assumes an excessively wooden view of poetic structure, the fact that commentators seem compelled to perpetuate it suggests the force of the anaphora and its impact on the reader or hearer.

[51] For departure from an established pattern as a closural device, see Smith, *Poetic Closure*, 28, 43–4, 92–3.

[52] Cloete, *Versification and Syntax*, 26–7; Stephen A. Geller, *Parallelism in Early Biblical Poetry* (HSM 20; Missoula, Mont.: Scholars Press, 1979), 6, 11–14; Pardee, *Ugaritic and Hebrew Poetic Parallelism*, 198–200.

[53] MT *rō'û* appears to come from the root *r''* II, "be shattered." Verse 9b, however, calls the nations to take defensive action (*hit'azzĕrû*, "gird yourselves") before repeating the command "be dismayed." If the same pattern holds for v. 9a, then a derivation from √*r'h* II ("associate, join together") or √*rw'* ("raise the war-cry") is preferable, either of which requires only a change in vocalization. The former, followed here, has support from Aq.; Sym.; Theod.; Tg., and is adopted by Wildberger (*Isa 1–12*, 349–50). The second option, however, is not implausible; see Magne Sæbø, "Traditio-Historical Perspectives on Isaiah 8:9–10: An Attempt to Clarify an Old *Crux Interpretum*," in *On the Way to Canon: Creative Tradition History in the Old Testament* (JSOTSup 191; Sheffield: Sheffield Academic Press, 1998), 108–21; trans. Birgit Mänz-Davies and repr. of "Zur Traditionsgeschicte von Jesaia 8, 9–10," *ZAW*

hitʾazzĕrû wāḥōttû
hitʾazzĕrû wāḥōttû
[10] *ʿuṣû ʿēṣâ wĕtūpār*
dabbĕrû dābār wĕlōʾ yāqûm
kî ʿimmānû ʾēl

[9] Join together, peoples, and be dismayed!
Give ear, all distant places of the earth—
Gird yourselves and be dismayed!
Gird yourselves and be dismayed!
[10] Plan a plan, but it will be frustrated;
Speak a word, but it will not stand;
For God is with us.

Five of these seven lines contain pairs of verbs and must be treated as internally parallel, since one could not divide them without producing awkward, single-word lines. If the proposed emendation in the first line of v. 9 has merit, then all of them follow a similar pattern, in which the action of the second verb tempers or undoes the action of the first. The internal parallelism quickens the pace of the poetry by allowing multiple verbs in a single line, instead of isolating them in their own respective lines and forcing the reader or hearer to wait longer for the next action. The effect becomes especially striking in v. 10a, which draws on a favorite theme of First Isaiah—ill-conceived human plans that are bound to fail, in contrast to the inexorable plan of God (see Isa 14:26–27; 30:1). The prophet sarcastically invites the nations to make such plans in the first half of each line, and the cognate accusative creates the expectation of perfect correspondence between action and result, an expectation which the second verb quite literally "frustrates." In this way, the internal parallelism reinforces the futility of military hostilities against Judah by its enemies. Every action to which the poet tauntingly calls them is immediately thwarted, all within the space of a single line.

The possibility of internal parallelism forces the interpreter to consider whether any given pair of consecutive, brief clauses forms a single line or a couplet with two short lines. Isaiah 3:8 illustrates the problem well:

---

76 (1964): 132–44. Emending the verb to *dēʿû* ("know"), following LXX and supported by the frequency of *r/d* confusion, seems less attractive despite its widespread appearance in commentaries (for example, Blenkinsopp, *Isa 1–39*, 240; Gray, *Isa I–XXVII*, 149; Kaiser, *Isa 1–12*, 115).

> kî kāšĕlâ yĕrûšālaim
> wîhûdâ nāpāl
> For Jerusalem will stumble,
> and Judah will fall.

Interpreters differ over whether to treat this segment as one line or two.[54] The question is finally how one hears the clauses: do they bear individual emphasis or form a continuous thought? Favoring the former option, the verbs *kāšal* ("stumble") and *nāpal* ("fall") depict separate, sequential events. In this case, the capital Jerusalem "will stumble" as its leadership gives way to the anarchy described in the preceding verses. The effects of this power vacuum then prove detrimental to the entire nation, and so the nation as a whole "will fall."[55] Although couplets of two-word lines are the exception in First Isaiah, they do occur. In this case, the short lines encapsulate the effects of the social disorder detailed in the longer, preceding lines, and their brevity calls attention to them. Moreover, the succession of brief lines produces a halting effect as one hears or reads the poem, a poetic mimesis of the actions of stumbling and falling.[56]

In other cases it may be less clear whether an internally parallel line or two short lines better match the tenor of the poem. The decision will be made easier by an awareness of circumstances in which one is likely to find the phenomenon. For instance, Wilfred G. E. Watson notes that internally parallel lines often occur in clusters, ranging from two to five lines in length.[57] I have already discussed Isa 8:9–10 as one example of such a cluster. Isaiah 1:16b–17 is another. A second likely scenario is a couplet with an internally parallel first line. These couplets typically appear as a series of two short clauses followed by a third, longer clause, which is often roughly the same length as the two

---

[54] Among those who treat it as a single line are Lowth, *Isaiah*, 6; Wilfred G. E. Watson, *Traditional Techniques in Classical Hebrew Verse* (JSOTSup 170; Sheffield: Sheffield Academic Press, 1994), 45. Those who divide it into two lines include *BHS*; Gray, *Isa I–XXVII*, 61; Wildberger, *Isa 1–12*, 124; Williamson, *Isa 1–5*, 242.

[55] Berlin, *Dynamics*, 145, n. 14.

[56] Contrast the similarly worded line in Isa 31:3b: *wĕkāšal 'ôzēr wĕnāpal 'āzūr* ("then the helper will stumble, and the one helped will fall"). This line is the second line of a triplet, and treating it as two short, parallel lines would leave the preceding clause isolated as a single line; consequently, it should be regarded as internally parallel.

[57] Watson, *Traditional Techniques*, 155–8, 174–5.

shorter clauses together. Watson has labeled this phenomenon the "A- A- // A— line."[58] Examples include Isa 1:6b; 5:2a, 15; 10:6b; 14:31a; 15:6b; 16:4b; 22:16; 30:11. Couplets with an internally parallel second line (A— // A- A-) are less common, but one finds them in Isa 8:13 and 10:14b.

The second possibility for parallelism beyond the line is parallel couplets—that is, successive couplets whose corresponding lines are parallel.[59] Again, it may be difficult to decide whether two, exceptionally lengthy parallel segments should be analyzed as a single couplet with long lines or as two parallel couplets. In some cases, though, internal pauses or other stylistic features will encourage further division of each parallel segment, as in the following example:

wĕniggaś hāʿām ʾîš bĕʾîš
wĕʾîš bĕrēʿēhû
yirhăbû hannaʿar bazzāqēn
wĕhanniqleh bannikbād

And the people will oppress themselves, each against another,
    and each against his neighbor;
they will rise up, the lad against the elder,
    and the scorned against the honored. (Isa 3:5)

It would be possible to take the verse as a pair of parallel lines, longer than usual but within allowable limits.[60] Alternatively, following *BHS*, one might divide each half of the verse at the conjunction, since it forces a syntactic pause that could mark the end of a line. This division produces several pleasing effects. It highlights the gapping of the verbs, a phenomenon more appropriate within a pair of lines than a single line. The imbalance of the alternating long and short

---

[58] Watson, *Traditional Techniques*, 176; see also Alonso Schökel, *Manual*, 56; Geller, *Parallelism in Early Biblical Poetry*, 28.

[59] Terminology for the phenomenon is inconsistent. Some possibilities include "alternating" or "ABAʹBʹ parallelism": John T. Willis, "Alternating (ABAʹBʹ) Parallelism in the Old Testament Psalms and Prophetic Literature," in *Directions in Biblical Hebrew Poetry* (ed. Elaine R. Follis; JSOTSup 40; Sheffield: Sheffield Academic Press, 1987), 49–76; "external parallelism": Norman K. Gottwald, "Poetry, Hebrew," *The Interpreter's Dictionary of the Bible* 3:833; "interlinear parallelism": Alter, *Art of Biblical Poetry*, 14, 20; and "near parallelism": Pardee, *Ugaritic and Hebrew Poetic Parallelism*, 188–9, 198–9. Each of these terms has its problems, so I refer to such units simply as "parallel couplets," as distinguished from a single couplet that contains two parallel lines.

[60] See Lowth, *Isaiah*, 6.

lines feels appropriate for the social disorder that the verse describes. At the same time, the parallelism becomes perceptually stronger as it is sustained across four lines instead of two, and this sense of greater structure perhaps plays against the theme of disorder. Keeping in mind Pinsky's suggestion that the best lineation most readily illuminates the poem's meaning, dividing the verse into four lines thus seems preferable.

For all of this attention to parallelism, of course, not all Biblical Hebrew verse is parallelistic. The most common alternative is enjambment, where the line break falls within a clause instead of at its boundary. This phenomenon is common in poetries from many different historical periods and cultures. While the majority of line groups in Isaianic poetry are parallel, enjambed lines occur with some frequency. By their nature, such lines are syntactically and often semantically incomplete, which increases the difficulty of determining line boundaries. Delbert R. Hillers comments on this difficulty for the poetry of Lamentations, which contains the highest concentration of enjambed lines in the Hebrew Bible: "To make two parts out of these lines with only one sentence, it is necessary to divide at a great variety of places with respect to the syntax."[61] As he rightly observes, one cannot easily predict where the line break will occur in a pair of enjambed lines, since it will not correspond with clausal boundaries. Indeed, a key effect of enjambment is often subversion of the closure that end-stopping secures for the line, the very feature that makes parallelism such a prominent marker of lineation.[62]

Even in enjambed lines, however, syntactic or stylistic features will frequently create a slight pause in the sentence that may be taken to correspond to the line end.[63] Due to "the relatively conservative nature of enjambment" in Biblical Hebrew verse, as F. W. Dobbs-Allsopp puts it, line breaks generally do not occur within a construct chain or prepositional phrase.[64] When such a syntactic unit is isolated at the beginning or end of a long sentence, consequently, its position limits the options for dividing the lines, especially when it is the longest grammatical unit in the sentence (for example, Isa 5:1a;

---

[61] Delbert R. Hillers, *Lamentations: A New Translation with Introduction and Commentary* (2nd ed.; AB 7A; New York: Doubleday, 1992), 20; see also Dobbs-Allsopp, "Enjambing Line," 231–2.
[62] Kinzie, *Poet's Guide*, 52–6, 67–9.
[63] Collins, *Line-Forms*, 56–7; Dobbs-Allsopp, "Enjambing Line," 230–3, 237.
[64] Dobbs-Allsopp, "Enjambing Line," 233.

23:12a; 28:3). In other cases, a subordinate clause forms the second line of an enjambed couplet, and its beginning is clearly marked by a conjunctive *w-* (for example, Isa 5:4; 10:19; 28:18b) or a clause-initial particle such as *kî* ("for"; for example, Isa 3:9b–11; 14:29a), *pen* ("lest"; Isa 28:22a), or the relative *ʾăšer* (for example, Isa 18:1; 28:4a, 4bα). In still other cases, particular stylistic features will locate the line break. For instance, one of the enjambed lines may be internally parallel, as in Isa 28:11:

> *kî bĕlaʿăgê śāpâ ûbĕlāšôn ʾaḥeret*
> *yĕdabbēr ʾel-hāʿām hazzeh*
> For with stammering lips and with foreign speech
> he will speak to this people.

As noted already, the break will not likely fall within a prepositional phrase, and here the parallelism of the prepositional phrases at the beginning of the verse mitigates against dividing the line between them. From the experience of other internally parallel lines, one expects a pause to follow the second phrase, although here the syntactic incompleteness of the line more quickly pulls the reader or hearer forward. Couplets like this one are a variation on the "A- A- // A— line" discussed earlier; the second line is not parallel to the two halves of the first line but is approximately equivalent in length. Other examples are Isa 3:18; 11:9; 15:2bα.

Attention to sound can also help determine the extent of lines when other features are inconclusive. Although not restricted to it, soundplay occurs most prominently at the level of the line in many poetic traditions.[65] When a cluster of similar sounds is concentrated at one end of a long sentence, consequently, one may divide the line accordingly. Following BHS, phonological considerations suggest the following division for Isa 28:13b, a series of five verbs depicting sequential actions:

> *lĕmaʿan yēlĕku wĕkāšĕlû ʾāḥôr*
> *wĕnîšbārû wĕnôqĕšû wĕnilkādû*
> Therefore, they will walk and stumble backwards;
> they will be broken, trapped, and captured.

---

[65] Hartman, *Free Verse*, 65, cited in Dobbs-Allsopp, "Enjambing Line," 222, n. 15; O'Connor, *HVS*, 140; Watson, *CHP*, 227. For an example from Ug. poetry (*KTU*² 1.2 iv.10), see Mark S. Smith, *Untold Stories: The Bible and Ugaritic Studies in the Twentieth Century* (Peabody, Mass.: Hendrickson, 2001), 132–3.

The consonant *l* occurs in the first two verbs as well as the conjunction *lĕmaʿan*, creating a link among these words. The final three verbs, on the other hand, are all *nipʿal* perfects and thus share the prefix *n-*. While these sounds demarcate the separate lines of the couplet, the repetition of the consonant *š* in the three middle verbs bridges the lines and holds them together as a couplet, as does the recurrence of the sound *l* in the final word. The succession of similar sounds lends an air of logical progression to the chain of verbs, creating an impression of inevitability for the unfolding destruction that they depict. One may contrast Isa 8:15, which has a series of verbs nearly identical to 28:13b. The major differences in 8:15 are the placement of the verb *kāšĕlû* ("they will stumble") at the beginning of the series, the absence of *yēlĕkû* ("they will walk"), and the occurrence of *nāpĕlû* ("they will fall") in its stead as the second verb. These differences, however, make it more difficult to divide this verse into lines on the basis of sound. The rhyming of *kāšĕlû* and *nāpĕlû* suggest that they belong in the same line, but the initial *n* links *nāpĕlû* with the three *nipʿal* verbs that follow.

Rhythm and Line Length

Already, the discussion in this chapter has turned repeatedly to the question of line length. Meter, the regular recurrence of selected phonological phenomena such as stress, controls the lengths of lines in many poetic traditions, and it would provide an invaluable key to lineation if its existence in biblical poetry could be demonstrated. This task is easier said than done. Most scholars identify stress as the decisive phonological element of Biblical Hebrew verse, often noting that the location of the accent can sometimes be the sole distinction between different words.[66] Stress-based scansion of Biblical Hebrew

---

[66] For example, Alonso Schökel, *Manual*, 36; Alan M. Cooper, *Biblical Poetics: A Linguistic Approach* (Ann Arbor, Mich.: University Microfilms, 1977), 29-31; Cloete, *Versification and Syntax*, 7; Geller, "Hebrew Prosody," 510; Benjamin Hrushovski, "Prosody, Hebrew," in vol. 13 of *Encyclopedia Judaica* (16 vols; Jerusalem: Keter, 1971), col. 1201; Johannes C. de Moor, "The Art of Versification in Ugarit and Israel. I: The Rhythmical Structure," in *Studies in the Bible and the Ancient Near East Presented to Samuel E. Loewenstamm on His Seventieth Birthday* (eds. Y. Avishur and J. Blau; Jerusalem: E. Rubenstein's Publishing House, 1978), 122-3, 139; Petersen and Richards, *Interpreting Hebrew Poetry*, 39, 43; Watson, *CHP*, 97. The major alternative position argues that the phonological structure of Hebrew poetry is best described

poems usually takes account of the number of stresses per line with little concern for where they occur or the number of unstressed syllables between them.[67] This practice avoids the problematic question of where stresses would originally have fallen in Biblical Hebrew, which the Masoretic accentual system does not always accurately reflect.[68] In other words, the rhythmic structure of Biblical Hebrew verse seems to have been pure accentual, as opposed to syllabic-accentual, to borrow categories from John Hollander.[69] A more pressing question, however, concerns the nature of the rhythmic structure created by the stresses: is it appropriate to describe it as "metrical"? The answer, of course, depends as much on the definition of the term "meter" as it does the analysis of poetic texts. Despite a growing consensus that Biblical Hebrew poetry lacks meter, the voluminous literature on this topic is complicated enough that an admittedly selective review of the problem may be useful here.

Almost all interpreters recognize that the number of stresses per line varies noticeably in Hebrew poetry, often with more consistency between parallel lines—owing to the repetition of frames with similar numbers of syntactic components—but with considerable disparity from one group of lines to the next. Wildberger's scansions of poetic texts in his Isaiah commentaries, for example, reveal no uniform patterns within most poems.[70] On this basis, most contemporary interpreters argue that the term "meter" does not fit Biblical Hebrew

---

through counting syllables; see, for example, Bartelt, *Book Around Immanuel*, 2-8, 23-6; Fokkelman, *Reading Biblical Poetry*, 22-4, 46-9; David Noel Freedman, "Another Look at Biblical Hebrew Poetry," in *Directions in Biblical Hebrew Poetry* (ed. Elaine R. Follis; JSOTSup 40; Sheffield: Sheffield Academic Press, 1987), 18-23; Freedman, "Pottery, Poetry, and Prophecy: An Essay on Biblical Poetry," in *Poetry, Pottery, and Prophecy: Studies in Early Hebrew Poetry* (Winona Lake, Ind.: Eisenbrauns, 1980), 6-11; repr. from *Journal of Biblical Literature* 96 (1977); Tremper Longman III, "A Critique of Two Recent Metrical Systems," *Bib* 63 (1982): 232-8; O'Connor, *HVS*, 34-8.

[67] As de Moor argues, the similar line structures of Ugaritic and Biblical Hebrew poetry suggest that the placement of the stress had little rhythmic significance, as the former retained final short vowels and the latter did not ("Art of Versification I," 122-3). For a discussion of different approaches to the question of unstressed syllables, see Cloete, *Versification and Syntax*, 30.

[68] Petersen and Richards, *Interpreting Hebrew Poetry*, 43.

[69] Hollander, *Rhyme's Reason*, 4-11, 21-3.

[70] Wildberger, *Isa 28-39*, 669; so also Edward J. Kissane, *The Book of Isaiah: Translated from a Critically Revised Hebrew Text with Commentary* (2 vols; rev. ed.; Dublin: Browne and Nolan, 1960), 1:xlix-l; Petersen and Richards, *Interpreting Hebrew Poetry*, 40-1; Williamson, *Isa 1-5*, 24-5.

poetry, because the *sine qua non* of meter is the very regularity of line lengths that this corpus lacks.[71] Brogan's definition of meter in *The New Princeton Encyclopedia of Poetry and Poetic Terms* favors this assessment: "M[eter] selects one phonological feature of lang[uage] (stress, pitch, length) . . . *Regular patterns* of these contrastive features create units of structure (feet, measures, metra, cola) which in turn comprise the line."[72] In the absence of such regularity, the phonological structure of Biblical Hebrew verse is better described as rhythmic rather than metrical, since rhythm—a broader category of which meter is a subset—allows for recurring patterns without requiring that they be strictly regular.[73] In short, then, biblical poems are ancient examples of non-metrical, free verse poetry. Free verse, unlike metrical verse, is not governed by a regular, quantifiable pattern of sounds. Instead, variable patterns appear throughout a poem. The inconsistent occurrence of these patterns does not necessarily mean that they are random. On the contrary, they may be carefully constructed to enhance the effects of a single line or group of lines, in conjunction with syntax and other linguistic features; they simply do not extend throughout the entire poem.[74]

Despite their awareness of its irregular line lengths, a few scholars still insist on describing biblical verse as metrical. Watson, for instance, speaks of meter in his work on biblical poetry, but with

---

[71] For example, de Moor, "Art of Versification I," 127–8; Dennis Pardee, "Ugaritic and Hebrew Metrics," in *Ugarit in Retrospect: Fifty Years of Ugarit and Ugaritic* (ed. George Douglas Young; Winona Lake, Ind.: Eisenbrauns, 1981), 115–16; O'Connor, *HVS*, 64–5; Petersen and Richards, *Interpreting Hebrew Poetry*, 41.

[72] T. V. F. Brogan, "Meter," in *TNPEPP* (eds. Alex Preminger and T. V. F. Brogan; Princeton: Princeton University Press, 1993), 768–9, emphasis added. Cloete cites a definition of meter that allows for varying numbers of stresses per line, on the basis of which he condescendingly concludes that scholars who deny the existence of meter in biblical poetry do not really understand it (*Versification and Syntax*, 9–11, 14). His idiosyncratic definition, however, does not reflect the typical sense of the term as used by most literary critics.

[73] Brogan, "Meter," 772; Hartman, *Free Verse*, 14. For biblical interpreters who use the language of "rhythm," see Alter, *Art of Biblical Poetry*, 9; Dobbs-Allsopp, "Poetry, Hebrew," 553–4; Hrushovski, "Prosody, Hebrew," cols. 1201–2; Petersen and Richards, *Interpreting Hebrew Poetry*, 40–2.

[74] Hartman, *Free Verse*, 24–8; Benjamin Hrushovsky, "On Free Rhythms in Modern Poetry," in *Style in Language* (ed. Thomas A. Sebeok; Cambridge, Mass.: Technology Press of the Massachusetts Institute of Technology; New York: John Wiley & Sons, 1960), 183–9; Donald Wesling and Enriko Bollobás, "Free Verse," in *TNPEPP*, 425–7. Hrushovski notes that post-biblical Hebrew poetry is predominantly metrical ("Prosody, Hebrew," col. 1198).

the seemingly contradictory qualification that it is "not regular metre."[75] It seems preferable to avoid the term altogether, given its common association with poetic traditions that are very different from Biblical Hebrew poetry. One wonders whether the refusal to abandon the term follows from the mistaken notion that poetry must by nature be metrical.[76] Lowth himself believed that to be the case and insisted that biblical poems must have been metrical, even if the bases for that meter have become unrecoverable.[77] The identification of meter as the necessary condition for poetry, however, should seem as misguided to a contemporary critic as it seemed obvious to an eighteenth-century one. Alternatively, an unfortunate disregard for the quality of free verse poems may be at play, perhaps coupled with a theological presupposition of the high literary quality of the Bible, or it could be that the relatively recent advent of free verse forms in English-language poetry has led to the mistaken conclusion that it is a modern phenomenon that could not possibly be found in an ancient text. Many contemporary free verse poems are different from biblical poems in many striking ways, to be sure, but they may be just as different from other free verse poems.[78]

Whatever it is finally called, the observable phonological structure of Biblical Hebrew poetry is not sufficiently regular to allow the prediction of the number of accents per line. Thus, no putative "meter" can establish the lineation of Biblical Hebrew poetry. This fact does not mean, however, that the issue of line length is irrelevant to this discussion. Lines in biblical free verse are consistently and remarkably terse.[79] As a result, they seldom vary substantially in length, as do lines of some twentieth-century English free verse.[80]

---

[75] Watson, CHP, 92.
[76] Ronald L. Giese, "Strophic Hebrew Verse as Free Verse," JSOT 61 (1994): 29. This idea seems in part to underlie Kugel's denial of the existence of poetry in the HB, given his emphasis on regularity as the defining characteristic of Western poetry and his recognition of the absence of meter in biblical texts (Kugel, Idea, 69–75, 298–302; see Rebecca Raphael, "That's No Literature, That's My Bible: On James Kugel's Objections to the Idea of Biblical Poetry," JSOT 27 (2002): 37–45).
[77] Lowth, Lectures, 31.
[78] On the comparability of Biblical Hebrew poetry and contemporary free verse poems, see Hrushovski, "Free Rhythms," 189; Wesling and Bollobaś, "Free Verse," 425.
[79] For this quality of Hebrew poetry, see Berlin, Dynamics, 5–7, 16; Dobbs-Allsopp, "Poetry, Hebrew," 551–2; Kugel, Idea, 87; Miller, "Theological Significance," 215.
[80] Even within free verse, some sense of limit—albeit very broadly conceived—controls line length (Hartman, Free Verse, 24–5; Smith, Poetic Closure, 86; Hrushovski, "Free Rhythms," 189).

Indeed, Dennis Pardee identifies "approximately comparable length of line" as "the main quantitative element" in Hebrew poetry.[81] For many lines, although certainly not all of them, the syntactic shape imposed by parallelism contributes significantly to this effect.[82] In light of this approximate regularity, a count of stresses—or, for all practical purposes, the number of words—might suggest whether a proposed line division results in a suspiciously short or long poetic line.[83] It must be stressed (pun intended) that scansion offers an approximate handle on line length for descriptive purposes, not the key to uncovering the compositional principles of ancient Hebrew poets. Although stress/word counting takes best account of the apparent phonological structure of Biblical Hebrew verse, other approaches to scansion such as syllable counting may offer an equally, if not in some cases more, effective means to quantify and discuss line length.[84]

There is some room for flexibility when counting stresses or words, and many interpreters' attempts at scansion have been criticized for arbitrarily applying unclear principles in disputed cases.[85] Often, this inconsistency results from the attempt to force lines into consistent patterns, usually to achieve more regular results that could provide evidence for meter.[86] Recognition of the non-metrical character of Biblical Hebrew verse should eliminate this tendency. Ultimately, the persuasiveness of one's results depends on a degree of consistency in the counting of stresses. On the other hand, as I have

---

[81] Pardee, "Ugaritic and Hebrew Metrics," 127.

[82] Berlin, *Dynamics*, 6–7; Geller, "Hebrew Prosody," 510; de Moor, "Art of Versification," 128; see also G. Douglas Young, "Ugaritic Prosody," *Journal of Near Eastern Studies* 9 (1950): 132.

[83] Freedman, "Pottery, Poetry, and Prophecy," 8; Geller, "Hebrew Prosody and Poetics," 510; Hrushovski, "Prosody, Hebrew," col. 1201; Simon B. Parker, "Parallelism and Prosody in Ugaritic Narrative Verse," *UF* 6 (1974): 283. It is possible, as Alonso Schökel (*Manual*, 40) and Geller ("Hebrew Prosody," 510) maintain, that longer words should be assigned two stresses, especially words with prefixed prepositions or pronominal suffixes. Still, it seems safe to assume one stress per word as a general rule and deal with longer words on a case-by-case basis.

[84] Freedman, "Pottery, Poetry, and Prophecy," 7–8.

[85] See, for example, Longman's criticism of the systems of Jerzy Kurylowicz and Alan Cooper, who posit the existence of "word complexes" bearing a single stress but do not provide precise guidelines for identifying them ("Critique," 252–3).

[86] Alonso Schökel explicitly proposes that certain words be assigned stress in some lines but not others in order to "harmonise the verse in the series to which it belongs" (*Manual*, 40).

argued for the question of lineation as a whole, scansion must not be divorced from other questions of interpretation, which allows for some variation when the meaning of the poem seems to require it. Still, a clear statement of one's principles for scansion remains a desideratum, and the interpreter should then take care to justify possible exceptional cases so that the practice does not appear haphazard. Two areas where clarity is especially needed are the status of grammatical particles and groups of closely related words such as construct chains.

The question of particles is especially pertinent for prophetic poetry such as that of First Isaiah, which uses particles more frequently than other genres of biblical poetry due to its argumentative character. William L. Holladay's comprehensive proposals offer useful guidelines in most cases. He concludes that the following particles should be excluded from word-counts: mono- and biconsonantal prepositions, most negative particles, most clausal adverbs (for example, *kî, pen, 'ap*), the particle of entreaty *nā'*, and the interjection *hinnēh/hēn*. By contrast, prepositions with pronominal suffixes; longer prepositions; adverbs of location, time, or manner; demonstratives; most interrogative words; particles of existence; the relative *'ăšer;* the adjective *kōl/kol-;* and the interjections *'ôy* and *hôy* all "count" for purposes of scansion.[87] Nonetheless, aspects of a poem's meaning may sometimes demand adjustments to these guidelines; consequently, I follow Geller in treating many monosyllabic particles flexibly in terms of their role in phonological structure. The negative particle *lō'* ("not") in Isa 1:3 is one such case:

> *yāda' šôr qōnēhû*
> *wahămôr 'ēbûs bě'ālāyw*
> *yiśrā'ēl lō' yāda'*
> *'ammî lō' hitbônān*
>
> The ox knows its owner,
>   and the ass its master's trough;
> Israel does not know;
>   my people do not understand.

---

[87] William L. Holladay, "*Hebrew Verse Structure* Revisited (I): Which Words 'Count'?," *JBL* 118 (1999): 24–32; see also the discussions in Geller, *Parallelism in Early Biblical Poetry*, 6–8; O'Connor, *HVS*, 300, 305–6.

The animals' knowledge in v. 3a is contrasted with Israel's ignorance in v. 3b, which is reinforced by the repetition of *yāda'* ("knows") and the reversed word order in the second couplet. This being the case, semantic emphasis falls on *lō'* in both lines, especially since the verbs lack objects. Although semantics and phonology need not coincide completely, it seems odd for such a thematically important word to have no rhythmic stress. One should therefore allow for the possibility that *lō'* bears stress in the second couplet, yielding two lines with three stresses each.[88] This case is somewhat exceptional, though, and I exclude *lō'* from word counts much more often than not.

Words in close semantic and syntactic relationship create further uncertainty for scansion. For instance, many interpreters assign only one stress to a construct chain.[89] The use of construct chains in couplets with ellipsis, however, suggests that they can bear multiple stresses. The first couplet of Isa 1:3 proves instructive. The verb *yāda'* is left out of the second line of the couplet; to retain approximate rhythmic balance between the lines, the one-word object in the first line (*qōnēhû*, "its owner") is matched by a construct chain in the second line (*'ēbûs bĕ'ālāyw*, "its master's feed trough").[90] One finds many examples of similar expansion by construct chain in Biblical Hebrew poetry, which would be difficult to explain if the construct chain were regarded as a single rhythmic unit.[91] Some interpreters also assign a single stress to words joined by the Masoretic *maqqēp*.[92] Isaiah 15:1b provides strong empirical evidence against this practice. The single difference between these two couplets is the first word of their respective second lines (*'ār*, "city," versus *qîr*, "town"), both of which are monosyllabic; otherwise, the lines are identical, and the

---

[88] So Alonso Schökel, *Manual*, 40, 44; Gray, *Forms*, 139–40; Williamson, *Isa 1–5*, 25.
[89] Cloete, *Versification and Syntax*, 200; Cooper, *Biblical Poetics*, 33; Watson, *CHP*, 101. Watson cites a broken construct chain in Isa 19:8 (*kol-maśkîlê bay'ôr ḥakkâ*, "all who cast hook into the Nile") as evidence, arguing that it is broken precisely to create an additional stress to produce a uniform couplet. The use of construct forms with prepositions, however, is hardly anomalous in First Isaiah (for example, Isa 5:11; 28:9; 30:18; see GKC §130a). The syntax of Isa 19:8, then, should be taken simply as a feature of Isaianic style, with no necessary rhythmic implications.
[90] Kugel, *Idea*, 46.
[91] See the examples in Geller, *Parallelism in Early Biblical Poetry*, 301–5; Gray, *Forms*, 76–8; Watson, *CHP*, 343–8. For Ug. examples, see Cyrus H. Gordon, *Ugaritic Textbook: Grammar* (Analecta Orientalia 38:1; rev. ed.; Rome: Pontifical Biblical Institute, 1998), §113.16.
[92] For example, Watson, *CHP*, 101.

reader or hearer would likely regard them as equal in length. The *maqqēp*, however, joins *qîr* and *môʾāb* ("Moab") in the second couplet but not *ʿār* and *môʾāb* in the first couplet in most manuscripts (see BH³). If one takes the *maqqēp* into account, one must conclude despite strong internal evidence that these lines are not equally long. Given the relative lateness of this Masoretic convention, it seems best to ignore it for purposes of scansion.[93]

To reiterate, none of these guidelines should be regarded as absolute, particularly when other features in a line hint at rhythmic anomalies. Still, they facilitate the practice of scansion and offer a basis for describing the relative lengths of lines. Descriptions of line length make it possible to discuss certain rhythmically significant, even if not metrically regular, patterns that occur in biblical poems, such as the recurrence of unbalanced couplets. Given the frequent occurrence of this pattern in laments, it is often labeled "*qînâ* (lament) meter" or, better, "*qînâ* rhythm."[94] These descriptions also allow the specification of acceptable ranges of line lengths in Biblical Hebrew verse, which provides a useful control for proposed line divisions. There seems to be relative consensus that a line can have no fewer than two words.[95] One finds disagreement, though, about the maximum number of words in a line, with proposals ranging

---

[93] Gray, *Forms*, 138–40. The placement of the *maqqēp* in Isa 15:1b can be explained entirely by the rules of the Masoretic system of accentuation. The accent for *môʾāb* in the second couplet is the *ṭipḥâ*, which may only have one conjunctive accent preceding it—typically the *mêrĕkāʾ*, which occurs here two words prior. As a result, *qîr* and *môʾāb* are joined by the *maqqēp* to limit the number of accents to the allowable quantity. See Israel Yeivin, *Introduction to the Tiberian Masorah* (trans. E. J. Revell; Masoretic Studies 5; Atlanta: Scholars Press, 1980), §§231, 300.

[94] Hrushrovski argues that one may speak meaningfully of this rhythmic pattern even while maintaining that Biblical Hebrew poetry lacks meter ("Prosody, Hebrew," col. 1202). On the pattern and its association with lament, see Frank More Cross, "Studies in the Structure of Hebrew Verse: The Prosody of Lamentations 1:1–22," in *The Word of the Lord Shall Go Forth: Essays in Honor of David Noel Freedman in Celebration of His Sixtieth Birthday* (eds. Carol L. Meyers and M. O'Connor; ASOR Special Volume Series 1; Winona Lake, Ind.: Eisenbrauns, 1983), 129–55; F. W. Dobbs-Allsopp, *Weep, O Daughter of Zion: A Study of the City-Lament Genre in the Hebrew Bible* (BibOr 44; Rome; Pontifical Biblical Institute, 1993), 43–4, 170; W. Randall Garr, "The *Qinah*: A Study of Poetic Meter, Syntax, and Style," *ZAW* 95 (1983): 60–2; Hillers, *Lamentations*, 17–24; William Shea, "The Qinah Structure of the Book of Lamentations," *Bib* 60 (1979): 103–7.

[95] Cloete, however, argues for the integrity of lines consisting of a single verb with a suffixed object pronoun in Jer 5:14 and 15:6 (*Versification and Syntax*, 209).

from four to five to six words.⁹⁶ While rare, apparent examples of six-word lines can be found in First Isaiah. If one counts the units of the construct chain individually, the first line of the following couplet, the bounds for which are clearly indicated by the parallelism, has six words:

kî ʿăśeret ṣimdê-kerem yaʿăśû bat ʾeḥāt
wĕzeraʿ ḥōmer yaʿăśeh ʾêpâ
For ten yokes of a vineyard will produce one *bath*,
and a homer of seed will produce one *ephah*. (Isa 5:10)

Geller's proposed range of two to six words for lines of biblical verse, then, best matches the evidence from First Isaiah. When a proposed line does not fall within these bounds, one should reconsider the location of line breaks. For instance, excessively long parallel lines may be divided further to produce parallel couplets, as discussed in the previous section.

Geller's position is actually more nuanced. While allowing for two- and six-word lines, he suggests that "the great majority" of lines contain between three and five words or stresses.⁹⁷ This relatively constricted range quantitatively codifies the characteristic terseness of Biblical Hebrew verse. Indeed, three- and four-word lines are by far most common in First Isaiah, with the result that two-word lines seem conspicuously short and five- and six-word lines conspicuously long. Few Isaianic poems are composed predominantly of such long or short lines.⁹⁸ Instead, they most frequently appear interspersed throughout poems among lines of more standard length—often, but not exclusively, in a couplet or triplet that also contains a three- or four-word line. The greater or shorter length of these lines often

---

⁹⁶ For four words as the maximum, see Alonso Schökel, *Manual*, 37; Hrushovski, "Prosody, Hebrew," col. 1201; it is not clear whether they assign only one stress to construct chains, in which case they actually would allow for five-word lines. For five words as the maximum, see Cloete, *Versification and Syntax*, 207–8; O'Connor, *HVS*, 75, 87, 315; both specifically include the individual terms of construct chains in word counts. For six words as the maximum, see Geller, "Hebrew Prosody," 509; Gray, *Forms*, 59.

⁹⁷ Geller, "Hebrew Prosody," 509.

⁹⁸ Two exceptions are Isa 21:1–10 and 32:9–14, which both contain a high number of two-word lines, but the Isaianic authorship of both poems is disputed by many commentators.

emphasizes and reinforces their content, as I argued earlier for Isa 3:8. Note also the following exceptional 5:5 couplet:

zō't hā'ēṣâ hayyĕ'ûṣâ 'al-kol-hā'āreṣ
wĕzō't hayyād hannĕṭûyâ 'al-kol-haggôyīm
This is the plan that is planned concerning the whole earth,
and this is the hand that is outstretched over all the nations. (Isa 14:26)

In this couplet, Isaiah describes the far-reaching control that Yhwh exercises over all nations. The conspicuous length of the two lines creates a sense of expansiveness appropriate for the grand theological claim. In this way, rhythm may have rhetorical effects, as the prophetic poet takes advantage of its subtle effects to augment the persuasiveness of his message.

Syntactic Constraints

While considerably helpful, limits on line length in biblical poetry only suggest that a given poetic sequence should be divided, without necessarily offering guidance for dividing it. Syntactic descriptions of the line move us further in this direction. Increased awareness of the importance of syntax for poetic meaning has been a significant advance in work on Biblical Hebrew poetry over the past thirty-five years, which echoes trends in the study of poetry more generally.[99] While patterns of syntax operate at all levels of the poem—just like sound, imagery, and other poetic features—the question here is the relationship between syntax and the line. The predominance of end-stopping in biblical poetry, as well as the conservative nature of enjambment where it occurs, leads the reader or hearer to expect pauses not only at certain intervals of time but usually at certain syntactic boundaries. This fact makes possible syntactic descriptions of the shapes of poetic lines, which may highlight unacceptable line breaks, point to specific junctures at which breaks should occur, or suggest specific configurations of syntactic elements that are likely to occur within single lines. In this way, syntax offers an additional

---

[99] Berlin, *Dynamics*, 18; Collins, *Line-Forms*, 10–13, 18–19. On the rationale for attention to syntax in poetic interpretation, see Terence Collins, "Line Forms in Hebrew Poetry," *JSS* 23 (1978): 230; Eagleton, *How to Read a Poem*, 121–3; O'Connor, *HVS*, 13–20.

check against proposed line divisions and, most helpfully, additional criteria for division when other indicators prove inconclusive.

Studies in this area by Terrence Collins and Michael O'Connor both assume that the shapes of lines in Biblical Hebrew poetry are governed primarily, if not exclusively, by syntactic principles.[100] Indeed, taking the non-metrical character of Biblical Hebrew poetry to an extreme conclusion, O'Connor suggests that the structural grounds for the biblical verse line are entirely syntactic, with no significant phonological elements, and he offers other examples of such systems from a small number of poetic corpora from world literature.[101] Both authors describe the line syntactically with the goal of identifying common linear structures and distinguishing them from exceptional ones. Collins proposes a series of basic forms that can account for the majority of biblical verse lines, based on different combinations of four simple sentence types, and he discusses numerous examples of each form from prophetic poetry. His focus on the prophets makes his work especially useful for the study of First Isaiah, as one can use his proposed divisions as a basis for comparison in specific cases and find other examples of lines from prophetic books with similar syntactic structures. On the other hand, Collins unhelpfully equates the line with the couplet, and, for all of his methodological rigor, he never satisfactorily discusses the criteria by which one might divide the lines ("hemistiches" in his parlance) within the couplet, which limits the usefulness of his work for the question at hand.

The system proposed by O'Connor is much more flexible than Collins's and potentially applicable to any line of Biblical Hebrew poetry. Rather than beginning with specific structures, he identifies possible syntactic components that can be combined in myriad ways to form poetic lines. In brief, three hierarchical, linguistic levels are the basis for his system: (1) "units," by which he means individual substantives, pronouns, adjectives, adverbs, and verbs; (2) "constituents," the nominal phrases dependent on verbs or combined in verbless clauses; and (3) "clause predicators," which include verbal

---

[100] Collins, *Line Forms*, 16, 227–8; O'Connor, *HVS*, 55.
[101] O'Connor, *HVS*, 65–7, 147–59, 643; for additional bodies of verse that build the line solely on syntactic constrictions, see Cloete, *Versification and Syntax*, 50–61. Collins considers this possibility but is unwilling to commit firmly to it (*Line-Forms*, 251–2).

The Line in First Isaiah

predicates, particles of existence, vocatives, and verbless clauses. Drawing on data from a large corpus of pre-exilic biblical poems, he proposes a series of constraints that consist of minimum and maximum numbers of these components per line and various restrictions for their combination within a single line.[102] Although a variety of syntactic shapes can be found in verse lines from his corpus, O'Connor concludes that the "dominant line form" is "one clause and either two or three constituents of two or three units."[103] In situations where more than one possible line division conforms to his constraints, he suggests that this structure should be preferred.

In many cases, O'Connor's constraints identify lines that fall within acceptable limits for line length but should be further divided, as in the following example:

> kî yhwh ṣĕbā'ôt yā'aṣ
> ûmî yāpēr
> wĕyādô hannĕṭûyâ[104]
> ûmî yĕšîbennâ
>
> Indeed, Y<small>HWH</small> of Hosts has planned—
> and who will frustrate it?
> And his hand is the one that is outstretched—
> and who will turn it back? (Isa 14:27)

BHS divides the verse into two long lines, as suggested by parallelism and the placement of the 'atnāḥ in the Masoretic Text. According to O'Connor, however, a line with two clause predicators may only contain one dependent noun phrase—that is, in a line with two finite

---

[102] O'Connor, *HVS*, 68–87, 297–316. For overviews of O'Connor's system, see Cloete, *Versification and Syntax*, 80–98; Holladay, "*HVS* Revisited (I)," 21–4; Kuntz, "Biblical Hebrew Poetry, I," 42–4. In the afterword to the 2nd ed. of *HVS*, O'Connor himself offers a concise restatement and defense of his system (*HVS*, 631–61).

[103] O'Connor, *HVS*, 87.

[104] Following Syr., Wildberger removes the definite article from the passive participle *hannĕṭûyâ* ("the one that is outstretched") so that it can function as a simple predicate ("his hand is outstretched"; *Isaiah 13–27* [trans. Thomas H. Trapp; CC; Minneapolis: Fortress, 1997], 79). The point of the couplet, however, is not simply that the divine hand is outstretched, but rather that the hand already outstretched "over all the nations" in v. 26 belongs to Y<small>HWH</small>, not Assyria. In both vv. 26 and 27, *nĕṭûyâ* functions as a relative clause; when so used, a participle may have the definite article, even when serving as a predicate nominative (for example, Gen 2:11; Deut 3:21; Mal 3:2; see GKC §126i-k; *IBHS*, 621). It seems best, then, to retain the article with <small>MT</small> (Blenkinsopp, *Isa 1–39*, 289; Duhm, *Jesaia*, 124; Gray, *Isa I–XXVII*, 262).

verbs, only one can have a separate subject or object, and in a line with a verbless clause and a finite verb, the verb cannot have a separate subject or object.[105] On that basis, each half of v. 27 must be further divided into two lines, resulting in a pair of parallel couplets.[106] The common occurrence of such couplets in First Isaiah supports this move. This division establishes a separate couplet for each of the major motifs of the verse: the "planned plan" and "outstretched hand," which were introduced in the preceding verse as the basis for the imminent defeat of Assyria. Both belong to Yhwh, and neither can be opposed. The succession of shorter lines also creates a sense of closure for this brief poem, following the unusually long lines in v. 26.

O'Connor's constraints allow as many as three verbs in a single line, provided that the line contains no dependent nominal phrases.[107] This criterion supports the divisions of Isa 8:15 and 28:13b that were proposed earlier on the basis of soundplay. In other cases, it may force the subdivision of longer poetic units, again resulting in parallel couplets:

> ʾim-tōʾbû ûšĕmaʿtem
> ṭûb hāʾāreṣ tōʾkēlû
> wĕʾim-tĕmāʾănû ûmĕrîtem
> ḥereb tĕʾukkĕlû

> If you are willing and obey,
>   the good of the land you will eat;
> but if you refuse and rebel,
>   by the sword you will be eaten. (Isa 1:19–20)

Although one might initially take these verses as two long, parallel lines, interpreters almost universally divide them into four lines, as indicated earlier, reflecting the natural pause between the protasis and apodosis of the conditional sentences. O'Connor's constraints offer concrete grounds for this impressionistic division. The subdivision of the verses places more equal weight on the respective protases and

---

[105] O'Connor, HVS, 87, 307.

[106] So also Willis, "Alternating Parallelism," 27. This matches the lineation of the second couplet in BH³; in the first couplet, the verb yāʿaṣ ("has planned") is inexplicably taken with the second line instead of the first.

[107] O'Connor, HVS, 75–6, 87, 307. Although he classifies verbless clauses, vocatives, and verbs as "constituents," he only allows lines with three constituents in the case of verbs.

apodoses, thereby bringing into clearer focus the moral calculus that the prophet wishes to establish. Moreover, the continuation of the parallelism across a longer sequence than usual creates a stronger impression of structure that is appropriate for the strict causality imagined in these lines. Isolating the apodoses as separate lines also draws greater attention to the wordplay that they develop through the pun on the active and passive forms of √'kl. One can make a strong case, then, that the lineation suggested by O'Connor's constraints best coincides with the meaning of the lines, as suggested both by content and style.

All of these guidelines, however, must be used judiciously in consideration with other factors. As the preceding examples indicate, the application of O'Connor's constraints often forces further division of otherwise acceptable lines, usually with pleasing effects. The impulse toward shorter lines is appropriate insofar as terseness is a hallmark of Biblical Hebrew poetry, and O'Connor has convincingly demonstrated the role of syntactic constriction in producing this effect. One should not privilege brevity over all other poetic features, however, particularly when aspects of style demand a longer or more syntactically complex line. Consider the following example:

> hêlîlî ša'ar za'ăqî-'îr
> nāmôg pĕlešet kullēk
>
> Howl, O gate; cry out, O city;
> Melt in fear, Philistia—all of you. (Isa 14:31a)

O'Connor would have us divide the first line again to form a triplet, since two verbs with dependent noun phrases should not occupy a single line. On the other hand, as noted by Dobbs-Allsopp, this verse displays many affinities with the city-lament genre, which favors treating it as an unbalanced (4:3) couplet, a generic feature of biblical laments.[108] As discussed already, couplets like this one, in which one of the parallel lines is also internally parallel—the so-called "A- A- // A— line"—occur with some frequency in Isaianic poetry. A few such couplets are consistent with O'Connor's guidelines (for example, Isa 1:6b; 5:2a), but many more are not, as in this case.[109] To account for these

---

[108] Dobbs-Allsopp, *Weep, O Daughter of Zion*, 133; see Isa 15:6b for a similar case.
[109] In his review of O'Connor's analysis of Exod 15, Holladay notes the existence of "pairs of short cola that parallel longer cola": Holladay, "*Hebrew Verse Structure* Revisited (II): Conjoint Cola and Further Suggestions," *JBL* 118 (1999): 404. Because

couplets, I propose a slight modification to O'Connor's constraints: a line with two clause predicators may also contain two associated noun phrases, so long as both the clause predicators and noun phrases consist only of a single word (for example, verb–subject verb–subject).

This proposed modification—others could be adduced—hardly delegitimizes O'Connor's system.[110] In the majority of cases in First Isaiah, his guidelines confirm or improve line divisions suggested by other factors, and they typically point to agreeable divisions for segments of verse that otherwise lack clear markers of lineation. They should not, however, be taken as absolute—nor for that matter should any of the indicators discussed in this chapter, although parallelism may usually be regarded as the most secure. The foregoing discussion has shown that the lineation of Biblical Hebrew verse is seldom cut and dried. Because of this fact, interpretations of biblical poems should address the question more explicitly, marshalling as many different kinds of evidence as possible, and clearly explaining the basis for decisions about line division, with the ultimate goal of showing how the proposed lineation contributes productively to the poem's meaning.[111] When different indicators suggest conflicting line breaks, one must consider the larger interpretive issues at stake and decide accordingly, remaining open to the possibility that the tension between opposing possibilities for division may itself be meaningful.

READING OF ISAIAH 22:1B–14

On the basis of the many textual examples surveyed in this chapter, one may tentatively identify some trends in the lineation of Isaianic

---

O'Connor's system will not allow it, Holladay never considers the possibility that the "pairs of short cola" could be examples of internal parallelism. Instead, he coins the label "conjoint cola" for the phenomenon.

[110] Pardee, *Ugaritic and Hebrew Poetic Parallelism*, 45. Paul R. Raabe offers several examples from the Psalms that do not fit O'Connor's constraints: *Psalm Structures: A Study of Psalms with Refrains* (JSOTSup 104; Sheffield: Sheffield Academic Press, 1990), 17. O'Connor himself recognizes that further syntactic study of specific poetic texts might necessitate revisions to his system (*HVS*, 5).

[111] See Tod Linafelt and F. W. Dobbs-Allsopp, "Poetic Line Structure in Qoheleth 3:1," *VT* 60 (2010): 258–9.

poetry. The typical line in this corpus contains three or four words. Shorter lines (two words) or longer ones (five to six words) appear less frequently and typically in isolated cases within a particular poem. Most lines consist of a single clause that is syntactically parallel to contiguous clauses, in which case line breaks usually correspond to clausal boundaries. Parallelism may also occur at the level of the couplet, especially when the parallel frames are longer than normal and natural syntactic pauses occur within them, or when multiple independent and subordinate clauses alternate. Similarly, parallelism also occurs within the line, typically either in a run of syntactically parallel clauses that are shorter than normal or in a couplet in which two short clauses match a single, longer clause (Watson's "A- A- // A— line"). In other cases, line breaks occur within a single clause or between a single independent and dependent clause—a phenomenon known as enjambment. Even in these cases, the options for line breaks are limited because they do not violently sever the components of smaller syntactic units like construct chains, and one of the lines will often be the longest indivisible unit within the clause. Soundplay often occurs at the level of the line, so that runs of similar sounding words within acceptable limits usually constitute discrete lines. Although most lines contain only a single verb with various supporting syntactic units, lines with three verbs do occur when they are the only stressed words in the line. Lines with two verbs also occur, including, but not limited to, cases of internal parallelism. Sometimes line breaks have no further significance beyond their necessary occurrence in verse. Often, however, they have specific stylistic effects at local levels within poems in First Isaiah, especially unusually long or short lines, lines in parallel couplets, and lines with atypical syntactic shapes.

By way of conclusion to this chapter, I offer the following reading of Isa 22:1b–14 to illustrate the interpretive payoff of attention to lineation on a larger scale than the excerpts discussed to this point. The superscription *maśśāʾ gêʾ ḥizzāyôn* ("oracle of the valley of vision") in v. 1a marks the beginning of the poem and locates it within a series of oracles so marked in chapters 13–23 (see 13:1; 15:1; 17:1; 19:1; 21:1, 11, 13; 23:1), and the divine directive to prophecy against the individual Shebna in v. 15 signals a new oracle. The poem contains examples of a variety of markers of lineation; moreover, it displays a low concentration of figurative language and other poetic tropes, with the notable exception of soundplay. As a result, its

56   *Reading the Poetry of First Isaiah*

lineation is the primary locus of its poetic meaning. For this reason, the poem provides a fitting text against which to test the principle asserted throughout this chapter, that the determination of lineation should be undertaken in concert with interpretation.

[1] *mah-lāk 'ēpô' kî-'ālît*
    kullāk laggaggôt
[2] *tĕšū'ôt mĕlē'â 'îr hômîyâ*
    qiryâ 'allîzâ
    ḥălālayik lō' ḥallê-ḥereb
    wĕlō' mētê milḥāmâ
[3] *kol-qĕṣînayik nādĕdû-yaḥad*
    miqqešet 'ussārû
    kol-nimṣā'ayik 'ussĕrû yaḥdāw
    mērāḥôq bārāḥû
[4] *'al-kēn 'āmartî šĕ'û minnî*
    'ămārēr babbekî
    'al-tā'îṣû lĕnaḥămēnî
    'al-šōd bat-'ammî
[5] *kî yôm mĕhûmâ ûmĕbûsâ ûmĕbûkâ*
    la'dōnāy yhwh ṣĕbā'ôt bĕgê' ḥizzāyôn
    mĕqarqar qīr wĕšôa' 'el-hāhār
[6] *wĕ'êlām nāśā' 'ašpâ*
    bĕrekeb 'ărām[112] *pārāšîm*
    wĕqîr 'ērâ māgēn
[7] *wayhî mibḥar-'ămāqayik mālĕ'û rākeb*
    wĕhappārāšîm šōt šātû haššā'ĕrâ
[8] *waygal 'ēt māsak yĕhûdâ*
wattabbēṭû[113] *bayyôm hahû' 'el-nešeq bêt hayyā'ar*
[9] *wĕ'ēt bĕqî'ê 'îr-dāwīd rĕ'îtem kî rābbû*
wattĕqabbĕṣû 'et-mê habbĕrēkâ hattaḥtônâ

---

[112] MT *bĕrekeb 'ādām* ("with human chariots") makes poor sense. Some translations take *'ādām* to refer to infantry (NJPS) or charioteers (NJB); see also Jan de Waard, *A Handbook on Isaiah* (Textual Criticism and the Translator 1; Winona Lake, Ind.: Eisenbrauns, 1997), 95, but this meaning is otherwise unattested. Although the versions support MT, the frequently proposed emendation of *'ādām* to *'ărām* is plausible, given the geographic names in surrounding lines and the frequency of d/r confusion; for other cases involving these very words, see Judg 18:7, 28; Zech 9:1; Ps 76:11 (Eng. 76:10).

[113] For the singular verb *wattabbēṭ* in MT and 1QIsaᵃ, it seems preferable to read a second-person plural verb to match the other verbs in vv. 9–11 (see Gray, *Isa I–XXVII*, 373; Wildberger, *Isa 13–27*, 352). LXX has a third-person plural verb here and in vv. 9–10.

[10] wĕʾet-bāttê yĕrûšālaim sĕpartem
wattitṣû habbāttîm lĕbaṣṣēr haḥômâ
[11] ûmiqwâ ʿăśîtem bên haḥōmōtayim
lĕmê habbĕrēkâ hayšānâ
wĕlōʾ hibbaṭṭem ʾel-ʿōśêhā
wĕyōṣĕrāh mērāḥôq lōʾ rĕʾîtem
[12] wayyiqrāʾ ʾădōnāy yhwh ṣĕbāʾôt bayyôm hahûʾ
libkî ûlĕmispēd ûlĕqorḥâ wĕlaḥăgōr śāq
[13] wĕhinnēh śāśôn wĕśimḥâ
hārōg bāqār wĕšāḥōṭ ṣōʾn
ʾākōl bāśār wĕšātôt yāyin
ʾākôl wĕšātô
kî māḥār nāmût
[14] wĕniglâ bĕʾoznāy yhwh ṣĕbāʾôt
ʾim-yĕkuppar heʿāwōn hazzeh lākem ʿad-tĕmūtûn
ʾāmar ʾădōnāy yhwh ṣĕbāʾôt[114]

[1] What are you doing, that you go up—
all of you—to the rooftops,
[2] shout-filled, tumultuous city,
exultant town?
Your slain are not slain by the sword,
nor your dead from battle.
[3] All your leaders have fled together,
without bow they were captured;
all found among you were captured together;
afar they fled.
[4] Therefore I say, "Look away from me,
that I may weep bitterly!
Don't try to comfort me
over the destruction of my poor people!"
[5] For a day of dismay, devastation, and disarray[115]
belongs to YHWH of Hosts in the valley of vision—

---

[114] LXX lacks this final line; as a result a number of commentators take it as a later addition (for example, Duhm, *Jesaia*, 162; Clements, *Isa 1–39*, 187; Gray, *Isa I–XXVII*, 373; Wildberger, *Isa 13–27*, 353). It is attested in 1QIsa[a]; Syr.; Tg.; Aq.; Theod.

[115] For other attempts to convey the soundplay of *mĕhûmâ ûmĕbûsâ ûmĕbukâ* in English, note REB "tumult, trampling, and turmoil," adopted by Blenkinsopp (*Isa 1–39*, 331), and NIV "tumult, trampling, and terror," endorsed by Tull (*Isa 1–39*, 345). Wildberger notes the attempt by Eichrodt in German: "*Sturm, Sturz, und Bestürtzung*" (*Isa 13–27*, 350).

resounding noise[116] and a cry[117] to the mountain.
[6] Elam lifted up the quiver,
   with chariots of Aram and horses,
   and Qir uncovered the shield.
[7] Your choicest valleys were full of chariots,
   and the cavalry stationed themselves at the gate,
[8] and Judah's covering was laid bare.
   You looked on that day to the weaponry of the Forest House,
[9] and the breeches of the city of David you saw—they were many.
   You gathered the waters of the lower pool,
[10] and the houses of Jerusalem you counted.
   You tore down the houses to make the wall inaccessible,
[11] and a reservoir you made between the two walls
   for the water of the old pool.
   But you did not look to the one who did this,
   and the one who formed this long ago you did not see.
[12] My Lord YHWH of Hosts called on that day
   for weeping, lamentation, baldness, and wearing sackcloth.
[13] Instead—gaiety and gladness,[118]
   killing cattle and slaughtering sheep,
   eating meat and drinking wine.

---

[116] This translation follows G. R. Driver, "Isaiah I–XXXIX: Textual and Linguistic Problems," *JSS* 13 (1968): 47–8 and Manfred Weippert, "Mitteilungen zum Text von Ps 19 5 und Jes 22 5," *ZAW* 73 (1961): 97–9, whose proposals are adopted in part by Willem A. M. Beuken, *Jesaja 13–23* (trans. Ulrich Berges; HTKAT; Freiburg: Herder, 2007), 245; Blenkinsopp (*Isa 1–39*, 333); NJPS; REB. The participle *měqarqar* derives from a reduplicated verb *qrqr* ("make noise"), with cognates in Arab., Aram., and Mid. Heb. *Qîr* is most likely a cognate accusative of this verb (see also Ug. *qr*, "noise"; Syr. *qûrqārā'*, "breaking wind"). This meaning best fits the context, and the prominent repetition of sounds is consistent with a phrase that communicates the idea of making noise. Alternatively, *qîr* may be a defective spelling of the geographic name *qîr* ("Kir"), which appears in the next verse (see A. Guillaume, "A Note on the Meaning of Isaiah XXII.5," *JTS* [NS] 14 [1963]: 383–4; NJPS). In all other occurrences, however, this name is spelled fully (v. 6; 2 Kgs 16:9; Amos 1:5; 9:7). Earlier commentators typically took *qîr* as a defective spelling of *qîr* ("wall") and *měqarqar* as the participle of a denominative verb meaning "break down a wall" (for example, Duhm, *Jesaia*, 159–60; Gray, *Isa I–XXVII*, 336).

[117] The rare term *šôa'* is best taken as a noun from the root *šw'* ("cry for help"), related to the nouns *šewa'* (Ps 5:3); *šûa'* (Job 30:24); and *šaw'â* (Exod 2:23; Jer 8:19; Ps 40:2 [Eng. 40:1]; etc.). Alternatively, one could take it as a geographic name, as in Ezek 23:23 (see Guillaume, "Isaiah XXII.5," 384–5; NJPS).

[118] The translation "gaiety and gladness," reflecting the alliteration of *śāśôn wěśimḥâ*, follows NASB.

"Eating and drinking,
  for tomorrow we die!"
[14] It is revealed in my ear by Yhwh of Hosts:
"This iniquity will not be covered for you until you die!"
says my Lord Yhwh of Hosts.

Most interpreters identify at least an Isaianic core to this poem, minimally including vv. 1-3 or 4 and vv. 12-14, which they date to the aftermath of Sennacherib's invasion of Judah in 701 BCE. This original oracle would have castigated the citizens of Jerusalem, who blithely rejoiced that they survived the catastrophe. Verses 5-11 are often regarded as additions from the time of the Babylonian conquest of Jerusalem in 587 BCE, if not even later, on literary and historical grounds.[119] Proponents of the later date typically classify vv. 8b-11 as prose and not poetry; however, while these verses do contain some prosaic features, there are convincing reasons to read them as poetry, as I will argue. The reference to Elam in v. 6 does pose problems for an eighth-century BCE date because Elam was allied with Babylon against Assyria, which calls into question the likelihood of its participation in Sennacherib's campaign. Against this majority view, however, Seitz, Sweeney, and Wildberger take vv. 1-14 as a unified composition by Isaiah of Jerusalem in response to the events of 701 BCE.[120] They explain v. 6 by noting that the Assyrian forces included captives and mercenaries, some of whom would have been Elamite. More recently, William R. Gallagher has also argued for the poem's original unity but associates it with Sennacherib's defeat of Babylon at

---

[119] For example, Clements (*Isa 1-39*, 82; "The Prophecies of Isaiah and the Fall of Jerusalem in 587 B.C.," *VT* 30 [1980]: 429-31); Gray (*Isa I-XXVII*, 363-5); Kaiser (*Isa 13-39*, 139-40). Blenkinsopp regards v. 5 as a late, apocalyptic addition, but he thinks that vv. 6-8 can plausibly be dated either to 701 or 587 BCE (*Isa 1-39*, 334-5). Beuken reverses the typical view, arguing that vv. 2b-3 better match the events of 587 BCE, vv. 5-7 fit either 701 or 587, and vv. 8b-11a better match 701 BCE (*Jesaja 13-27*, 248; see also Tull, *Isa 1-39*, 345). A few scholars date the text entirely to the Babylonian invasion, for example: Uwe Becker, *Jesaja, von der Botschaft zum Buch* (Forschungen zur Religion und Literatur des Alten und Neuen Testaments 178; Gottingen: Vandenhoeck & Ruprecht, 1997), 278-9; de Jong, *Isaiah Among the Ancient Near Eastern Prophets*, 154.

[120] Seitz, *Isa 1-39*, 159-62; Sweeney, *Isa 1-39*, 295-6; Wildberger, *Isa 13-27*, 357-8; see also Childs, *Isaiah*, 159-60. Hayes and Irvine date the text to 711 BCE, following Sargon's campaigns against Philistia, but their reading does not otherwise differ significantly (*Isaiah*, 277-9).

Kish in 704 BCE.[121] The defeat of the Chaldean leader Merodach-baladan, who was apparently an ally of Hezekiah (2 Kgs 20:12-13 = Isa 39:1-2; 2 Chr 32:31), virtually guaranteed the invasion of Judah, as it freed Sennacherib to deal with their uprising.[122] On this reading, the poem criticizes Jerusalem's preparation for and fatalistic attitude concerning the coming invasion, rather than its response to surviving the invasion. Although not without problems, this background makes good sense of the description of captured leaders in v. 3, the presence of Elamite and Aramaean archers and chariots in v. 6, and the enigmatic reference to "Judah's covering" in v. 8.[123] I tentatively follow Gallagher's proposal in my reading of the poem, although most of the interpretation would still hold for other proposals.

Based on structural indicators, the poem may be divided into four sections: vv. 1b-4, 5-8a, 8b-11, and 12-14. The particle *kî* ("for") introduces the transition between the first and second sections. The beginnings of the third and fourth sections are marked by the repetition of *bayyôm hahû'* in vv. 8b and 12a, which echo the announcement of the day of YHWH at the beginning of the second section in v. 5a. Inclusio reinforces the limits of the third and fourth sections; observe the repetition of the pair *nābaṭ* ("look")/*rā'â* ("see") in vv. 8b-9a and 11b and the divine name *'ădōnāy yhwh ṣĕbā'ôt* ("my Lord YHWH of Hosts") in vv. 12 and 14. At the same time, a number of verbal connections across unit boundaries function loosely to hold the poem together as a whole: the multiple occurrences of *yôm*; the repetition of *mērāḥôq* ("afar, long ago") in the first and third sections (vv. 3, 11); the verb *bkh* ("to weep") in the first and fourth sections (vv. 4, 12); the verb *glh* ("to uncover, reveal") in the second and fourth sections (vv. 8, 14); and the name *'ădōnāy yhwh ṣĕbā'ôt* in the second and fourth sections (vv. 5, 12, 14).[124]

---

[121] William R. Gallagher, *Sennacherib's Campaign to Judah: New Studies* (Studies in the History and Culture of the Ancient Near East 18; Leiden: Brill, 1999), 60-71.

[122] Gallagher, *Sennacherib's Campaign*, 270-2.

[123] Beuken objects that the Battle of Kish would have been too remote to attract Isaiah's notice (*Jesaja 13-27*, 249). On Gallagher's reading, however, its implications for Judah's future would not have been lost on Hezekiah's court, and Isaiah elsewhere assumes that his audience is aware of geographically distant Assyrian conquests (for example, Isa 10:9).

[124] Throughout the poem, the divine name appears as part of the phrase *'ădōnāy yhwh ṣĕbā'ôt* (vv. 5a, 12a, 14b). The single exception is v. 14a, where only *yhwh ṣĕbā'ôt* appears. Here, however, the immediately preceding word *bĕ'oznāy* ("in my ears") might play phonologically on the audience's expectation of the word *'ădōnāy*.

The first section is characterized by couplets with unbalanced lines, the so-called *qînâ*-rhythm typically associated with lament.[125] Within the opening couplet (v. 1b), the Masoretic accents suggest a line break following *'ēpô*, but the succession of unbalanced lines in vv. 2–4 support the lineation in *BH*[3] and *BHS*, which divide after *'ălît* to create a longer first line. Morphological and phonological considerations corroborate this division: the second-person feminine suffix *-āk* marks the initial word in both lines,[126] while the final words in each end with the consonant *t*, again designating them as feminine. In v. 2, parallelism demarcates the lines of the two couplets, with the lack of parallels for *těšū'ōt mělē'â* ("full of shouting") in v. 2a and *ḥălālayik* ("your slain") in v. 2b yielding unbalanced lines. Verse 3 contains a pair of parallel couplets, in which morphological and grammatical matching mark the lineation: the first lines of each couplet begin with *kol-* ("all") and end with *yaḥad/yaḥdāw* ("together"), while the shorter second lines both begin with words with the prefixed preposition *min-* and end with third-person plural perfect verbs. Soundplay delimits the lines in the two couplets of v. 4. The final sound in the concluding word of all four lines is the first-person singular morpheme *-î*, while the opening words in the four lines begin with the gutturals ʿ or ʾ; moreover, three of the four lines begin with rhyming words (*'al/ 'al*). Indeed, the entire section as a whole contains a striking concentration of rhyming words, nearly all of them occurring in the initial or final positions of lines and thus demarcating their limits.[127]

Initially, the unbalanced couplets of the *qînâ*-rhythm, with their evocation of lament, conflict with the description of the unnamed city's joyful festivity.[128] This tension between form and content

---

[125] Dobbs-Allsopp, *Weep, O Daughter of Zion*, 142–3; Kaiser, *Isa 1–39*, 140. Dobbs-Allsopp notes several other connections between this poem and the city-lament genre.

[126] The form *kullāk* ("all of you") is exceptional in First Isaiah (but see Song 4:7); elsewhere, it appears as *kullēk* (Isa 14:29, 31). The unusual form here enhances the assonance of the line (Gray, *Isa I–XXVII*, 366).

[127] On this use of rhyme, see Jeremy Corley, "Rhyme in the Hebrew Prophets and Wisdom Poetry," *Biblische Notizen* 132 (2007): 61–7; Watson, *CHP*, 233.

[128] Blenkinsopp, *Isa 1–39*, 333. Some recent interpreters claim that the actions described in vv. 1–2a are not celebratory, but this requires identifying the city as Jerusalem (Willem A. M. Beuken, "Obdurate Short-Sightedness in the Valley of Vision: How Atonement of Iniquity is Forfeited [Isa 22:1–14]," in *One Text, A Thousand Methods: Studies in Memory of Sjef van Tilborg* [eds. Patrick Chatelion

powerfully reinforces Isaiah's charge that the celebration is grossly inappropriate. Beginning in v. 2b, however, the themes become more consistent with the tone of lamentation suggested by the rhythm. The prophet describes the city's humiliating defeat (vv. 2b–3), including the capture and shameful defection of its leaders, who were not even capable of self-defense (v. 3). According to Gallagher, the celebratory city addressed in these verses is likely Babylon, which welcomed the victorious Sennacherib as a liberator, at least according to Assyrian sources.[129] For Isaiah, however, the outcome of the Battle of Kish represents a national tragedy in light of its implications for Judah, and so he cannot understand the Babylonians' celebration. His sorrow over the impending destruction of his own people (v. 4) stands in stark contrast to their exultation, and it embodies the lamentation to which God has called all of Jerusalem in the fourth section (v. 12), which will also depict the tension between unseemly celebration and appropriate lamentation.

The lines of the second section are longer and more balanced. Sound is the key for dividing v. 5. The repetition of *m* and striking rhyme in *yôm měhûmâ ûměbûsâ ûměbûkâ* ("a day of dismay, devastation, and disarray") bind together the first line, while the appositional phrase *la'dōnāy yhwh ṣěbā'ôt* ("belongs to my Lord YHWH of Hosts") resists division and forms the beginning of the next line. Based on the punctuation in the Masoretic Text, Septuagint, and Peshitta, the phrase *běgê' hizzāyôn* ("in the valley of vision") belongs to this line as well, but *BH*³ and *BHS*, followed by many commentaries and translations, take it with the second half of the verse, which they further divide following *qîr* ("noise").[130] Presumably, the attraction of this division lies in its unbalanced lines, which maintain the predominant rhythm of the first section, although a simple preference for couplets may also underlie the decision. The final four words of v. 5, however, are best taken as a single line on phonological grounds, in light of the final *r* in three of the four words, as well as the partial internal parallelism created by the synonyms *qîr* and *šôa'* ("alarm"). If

---

Counet and Ulrich Berges; Biblical Interpretation Series 71; Leiden: Brill, 2005], 51–3; de Jong, *Isaiah Among the Ancient Near Eastern Prophets*, 154; Sweeney, *Isa 1–39*, 296).

[129] Gallagher, *Sennacherib's Campaign*, 68–9, 71; see also the depiction of Babylon's acceptance of Cyrus in the Cyrus Cylinder, lines 18–19.

[130] For example, Duhm, *Jesaia*, 159; Gray, *Isa I–XXVII*, 362; Wildberger, *Isa 13–27*, 348, 350. Blenkinsopp regards v. 5 as prose (*Isa 1–39*, 331, 333; see also REB).

one then follows the traditional punctuation and divides the second line after *bĕgê' ḥizzāyôn*, the result is a triplet of roughly balanced lines (4:5:4). Parallelism indicates the division of v. 6 as a similarly balanced triplet, with a geographic name and at least one military term in each line. Likewise, vv. 7–8b form a triplet; although the lines are not tightly parallel, the repeated conjunction *w-* marks their limits.[131]

The lineation in this section is relatively straightforward by comparison to the rest of the poem. One finds little play between lineation and content; rather, the sequence of lines with their attendant pauses effectively presents a staccato collage of sounds and images. The opening lines proclaim a "day for . . . YHWH" that has taken place in the enigmatic "valley of vision" (v. 5a). Subsequent verses identify this day of YHWH as the Battle of Kish, the events of which the prophet apparently witnessed in a vision. Through his poetry, he recreates the experience of this vision for his audience. The first triplet suggests the noise of the battlefield through its content and use of soundplay.[132] The aural emphasis is at slight odds with the theme of "vision," but the poetry becomes more visual in the second and third triplets. These lines evoke a freeze-frame sequence of battlefield scenes with compact, suggestive statements that show soldiers poised for action without describing actual conflict. The point here is not to provide an ordered narrative of the events of the battle, like one might find in Assyrian annals.[133] Despite similarities in detail, Isaiah's poetic account is more interested in evoking the feel of the battle than recounting its outcome, which was presumably already known to his audience. Its consequences for the prophet and his audience are announced with striking conciseness in the final line of the section (v. 8a). The word "covering" (*māsāk*, "curtain") is a metaphor for Merodach-baladan's rebellion, the suppression of which has now left

---

[131] I find no persuasive reason to treat *mālĕ'û rekeb* ("were full of chariots") as a separate line in v. 7a (so *BH*³; *BHS*; Wildberger, *Isa 13–27*, 348). Duhm's lineation is even more idiosyncratic (*Jesaia*, 160). In all of these cases, the primary motivation appears to be a predilection for unbalanced couplets.

[132] Watson, *CHP*, 233.

[133] The differences between the two are comparable in some respects to the differences between narrative and poetic accounts of the same battle in Judges 4–5; see Alter, *Art of Biblical Poetry*, 50–8; Robert S. Kawashima, *Biblical Narrative and the Death of the Rhapsode* (Indiana Studies in Biblical Literature; Bloomington: Indiana University Press, 2004), 17–34.

Judah open for attack.¹³⁴ The impersonal third-person verb, without a specific subject, raises questions about who, in fact, "laid bare" Judah's defenses.

Some commentators and most English translations take at least some verses of the third section as prose.¹³⁵ The poetic character of v. 11b seems clear in light of the tight semantic and syntactic parallelism, including the verb pair *nbt/r'h*, which occurs elsewhere in Isaianic poetry (Isa 5:12; see also Hab 1:13; Pss 33:13; 84:10 [Eng. 84:9]; Job 28:24), and the chiastic structure. By contrast, vv. 8b–11a display only slight parallelism, and the accusative marker *'et*, more typically associated with prose, occurs in vv. 9–10. These objections are not decisive, however, and multiple stylistic features indicate the presence of poetry here.¹³⁶ The six sentences in vv. 8b–11a show consistently alternating structures, with clauses beginning with the verb (vv. 8b, 9b, 10b) followed by clauses beginning with the direct object (vv. 9a, 10a, 11a), as seen also in the clearly poetic v. 11b. Likewise, the verb forms in these sentences alternate regularly, with *yqtl* forms in one line and *qtl* forms in the next, a common variation which Adele Berlin has identified as a type of morphological parallelism.¹³⁷ These alternating patterns group the lines into two couplets and a triplet. Features such as these may occur in highly stylized prose, but their concentration across a small unit of text considerably increases the likelihood that these verses are, in fact, verse. Line and

---

¹³⁴ Gallagher, *Sennacherib's Campaign*, 68.

¹³⁵ For example, Blenkinsopp, *Isa 1–39*, 333–4 (vv. 8b–11); Duhm, *Jesaia*, 161 (vv. 9b–11a); Gray, *Isa I–XXVII*, 362, 370 (vv. 9b–11a); Tull, *Isa 1–39*, 346 (vv. 8b–11); NJPS (vv. 9b–11a); NRSV (vv. 8b–11); REB (vv. 8b–11a). As noted earlier, the commentators who take this view typically regard these verses as a later addition. BH³, BHS, NIV, NJB, and Wildberger (*Isa 13–27*, 348, 356) present the entire section as poetry—rightly, as I argue. The fullest discussion of the question appears in J. A. Emerton, "Notes on the Text and Translation of Isaiah XXII 8–11 and LXV 5," VT 30 (1980): 439–40. Emerton concludes that arguments against the poetic character of the passage are unpersuasive but does not dismiss the possibility that it is "exalted prose."

¹³⁶ Emerton, "Text and Translation," 438. Infrequent use of so-called prose particles may indicate the presence of poetry in biblical texts (Francis I. Andersen and A. Dean Forbes, "Prose Particle Counts of the Hebrew Bible," in *The Word of the Lord Shall Go Forth: Essays in Honor of David Noel Freedman in Celebration of his Sixtieth Birthday* [eds. C. Meyers and M. O'Connor; Winona Lake, Ind.: Eisenbrauns, 1983], 165–83). It does not follow, however, that the presence of these particles means that a text cannot be poetic; David Noel Freedman argues for the greater presence of such particles in prophetic poetry relative to other Biblical Hebrew poems ("Another Look," 15–16; see also Bartelt, *Book Around Immanuel*, 26).

¹³⁷ Berlin, *Dynamics*, 36.

sentence typically coincide in this section, except for v. 11a, the length of which necessitates its division into two lines as in *BHS*.[138]

The section describes the actions undertaken in Jerusalem "on that day" (v. 8b), that is, the day of YHWH described in the previous unit. Apparently, the city's leaders recognize with the prophet the precariousness of Judah's situation following Merodach-baladan's defeat, and they prepare for the inevitable Assyrian invasion with careful defensive measures. These include taking inventory of weaponry (v. 8b), strengthening the city's fortifications (vv. 9a, 10; see also 2 Chr 32:5), and securing its water supply (vv. 9b, 11a; see also 2 Kgs 20:20; Siloam Tunnel Inscription, lines 5–6). The repeated, alternating structures of these lines connote the orderliness of the city's defensive preparations. At the same time, the relatively weak parallelism may suggest some degree of futility to these actions, especially when compared to the concise, compact poetry of v. 11b, which describes the divine actions of which the city has failed to take note. The human military measures undertaken "on that day" (v. 8b) cannot overcome what YHWH has already done on his "day" (v. 5), which was in fact planned "long ago." The true identity of the unspecified subject in v. 8a, who removed "Judah's covering," now becomes clear. The tight parallelism of the final couplet in contrast to the preceding lines also achieves a sense of closure for the section. As Edward Greenstein explains, "Parallelism can achieve closure... by setting up a series of lines that are roughly parallel in structure, and then rounding them off with two lines that are neatly parallel to one another."[139]

The fourth section opens with an enjambed couplet (v. 12), which is best divided at the *'atnāḥ* in the Masoretic Text, as the repetition of the preposition *l-* marks v. 12b as a single line.[140] The phrase *bayyôm*

---

[138] So also Emerton, "Text and Translation," 437–8. He further divides vv. 8b–9a into four lines, but they fall into acceptable limits when taken as two.

[139] Greenstein, "How Does Parallelism Mean?" 62.

[140] One finds a wide range of line divisions for this verse, which are almost never defended. Gray's lineation matches that proposed here, except that he regards *bayyôm hahû'* ("on that day") as a gloss (*Isa I–XXVII*, 362). Duhm also divides the verse into two lines, but he deletes *bayyôm hahû'* and includes *libkî* with the first line (*Jesaia*, 162; see also Blenkinsopp, *Isa 1–39*, 331). *BH*³ and *BHS* divide each half of the verse into two lines, following the divine name in v. 12a and *ûlĕmispēd* ("and for lamentation") in v. 12b (see also NIV). Wildberger also treats the verse as two couplets, but he includes *libkî* ("for mourning") in the second line of the first couplet, and divides the second couplet following *ûlĕqorḥâ* ("and for baldness"; *Isa 13–27*, 348). NJPS, NRSV, and REB take the verse as a triplet, dividing v. 12b after *ûlĕmispēd*.

hahû' locates these verses in the same temporal realm as the preceding two sections, depicting an interlocking series of divine and human actions. This schema may not be precisely factual, as all of the events described in vv. 5–14 did not happen simultaneously, but the reduction of their temporal extent to the ubiquitous "that day" effectively communicates their interconnectedness in Isaiah's view. Verse 13 contains a triplet of internally parallel lines depicting the decadent festivities of the Jerusalemites. Note especially the phonological interplay between words in parallel slots in the second and third lines: *bāqār* ("cattle")/*bāśār* ("meat"); *šāḥōṭ* ("slaughtering")/*šātôt* ("drinking");[141] *ṣō'n* ("sheep")/*yayin* ("wine"). This soundplay provides strong grounds for treating these lines as internally parallel, rather than dividing them into shorter parallel lines. The quickened pace of the internal parallelism suggests the frenzy with which the citizens of Jeruaslem celebrated in the shadow of impending disaster, in striking contrast to the slower movement of the unusually long lines that call for mourning rituals in v. 12. The first-person plural verb in v. 13b, in contrast to the second-person plural verbs in vv. 9b–11a, indicates that it represents the speech of the people, although it seems likely that the prophet has sarcastically put words into their mouths, as he also does in Isa 28:15, 29:11, and other passages. The repetition of *'ākôl* ("eating") and *šātô* ("drinking") leads the audience to expect further description of the festivities; as a result, the final clause (*kî māḥār nāmût*, "for tomorrow we die") comes as a shock, revealing the fatalism that hangs over the people's activities. Following O'Connor's constraints, v. 13b should be divided after *šātô*, which isolates and further emphasizes this final clause.

Verse 14 displays no parallelism save the repetition of the divine title *yhwh ṣĕbā'ôt*. REB takes the first line, and NIV the entire verse, as prose. If one divides the verse at the major clause junctures, following the punctuation in the Masoretic Text and Peshitta, the result is a roughly balanced triplet (4:5:4), bounded by the repetition of *yhwh ṣĕbā'ôt*, just like the section as a whole. In contrast to the short clauses of the preceding internally parallel lines and their depiction of festivity, the longer clauses in v. 14 suggest the seriousness of the judgment

---

[141] The unusual form of the infinitive absolute *šātôt* enhances the soundplay (GKC §75n; Wildberger, *Isa 13–27*, 353). The expected form (*šātô*) occurs later in the same verse.

that they communicate. This statement ironically echoes the Jerusalemites' own grave assessment of their situation from the preceding verse, confirming that they will indeed die. Given the predominance of couplets in Biblical Hebrew poetry, a triplet at the end of a poem serves as a form of terminal modification and helps to create a sense of closure, an effect made even stronger in this case by the absence of parallelism.[142] Thematically, the divine death sentence punctuates the poem with a chilling note of finality, beyond which nothing remains to be said.[143] Finally, the repeated indication of God's speech also indicates the end of the oracle and claims for it the incontrovertible authority of the divine. In this way, the verse provides both strong formal and thematic closure to the poem.

Despite its obscure historical referents and occasionally difficult language—both of which would presumably have been more intelligible to Isaiah's audience—the substance of this poem is straightforward enough. The subtle effects of the lineation, however, produce undercurrents of meaning that interact in complex ways with the surface content of the poem to heighten its persuasiveness. Among these undercurrents are the tension between lamentation and celebration, the evocation of the atmosphere of the battlefield, the futility of misguided human action against the efficiency of divine action, and the fervor of Jerusalem's festivities against the seriousness of its fate. These effects both result from and support the lineation I propose, and it is difficult to discern similarly meaningful effects among the bewildering variety of line divisions for this poem among critical editions, commentaries, and translations. The striking lack of other poetic devices in the poem magnifies the communicative potential of its lineation, making careful attention to it all the more indispensable for the interpretation of this text. Nonetheless, matters of lineation deserve close consideration in any poem, as the lined language of verse provides the conceptual space in which all other poetic features function.

---

[142] Alter, *Art of Biblical Poetry*, 35; Greenstein, "How Does Parallelism Mean?" 54; Watson, *CHP*, 183; see further Smith, *Poetic Closure*, 76–7. For other examples of concluding triplets, see, for example, Pss 19:15 (Eng. 19:14); 125:5; 133:3; Song 1:5–8.
[143] On the closural force of allusions to death, see Smith, *Poetic Closure*, 102.

2

Structure and Movement

The preceding chapter argued for the definitive character of lineation in poetry; however, a series of isolated, unconnected lines does not a poem make. In order to establish the perception of movement, a variety of devices join one line to the next, acting as the counterpoint to the series of pauses created by line breaks. While careful discernment of line breaks remains crucial for the interpretation of Biblical Hebrew poetry, the interpreter must also take the next step of elucidating the network of relationships among lines that ultimately constitutes the poem. Broadly speaking, these concerns fall under the category of poetic structure, which Barbara Herrnstein Smith helpfully defines as follows:

> The structure of a poem...consist[s] of the principles by which it is generated or according to which one element follows another. The description of a poem's structure, then, becomes the answer to the question, "What keeps it going?" To think of poetic structure this way, instead of as an organization of, or relationship among, elements, is to emphasize the temporal and dynamic qualities that poetry shares with music.[1]

Two additional observations by Smith are relevant here. First, the structural principles of a poem may be formal or thematic—functions of the "physical features of words" or of "the symbolic or conventional nature of words."[2] As free verse, Biblical Hebrew poetry relies heavily on thematic elements for its structure, but formal elements often reinforce thematic ones. Second, this account of poetic structure emphasizes the audience's experience of a poem as an event that unfolds in real time. Even so, poetic movement is hardly a straightforward

---

[1] Smith, *Poetic Closure*, 4. [2] Smith, *Poetic Closure*, 6.

Structure and Movement 69

progression from beginning to end. The audience is continually processing new lines of a poem, and the devices that move the poem forward may also send the audience back to preceding lines with new insights. Smith dubs this process "retrospective patterning."[3]

This chapter examines the thematic and formal elements that create structure in the poetry of First Isaiah and, to borrow Smith's language, keep Isaianic poems going. The first part of the chapter discusses the dynamics of parallelistic and enjambed couplets. As the most common combination of lines in Biblical Hebrew poetry, the couplet provides the basis for the audience's impression of a poem's structure; consequently, any discussion of poetic movement should begin here. Triplets, quatrains, and even larger groups of lines, along with single lines, are treated in the second section of the chapter. Although they occur much less often than couplets, these line configurations have important structural functions in First Isaiah. The third part of the chapter details some common techniques in this corpus for holding together multiple groups of lines and whole poems. Structure at these levels is much more variable and diffuse. In many cases, smaller line groups form larger units, variously called "strophes," "stanzas," or "cantos" by interpreters, that in turn comprise the whole poem. These units are usually not as tightly defined as smaller line groups. A reading of Isa 3:1–15, with special attention to structural elements at all levels of the poem, concludes this discussion.

THE COUPLET

Couplets, or pairs of lines, comprise by far the most common structural unit in Biblical Hebrew poetry.[4] Their boundaries are maintained by the pronounced pause following the second line, which is much stronger than the one separating the two lines from each other. Because of the frequent and measured repetition of these pauses, the

---

[3] Smith, *Poetic Closure*, 10
[4] Geller, *Parallelism*, 5–6; Stephen A. Geller, "The Dynamics of Parallel Verse: A Poetic Analysis of Deut 32:6–12," *HTR* 75 (1982): 36; Kugel, *Idea*, 1; O'Connor, *HVS*, 134–5, 392; Petersen and Richards, *Interpreting Hebrew Poetry*, 23–4; Watson, *CHP*, 174, 177.

binary structure of the couplet profoundly shapes the reader or hearer's temporal experience of a poem. The audience begins to expect that the poem will continue to move forward in like fashion—one line, then another, one line, then another, and so forth. In this way, the consistent repetition of the couplet becomes a structural device, a form of "systematic repetition," to borrow another term from Smith, that lends stability and coherence to the poem.[5] Deviations from this structure have their own effects that the poet will exploit, of course, but only because the structure has been established so thoroughly.

In the majority of couplets, the lines are joined together by the complex network of relationships among their parts known as parallelism; concurrently, groups of lines held together by parallelism most often occur as couplets. As a result, many critics fail to distinguish adequately between the two phenomena. This failure arises, at least in part, from the prevalent but unhelpful tendency to refer to "whatever goes on between two lines" in biblical poetry as "parallelism," as noted by Greenstein.[6] To be sure, the coincidence of couplets with parallelism is so frequent that the reader or hearer of biblical poetry will come to associate them almost intuitively. There are, however, good reasons for keeping the two phenomena distinct. Couplets comprised of non-parallel lines are not infrequent, and parallel lines also form groups larger than the couplet, such as the triplet. A clear distinction between couplets and parallelism appropriately differentiates between a discrete grouping of individual lines and a pattern of expression that may be employed at almost any level of the poem. This distinction makes possible a fuller appreciation of the dynamics of the parallelistic couplet, in which the poet has employed a structural *device* to forge two lines into a structural *unit* of the larger poem.

Other options for joining the lines are possible, most notably syntactic dependency or enjambment. Dobbs-Allsopp proposes that these possibilities for joining lines rest on a continuum.[7] The majority of couplets may be clearly identified as parallelistic or enjambed, but less certain cases also exist. In these cases, the audience's perception of the dominance of one technique or the other comes to the fore. By virtue of their role in joining pairs of lines, parallelism and

---

[5] Smith, *Poetic Closure*, 38–42, 70–5.
[6] Greenstein, "How Does Parallelism Mean?" 45; see also O'Connor, *HVS*, 88–9.
[7] Dobbs-Allsopp, "Enjambing Line," 237–8.

enjambment also demarcate couplets as discrete units. Both kinds of couplets are usually end-stopped—that is, the end of the couplet coincides with a strong syntactic juncture—and therefore closed.[8] In couplets joined by parallelism, the emphatic character of the second line, which is connected to the preceding line but not the following one, marks the couplet as a closed entity.[9] In couplets joined by enjambment, the syntactic stop at the end of the second line carries similar force as a result of its being delayed.[10] These typically distinct boundaries contribute greatly to the perceptibility of couplets as structural units of the poem.

In most Isaianic poems, as with Biblical Hebrew poetry generally, parallelism is the more common strategy for forming couplets, but non-parallelistic couplets occur often enough to have perceptual integrity of their own. Even when non-parallelistic couplets play on the audience's expectation of parallelism, as they sometimes do, they should not be regarded as dependent phenomena.[11] The following treatment of couplets in First Isaiah examines first the dynamics of parallelistic and then enjambed couplets, giving greater attention to the former in light of their higher incidence, with some comment on the interplay between the two and its impact on the shape of a poem.

Parallelism

Throughout the nineteenth and twentieth centuries, Robert Lowth's work set the trajectory for treatments of parallelism in biblical poetry; while critics modified or expanded his categories of synonymous, antithetical, and synthetic parallelism, their validity was assumed largely without question.[12] Over the last thirty years, however, the

---

[8] For the closed couplet in English poetry, which is also typically the result of end-stopping, see Smith, *Poetic Closure*, 73–4, n. 41.
[9] Kugel, *Idea*, 55–6.
[10] F. W. Dobbs-Allsopp, "The Effects of Enjambment in Lamentations (Part 2)," *ZAW* 113 (2001): 372.
[11] *Contra* Geller, *Parallelism*, 6.
[12] Of course, Lowth did not "discover" the phenomenon of parallelism in Biblical Hebrew poetry, as is sometimes suggested; he himself notes that the sixteenth-century Jewish interpreter Azariah de Rossi ("Rabbi Azarias") had recognized the phenomenon and explained it similarly (*Isaiah*, liii–lxvi). See further Adele Berlin, *Biblical Poetry through Medieval Jewish Eyes* (Bloomington, Ind.: Indiana University Press, 1991); Gordon, "Legacy of Lowth," 74–7; Robert Allen Harris, *Discerning Parallelism:*

study of the phenomenon has received fresh life from a series of studies proposing new approaches, including a renewed emphasis on its non-semantic aspects.[13] To better appreciate the function of parallelism as a structural device, the work of James Kugel, Robert Alter, and Adele Berlin deserves particular attention. Despite sometimes vehement disagreements, both Kugel and Alter argue that the second of two parallel lines frequently moves beyond the first in some fashion.[14] This assertion counters descriptions that focus on the ostensible semantic redundancy of parallelism and recasts it as a vehicle for, rather than an impediment to, poetic movement. Parallel lines are not simply interchangeable paraphrases of each other; rather, the second line introduces additional semantic content, however subtle or nuanced, not present in the first line. Both Kugel and Alter appeal to a pair of couplets in Isa 1:3:

> *yādaʿ šôr qōnēhû*
> *waḥămôr ʾēbûs bĕʿālāyw*
> *yiśrāʾēl lōʾ yādaʿ*
> *ʿammî lōʾ hitbônān*
>
> The ox knows its owner,
>   and the ass its master's trough;
> Israel does not know;
>   my people do not understand.

Kugel argues for a negative progression in these lines, based on a perceived difference in intelligence between the two animals in the first couplet. The more intelligent ox obeys its master, while the less

---

A Study in Northern French Medieval Jewish Exegesis (Brown Judaic Studies 341; Providence: Brown University Press, 2004); Kugel, *Idea*, 96–170.

[13] For an overview of important studies, see Kuntz, "Biblical Hebrew Poetry in Recent Research," 40–7, 57–8; Joel M. LeMon and Brent A. Strawn, "Parallelism," in *Dictionary of the Old Testament: Wisdom, Poetry & Writings* (eds. Tremper Longman III and Peter Enns; Downers Grove, Ill.: InterVarsity Press, 2008), 507–10; Petersen and Richards, *Interpreting Biblical Poetry*, 21–35.

[14] Alter, *Art of Biblical Poetry*, 3–26; Kugel, *Idea*, 1–58. Alter discusses and develops the structural implications of parallelism across whole poems in ways that Kugel does not. Kugel focuses almost entirely on individual lines and line groups, a shortcoming for which he has been criticized: Daniel Grossberg, *Centripetal and Centrifugal Structures in Biblical Poetry* (SBLMS 39; Atlanta: Scholars Press, 1989), 3–4; Francis Landy, "Poetics and Parallelism: Some Comments on James Kugel's *The Idea of Biblical Poetry*," *JSOT* 28 (1984): 74–5.

intelligent ass at least recognizes the source of its food.[15] The first line of the second couplet contends that Israel does not even know as much as the ass, much less the ox, and the final line suggests that the nation lacks understanding altogether. Alter, by contrast, sees a positive progression, at least in the first verse. An ass typically enjoys closer relations with humans than an ox, and knowledge of the owner's crib is more concrete than mere knowledge of the owner.[16] The denunciatory character of these lines seems to favor a negative progression, but on either account this verse demonstrates the forward-moving character of parallelism.

Although it represents a significant advance, this focus on emphasis does not adequately account for the complexity of parallelism and, at times, smacks of reductionism. Kugel in particular seems to have responded to one extreme by adopting the other, finding no significant role for semantic similarity.[17] Alter likewise goes to great lengths to find subtle progressions of meaning in as many lines as he can, although he does recognize that some parallel lines are strictly synonymous.[18] On the other hand, Berlin advances the discussion by broadening the conception of parallelism to include both contrast and equivalence.[19] Parallel lines equate certain entities while differentiating between others, and the tension between these two impulses gives the phenomenon its dynamic character. By creating a sense of equivalence, parallelism slows the progress of the poem; by creating a sense of contrast, it moves the poem along. Further, parallelism simultaneously involves multiple facets of language.

---

[15] Kugel, *Idea*, 9. The possibility of this progression is lost in David Noel Freedman's reading, which takes "trough" as the object of both lines, although only specified in the second: "What the Ass and the Ox Know—But the Scholars Don't," *BRev* 1 (February 1985): 42-4.

[16] Alter, *Art of Biblical Poetry*, 25. Both readings would be more persuasive if Alter and Kugel supported their claims about attitudes toward livestock with relevant data from biblical and ancient Near Eastern sources.

[17] To avoid completely dismissing it, Kugel claims, "This is not to say that paralleling is not important—of course it is, it is the most striking characteristic of this style. But focusing on it is just somewhat beside the point" (*Idea*, 56). It seems oddly counterintuitive to suggest that one should not in fact focus on "the most striking characteristic" of a literary device!

[18] Alter, *Art of Biblical Poetry*, 22.

[19] Berlin, *Dynamics*, 11-17; see also Alonso Schökel, *Manual*, 71. Kugel also recognizes the possibility of contrasting elements in parallel lines, which he refers to as "differentiation," but he does not regard it as part of the phenomenon of parallelism proper (*Idea*, 15).

Berlin distinguishes among three linguistic aspects of parallelism—syntactic, lexical–semantic, and phonological—that may occur at two levels of the line, either the single word or the whole clause.[20] Parallelism at certain levels creates the impression of parallelism at other levels, encouraging the reader to search for less overt connections between lines.[21] In this way, the complexity and variability of parallelism increases its capacity to engage the attention of the audience.

Like Kugel and Alter, Berlin uses Isa 1:3 as a test case for her understanding of parallelism. She also finds a sense of progression in these lines but is unwilling to abandon the language of equivalence, arguing instead for a productive tension between the two. In the first couplet, the implied presence of the verb *yādaʿ* ("to know") in both lines creates a sense of equivalence, suggesting that the ox and ass possess the same kind of knowledge, while the different objects create a sense of contrast, hinting at a varying degree of knowledge between the animals. In the first line of the second couplet, *yādaʿ* has no object, suggesting that Israel, in fact, knows nothing. At the same time, the repetition of the verb from the first couplet indicates that the same sort of knowledge is in mind here. Israel lacks what any dumb animal possesses, knowledge of the identity of one's master—in this case, Yhwh.[22] The progression culminates in the final line, where Berlin suggests that the reflexive sense of the *hitpolel* works best, translating the line as, "My people does not understand itself."[23] Ironically, the poet indicates the lack of self-understanding with the appellative, "my people," the tenderness of which adds emotional poignancy to the line.[24] Although she agrees on many points with Kugel and Alter, Berlin's reading of Isa 1:3 uncovers a more intricate web of connections among the four lines. It ultimately appears that distinct

[20] Berlin, *Dynamics*, 28–9; see further O'Connor, *HVS*, 642–3.
[21] Berlin, *Dynamics*, 111–12, 134; see also Greenstein, "How Does Parallelism Mean?" 64–6.
[22] LXX makes this interpretation explicit by adding the first-person accusative pronoun in both lines of the couplet: "But Israel does not know *me*; my people does not perceive *me*." Poetically, the ambiguity created by the omission of the object in MT proves more effective. Indeed, one wonders if the lack of an object may be meant to suggest that Israel does not even know what awareness it lacks, ignorant finally of its own ignorance.
[23] Berlin, *Dynamics*, 98. She is rightly suspicious of Kugel's claim of an emphatic meaning for the verb *hitbônān*.
[24] Berlin, *Dynamics*, 137.

understandings of poetry itself, and not simply parallelism, are at stake for Kugel and Berlin.[25]

Perhaps the most one can say is that parallelism typically moves a poem forward but does so in varied and unpredictable ways. The following discussion explores the structural dimensions of parallelism at the level of the couplet in First Isaiah, with the goal of demonstrating how the poet creates couplets with complex interlinear dynamics. While the examples are more illustrative than exhaustive, they will help us begin to chart some typical features of Isaianic style. The discussion will move from couplets with more overt movement to those with less overt movement.

Parallelism and Narrativity

The impression of sequential progression in a poem produces a highly perceptible sense of movement. Such progression is characteristic of narrative poetry, in which temporal sequence suggests causal connection.[26] Despite the much discussed absence of epic narrative poetry in the biblical corpus, one does find brief sequences of lines with what Alter calls an "incipiently narrative" character.[27] This impression of narrativity is sustained by apparent sequential relationships between lines. Alter holds that these relationships depend on semantically parallel terms that remain close enough in meaning to create a sense of equivalence, even as they depict temporally consecutive actions.[28] While narrative development can unfold between parallel lines by means of such nuanced synonymy, the corresponding terms often exhibit minimal semantic equivalence. These cases may be better explained with reference to Berlin's categories. The

---

[25] Appealing to Isa 1:3 elsewhere, Kugel suggests that parallelism is most effective when it is least perceptible: "An awkward poem, one that tramples rhythm and perhaps good sense in its struggle to rhyme, will have no difficulty in making the reader notice the fact of its rhyming; a more subtle poet will meet the requirements of form without letting them take over the poem, and unless we are looking for them, these formal elements will tend to recede" (*Idea*, 102). Berlin, following the linguist Roman Jakobson, identifies parallelism as an expression of the poetic function of language, which calls attention to its message for its own sake. Thus, perceptibility becomes paramount: "It is really a question of the 'poetic effect' of these parallelisms—their 'psychological validity' or 'perceptibility,' or how striking they are" (*Dynamics*, 9–10).

[26] Leonard Nathan, "Narrative Poetry," in *TNPEPP*, 814.
[27] Alter, *Art of Biblical Poetry*, 29.   [28] Alter, *Art of Biblical Poetry*, 39.

sense of temporal or causal development results from semantic contrast, while the equivalence between the lines resides primarily in their grammatical and phonological aspects. In other words, non-semantic effects hold the two lines together, allowing the poet greater flexibility to make semantic distinctions to create an impression of narrative progression.

While this phenomenon sometimes persists over a number of lines, creating brief narrative sequences within a poem, it is often restricted to a single couplet. One finds several examples at this level in First Isaiah, such as Isa 28:20:

> kî qāṣar hammaṣṣāʿ mēhiśtārēaʿ
> wĕhammassēkâ ṣārâ kĕhitkannēs[29]
> For the bed is too short to stretch out upon it,
> and the blanket too narrow when one draws up in it.

A number of grammatical and phonological equivalences establishes the relationship between the two lines. They have identical syntactic structures, including matching infinitives in the infrequent *hitpaʿel* stem, and they share the repeated consonants s/ṣ/ś and k/q, along with the assonance created by the repeated verbal patterns. The actions depicted by the verbs, on the other hand, are hardly synonymous. In fact, they could logically occur in sequence, and the tightness of their parallelistic frame encourages such a reading. Someone lies down in a bed, only to discover that it is too short; as a result, the person draws up to fit more comfortably in the bed, but then the blanket no longer covers the entire body, making for a terrible night's sleep.[30] The narrativity is the cumulative effect of the opposing pulls of the

---

[29] MT *kĕhitkannēs* is problematic, since the preposition *k-* is not normally used comparatively in Bibl. Heb., as the sense seems to demand here. 1QIsa[a] reads *bhtkns*, and Dahood has argued for a comparative sense for the preposition *b-*: *Psalms III, 100–150* (AB 17A; Garden City: Doubleday, 1968), 394, 397–8. Many of his proposed examples, however, are unconvincing; moreover, as William H. Irwin observes, 1QIsa[a] also reads *b-* for MT *k-* twice in the next verse, in contexts in which *k-* seems more likely: *Isaiah 28–33: Translation with Philological Notes* (BibOr 30; Rome: Pontifical Biblical Institute, 1977), 35. The reading *k-* is attractive for the resultant soundplay, given the predominance of the sounds *k* and *q* in the couplet. I follow MT, then, taking *k-* + infinitive with its usual temporal meaning in the second line, but I assume that the comparative element still carries over from the first line.

[30] For this interpretation, see Arnold B. Ehrlich, *Jesaja, Jeremia* (vol. 4 of *Randglossen zur Hebräischen Bibel: textcritisches, sprachliches und sachliches*; Leipzig: J. C. Hinrichs, 1912), 101.

couplet's contrasting and equivalent elements. The depiction of successive frustrations heightens the sense of futility that the prophet wishes to convey, as he declares the certainty of Assyrian military action despite Judahite attempts to resist it.[31]

In another example, with much less pronounced parallelism, phonological effects hold the lines together even as syntactic and semantic effects create a perception of temporal movement:

> hinnēh dammeśeq mûsār[32] mē'îr
> wĕhāyĕtâ mĕ'î[33] mappālâ
> Damascus will soon be removed from being a city
> and will become a heap of ruins. (Isa 17:1b)

The temporal progression in these lines is marked by the syntactic sequence *hinnēh* + participle + consecutive perfect, a sequence more commonly associated with prose (for example, Gen 17:4; Exod 17:6; 1 Kgs 20:36). A more poetic effect is the repetition of the sound *m* in five of the seven words in the couplet, which seems to result from careful word choice. The initial *m-* has been added as a prefix in two of the terms (the *ho'pal* participle *mûsār*, "will be removed," and the

---

[31] Compare the similar narrative effect of Amos 5:19, in which the protagonist escapes from a lion and then a bear, only to be bitten by a snake on arriving home. Several commentators resist finding narrative progression in these verses, arguing instead that they contain a series of separate images: for example, Francis I. Andersen and David Noel Freedman, *Amos: A New Translation with Introduction and Commentary* (AB 24A; New York: Doubleday, 1989), 522. Hans Walter Wolff, however, points to the series of *waw*-consecutive perfect verbs as evidence for the narrative unity of the verse: *Joel and Amos* (trans. Waldemar Janzen et al.; Hermeneia; Philadelphia: Fortress, 1977), 256–7.

[32] MT *mûsār* ("be removed"), supported by 1QIsa^a, is problematic; one expects a feminine verb with Damascus as the subject, as in the second line. Some commentators emend to *mûsārâ*: for example, Blenkinsopp, *Isa 1–39*, 302; Duhm, *Jesaia*, 132; Wildberger, *Isa 13–27*, 156. According to GKC §121b (followed by Gray, *Isa I–XXVII*, 298), the verb is an impersonal passive with Damascus as the object, in light of examples of similar gender discrepancy (see Isa 16:10; 21:2). The masculine form enhances soundplay within the line by emphasizing the final *r* sounds in consecutive words.

[33] MT *mĕ'î* ("heap") is a *hapax*, and some older commentators, appealing to the versions, propose deleting it (Duhm, *Jesaia*, 132; Gray, *Isa I–XXVII*, 298–9). The variety of renderings in the versions (contrast LXX; Tg.; Syr) likely represents varying understandings of a difficult word, and *mĕ'î* may best be taken as a biform of the more common *'î* ("heap"), used here for soundplay (so Wildberger, *Isa 13–27*, 156). Ironically, the suggestion that it is a dittograph of *mē'îr* ("from a city") testifies to the effectiveness of the soundplay.

noun plus preposition *mēʿîr*, "from being a city"), while another (*měʿî*, "heap") is a rare biform of a more common word (*ʿî*) that does not begin with *m-*. This phonological parallelism is the primary point of equivalence between the lines. Not only do their syntactic structures differ, but the sequential development marks the second clause as dependent. Further, at the lexical level, the nouns *ʿîr* and *měʿî* would not normally be regarded as synonyms.[34] Despite these contrasts, the phonological similarity encourages the reader or hearer to rethink the connectedness of the lines in general, and the terms *mēʿîr* and *měʿî* in particular. In this case, the terms are connected with reference to the city of Damascus, and the similar sounds ironically highlight the disparity between its present state as a populous fortified city and its future state as a deserted heap of ruins. The contrasting elements of the parallelism thus draw attention to the progression, while the equivalent elements convey a sense that the progression is natural.[35]

Recognition of the potentially narrative character of parallelism may even bear on text-critical decisions, as in Isa 11:1:

> *wĕyāṣāʾ ḥōṭer miggēzaʿ yīšāy*
> *wĕnēṣer miššārāšāyw yipreh*
>
> A shoot will come forth from the stump of Jesse,
> and the sprout from his roots will bear fruit.[36]

---

[34] See, however, Alter, *Art of Biblical Poetry*, 20.

[35] It is possible for the sense of progression to overwhelm any points of equivalence between the lines of a couplet, such that they will not be perceived as parallel at all, as in Isa 19:1b: *hinnēh rōkēb ʿal-ʿāb qal/ûbāʾ miṣrayim* ("Yhwh will soon mount a swift cloud / and come to Egypt"). Syntactically, the verbal sequence indicates temporal progression from one line to the next, as in Isa 17:1. Here, however, no prominent repetition of sound holds the lines together. Given the further absence of semantic similarity and the divergent syntactic structures, it makes little sense to speak of these lines as parallel.

[36] Many commentators date these verses to the post-exilic period, taking the image "stump of Jesse" as a reference to the end of the monarchy (Blenkinsopp, *Isa 1–39*, 264; Clements, *Isa 1–39*, 121–2; Gray, *Isa I–XXVII*, 214), although Wildberger interprets the expression similarly but defends Isaianic authorship (*Isa 1–12*, 468–9). The image need not presuppose the end of the monarchy, however; for alternative explanations, see Hayes and Irvine, *Isaiah*, 212–13; H. G. M. Williamson, "The Messianic Texts in Isaiah 1–39," in *King and Messiah in Israel and the Ancient Near East: Proceedings of the Oxford Old Testament Seminar* (ed. John Day; JSOTSup 270; Sheffield: Sheffield Academic Press, 1998), 262–4; Seitz, *Isa 1–39*, 96–8. Once the possibility of a pre-exilic date is accepted, the case for Isaianic authorship becomes significantly more compelling; however, Sweeney and Vermeylen date the text to the reign of Josiah (Sweeney, *Isa 1–39*, 204–5; Vermeylen, *Isaïae*, 269–75).

The verbs in these lines create the narrative dynamic of the couplet, depicting first the emergence of new growth from the stock, then its subsequent maturation and production of fruit; on the basis of v. 4a, the expected fruit may be understood as *ṣedeq* ("righteousness") and *mîšôr* ("uprightness").[37] With the plant imagery depicting the fortunes of the Davidic line, the poet thus proclaims the complete regeneration of the monarchy in the space of two lines. Many commentators, however, emend the verb *yipreh* ("bear fruit") to *yipraḥ* ("sprout, grow"), which would negate this effect.[38] Wildberger's argument is telling; he appeals to the versions, but his proposal ultimately rests on his observation that *yipreh* "is not a close parallel" to *wĕyāṣā'*.[39] The evidence from the versions alone, however, is unconvincing.[40] More to the point, the possibility of narrative development between parallel lines eliminates this stylistic objection. The lines share the same syntactic structure, and the respective nouns and prepositional phrases are semantically equivalent.[41] These matches reduce the need for pronounced synonymy between the verbs, which allows the poet to fill those syntactic slots with terms denoting successive stages of vegetative growth. Note further that Isaiah 14:29b also contains the sequential actions "come forth" and "(bear) fruit" in parallel lines, although with the noun *pĕrî* ("fruit") instead of the verb *pārâ*. The appearance of the term *šōreš* ("root") further connects this verse to Isa 11:1.[42]

---

[37] This image is developed further in the song of the vineyard in Isa 5:1-7, where the expected yield of the metaphorical vineyard is *mišpāṭ* ("justice") and *ṣĕdāqâ* ("righteousness") in v. 7 (see Isa 32:15-18; 45:8); see the discussion in William P. Brown, *The Ethos of the Cosmos: The Genesis of Moral Imagination in the Bible* (Grand Rapids: Eerdmans, 1999), 254-6.

[38] Blenkinsopp, *Isa 1-39*, 263; Ehrlich, *Jesaja*, 46; Gray, *Isa I-XXVII*, 216; Hayes and Irvine, *Isaiah*, 212-13; Wildberger, *Isa 1-12*, 461; so also NAB; NJPS; NRSV.

[39] Wildberger, *Isa 1-12*, 461.

[40] *Contra* Wildberger, LXX *anabēsetai* ("will go up") and Tg. *ytrby* ("will be made great") need not reflect the reading *yipraḥ*, as √*prh* denotes vegetative growth, not simply upward motion or exaltation. Syr. *npr'* ("will spring up, bud") may suggest a *vorlage* with *yipraḥ*, but this reading could have arisen from the interchange of *h* and *ḥ* at some earlier stage of textual transmission. 1QIsaᵃ agrees with MT.

[41] For the pair *gēza'/šōreš* ("stump/root"), see also Job 14:8.

[42] Ancient readers were already aware of this connection, as demonstrated by the expansionistic rendering of Isa 14:29bα in Tg.: "for from the descendants of Jesse will come forth the Messiah" (*'ry mbny bnwhy dyšy ypwq mšyḥ*).

Non-narrative Development

Couplets with narrative development clearly demonstrate the forward-moving character of parallelism, as lines that refer to distinct, successive events cannot be taken as mere restatements of a single idea. On the other hand, some parallel lines in Biblical Hebrew poetry do seem to refer to a single action or event, and attempts to read narrative progression into them may result in mistaken interpretations. An infamous example can be found in the New Testament in Matt 21:1–5, which takes the parallel pair ḥămôr/ben-'ătōnôt ("he-ass/foal of she-asses") in Zech 9:9 as a reference to two animals![43] Parallelism of both sorts may occur in the same poem. In Isaiah's vineyard song (5:1–7), a series of couplets in v. 2 form a brief narrative vignette that describes the successive actions of cultivating a vineyard, planting it, building a watchtower, and digging a wine-vat. Later, two parallel lines that describe the destruction of the vineyard are best taken as portraying a single action:

hāsēr měśûkātô[44] wěhāyâ lěbāʿēr
pārōṣ gědērô wěhāyâ lěmirmās
Removing its hedge, it will be devastated;[45]
breaking down its wall, it will be trampled. (Isa 5:5b)

It makes little sense to read separate actions into these lines. There would be nothing left to trample after the vineyard had already been devastated, and one would be forced to assume that it had both a

---

[43] Mayer I. Gruber, "The Meaning of Biblical Parallelism: A Biblical Perspective," *Prooftexts* 13 (1993): 289–93.

[44] MT points this word as měśukkâ with doubled k, presumably from √s/śkk ("to shut off"; see Exod 25:30; 1 Kgs 8:7). The full spelling suggests a vocalization měśûkâ (see měśûkâ/měśūkâ ["thorn hedge"] in Mic 7:4; Prov 15:19), from √śwk ("to hedge about"; see Hos 2:8; Job 1:10). The two roots may be related, so there is little at stake semantically in the distinction; see Gray, *Isa I–XXVII*, 87; Wildberger, *Isa 1–12*, 177; Williamson, *Isa 1–5*, 321.

[45] The verb bāʿar also occurs with "vineyard" as its object in Isa 3:14. It has a wide semantic range, such that lexicons routinely list multiple homophonous roots (for example, *HALOT* 145–6). The most common meanings are "burn, consume" and, more generally, "destroy," all of which fit here. Most commentators argue that destruction by livestock or wild animals is in view, since there is no longer a fence to keep them out (Gray, *Isa I–XXVII*, 87; Wildberger, *Isa 1–12*, 176; Williamson, *Isa 1–5*, 321); however, the parallel term mirmās may refer to "trampling" by livestock (Isa 7:25; Ezek 34:19) or an invading army (Isa 10:6; Mic 7:10), and the latter sense cannot be ruled out here.

hedge and a wall.[46] Rather, at a climactic moment in the poem, the prophet slows down and forces the reader or hearer to pay closer attention to the fate of the vineyard—and the impending judgment of Israel and Judah to which the metaphor points—by devoting multiple lines to the single event of its ransacking. Even so, the verse still conveys a subtle sense of development. In two of the four lexical pairs, the term in the second line seems more forceful than the first. "Wall" (*gĕdērô*) in the B-line denotes a more substantial form of protection than "hedge" (*mĕśûkātô*) in the A-line, and correspondingly the verb "break down" (*pārōṣ*) seems more violent than "remove" (*hāsēr*).

Alonso Shökel nicely describes this sort of subtle development, which he specifically identifies as characteristic of the style of First Isaiah: "The poet takes a totality and expresses it in a sentence. When he has finished he takes the same totality again and expresses it with another series of words which are similar or equivalent.... He presents a contemplation of the same object which reveals new details, new facts."[47] As in Isa 5:5, these subtle effects of parallelism are often concentrated at the level of paired words, as opposed to narrative parallelism, in which the development more often encompasses the sense of the whole line. The second term develops the first with new— at least in the audience's temporal experience of the poem—and complementary semantic information and thus evokes a sense of progression, albeit in a more impressionistic or imagaic fashion. More often than not, Kugel and Alter have these effects in mind in their respective claims that the second of two parallel lines typically moves beyond the first in some fashion. Without attempting to provide an exhaustive account, Alter suggests a number of ways that this might unfold: the term in the second line may be an epithet or metaphor for the first, a "synecdochic substitution," or a "hyperbolic stepping-up of the initial verb."[48] The following examples illustrate some of these possibilities.

Isaiah's oracle against Shebna, Hezekiah's chief of staff, castigates him for constructing an elaborate tomb. A couplet that describes his building activities displays several cases of lexical elaboration, including metaphoric substitution:

---

[46] Wildberger cites evidence that some ancient vineyards possessed both structures (*Isa 1–12*, 183). It seems unnecessary at best and excessively literalistic at worst, however, to assume that this must be the case because both are mentioned within the poem; see Williams, "Frustrated Expectations," 461, n. 15.
[47] Alonso Schökel, *Manual*, 71; see further Alonso Schökel, "Isaiah," 168.
[48] Alter, *Art of Biblical Poetry*, 15–21.

ḥōṣĕbî mārôm qibrô
ḥōqĕqî bassela' miškān lô
One who hews his grave up high,
who carves in the cliffs a residence for himself. (Isa 22:16b)

Any distinction between *ḥōṣĕbî/ḥōqĕqî* ("hews/carves") is slight at best. Their synonymy is underscored by phonetic parallelism, as both words begin with *ḥ*, share an identical vocal pattern (*qal* participle), and end with *-î*.[49] With *mārôm/bassela'* ("up high/in the cliffs"), we move from a general spatial designation to a specific topographical feature. Height is a common image for human pride in First Isaiah (see Isa 2:12–17; 5:15–16), concretized here by the designation of the tomb's location. The reference to the cliffs also clarifies the material of the tomb, already implied by the initial verb *ḥāṣab*, which almost always refers to the act of cutting stone or stone objects (Isa 5:2; Job 19:24; Siloam Tunnel Inscription, line 4; etc.). The third set of terms (*qeber/miškān*, "tomb"/"residence") involves figurative development, with the second term as a metaphor for the first. The metaphor of the grave as a home for the deceased person is amply attested in the Bible and ancient Near Eastern sources.[50] The image emphasizes Shebna's personal attachment to his tomb, in light of which Isaiah's

---

[49] This ending is typically understood as a *ḥireq compaginis*: Wildberger, *Isa 13–27*, 379; John T. Willis, "Textual and Linguistic Issues in Isaiah 22, 15–25," *ZAW* 105 (1993): 381; *contra* Hayes and Irvine, *Isaiah*, 285.

[50] *Miškān* appears in this context in Ps 49:12 (Eng. 49:11), parallel to *bayit* ("house"), which serves as a metaphor for the grave in Isa 14:18; Job 17:13; 30:23; see *bêt 'ôlām* ("house of eternity") in Qoh 12:5, Deir 'Alla 2.6, and Palmyranean tomb inscriptions (*DNWSI* 1, 160; see Avi Hurvitz, "*BYT-QBRWT* and *BYT-'LM*: Two Funerary Terms in Biblical Literature and their Linguistic Background," *Maarav* 8 [1992]: 64–6). Wildberger notes that the tomb of the royal steward in Silwan, which is roughly contemporary with this oracle and sometimes identified as Shebna's actual grave, resembles a house in size and layout: Wildberger, *Isa 1–12*, 387; see Nahman Avigad, "The Epitaph of a Royal Steward from Siloam Village," *Israel Exploration Journal* 3 (1953): 137–52; David Ussishkin, "The Necropolis from the Time of the Kingdom of Judah at Silwan, Jerusalem," *Biblical Archaeologist* 33 (1970): 34–46. These facts may reflect the conventional association of "grave" and "home," but they should not be taken as the specific justification for the parallelism of *qeber/miškān* in Isa 22:16. The metaphor of grave as home occurs in modern poetry as well; see the discussion of Emily Dickinson's "Because I Could not Stop for Death," in George Lakoff and Mark Turner, *More than Cool Reason: A Field Guide to Poetic Metaphor* (Chicago: University of Chicago Press, 1989), 4–8.

Structure and Movement 83

prediction that he will die in exile and thus not be buried in his magnificent tomb (v. 18) rings all the more harshly.[51]

Isaiah 1:23aβ is an example of "hyperbolic stepping-up," to borrow Alter's phrase. In this couplet, the prophet indicts the political leadership of Jerusalem with the parallel charges that each one "loves a bribe" (*'ōhēb šōḥad*) and "pursues gifts" (*rōdēp šalmōnîm*). The semantic heightening of the verbs is striking, moving from the emotive "loves" to the more dynamic "pursues." The first term suggests an affinity for dishonest activity; the second implies that these activities are carried out with reckless enthusiasm. There does not appear to be any inherent semantic difference between the objects *šōḥad* ("bribe") and **šalmōn* ("gift").[52] Note, however, that the former occurs in the singular in the first line and the latter in the plural in the second line. This contrast enhances the sense of increased magnitude by providing the more dynamic verb with multiple objects ("loves a bribe" vs. "*pursues* [many] gifts"). The accusation in the first line is damning enough, but the even starker language of its restatement in the second line portrays Jerusalem's officials as hopelessly dishonest, leaving no doubt that they must be removed. Indeed, the multiple articulation of the charge may itself gesture toward the ongoing and repeated nature of their offenses.

Deletion compensation offers another possibility for development within parallel lines that do not necessarily depict successive events. Instead of exploiting subtle differences between parallel words, the poet introduces new semantic material in the second line with no

---

[51] The threat that Shebna will not be buried in his grave thus displays affinities to biblical curses associated with exile, especially the threat that one will not be able to live in the home one has built: Deut 28:30; Amos 5:11; Zeph 1:13; etc.; see Delbert R. Hillers, *Treaty-Curses and the Old Testament Prophets* (BibOr 16; Rome: Pontifical Biblical Institute, 1964), 28–9.

[52] Because **šalmōn* is a *hapax legomenon*, its semantic range is unclear. Although it may be connected to Heb. √*šlm* (*HALOT*, 1542; Wildberger, *Isa 1–12*, 66), it is more likely a loanword: compare Akk. *šulmānu*; so Harold R. (Chaim) Cohen, *Biblical Hapax Legomena in the Light of Akkadian and Ugaritic* (SBLDS 37; Missoula, Mont.: Scholars Press, 1978) 40–1; Paul V. Mankowski, *Akkadian Loanwords in Biblical Hebrew* (Harvard Semitic Studies 47. Winona Lake, Ind.: Eisenbrauns, 2000), 143–6; Williamson *Isa 1–5*, 122. It is possible, then, that a common term in the first line has been replaced with a more literary term in the second; see the comparable case of *'ŏnîyôt* ("ships")/*śĕkîyôt* ("armadas") in Isa 2:16, in which the latter is an Egyptian loanword, according to Cohen, *Hapax Legomena*, 41–2; Yoshiyuki Muchiki, *Egyptian Proper Names and Loanwords in North-West Semitic* (SBLDS 173; Atlanta: Society of Biblical Literature, 1999), 255–6. On this phenomenon more generally, see Alter, *Art of Biblical Poetry*, 13.

counterpart in the first line, which appears in place of a prior term that has no match. In other words, deletion compensation gives the poet a way to overload the second line with meaning, since the meaning of the deleted term must be assumed in addition to the explicit presence of the new material. Many treatments of biblical poetry use the appellative "ballast variant" for the new material, as if it were mere rhythmic padding. By contrast, Kugel and Alter rightly regard the elaboration made possible by the new material as the salient feature of this technique, to which the absence of the deleted term draws attention.[53] Deletion compensation occurs throughout First Isaiah, as in the following example:

> *wayyibṭĕḥû ʿal-rekeb kî rāb*
> *wĕʿal pārāšîm kî-ʿāṣĕmû mĕʾōd*
> They trusted in chariots, for they were many,
> and in cavalry, for they were very numerous. (Isa 31:1b)

The addition of *mĕʾōd* ("very") in the second line counters the deletion of *wayyibṭĕḥû* ("they trusted") in the first. By its very nature, the adverb functions as an intensifier, and it receives special emphasis because it has no parallel and occurs at the end of the line. The heightened expression underscores the futility of alliance with Egypt, as their many chariots and even their very numerous riders will not save Judah from Assyria.

This technique makes possible even more extensive elaboration than simple lexical differentiation. In the following example, the added material develops a metaphor along a trajectory implied but not made explicit in the first line:

> *lākēn hirḥîbâ šĕʾôl napšāh*
> *ûpāʿărâ pîhā liblî-ḥōq*
> Therefore, Sheol has widened her gullet,
> and opened her mouth without limit. (Isa 5:14a)

In the first line, the prophet personifies the underworld as a ravenous monster.[54] Because the single subject "Sheol" governs both verbs in the couplet, it need not be repeated; in this regard, the couplet

---

[53] Alter, *Art of Biblical Poetry*, 23–5; Kugel, *Idea*, 46–7.
[54] In the Ug. Baal myths, the deity Mot ("Death") is similarly depicted as a ravenous monster; note especially the repeated references to Mot's *npš* ("throat, appetite"); *KTU*² 1.5 i.6–7, 14–22; 1.5 ii.2–6; 1.6 ii.15–20).

Structure and Movement   85

behaves no differently than a clause with a compound verb in Biblical Hebrew prose.[55] In a characteristically poetic move, however, the adverbial phrase *liblî-ḥōq* ("without limit") fills the corresponding slot in the second line. This addition advances the depiction of the underworld by introducing the idea of its infinite rapacity. Death is not only imminent but inescapable for the prophet's audience, as the following couplet makes clear: "and its magnificence and multitude go down into her, / its throng and those who exult in it" (Isa 5:14b). In this way, the second line of v. 14a creates a sense of progression through a phrase with no parallel in the first line, even though both lines are variations on the same image. Other examples of compensation as a vehicle for poetic movement include Isa 3:13; 5:9b; 10:3a; 30:10a; 31:4aβ.

Non-Semantic Development

Even Alter admits that "there are semantically parallel versets where only tortured ingenuity would infer development and where it looks as though the line has really been shaped on a principle of relatively static synonymity."[56] As an example, he notes Isa 10:2b, which he translates as follows:

> *lihyôt ʾalmānôt šĕlālām*
> *wĕʾet-yĕtômîm yābōzzû*
> For widows to be their booty
> and they plunder orphans.

While conceding the overwhelmingly synonymous character of these lines, he cannot entirely relinquish the notion of dynamic progression; he observes that only the second line of the couplet contains "a transitive form of the verb," suggesting that some kind of development has taken place at the grammatical level. As a matter of fact, it is not simply a contrast between intransitive and transitive verbs but between non-finite and finite verbs, respectively an infinitive and an imperfect, and the finite verb stands out all the more because not only the verb in the first line but also those in the previous couplet (v. 2a) are infinitives. Such contrast in tense constitutes a form of morphological parallelism in Berlin's terms, although she only treats the more

---

[55] See O'Connor, *HVS*, 122.   [56] Alter, *Art of Biblical Poetry*, 22.

common parallelism of *qtl* and *yqtl* verbs under this category.[57] Since the finite verb appears in the second line, one may reasonably speak of grammatical development within the couplet, as Alter suggests.[58] In discussing poetic movement within a couplet, then, one must be attentive to non-semantic features of the lines, although these will likely be even less perceptible to the reader or hearer than the most subtle lexical variations.

An example from Isa 29 illustrates the kind of poetic movement produced by non-semantic features of the lines:

wĕṣartî ʿālayik muṣṣāb
wahăqîmōtî ʿālayik mĕṣūrōt

I will lay siege against you with garrisons,[59]
and I will raise against you siege-works.[60] (Isa 29:3b)

---

[57] *Dynamics*, 35-6. Parallelism between non-finite and finite verbs occurs with relative frequency in Isaianic poetry; for other cases involving an infinitive and imperfect, see Isa 5:24aα; 14:25; 30:12. One may also note a number of couplets in which a participle and imperfect are parallel, especially in *hôy*-oracles, such as the one under discussion; see Isa 5:8a, 11a, 23; 30:2a; 31:1a. In all of these examples, the finite verb occurs in the second line.

[58] According to GKC §114r, the extension of an infinitive with a prefixed preposition by a finite verb is a standard construction in both poetry and prose, although many of the examples come from poetic texts (1 Sam 2:8b; Isa 45:1aβ; Job 38:7; Prov 1:27a; etc.). This syntactic construction explains the consistent placement of the finite verb in the second line of couplets in which a non-finite and finite verb are parallel. At the same time, one should not dismiss the poetic character of such parallelism; although its shape may be syntactically determined, the division into lines remains a stylistic move with particular effects.

[59] MT *muṣṣāb* is a *hapax*. The related noun *maṣṣab* denotes a place where troops are stationed (1 Sam 14:1, 4; 2 Sam 23:14), and *maṣṣābâ* designates a unit of troops (1 Sam 14:12; Zech 9:8 emended). LXX *charaka* ("palisade, bulwark") is probably extrapolated from the parallel term *mĕṣūrôt*, "siege works" (LXX *purgos*, "tower"). Syr. *mqbt*ʾ ("drill") also suggests a weapon; however, Syr. has *mṭrq*ʾ ("guards, camp") for the parallel, so the translator may have reversed the terms. The most likely meanings, then, are a group of soldiers or the location of their station, either of which may be meant by the English term "garrison."

[60] MT *mĕṣûrâ* typically refers to defensive fortifications (Nah 2:2 [Eng. 2:1]; 2 Chr 12:4), but here it apparently refers to a siege instrument, a meaning typically associated with the related term *māṣôr* (Deut 20:20; Ezek 4:2; Mic 4:14; *KAI* 202.A.9, 15). 1QIsaᵃ reads *mṣwdwt*, which Irwin takes to be an interchangeable synonym, as the same terms are confused in Isa 29:7; Qoh 9:14 (*Isa 28-33*, 49). Elsewhere, however, *mĕṣād/mĕṣûdâ* refer to defensive structures (1 Sam 22:4; Isa 33:16; Ps 31:3-4 [Eng. 31:2-3]), so they should not be regarded as synonyms: C. L. Seow, *Ecclesiastes: A New Translation with Introduction and Commentary* (AB 18C. New York: Doubleday, 1997), 309. Rather, the variants result from *d/r* confusion.

It is difficult to discern significant semantic differentiation in these two lines. They share the same syntactic structure (verb + prepositional phrase + object), and the syntactic pairs, which occur in the corresponding positions in each line, exhibit varying degrees of phonological equivalence (*wĕṣartî/wahăqîmōtî*; *muṣṣāb/mĕṣūrōt*). The verb that opens the first line and the noun that closes the second line also share a common root (√*ṣwr*), forming a phonological and semantic inclusio that reinforces the magnitude of the threatened siege of Jerusalem.[61] At the same time, grammatical contrasts occur at the level of individual words. One verb occurs in the *qal* stem and the other in the *hipʿil*; the object in the A-line is a masculine singular noun, while the object in the B-line is feminine plural. This shift from less marked to more marked forms creates some impression of progression, achieved largely by the play between equivalence and contrast of morphological and phonological features.

Syntactic transformation offers further possibilities for non-semantic development. In couplets in which transformation has taken place, the two lines share an underlying syntactic structure but display grammatical differences at the surface level. Both Edward Greenstein and Adele Berlin have treated this phenomenon at great length; despite differing accounts of its relationship to parallelism, they agree that transformation elicits greater audience engagement.[62] Berlin explains:

> Something processed easily, which matches the reader's knowledge or expectation perfectly possesses low "informativity." ... If we apply this to parallelism we see that, for instance, changing the surface structure of a parallel line makes it more interesting.[63]

By requiring greater engagement on the part of the reader or hearer and eliciting curiosity about the relationship between two lines, transformation serves poetic movement. Berlin identifies four types

---

[61] Exum, "Broken Pots," 341; Irwin, *Isa 28–33*, 49.
[62] Greenstein suggests that transformation obscures parallelism and must be "peel[ed] away" in order to reveal the parallelism between two lines ("How Does Parallelism Mean?" 47). For Berlin, by contrast, transformation is a form of grammatical contrast at the level of the line and is thus a form of parallelism, albeit a less perceptible one (*Dynamics*, 53–4, 132–3).
[63] Berlin, *Dynamics*, 53–4; see also Greenstein, "How Does Parallelism Mean?" 54. Of course, increasingly complex transformations produce diminishing returns when the effort required to negotiate them outstrips the interest that they create, so some balance is required (Berlin, *Dynamics*, 135).

of transformation that commonly take place between parallel lines: nominal–verbal, positive–negative, subject–object, and contrast in mood. All of these are attested in Isaianic poetry: for nominal–verbal, see Isa 3:12b; 23:3; for positive–negative, see Isa 8:10bα; 9:6aα (Eng. 9:7);[64] 17:10; 28:8, 18a; for subject–object, see Isa 3:4; 19:4; 22:23; 28:26; for contrast in mood, see Isa 10:11; 14:27a.

A few examples will illustrate the dynamics of transformation in parallel lines. Positive–negative transformation can be found in Isa 28:18a:

> wĕkuppar bĕrîtĕkem ʾet-māwet
> wĕḥāzûtĕkem ʾet-šĕʾôl lōʾ tāqûm
> And annulled will be your covenant with death,
> and your pact[65] with Sheol will not stand.

The philological difficulties associated with ḥāzût ("pact") notwithstanding, these lines appear to be variations of the same idea, expressed respectively by affirmative and negative verbal constructions.[66] Although a competent reader or hearer will quickly grasp the semantic equivalence of the lines, the transformation creates the impression that the second line has developed the meaning of the first

---

[64] Reading rabbâ hammiśrâ ("dominion will increase") for MT Q lĕmarbê hammiśrâ ("to increase of dominion") in the first line. The Kethib in both MT^L (lmrbh, with anomalous orthography) and MT^A (lm rbh) suggests that the letters lm result from dittography with šālôm ("peace") in the preceding line (see Duhm, Jesaia, 91; Gray, Isa I–XXVII, 176; etc.). Alternatively, one could take them as a prepositional phrase, either lām ("for them"; see Blenkinsopp, Isa 1–39, 247) or lāmô ("for him").

[65] Ḥāzût is a crux in Isa 28:18 (see ḥōzeh in v. 15). Its usual meaning ("vision") make little sense; instead, it appears to be synonymous with bĕrît ("covenant") and is translated as such in LXX and Vulg. G. R. Driver seeks an etymology from a separate √ḥzh, appealing to Arab. and Sabaean cognates: "Linguistic and Textual Problems: Isaiah I–XXXIX," JTS 38 (1937): 44; see also Ehrlich, Jesaja, 100–1. Most critics propose scenarios in which "vision" could take the extended meaning of "covenant." Blenkinsopp suggests that it recalls the theophany at Sinai: "Judah's Covenant with Death (Isaiah XXVIII 14–22)," VT 50 (2000): 475–6; see Exod 24:9–11. Irwin, following Moshe Weinfeld, notes that √ḥzh occurs in covenantal contexts with reference to the favorable gaze of the suzerain: Isa 28–33, 27; see also Weinfeld, "Covenant Terminology in the Ancient Near East and its Influence on the West," JAOS 93 (1973): 196.

[66] As Berlin notes, this phenomenon should not be confused with Lowth's category of antithetical parallelism, which need not involve transformation (Dynamics, 56). Indeed, parallel lines that show transformation are typically synonymous, not antithetical, the point of the transformation being that "x will happen" and "the opposite of x will not happen," not "x will happen" and "the opposite of x will happen."

one. The pairing of a verb possessing negative semantic import with a negated verb possessing positive semantic import further creates the impression of totality, in which the Judahites' ill-advised treaty will be rendered completely null and void. Both the chiastic structure of the couplet, which emphasizes the verbs by placing them at the beginning and end of the couplet, and the parallelism of a perfect and imperfect verb further contribute to this totalizing effect.

Isaiah 19:4 nicely demonstrates subject–object parallelism:

wĕsikkartî 'et-miṣrayim bĕyad 'ădōnîm[67] qāšeh
ûmelek 'az yimšol-bām
And I will dam up[68] Egypt into the power of a harsh lord,
and a mighty king will rule over them.

The matched noun + adjective phrases 'ădōnîm qāšeh/melek 'az ("a harsh lord/a mighty king") are the focal point of the parallelism. The former appears in the first line in a prepositional phrase functioning as an accusative, while the latter is the subject in the second; the respective placement of the phrases at the end and beginning of their lines draws attention to this transformation. In the first line, Yнwн places Egypt under the authority of a cruel dictator. The second line elaborates the consequences of this divine action, as the dictator becomes the subject and assumes political power. In this way, the object–subject transformation speaks to the interplay of divine and human agency. It also underscores Egypt's total passivity, as they alone of the entities named in the couplet never act as subject. While the transformation creates a sense of development syntactically, it

---

[67] For 'ădōnîm as a plural of majesty—note the singular adjective—see Blenkinsopp, *Isa 1–39*, 313; GKC §§124i, 132h; Wildberger, *Isa 13–27*, 230. Alternatively, but less likely, Horace D. Hummel has suggested reading the singular noun with enclitic -*m*: "Enclitic *Mem* in Early Northwest Semitic, Especially Hebrew," *JBL* 76 (1957): 101.

[68] The verb √*skr* occurs only here in the *pi'el* in Bibl. Heb.; it is attested in the 'ap'el in Old Aram. in the Sefire inscriptions with the meaning "hand over" (*KAI* 224.2–3). Most commentators take this for its meaning in Isa 19:4, as suggested by the versions, and argue that √*skr* was a dialectical variant of √*sgr* in Bibl. Heb.: *HALOT*, 756; E. R. Rowlands, "The Targum and the Peshitta Version of the Book of Isaiah," *VT* 9 (1959): 189–90; Wildberger, *Isaiah 13–27*, 230. On the other hand, √*sgr* appears multiple times in the Book of Isaiah (for example, Isa 22:22; 24:10; 45:1). Christopher B. Hays has recently argued that √*skr* means "block, dam up" in Isa 19:4, similar to its *nip'al* occurrences in Gen 8:2; Ps 63:12 (Eng. 63:11), with a wordplay on the more common √*sgr*: "Damming Egypt/Damning Egypt: The Paranomasia of *skr* and the Unity of Isa 19,1–10," *ZAW* 120 (2008): 612–17.

also functions semantically to create the impression of narrative movement.⁶⁹ The parallelism implies both a casual and sequential relationship between the lines, as the subject's capacity to act in the second line depends on action performed on it in the first line. Another common form of transformation in Biblical Hebrew poetry is gapping of the verb, even when the following line contains no compensatory terms. When gapping occurs in a couplet, the reader or hearer must subconsciously supply the missing term in order for the second line to make any sense. In some cases, the grammatical form of the deleted material must even be modified to fit the new clause.⁷⁰ At the same time, the otherwise similar syntactic structures and shared verb tightly connect the two lines.⁷¹ Consider the following couplet:

> mĕtayik baḥereb yippōlû
> ûgĕbûrātēk⁷² bammilḥāmâ
> Your men by the sword will fall,
> and your strength in battle. (Isa 3:25)

In a nice example of morphological contrast, the masculine plural mĕtayik ("your men") and the feminine singular gĕbûrātēk ("your strength") are parallel. As a result, the deleted verb yippōlû ("they [masculine] will fall") would need to be changed in number and gender to tippōl ("she will fall") if it appeared in the second clause. It seems unlikely that the reader or hearer consciously engages in such mental gymnastics in decoding the line, but some effort is necessary beyond simply repeating the verb. This required effort heightens the sense of connectedness between the two lines and thus the impression of movement between them.

This discussion has foregrounded the kinds of development possible within parallelistic couplets. Still, it is important not to dismiss

---

⁶⁹ See Dobbs-Allsopp, "Enjambing Line," 236.
⁷⁰ Greenstein, "How Does Parallelism Mean?" 46–7, 52–3; Miller, "Linguistic Approach to Ellipsis," 253–5, 262.
⁷¹ Miller, "Relation of Coordination," 44.
⁷² For MT gĕbûrātēk ("your strength"), 1QIsaᵃ reads gbwryk ("your warriors"), with a supralinear correction to gbwrwtk (plural of MT). LXX, Sym., Syr., and Tg. offer rough equivalents to gbwryk, but it is unclear whether they actually read this term or simply approximated its sense from parallelism. MT is the *lectio difficilior* and may be explained stylistically as the substitution of a singular abstract noun for a plural concrete one: Duhm, *Jesaia*, 50–1; Williamson, *Isa 1–5*, 293; see also Watson, *CHP*, 314–16.

the poetic value of synonymy. After all, the very conception of parallelism depends finally on equivalence.[73] It is against this backdrop that contrast and any resulting poetic movement occur. Synonymy, moreover, has artistic effects in its own right, independent of any contrast that may accompany it. Even as it develops the first line, the second line of the couplet forces the reader or hearer to linger just a bit longer on a thought before moving forward. Parallelism, in other words, encourages a type of contemplation, as Alonso Schökel eloquently observes: "Taken simply we can see in the poetic use of synonymy the tendency to preserve and prolong.... Emotion persists until it is fully expressed, contemplation remains gazing at the object under consideration."[74] One cannot finally deny the existence of parallel lines in which no movement is discernible. Even then, however, the reader or hearer's experience of the lines will be flavored by the others in which movement is apparent, minimizing any retarding effects that they might have on the forward progress of the poem.

Enjambment

As discussed in Chapter 1, enjambed poetic lines are syntactically dependent on each other, such that a group of these lines makes up a single sentence. Together with parallelism, enjambment is one of two basic strategies for joining lines into couplets in Biblical Hebrew poetry. Whereas parallelism serves this structural function in a more subtle fashion, enjambment creates an overt sense of connection between successive lines. As Dobbs-Allsopp explains: "One of the more obvious effects of enjambment is to provide a sense of forward movement.... [Enjambment] markedly de-emphasizes the significance of the pause at the end of the first line and increases instead the sense of progression and onward thrust."[75] Consider the following example:

> wĕʿattâ ʾôdîʿâ-nāʾ ʾetkem
> ʾēt ʾăšer-ʾănî ʿōśeh lĕkarmî
>
> And now, let me make known to you
> what I will do to my vineyard. (Isa 5:5a)

---

[73] Berlin, *Dynamics*, 2, 11; LeMon and Strawn, "Parallelism," 510.
[74] Alonso Schökel, *Manual*, 66.
[75] Dobbs-Allsopp, "Effects of Enjambment," 371–2; see also O'Connor, *HVS*, 409.

In this couplet, the second line or *rejet* is the object of the verb in the first line; the first line seems incomplete without it, which compels the reader or hearer to continue to the next line for resolution. Since enjambment is less common than parallelism and its structural function more straightforward, it need not be discussed as extensively; nevertheless, a brief treatment of its distinctive effects is in order here.

By dividing a single sentence into two or more lines, enjambment allows for the articulation of longer thoughts than parallelism. In the previous example, for instance, the sentence contains seven words, counting the relative particle 'ăšer ("what"). As such, it is too long to form a single, end-stopped line and thus requires an enjambed couplet. A more ambiguous case is Isa 9:1 (Eng. 9:2), which could be divided as a pair of long (six-word) parallel lines. By treating it as a pair of enjambed lines that form parallel couplets, however, the line lengths become more standard:

> hā'ām hahōlĕkîm baḥōšek
> rā'û 'ôr gādôl
> yōšĕbê bĕ'ereṣ ṣalmāwet
> 'ôr nāgah 'ălêhem

> The people who walk in darkness
> have seen a great light;
> the ones who dwell in a land of deep darkness—
> light has shone upon them.

In both couplets, the longest sentence constituent takes up the entire first line, leaving the rest of the sentence—including the verb—as the second line.[76] Dividing the lines in this way isolates the language of darkness in the respective first lines of the couplets and the language of light in the second lines. At the same time, subject–object transformation takes place across the two couplets; the semantically matching first lines are respectively the subject and object in their sentences. All of these effects reinforce the sense of reversal conveyed by the poetry.

---

[76] Because he arbitrarily insists that a line break cannot separate a subject and verb, Holladay analyzes these couplets as single lines; at the same time, because he takes five words as the maximum possible in a line (following O'Connor), he deletes hā'ām ("the people") in v. 1a and 'ôr ("light") in v. 1b: Holladay, "*HVS* Revisited (II)," 410–12; see also *BHS*. These conjectural emendations have no support from the versions.

The first line of an enjambed couplet may express a relatively complete thought that runs counter to the sense of the whole couplet. In such cases, the reader or listener forms an initial (mis-)impression of the line during the pause accompanying the line break, but the content of the following line forces reconsideration of this impression. In other words, enjambed lines by their very nature may demand retrospective patterning.[77] The effect can be unsettling, as we see in Isa 1:10a:

> šim'û děbar-yhwh
> qěṣînê sědōm
> Hear the word of YHWH,
> O rulers of Sodom![78]

By itself, the first line of v. 10a offers a straightforward injunction to listen to the prophetic word. The audience may well expect some word of comfort in response to the national tragedy described in preceding verses—presumably Sennacherib's invasion in 701 BCE. The vocative in the second line comes with a jolt, however, acerbically addressing the city's elite as "rulers of Sodom." It forcefully contradicts the people's assertion in v. 9 that Jerusalem is not like Sodom; although they may not have suffered the same fate as the legendary city, they are in fact no less wicked.[79] These impressions are all the more effective because they are unexpected. The next couplet parallels this one: "Give ear to the instruction of our God / O people of Gomorrah" (v. 10b). This time, the comparison to Gomorrah is not shocking. It reinforces the central theme of the first couplet, while also implicating the people as a whole in the indictment.

Quotations are one of the most frequent contexts for enjambment, so much so that O'Connor treats them as a special category of

---

[77] Dobbs-Allsopp, "Effects of Enjambment," 378–9; Kinzie, *Poet's Guide*, 49.

[78] It would be possible to take vv. 10a and 10b as single, five-word lines; however, vocative enjambment is common in Biblical Hebrew poetry (for example, Isa 28:14a; Lam 2:13a, 18a; see also Dobbs-Allsopp, "Enjambing Line," 224).

[79] For this reading, see N. A. van Uchelen, "Isaiah I 9—Text and Context," in *Remembering All the Way: A Collection of Old Testament Studies Published on the Occasion of the Fortieth Anniversary of the Oudtestamentisch Werkgezelschap in Nederland*, ed. A. S. van der Woude (OtSt 21; Leiden: Brill, 1981), 155–63; Tull, *Isa 1–39*, 58–9; Williamson, *Isa 1–5*, 87–8. Berlin similarly understands the distinction between Sodom's fate and wickedness as the key to understanding Isa 1:10, but she also reads Isa 1:9 as an affirmation of Jerusalem's likeness to Sodom: Berlin, *Dynamics*, 151, n. 48.

syntactic dependency.[80] The most common form consists of a separate line introducing the quotation—the "quotative frame," as O'Connor terms it—followed by the line(s) containing the quotation itself. Typically, both the frame and the quotation are complete clauses, but the latter is syntactically subordinate to the former. As a result, one may still speak of the lines as enjambed, although the line breaks are noticeably less harsh than those that occur within a clause, as in many of the examples discussed earlier.[81] Enjambed couplets containing quotations in First Isaiah include Isa 14:13a; 18:4a; 30:7b. The first two are part of longer quotations, spanning seven and three lines respectively, but in both cases an emphatic break separates the opening line from those that follow and establishes the integrity of the couplet. In the second example, the quotative frame is a variation on the standard prophetic messenger formula, *kōh 'āmar yhwh* ("Thus says Yhwh"). The third example has a naming verb (*qārā 'tî*, "I call") in the first line, followed by the spoken name in the second line. Quotative frames with dependent quotations also form triplets (for example, Isa 14:32; 19:11b), quatrains (for example, Isa 3:7; 28:13), and one group of five lines (Isa 9:5b [Eng. 9:6]), several of which will be discussed in this chapter. This high count, which does not include unmarked speech, points to the frequency of quotations in this corpus.

On the whole, Isaianic poetry uses enjambment to a greater degree than other biblical poems.[82] It diminishes the dominance of parallelism, keeping the poetry less predictable.[83] As Dobbs-Allsopp has noted, moreover, a high concentration of enjambed lines has noticeable effects on the texture of a poem.[84] Some poems with extensive

---

[80] O'Connor, *HVS*, 409–14; so also Dobbs-Allsopp, "Enjambing Line," 235.

[81] For a range of possible manifestations of "clause external enjambment," see Dobbs-Allsopp, "Enjambing Line," 233–8.

[82] In the corpus treated by O'Connor, the percentage of enjambed lines in most poems is around one-third (*HVS*, 420). In Lam 1–4, over two-thirds of the lines are enjambed, with an even higher percentage in the first two chapters (Dobbs-Allsopp, "Effects of Enjambment," 371, 373–4). By an approximate count, the number of clearly enjambed lines in many Isaianic poems is just under fifty percent, with a few poems registering higher. Taking O'Connor's corpus as typical, then, First Isaiah displays a higher-than-average concentration of enjambment, while still below the extreme represented by Lamentations. The amount is roughly comparable to that in Zephaniah, where fifty-one percent of the lines are syntactically dependent (*HVS*, 524).

[83] See Watson, *CHP*, 333–5.

[84] Dobbs-Allsopp, "Effects of Enjambment," 370–1.

enjambment in First Isaiah also imitate the lament form, in most cases in ironic fashion (for example, Isa 14:1–21; 15:1–16:12; 23:1–16).[85] In these cases, enjambment serves as a generic marker, encouraging the reader or hearer to make the connection between these poems and the lament tradition. Not surprisingly, all of these poems contain a high number of couplets with unbalanced lines—the so-called *qînâ*-rhythm—and other features typical of lament poetry. Another example of a poem with a high concentration of enjambed lines is the song of the vineyard in Isa 5:1–7. In this poem, the prophet employs various literary techniques to create and then frustrate particular audience expectations, artistically mimicking the divine frustration that the poem seeks to communicate.[86] The enjambed lines further this rhetorical strategy, as the line breaks thwart the reader or hearer's expectations by creating misleading provisional meanings and delaying completion. In short, enjambment in Isaianic poems creates variation not only in the form of couplets but also in the dynamics of their movement.

TRIPLETS, QUATRAINS, LARGER GROUPS, AND SINGLE LINES

Despite its effectiveness as a structural unit, the perceived dominance of the couplet in Biblical Hebrew poetry may have the unfortunate side effect of monotony. This holds true for English poetry as well, as Smith observes: "The greatest danger to formal continuity created by the closed couplet is ... 'saturation,' or, in more familiar terms ... boredom and fatigue."[87] Like repetitive drumbeats in a song, the regular pauses in a run of couplets risk becoming an annoyance that diminishes the experience of the poem. The presence of other kinds of line groups helps maintain the reader or hearer's interest. O'Connor observes that couplets occur with less regularity in the

---

[85] For satirical elements in these texts, see especially Jones, *Howling over Moab*; Lessing, *Interpreting Discontinuity*; R. Reed Lessing, "Satire in Isaiah's Tyre Oracle," *JSOT* 28 (2003): 89–112; Gale A. Yee, "The Anatomy of Biblical Parody: The Dirge Form in 2 Samuel 1 and Isaiah 14," *CBQ* 50 (1988): 565–86.
[86] Williams, "Frustrated Expectations," 459.
[87] Smith, *Poetic Closure*, 75.

96 Reading the Poetry of First Isaiah

Prophets than in other kinds of biblical poetry.[88] Triplets and quatrains are the most common groups of lines besides the couplet, although one occasionally finds even larger units.

Triplets

As with couplets, parallelism and enjambment are the basic forms for joining lines into triplets in Biblical Hebrew poetry, and the dynamics of these forms are similar for both kinds of line groups. Nonetheless, triplets have their own structural integrity independent of couplets. Geller regards triplets as "a sequence of interlocking couplets," but this schema does not work for all cases. In Isa 1:25, for instance, continuous narratival development across three parallel lines makes it impossible to group them in any other fashion:

> wĕʾāšîbâ yādî ʿālayik
> wĕʾeṣrōp bakkûr[89] sîgāyik
> wĕʾāsîrâ kol-bĕdîlāyik
> And I will turn my hand against you,
> and I will smelt your silver dross in the crucible,
> and I will remove all your impurity.

These lines describe three successive events in God's punishment and restoration of Jerusalem, depicted metaphorically as the refinement of silver. They share similar syntactic structures of verb + object + prepositional phrase, although the latter is omitted in the final line. The opening word of each line contains the initial consonant cluster $w + ʾ +$ sibilant ($š/ṣ/s$), and all three lines end with words with the suffix –ayik, although one is a preposition and the other two are nouns. Because the equivalence of these lines is located primarily in

---

[88] O'Connor, HVS, 640.
[89] Although the versions support MT kabbōr ("as [with] lye"), evidence for the use of lye or potash in the smelting process is unclear; elsewhere, bōr/bōrît refer only to soap used for bathing or clothes washing (Jer 2:22; Mal 3:2; Job 9:30). Many commentators emend to bakkūr ("in the crucible"), supposing metathesis of b and k (see Blenkinsopp, Isa 1–39, 180; Ehrlich, Jesaja, 8; Gray, Isa I–XXVII, 34–5; for arguments for MT, see Wildberger, Isa 1–12, 60; Williamson, Isa 1–5, 144). Kûr designates a type of smelting furnace used with many metals, including silver (Isa 48:10; Ezek 22:18, 22). For more on the extraction of silver in antiquity, see P. R. S. Moorey, Ancient Mesopotamian Materials and Industries: The Archaeological Evidence (Oxford: Clarendon, 1994), 232–3; Philip J. King and Lawrence E. Stager, Life in Biblical Israel (Library of Ancient Israel. Louisville, Ky.: Westminster John Knox, 2001), 173–4.

their syntactic and phonological aspects, increased contrast—and thus narrative development—becomes possible in the semantic aspect.

In Isa 19:2, key features of the parallelism are grammatical, including subject–object transformation and verb gapping:

> wĕsiksaktî miṣrayim bĕmiṣrayim
> wĕnilḥămû ʾîš bĕʾāḥîw wĕʾîš bĕrēʿēhû
> ʿîr bĕʿîr mamlākâ bĕmamlākâ[90]
>
> And I will spur Egyptian against Egyptian,
> and each will fight against a relative and each against a neighbor,
> city against city, kingdom against kingdom.

The three lines of the triplet are held together by the repeated phrase "x against (b-) y." In the first line, YHWH acts as the subject and incites civil war among the Egyptians; in the second line, the Egyptians become the subject and make war against each other.[91] As with the previously discussed Isa 19:4a from the same poem, the subject–object transformation effectively traces divine action and its consequences. The verb is deleted in the final line, thus focusing the audience's attention on the even larger groups of Egyptians who will fight against each other. Note also the contrast in gender, with masculine nouns (ʾîš ["each one"]; ʾāḥ ["relative"]; rēaʿ ["neighbor"]) in the second line and feminine nouns (ʿîr ["city"]; mamlākâ ["kingdom"]) in the third. Watson claims that this arrangement of nouns heightens the portrayal of civil war—"like fighting with like."[92] These grammatical features work together to create a sense of movement within the triplet.

Occasionally, the three lines are joined entirely by syntactic dependency, with no parallelism. The concluding triplet in an oracle against Philistia is one example:

---

[90] The lineation follows BHS. It would be possible to divide the second two lines further, on analogy with Isa 3:5 (see Watson, CHP, 365). The contrast in gender between the second and third lines favors the lineation proposed here.

[91] The motif of conflict against a relative (ʾāḥ) and neighbor (rēaʿ) also occurs in Isa 3:5; 9:18–20 (Eng. 9:19–21). For this motif in ancient literature, see Robert Good, "Zechariah 14:13 and Related Texts: Brother Against Brother in War," Maarav 8 (1992): 39–47; in addition to the texts that he cites, note Erra 4. 131–5 (cited in O'Connor, HVS, 125–6).

[92] Watson, CHP, 365.

ûmah-yaʿăneh malʾăkê-gôy[93]
kî yhwh yissad ṣîyôn
ûbāh yeḥĕsû ʿăniyê ʿammô
And what will they answer the envoys of the nation?
That "Yhwh has founded Zion,
and in it the poorest of his people find refuge." (Isa 14:32)[94]

Here the prophet responds to Philistine overtures inviting Judah to join a rebellion against Assyria.[95] The triplet involves multiple levels of dependency. First, the B- and C-lines together are dependent on the A-line. This syntactic relationship can be construed in multiple ways. The first line poses a question to which the second and third lines respond. Because ʿānâ ("to answer") is a speech-act verb, the first line also functions as a quotative frame that introduces the recommended verbal response to the envoys, which is marked by the particle kî ("that") in the following line. In addition, the C-line is itself dependent on the B-line. They are linked by the w- conjunction, a weak form of clause external enjambment.[96] The relationship is most likely causal: the poor can find refuge in Zion because God has established it.

Many triplets contain both parallel and enjambed lines, providing additional evidence that these strategies for joining lines are not mutually exclusive. In such triplets, the second line is typically syntactically dependent on the first line, while the third line is parallel to the second, and thus also dependent on the first.[97]

---

[93] LXX, Syr., and Tg. all read a plural form for MT gôy ("nation"); 1QIsa_a supports MT. Since the oracle addresses a single nation (Philistia), the singular is preferable.

[94] Many commentators regard this verse, if not the whole oracle, as late (for example, Blenkinsopp *Isa 1–39*, 293; Gray, *Isa I–XXVII*, 267; Kaiser, *Isa 13–39*, 51–3). This judgment typically assumes that divine establishment of Zion is a late theme or takes ʿānî ("poor") as a term for a sectarian group, as in later texts (for example, Isa 66:2). Neither assumption is necessary. Even Clements attributes this verse to Isaiah, although he doubts that Isaiah believed in the inviolability of Jerusalem (*Isa 1–39*, 148). Wildberger argues that Isaiah could have used ʿānî to refer to the pious or faithful (*Isa 13–27*, 90–1); more likely, it has its more straightforward meaning here (Clements, *Isa 1–39*, 150).

[95] Clements, *Isa 1–39*, 150; Sweeney, *Isa 1–39*, 238; Wildberger, *Isa 13–27*, 99–101. The identification of the specific historical situation depends on the contested date of Ahaz's death (either 727 or 715 BCE), assuming that the heading in Isa 14:28 provides accurate information about the oracle's date.

[96] See Dobbs-Allsopp, "Enjambing Line," 235.

[97] Although it does not work for many cases, Geller's notion of the triplet as "a sequence of interlocking couplets" proves helpful here (Geller, *Parallelism*, 14; see further Kugel, *Idea*, 27–8; Watson, *CHP*, 181).

Consider the following lines, which refer to the broken pieces of a collapsed wall:

wĕlō' yimmāṣē' bimkittātô hereś
laḥtôt 'ēš miyyāqûd
wĕlaḥśōp mayim miggebe'
And there will not be found among its fragments a shard
for taking away fire from a fireplace
or for skimming water from a cistern. (Isa 30:14b)

The second and third lines are parallel infinitive phrases functioning as complements to the first line.[98] They display tight grammatical and phonological equivalence, including identical syntactic structures, the initial consonant clusters l-$ḥ$, and the repetition of the m sound. Semantically, the third line may move beyond the second, in Kugel's terms, as one could skim water with an even smaller shard than one would need to transport a hot coal, to avoid burning one's fingers. If so, the final line drives home the total destruction of the wall—not even the smallest possible usable shard remains. Other triplets with both parallel and enjambed lines include Isa 2:8, 12; 3:6; 8:10; 9:4 (Eng. 9:5); 23:7, 9; 31:3b. In addition, triplets in Isa 5:9; 14:24; 19:11b; 22:15; 28:12; and 31:4 consist of a one-line quotative frame and a two-line quotation. In each case, the two lines of the quotation are parallel and could conceivably stand alone as a self-contained couplet. The addition of the frame, however, creates a triplet.

Triplets offer some break from the structural dominance of couplets in Biblical Hebrew poetry. The third line comes instead of the sustained pause that normally follows two lines of poetry, and this variation helps sustain interest. Most often in First Isaiah, as in Biblical Hebrew poetry more generally, isolated triplets are scattered among couplets.[99] Occasionally, though, triplets occur in clusters. Examples include Isa 22:5–8, which was discussed in Chapter 1; Isa 23:7–9;[100]

---

[98] On this form of enjambment, see Dobbs-Allsopp, "Enjambing Line," 233.
[99] Watson, *CHP*, 183.
[100] *BH³* and *BHS* treat all three of these verses as pairs of couplets. In v. 7, however, there are no compelling reasons to divide the last four words. The parallelism in the second half of v. 10 strongly suggests a triplet, as does the punctuation in MT (Lessing, *Interpreting Discontinuity*, 137; Wildberger, *Isa 13–27*, 408). The structure of v. 8 is less certain. One could take the first half as a single line or plausibly divide it to produce enjambed line, with *BH³* and *BHS* (followed by most commentators and translations).

and 30:13, 14b. Such clusters often contain three triplets, although it is unclear how much one should make of this fact. Sometimes the form of the triplet calls attention to the content of its lines, but its location within the poem has no apparent significance. In other cases, triplets occur at crucial structural junctures. The cluster in Isa 23:7–9 occurs roughly at the middle of the poem, and the last of these triplets provides its rhetorical climax, attributing the devastation of the Phoenician cities to YHWH (v. 9). Similarly, triplets may mark the beginning or end of a section of a poem or the poem itself.[101] In Isa 31:3b, a triplet occurs at the end of a section of verses that opened with the particle *hôy*; the next verse begins with *kî* followed by the prophetic messenger formula ("Thus says YHWH"), marking a new unit. A description of the day of YHWH in Isa 2:12–17 begins and ends with a triplet, further marked by the inclusio of *yôm* ("day"). Other sections of this poem also end with triplets (vv. 8, 11), as does the poem itself, at least in its final form (v. 22).[102] Poems in Isa 14:28–32 and 22:1–14 also have concluding triplets, as discussed previously.

Quatrains

Four-line groups, or quatrains, occur much less frequently than couplets or triplets in Biblical Hebrew poetry, including First Isaiah. They are often difficult to distinguish from successive couplets.[103] Ostensibly, the difference depends on the pronounced pause at the end of a line group. Only one such pause would occur with a quatrain, whereas there would be two such pauses with paired couplets, and the reader or hearer would only sense a connection between them after processing them individually. This criterion is obviously subjective, and it may be impossible to decide without reference to the performance of the poem. Even so, it is worth maintaining the distinction for

---

[101] Alter, *Art of Biblical Poetry*, 35; Greenstein, "How Does Parallelism Mean?" 54; Watson, *CHP*, 183.

[102] LXX lacks v. 22, and most commentators take it to be a later addition (Gray, *Isa I–XXVII*, 57; Wildberger, *Isa 1–12*, 120–1; Williamson, *Isa 1–5*, 229–30, etc.). Almost all of them treat the verse as prose as well, even though it divides neatly at major syntactic junctures into three three-word lines.

[103] Gray, *Isa I–XXVII*, lxv; Watson, *CHP*, 185; John E. Worgul, "The Quatrain in Isaianic Poetry," *Grace Theological Journal* 11 (1990): 189–90. Worgul, in fact, regards parallel couplets as quatrains, which explains his high count of quatrains in First Isaiah (187–8).

theoretical reasons, even if the interpretive value of the decision proves minimal. The uncertainty reminds us that the division of a poem into smaller units is an interpretive act that serves the reading of the whole poem. It need not always reflect absolute divisions that are somehow inherent in the text.

A few quatrains in First Isaiah contain four parallel lines (for example, Isa 10:8–9, 15; 11:2). It would be difficult to maintain syntactic dependency across so many lines, and in fact no quatrains do. Most involve both parallelism and enjambment in a variety of configurations. The most common arrangement is three parallel lines dependent on a fourth, non-parallel line. The non-parallel line may come at the beginning of the couplet (ABBB), as in Isa 1:8, a chain of similes.[104] Alternatively, it may come at the end (AAAB), as in Isa 9:3 (Eng. 9:4), in which the first three lines contain the objects of the verb in the fourth line. These quatrains are structurally similar to triplets involving both parallelism and enjambment. Quatrains may also be formed by the addition of a quotative frame to three lines that would otherwise form a triplet (for example, Isa 3:7; 18:4; 29:13a). A more complicated configuration has two parallel lines in the middle that are syntactically dependent on the first line and a fourth line that is dependent on the third (ABBC; see Isa 28:2; 30:1, 9;[105] 31:4aα[106]). Runs of four lines with alternating parallel and enjambed lines (ABAB) are best treated as parallel couplets.

The poet may exploit the relationships among lines of a quatrain to create a complex, multivalent poetic unit:

> lākēn šimʿû děbar yhwh
> ʾanšê lāṣôn
> mōšělê hāʿām hazzeh
> ʾăšer bîrûšālāim
>
> Therefore, hear the word of Yʜᴡʜ
> men of scoffing,
> riddling rulers of this people,
> who are in Jerusalem. (Isa 28:14)

---

[104] On this structure, see O'Connor, *HVS*, 130–1, 416.
[105] Following the lineation of either *BHS*³ or *BHS*; see also Wildberger, *Isa 1–39*, 139. Alternatively, one may leave v. 9b undivided to form a triplet (see Irwin, *Isa 28–33*, 68).
[106] Alternatively, one could divide the last clause and treat it as a separate, enjambed couplet with the subject as the *rejet* (see *BH*³; *BHS*).

The first line contains an imperative; the second and third lines are dependent vocative phrases, and the final line is a relative clause. Two wordplays hold the unit together. The sound of *lāṣôn* ("scoffing") evokes *ṣîyôn* ("Zion") in a sarcastic characterization of the city's leaders. Further establishing the pun, the placement of *yĕrûšālaim* ("Jerusalem") at the end of the fourth line seems to match *lāṣôn* at the end of the second line; *ṣīyôn/yĕrûšālaim* is a common word pair, especially in the Book of Isaiah (for example, Isa 10:32b; 37:22; 40:9a). The second wordplay involves *mōšĕlê hāʿām hazzeh*, which could be translated either as "the rulers (√*mšl* II) of this people" or "the riddlers (√*mšl* I) of this people." The fact that the following verses concern political matters supports the first option.[107] On the other hand, the parallelism with *ʾanšê lāṣôn* supports the second option.[108] Recognition of the wordplay, however, eliminates the need to choose. J. J. M. Roberts explains:

> The point of the double entendre is to express Isaiah's contempt for Judah's rulers who have reduced themselves to scoffing "proverb-makers." ... The ability to coin a clever turn of phrase hardly constitutes the essence of genuine leadership.[109]

One should not miss the irony of the prophet's own use of wordplay to dismiss his opponents as "riddlers."

More often than not, the poet simply uses quatrains as a longer form of expression, with no obvious additional significance. In other cases, as with triplets, the quatrain secures rhetorical emphasis or occurs at a climactic juncture in a poem. A pair of quatrains in Isa 10:5–19 serves this function. Both units consist of parallel rhetorical questions, the first opening a speech by the king of Assyria:

kî yōʾmar hălōʾ śāray yaḥdāw mĕlākîm
hălōʾ kĕkarkĕmîš kalnô
ʾim-lōʾ kĕʾarpad ḥămāt
ʾim-lōʾ kĕdammeśeq šōmĕrôn

---

[107] See Clements, *Isa 1–39*, 230; see also Blenkinsopp, *Isa 1–39*, 392.
[108] See Ehrlich, *Jesaja*, 100; Irwin, *Isa 28–33*, 25; Kaiser, *Isa 13–39*, 250–1. Irwin notes the pairing of *lāyaṣ* and *māšal* in Hab 2:6; Prov 1:6.
[109] Roberts, "Double Entendre," 43. I have attempted to render the wordplay in Eng. with the translation "riddling rulers"; note also Irwin's "reigning wits" (*Isa 28–33*, 25).

Structure and Movement   103

> For he says, "Are not my commanders altogether kings?
> Is Calno not like Carchemish?
> Is Hamath not like Arpad?
> Is Samaria not like Damascus?" (Isa 10:8–9)

In these lines, the Assyrian ruler declares the prowess of his military commanders and alludes to past conquests to suggest that Jerusalem will inevitably fall before him (v. 11). The prophetic response to these claims similarly begins with a quatrain:

> *hăyitpā'ēr haggarzen 'al haḥōṣēb bô*
> *'im-yitgaddēl hammaśśôr 'al-měnîpô*
> *kěhānîp šēbeṭ 'et*[110] *měrîmāyw*
> *kěhārîm maṭṭeh lō'-'ēṣ*
>
> Should the axe glorify itself over the one who hews with it?
> Or should the saw exalt itself over the one who wields it?
> As if the rod should wield the ones who raise it?
> As if the staff should raise what is not wood? (Isa 10:15)

These questions reverse the earlier ones, reestablishing the view that the Assyrian king is simply an instrument of divine punishment (see v. 5) and ridiculing his attempts to supplant Yhwh. The quatrain form calls attention both to the connection between these line groups and their significance within the poem as a whole.

Larger Groups

Occasionally, one finds groups of five or more lines in Biblical Hebrew poetry that resist any further division.[111] As with quatrains, it may be difficult to distinguish between such groups of lines and clusters of discrete couplets or triplets connected by an overarching poetic device. Groups larger than a quatrain occur infrequently in First Isaiah, but a few cases deserve mention. The most syntactically complex example is a five-line unit in Isa 18:2:

> *lěkû mal'ākîm qallîm*
> *'el-gôy měmuššāk ûmôrāṭ*

---

[110] MT *wě'et*. The conjunction is absent in 1QIsa[a] and many Heb. mss.
[111] Watson, *CHP*, 187–9.

ʾel-ʿam nôrāʾ min-hûʾ wāhālěʾâ
gôy qawqāw[112] ûměbûsâ
ʾăšer-bāzěʾû[113] něhārîm ʾarṣô
Go, swift envoys
to a nation tall and smooth,
to a people feared from there to yonder,
a nation of strength and trampling,
whose land is divided by rivers.

The five lines form a single syntactic entity, characterized by extensive interplay between enjambment and parallelism. The first line is the main clause. Three parallel lines follow, each syntactically dependent on the first line, and the final line is a relative clause dependent on the middle three lines, with the relative ʾăšer referring to gôy/ʿam ("nation/people"). The middle three lines are closely connected by their parallelism—note the deletion of ʾel ("to") in the fourth line—which makes it difficult to divide the group as a triplet followed by a couplet, or vice versa. On the other hand, it would be unusual to find a triplet both preceded and followed by single lines. This group thus resists attempts at division into smaller units. Isaiah appears to take delight in describing the exotic prowess of the Cushites, heaping up phrase after phrase to emphasize the point; the intent is sarcastic, of course, as he does not believe that they will ultimately be able to withstand Assyria. The unusual length of the unit may also mimic the

[112] For MT qaw-qaw, 1QIsaª has the single word qwqw, which many commentators take as an adjective meaning "strong" (see also Arab. qawiya, "be strong"; Gray, Isa I–XXVII, 317–18; Driver, "Isa I–XXXIX: Textual and Linguistic Problems," 46; Wildberger, Isa 13–27, 208; see also NRSV). Others understand qaw-qaw as a reference to the Cushites' foreign speech in light of Isa 28:13, where the line qaw lāqāw qaw lāqāw mimics the incomprehensible speech of the Assyrians: Clements, Isa 1–39, 165; Herbert Donner, Israel unter den Völkern; die Stellung der klassischen Propheten des 8. Jahrhunderts v. Chr. zur Aussenpolitik der Könige von Israel und Juda (VTSup 11; Leiden: Brill, 1964), 122; Hayes and Irvine, Isaiah, 255; see also NIV. For less convincing proposals, see Marta Høyland Lavik, A People Tall and Smooth-Skinned: The Rhetoric of Isaiah 18 (VTSup 112; Leiden: Brill, 2007), 56; Meir Lubetski and Claire Gottlieb, "Isaiah 18: The Egyptian Nexus," in Boundaries of the Ancient Near Eastern World: A Tribute to Cyrus H. Gordon (ed. Meir Lubetski et al.; JSOTSup 273; Sheffield: Sheffield Academic, 1998), 374.

[113] The verb bāzaʾ is only attested here and in v. 7. Most LXX mss. have no equivalent, but other versions read a form of bāzaz, "to plunder" (LXX^L; Syr.; Tg.; Vulg.). Most commentators connect it to Syr. bzʿ (not bzʾ, contra Lavik, Wildberger), with the meaning "cut through" (Gray, Isa I–XXVII, 318; Lavik, Tall and Smooth-Skinned, 56–7; Wildberger, Isa 13–27, 208).

length of the journey to which the prophet sarcastically calls the envoys.

Poetic lists form even longer, albeit less tightly constructed, line units. Lists are common in First Isaiah. They typically consist of parallel lines containing nouns that are syntactically dependent on an earlier verb, with the enumerated items serving as a compound subject or object. The following couplet illustrates the standard form:

> wĕhāyâ kinnôr wānebel
> tōp wĕḥālîl wāyayin mištêhem[114]
> And there are lyres and harps,
> tambourines and flutes and wine at their festivals. (Isa 5:12a)

For similar couplets, compare Isa 41:19a; Hos 4:3b; Ps 76:4 (Eng. 76:3); etc. Lists are easily expanded to include multiple lines. In Isa 3:1–3, an initial participle *mēsîr* ("will remove") is followed by sixteen objects, including an extensive list of state and communal officials. While the lineation is uncertain, the absence of the conjunction on terms at the beginnings of vv. 2b and 3 (but not 3b) seems to mark these words as the heads of short groups that form poetic lines; this division is supported by the Masoretic punctuation and adopted in *BHS*.[115] So divided, the list comprises a poetic unit of six or seven lines, depending on whether one takes v. 1b as a gloss.

An even longer example, Isa 3:18–23, contains a list of twenty-one types of jewelry and fine attire worn by wealthy women of Jerusalem, which the prophet considers an inappropriate display of opulence. Most commentators regard these verses as a later, prosaic addition to Isa 3:16–24.[116] The arguments typically adduced against Isaianic authorship, however, are not entirely convincing, and the appearance of lists in other poems raises the possibility that these verses should

---

[114] *BH*³ lineates the verse as a triplet, beginning the third line at *wāyayin* ("and wine"). In many poetic lists, the line breaks are not readily apparent; as in other cases under discussion, I take the presence or absence of the conjunction as a potentially decisive factor.

[115] For differing proposals, see *BH*³; Wildberger, *Isa 1–12*, 27; Williamson, *Isa 1–5*, 244.

[116] Blenkinsopp calls it "the notorious catalogue of female attire and adornment from a well-informed but obsessive interpolator" (*Isa 1–39*, 201); see also Clements, *Isa 1–39*, 51; Gray, *Isa I–XXVII*, 71–2; Wildberger, *Isa 1–12*, 147–8; Williamson, *Isa 1–5*, 286.

also be taken as poetry.[117] While the list does not contain many overtly poetic features, the arrangement of items by gender produces some clusters of rhyming words with the same plural ending.[118] As with Isa 3:1-3, it is difficult to identify line breaks. The absence of the conjunction at the beginning of vv. 19-21, corresponding to the Masoretic versification, again offers some guidance, but it is possible that some of the groups should be divided further. In both Isa 3:1-3 and 18-23, the lists create a sense of comprehensiveness by virtue of their size, overwhelming the reader or hearer and suggesting the completeness of YHWH's judgment. The length of the line groups, with no pronounced pause until the very end, underscores this effect. The lists also impart concreteness to the prophet's proclamation, privileging specificity over abstract formulation.[119]

Other examples of longer line groups include Isa 3:24 (five lines); 9:5b (Eng. 9:6; five lines, counting each royal title as a separate line); 9:6a-bα (Eng. 9:7; six lines, dividing at each change in preposition); 28:4 (five lines); 28:16 (five lines, including a quotative frame).[120] Other possible cases, however, are open to alternative explanations. Isaiah 28:12 consists of a quotative frame followed by four lines, of which the first and the third are closely parallel at multiple levels. As a result, the reader or hearer likely expects the second and fourth of

---

[117] Although some interpolations in First Isaiah begin with *bayyôm hahû'* ("on that day"; for example, Isa 19:16-25), it occurs in likely Isaianic texts as well (for example, Isa 2:17). Even less persuasive are arbitrary assumptions that Isaiah would not have compiled such a list (for example, Wildberger, *Isa 1-12*, 147). While speculative, one can imagine plausible scenarios in which he would include these lines in a prophetic speech. Sweeney thinks that the list indicates a time of national prosperity, such as the reign of Hezekiah (*Isa 1-39*, 110), and Hayes and Irvine point out that such luxury items may have been confiscated to pay tribute in a time of national crisis (*Isaiah*, 95). Williamson designates the list as prose based on the presence of the accusative particle in v. 18 and the definite article throughout (*Isa 1-5*, 286). Although poetic texts, on the whole, use such particles less frequently than prose, their appearance in a given passage need not disqualify it from being poetic (Bartelt, *Book Around Immanuel*, 26; Emerton, "Text and Translation," 439; Freedman, "Another Look," 15-16).

[118] Alonso Schökel, *Manual*, 82; Watson, *CHP*, 231-3. While not consistent, the frequency of these groupings suggests some kind of pattern. Bartelt identifies additional numerical patterns, but these seem less obvious; it is perhaps notable, though, that the two construct chains occur in successive lines at the center of the list (*Book Around Immanuel*, 219).

[119] Gitay, *Isaiah and His Audience*, 66, 81-2.

[120] For the lineation of Isa 28:16, see J. J. M. Roberts, "Yahweh's Foundation in Zion (Isa 28:16)," in *The Bible and the Ancient Near East: Collected Essays* (Winona Lake, Ind.: Eisenbrauns, 2002), 292-310; repr. from *JBL* 106 (1987).

these four lines to be parallel as well, but the final line frustrates these expectations by deviating from the parallelism. This deviation likely corresponds to the people's refusal to listen to the divine word, as depicted in the verse.[121] Watson designates the verse a "pentacolon," but I prefer to analyze it as a triplet followed by a couplet, connected partially by interlocking parallelism.[122] An emphatic pause between the third and fourth lines of the verse would afford the audience an opportunity to process the structure of the triplet, more effectively setting them up to be surprised by the second line of the following couplet. The distinction may not prove crucial for the interpretation of the text, but it does impact how one hears the poem.

Single Lines

Single, unconnected lines—called "monocola" in many scholarly treatments—also occur in Biblical Hebrew poetry. Indeed, their existence is one of the most compelling reasons for identifying the colon as the line. They are unusual in First Isaiah, though, and their identification is often uncertain. Some quotative frames could be treated as single lines, although I have consistently analyzed them as part of the same group as the lines that follow (for example, Isa 5:9a; 14:24a; 18:4a). Most often, single lines appear at the beginning or end of biblical poems, but they also occur internally to mark a rhetorical climax.[123] The clearest example of an opening single line is Isa 30:6. Some superscriptions may also serve this function, such as Isa 15:1a; 17:1a; 22:1a; but one could just as easily take them as secondary titles and not parts of the poems. The final clause of Isaiah 9:6 (Eng. 9:7) is probably best treated as a concluding single line, although *BHS* subdivides it to form a couplet, and the lineation of the entire verse is uncertain. Watson also regards Isa 8:10b as a concluding single line, but its syntactic dependency on the preceding two lines suggests

---

[121] J. J. M. Roberts notes the lack of balance and proposes that a matching line, which he reconstructs as *hrgy' l'bywn* ("Let the needy repose"), has dropped out due to haplography; "A Note on Isaiah 28:12," *HTR* 73 (1980): 49–51. In response, Paul G. Mosca suggests that Roberts's proposed line may be close to what the audience might have expected, but the prophet has intentionally thwarted these expectations: "Isaiah 28:12e: A Response to J. J. M. Roberts," *HTR* 77 (1984): 116.

[122] Watson, *CHP*, 187.   [123] Watson, *CHP*, 170–2.

instead that it rounds off the triplet.[124] Either way, some form of terminal modification has taken place. Isaiah 22:22a is a climactic, internal single line. Overall, single lines seem to function much like triplets and other larger line groups in First Isaiah, although they occur even less frequently.

FROM LINE GROUPS TO POEMS

The discussion up to this point has focused on relatively small combinations of lines that serve as building blocks in Isaianic poems. These groups are typically self-contained units with clear boundaries, as one can see from the preceding examples. Their integrity enhances their structural function; because they are relatively brief yet clearly marked, their recurrence is easily perceptible, which makes them capable of systematic repetition. At the same time, the pronounced closure of these groups risks diminishing any sense of their connectedness. Kugel notes that the end-stopped character of couplets in the Psalms, for instance, leads to a high degree of "disjunction" among them.[125] The largely paratactic style of Biblical Hebrew poetry, which eschews explicit syntactic connection, contributes further to this effect, although prophetic poetry is less paratactic overall than other kinds of biblical poetry.[126] Structural devices such as repetition partly overcome this sense of disjunction, forging connections among line groups across a poem. Unlike smaller line groups, however, it is difficult to discern any consistent tendencies at the level of larger divisions or whole poems.

In many biblical poems, line groups are organized into larger units that in turn comprise the whole poem. Such units are easily observable in poems with overt structural schemes such as refrains, but they appear in other poems as well. The typical appellatives for these units in scholarly literature—"strophes," "stanzas," and the like—are problematic for a variety of reasons.[127] To avoid confusion, simpler and

---

[124] Watson, *CHP*, 172.   [125] Kugel, *Idea*, 55–6.   [126] Berlin, *Dynamics*, 6.

[127] For the use of these terms by biblicists, see Pieter van der Lugt, *Cantos and Strophes in Biblical Hebrew Poetry, with Special Reference to the First Book of the Psalter* (OtSt 53; Leiden: Brill, 2006), 3–68; Petersen and Richards, *Interpreting Hebrew Poetry*, 60–3; Raabe, *Psalm Structures*, 21–6. In literary studies, the uses of "strophe" and "stanza" are highly specialized in ways that make them a poor fit for a

more neutral terms such as "section" or "division" are preferable.[128] A rather wooden model of Biblical Hebrew poetry posits the existence of multiple, hierarchical levels of division within a poem. By this account, the description of poetic structure means identifying these units.[129] This high degree of uniformity assumed by this approach, however, turns out to be a chimera in many cases. Not all biblical poems share similar macrostructures, and recurring units of the same length are rare even within the same poem. Of course, any treatment of poetic movement should take account of larger divisions wherever they occur. One must be careful, however, not to reduce structure to "an organization of, or relationship among, elements," in the words of Smith. A poem is more than the sum of its component parts. While the outline of these parts may offer a suggestive sketch of the poem's movement, the interplay among the parts is variable and complex.

More judicious and useful is the flexible model of Gray, who outlines three broad possibilities for large-scale organization in Biblical Hebrew poetry.[130] Some poems, he suggests, contain no structural units beyond individual line groups. A good example is Isa 3:1–15, which is discussed at length at the end of this chapter. In other cases, one finds loosely structured sections of variable length that play some role in the movement of the poem. Most poems in First Isaiah fall into this category. As discussed in the previous chapter, for instance, Isa 22:1b–14 may be divided into four uneven

free verse tradition such as Biblical Hebrew poetry: see T. V. F. Brogan, "Stanza," in *TNPEPP*, 1212; Ernst Haüblein and T. V. F. Brogan, "Strophe," in *TNPEPP*, 1215; O'Connor, *HVS*, 455. At most, one might speak of biblical poems with refrains as quasi-stanzaic. Another possibility is Gray's preferred term, "verse paragraph," but even it is still associated most closely with different kinds of poetry than one finds in the Bible: see T. V. F. Brogan, Alex Preminger, and Edward R. Weismiller, "Verse Paragraph," in *TNPEPP*, 1352.

[128] See Pardee, *Ugaritic and Hebrew Poetic Parallelism*, 3, 70; Petersen and Richards, *Interpreting Hebrew Poetry*, 61. Watson also recognizes the problem but still uses the traditional terminology (*CHP*, 160).

[129] This approach is characteristic of the so-called "Kampen School," comprised largely of students and associates of Johannes C. de Moor; see Fokkelman, *Reading Biblical Poetry*, 37–47; Willem van der Meer and Johannes C. de Moor (eds.), *The Structural Analysis of Biblical and Canaanite Poetry* (JSOTSup 74; Sheffield: JSOT Press, 1988). David Noel Freedman and many of his students proceed on similar assumptions: for example, Bartelt, *Book Around Immanuel*, 31–2; Chris Franke, *Isaiah 46, 47, and 48: A New Literary Critical Reading* (Biblical and Judaic Studies 3; Winona Lake, Ind.: Eisenbrauns, 1994), 13–15; Raabe, *Psalm Structures*, 187; see also O'Connor, *HVS*, 527–33.

[130] Gray, *Forms*, 190–1.

units—the first one fourteen lines and the last three nine lines in length—by a combination of devices including rhythmic patterns, inclusio, keywords, and the like. Finally, some poems contain more highly structured sections with roughly comparable numbers of lines. They are sometimes marked by an acrostic or a recurring refrain, although these features need not be present. Despite their highly patterned, easily perceptible schemes, such poems should not be treated as the structural norm in Biblical Hebrew poetry because they occur infrequently.[131] The only Isaianic poem that fits this description is Isa 9:7-20 (Eng. 9:8-21) + 5:25-29, in which the repeated refrain *běkol-zōʾt lōʾ-šāb ʾappô/wěʿôd yādô něṭûyâ* ("For all of this, his wrath has not turned away / and still his hand is outstretched") divides the poem into five stanzas.[132]

In short, Biblical Hebrew poems make little use of established formal patterns, which is not surprising for free verse. A number of different devices play limited structural roles in the poetry of First Isaiah. They demarcate individual sections of poems as well as bridge contiguous sections, but rarely does a single one operate across the whole poem. Organization by theme is perhaps more common. Although its possibilities are even more variable, thematic structure often entails multiple iterations of a single image or idea that take different angles or emphasize new details. One might compare the musical technique of "variations on a theme."[133] Multiple strategies share the labor of creating structure in most of Isaiah's poems, and this process unfolds only as the poem is experienced temporally through reading or listening. Rather than established forms such as the sonnet or villanelle in English poetry, the reader or hearer must

---

[131] *Contra* Raabe, *Psalm Structures*, 9-10.

[132] For arguments that these texts originally comprised a single poem, see Duhm, *Jesaia*, 61-2; Gray, *Isa I-XXVII*, 179-80; Wildberger, *Isa 1-12*, 224-6; Williamson, *Isa 1-5*, 400-3; etc. Sweeney allows for their original unity—albeit with 5:25-30 as the introduction and not the conclusion of the poem—but is more concerned with the literary shape of the final form of the text (*Isa 1-39*, 128-9, 188-96). An increasing number of recent interpreters have argued for the literary or theological integrity of Isa 5 and 9-10 in their present shape; see Bartelt, *Book around Immanuel*, 96-114, 131-9; Andrew H. Bartelt, "Isaiah 5 and 9: In- or Interdependence?" in *Fortunate the Eyes that See: Essays in Honor of David Noel Freedman in Celebration of his Seventieth Birthday* (eds. A. B. Beck et al.; Grand Rapids: Eerdmans, 1995), 157-74; William P. Brown, "The So-Called Refrain in Isaiah 5:25-30 and 9:7-10:4," *CBQ* 52 (1990): 432-43; Childs, *Isaiah*, 41-9, 83-7.

[133] Alonso Schökel, *Manual*, 180; Smith, *Poetic Closure*, 99.

reckon with "organic" or "discovered" forms, as Dobbs-Allsopp observes.[134] Such unpredictable structures occur across the poetries of the world, and they do not indicate poor craft or diminished quality. Burton Raffel rightly remarks, "That does *not* mean the poem is formless: it is not. Rather, it means that the form has been developed in good part to meet the demands of the subject, the treatment, the tone, and the other imperatives that are important to the poet."[135] One might add that, as these demands change over the course of the poem, so too will the form.

In most biblical poems, structural features achieve only a tentative unity, one that allows the audience to experience the poem as a whole but also stands in creative tension with a sense of fragmentation among its smaller parts.[136] Because of their unpredictability, it is difficult to make broad statements about these features apart from the analysis of particular poems.[137] Nonetheless, certain formal devices occur with sufficient frequency throughout First Isaiah that one might judge them typical of this corpus. They include parallelism and enjambment at levels beyond the line, distant parallelism and repetition, and catalogues. In conjunction with various kinds of thematic development, these formal devices both demarcate component sections of poems and work across such divisions to hold together whole poems.

Parallelism and Enjambment at Larger Levels of the Poem

As noted already, parallelism and enjambment not only join lines to form couplets, triplets, and quatrains, but they also operate at the

---

[134] F. W. Dobbs-Allsopp, "The Psalms and Lyric Verse," in *The Evolution of Rationality: Interdisciplinary Essays in Honor of J. Wentzel van Huyssteen* (ed. F. LeRon Shults; Grand Rapids: Eerdmans, 2006), 359–61; see also Petersen and Richards, *Interpreting Hebrew Poetry*, 63.

[135] Raffel, *How to Read a Poem*, 226.

[136] Grossberg distinguishes between "centripetal" structures, which emphasize a poem's unity, and "centrifugal" structures, which emphasize its component parts. None of the biblical poetic collections that he discusses fall squarely at the centripetal end of the continuum. They are characterized by highly centrifugal structures, as in Song of Songs, or exhibit tension between the two extremes, as in Psalms 120–34 or Lamentations (*Centripetal and Centrifugal*, 5–7). The same holds true for poems from the Isaianic corpus.

[137] Alonso Schökel, *Manual*, 194; Petersen and Richards, *Interpreting Hebrew Poetry*, 63.

level of line groups, connecting discrete couplets and triplets within the poem. Typically, one will be employed to join the lines within the group, while the other links the groups together externally; that is, units joined by parallelism often consist of enjambed lines and vice versa.[138] These combinations are another example of the interplay between the two techniques in Biblical Hebrew poetry. Because the sense of connection does not overcome the pronounced pause that signals the end of a couplet or triplet, the line groups joined in this way retain perceptual integrity as separate units, just as lines within a couplet or triplet remain distinguishable as such. At the same time, they display an overarching unity that marks them as larger units, which may be part of even larger sections in some poems.

While both parallel and enjambed line groups are attested within the Isaianic corpus, parallelism is more common, as was the case within couplets. Indeed, parallelism occurs at this level with sufficient frequency in First Isaiah to be considered a characteristic of the prophet's poetic style.[139] Examples include Isa 1:10, 29; 2:7; 3:5, 12; 5:11; 9:1 (Eng. 9:2); 11:6b–7a; 14:27; 15:1b, 5b; 17:12; 30:16b. Most commonly, parallelism joins pairs of couplets, but other attested configurations are three couplets (Isa 3:9b–11; 5:20), a triplet followed by a couplet (Isa 28:12), and three couplets followed by a triplet (Isa 1:18b–19bα). The basic structural dynamics of parallel line groups should be clear from examples that have already been treated. More often than not, the effects of parallelism at the level of the line group do not differ significantly from those at the level of the line. They simply involve a larger swatch of the poem, which may increase the reader or hearer's impression of the strength of the parallelism. In some cases, though, the increased amount of text involved in the parallelism creates new possibilities for the poet to exploit.

For instance, parallel couplets are especially amenable to retrospective patterning, since they offer a greater number of lines over which the poet may establish a pattern and condition the audience's expectations, which then magnifies the surprise that accompanies the upsetting of those expectations. This happens in Isa 28:12, as treated

---

[138] See Alter, *Art of Biblical Poetry*, 52–3.
[139] Lowth, *Lectures*, 209.

earlier in the chapter. A pair of couplets in Isa 5 is another creative example:

> *hôy maškîmê babbōqer*
> *šēkār yirdōpû*
> *mĕʾaḥărê*[140] *bannešep*
> *yayin yadlîqēm*
> Hey, you who get up early in the morning
> and pursue beer,
> who linger late into the evening,
> and wine hotly chases[141] them. (Isa 5:11)

The A-line in both couplets contains a participle with the prefix *m-* and a temporal phrase with the preposition *b-*, while both B-lines have a noun denoting an alcoholic drink followed by an imperfect verb. At the lexical level, most of the pairs appear elsewhere in Biblical Hebrew poetry.[142] Encouraged by this matching, the reader or hearer expects sustained syntactic equivalence between the couplets, which appears to be the case until the very last syllable of the final word.[143] The suffix, however, reveals that the drunken revelers "who linger late in the evening" are actually the object of the verb, and "wine" is its subject. Roberts describes the effect as "a surprising reversal of roles. It is not just that the alcohol that the wealthy pursue inflames

---

[140] For MT *mĕʾaḥărê*, 1QIsaᵃ reads *mʾḥzy* ("who seize"). However one accounts for this discrepancy, MT is the better reading (see Williamson, *Isa 1–5*, 357). The versions support MT.

[141] This translation attempts to capture the pun on two possible meanings of √*dlq*, "enflame" and "chase." The latter sense is only clearly attested in the *qal* (Gen 31:36; 1 Sam 17:53; Ps 10:2; Lam 4:19), but, as Roberts observes, the *hipʿil* is not sufficiently attested for one to make definitive claims about its semantic range ("Double Entendre," 42). Cohen also notes that the parallel term √*rdp* is attested in the *hipʿil* with the meaning "pursue" in Judg 20:43 (Cohen, "The Enclitic-*mem* in Biblical Hebrew: Its Existence and Initial Discovery," in *Sefer Moshe: The Moshe Weinfeld Jubilee Volume: Studies in the Bible and the Ancient Near East, Qumran, and Post-Biblical Judaism* (eds. C. Cohen et al.; Winona Lake, Ind.: Eisenbrauns, 2004), 250.

[142] See Ps 127:2 for √*škm* ("get up early")/√*ʾḥr* ("linger late"); see Isa 5:22; 24:9; 56:12; Prov 31:4, 6 for *šēkār* ("beer")/*yayin* ("wine"); and see Lam 4:19 for √*rdp* ("pursue")/√*dlq* ("chase").

[143] Indeed, as an unwitting testimony to the power of this expectation, many commentators force total equivalence by deleting the object suffix and, in some cases, repointing the verb; see the discussion in Roberts, "Double Entendre," 41–2. Chaim Cohen takes the ending as an enclitic-*m*, but he allows for wordplay involving the reinterpretation of this ending as an object suffix: Cohen, "The Enclitic-*mem*," 248–50.

them.... The alcoholic is no longer in charge; the wine one began by pursuing ends up as the chaser."[144]

In Isa 29:4–5aα, the technique is artfully carried over a series of three couplets:

[4] wĕšāpalt mēʾereṣ tĕdabbērî
  ûmēʿāpar tiššaḥ ʾimrātēk
  wĕhāyâ kĕʾôb mēʾereṣ qôlēk
  ûmēʿāpār ʾimrātēk tĕṣapṣēp
[5] wĕhāyâ kĕʾābāq daq hămôn zārāyik[145]
  ûkĕmōṣ ʿōbēr hămôn ʿārîṣîm

[4] And low from the earth you will speak;
  And from the dust will your speech chirp;
  And like a ghost from the underworld will be your voice;
  And from the dust your speech will twitter.
[5] And like fine dust will be your enemy throng,
  And like chaff that blows away, the violent throng.

Having declared Yhwh's intention to attack Jerusalem, the prophet depicts the city on the brink of destruction in v. 4. A number of lexical connections hold these two couplets together: the repeated pair *mēʾereṣ/mēʿāpar* ("from the earth/dust"); the subject *ʾimrātēk* ("your speech") in both B-lines; the three imperfect verbs with the *t-* prefix; and the three second-person feminine suffixes. Similarly, one finds several links between the final couplet of v. 4 and v. 5a. Most notably, both A-lines begin *wĕhāyâ k-* ("and will be like"), suggesting a chain of similes, a common device in First Isaiah (Isa 1:8; 17:5; 29:8; etc.). These similar structures condition the audience to expect further description of Jerusalem's humiliation, but the poetry shifts course at the last moment. The final word of the first line in v. 5a identifies the subject of the line and target of the simile as the city's enemies, a

---

[144] Roberts, "Double Entendre," 42–3; see also Worgul, "Quatrain in Isainic Poetry," 193–4. For an extended poetic description of loss of control from alcohol, see Prov 23:29–35.
[145] For MT *zārāyik* ("your foreign ones"), 1QIsaᵃ reads *zdyk* ("your insolent ones"). Due to the frequency of *d/r* confusion and the inconclusive evidence of the versions (de Waard, *Handbook*, 122), it is difficult to decide between them; both terms occur in parallel with *ʿārîṣîm* ("violent ones") in Isaiah and Psalms (*zārîm*: Isa 25:5; Ps 54:5 [Eng. 54:3]; *zēdîm*: Isa 13:11; Ps 86:14). Favoring MT, Irwin and O'Connor suggest that the phrase *zārîm ʿārîṣê gōyīm* ("the foreigners, the most arrogant of the nations") in Ezek 28:7; 31:12 has been broken here to form a parallel pair: Irwin, *Isa 28–33*, 66; O'Connor, *HVS*, 647–8.

theme that successive lines develop.[146] The suddenness of this surprising shift poetically mirrors Isaiah's expectation for the reality of Jerusalem's deliverance, as suggested by v. 5bβ: "it will happen in a sudden instance" (*lĕpetaʿ pitʾōm*).

Enjambment, too, occurs at the level of line groups. O'Connor refers to syntactic dependency at this level as "mixing," which he regards as the "densest" and "rarest" trope of Biblical Hebrew poetry. He identifies its basic form as "two main clauses and two subordinate clauses, in that order; both the subordinate clauses modify both the main clauses."[147] A pair of couplets in Isa 10:6 perfectly fit this description:

bĕgôy ḥānēp ʾăšallĕḥennû
wĕʿal-ʿam ʿebrātî ʾăṣawwennû
lišlōl šālāl wĕlābōz baz
ûlĕśûmô mirmās kĕḥōmer ḥûṣôt

Against a godless nation I send him,
and against the people of my wrath I order him,
to spoil spoil and to plunder plunder,
and to trample them down like refuse in the streets.

In the first couplet, parallel lines describe God's dispatch of the Assyrian army against Judah. The three infinitives in the second couplet (note the "A- A- // A—" lines) complement the verbs in the first couplet. In this way, the lines of the second couplet are dependent on the lines of the first, even as the parallelism within the couplets clearly demarcates their limits. It would have been possible for the poet to alternate the parallel lines (i.e., *abab* instead of *aabb*, as here), creating a pair of parallel couplets with enjambed

---

[146] Some interpreters understand v. 5a very differently. Wildberger, for instance, reads *zēdim* ("insolent ones") with 1QIsa[a], which he takes as a reference to the oppressors within Jerusalem; thus, he argues that the verse continues the rhetoric of v. 4, and the surprise turn does not happen until v. 5bβ (*Isa 28–39*, 66). Benjamin D. Sommer argues that v. 5a is undecidably ambiguous, since the comparison of Jerusalem's invaders to dust could develop the earlier image of the city as a grave: Sommer, "Is it Good for the Jews? Ambiguity and the Rhetoric of Turning in Isaiah," in *Birkat Shalom: Studies in the Bible, Ancient Near Eastern Literature, and Postbiblical Judaism Presented to Shalom M. Paul on the Occasion of his Seventieth Birthday* (eds. Chaim Cohen et al.; 2 vols.; Winona Lake, Ind.: Eisenbrauns, 2008), 337; see also Childs, *Isaiah*, 215.

[147] O'Connor, *HVS*, 132, 421.

lines, not unlike many other examples from First Isaiah.[148] Although O'Connor's definition limits mixing to two couplets, consistent with the examples from his corpus, it spans three couplets in Isa 10:1–2, which otherwise displays a similar syntactic structure to the previous example. Mixing creates tightly integrated syntactic complexes containing multiple line groups. As such, it exemplifies the grammatical complexity that is a hallmark of Isaiah's poetic style.

Alternatively, the poet may use prepositions, conjunctions, or adverbs to create marked relationships of syntactic dependency between line groups. These particles connect contiguous line groups but need not involve all lines in the unit as mixing does. Terms used in this way in First Isaiah—many of which are used to mark enjambment within line groups as well—include ʾăšer ("that, which"; Isa 28:12; 30:10); yaʿan or yaʿan kî ("because"; Isa 3:16; 8:6; 29:13); kî ("for, because"; Isa 3:8; 14:27, 31; 28:10–11; etc.);[149] kēn ("so,"; Isa 31:4b); lākēn ("therefore"; Isa 5:13–14; 10:16; 30:12; etc.); lĕmaʿan ("so that"; Isa 28:13); ʿad ("until"; Isa 5:8); ʿal-kēn ("therefore"; Isa 5:25; 9:16 [Eng. 9:17]; 16:9; etc.); and ʿattâ ("now"; Isa 5:3). The logical, sequential connections marked by these lexemes serve clear rhetorical functions.[150] They also highlight the persuasive or argumentative purpose of Isaianic poetry, like prophetic poetry more generally.[151] On the whole, prophetic poetry displays less parataxis than other corpuses of Biblical Hebrew poetry, although line groups introduced simply by the w- conjunction, or not marked at all, still outnumber line groups with more explicit syntactic markers.

---

[148] According to Berlin, the parallelism of the aabb arrangement is more perceptible, as it maintains the parallel lines in closer proximity (Dynamics, 132).
[149] Because of its multivalence, the precise function of kî may be open to debate in particular texts; in the texts cited here, a logically sequential sense is at least plausible.
[150] Smith, Poetic Closure, 137.
[151] Particular connectors are formal conventions of prophetic judgment speeches; see R. B. Y. Scott, "The Literary Structure of Isaiah's Oracles," in Studies in Old Testament Prophecy Presented to Theodore H. Robinson on his Sixty-fifth Birthday, August 9th, 1946 (ed. H. H. Rowley; Edinburgh: T&T Clark, 1957), 175–86; Claus Westermann, Basic Forms of Prophetic Speech (trans. H. C. White; Louisville: Westminster John Knox, 1991), 129–98.

Distant Parallelism and Repetition

In addition to successive lines or line groups, parallelism also connects non-contiguous lines or line groups. Pardee refers to this phenomenon as "distant parallelism" and observes that its primary function, given the amount of text that it spans, is structural.[152] At the same time, the distance may impede the effectiveness of the parallelism; as Berlin notes, proximity plays a critical role in the perception of parallelism, such that a reader or hearer is less likely to recognize parallelism when intervening material separates the parallel elements.[153] To offset this risk of diminished perceptibility, distant parallelism relies heavily on semantic matching—frequently to the point of near repetition—rather than grammatical and phonological matching by themselves.[154] It may involve single words or phrases, entire lines, or entire line groups.

Inclusio, the repetition of material at the beginning and end of a section or whole poem, is a common form of distant parallelism in Biblical Hebrew poetry.[155] It provides structural stability and achieves closure by marking the outer limits of the material that it encloses.[156] Compared to other poetic corpuses such as the Psalms, inclusio occurs relatively infrequently in First Isaiah, but note the example in Isa 1:21–26:

> [21] ʾêkâ hāyĕtâ lĕzônâ
>   qiryâ neʾĕmānâ ...
> [26] ʾaḥărê-kēn yiqqārēʾ lāk
>   ʿîr haṣṣedeq
>   qiryâ neʾĕmānâ

> [21] How she has become a whore,
>   the faithful city....
> [26] Afterwards, you will be called
>   the city of righteousness,
>   the faithful city. (Isa 1:21a, 26b)

---

[152] Pardee, *Ugaritic and Poetic Parallelism*, 199; see further Grossberg, *Centripetal and Centrifugal*, 9.
[153] Berlin, *Dynamics*, 131–2.
[154] Pardee, *Ugaritic and Poetic Parallelism*, 170, 200–1.
[155] Alonso Schökel, *Manual*, 78; Martin Kessler, "Inclusio in the Hebrew Bible," *Semitics* 6 (1978): 44–9; Watson, *CHP*, 282–7.
[156] Stephen F. Fogle and T. V. F. Brogan, "Envelope," in *NPEPP*, 360–1; Smith, *Poetic Closure*, 65–7.

118   Reading the Poetry of First Isaiah

The avoidance of exact repetition is common in inclusios in Biblical Hebrew poetry.[157] In this case, the couplet and a triplet only repeat their common final lines, although they also share initial ʾ sounds and unbalanced rhythm. These formal similarities overlie important thematic differences—the opening couplet introduces Jerusalem's moral corruption, while the concluding triplet describes its restoration to its pristine righteousness. The poem framed by these lines charts the city's transformation from one state to the other. In this way, the inclusio encapsulates the movement of the poem, with its return to its opening line marking Jerusalem's return to its original state as "faithful city." Other examples of inclusio are Isa 1:2aβ, 20bβ and Isa 23:1bα, 14. In both cases, the line or lines in question display minor variation.[158]

Distant parallelism also occurs internally within poems, and the parallel material may take on new significance with each occurrence. In Isa 28:10, for instance, Isaiah's opponents derisively reduce his prophetic message to three lines of nonsensical chatter: *ṣaw lāṣāw ṣaw lāṣāw/qaw lāqāw qaw lāqāw/zěʿêr šām zěʿêr šām*. Especially in the first two lines, the unintelligibility of the utterance seems to be the point of the comparison, but the sounds are richly evocative on multiple levels. The reference to weaned infants in the preceding couplet suggests that they might be an onomatopoeic mimicry of repetitive baby sounds, like "goo-goo gaa-gaa" in English, or perhaps a child's attempt to learn the alphabet.[159] At the same time, the pairing of the consonants *q* and *ṣ* also recalls the lexical pair "vomit" and "dung" (*qîʾ/ṣōʾâ*) in v. 8.[160] The triplet is repeated exactly in v. 13, but the nonsensical sounds have now become the inaccessible

---

[157] According to Kessler, inclusio in classical rhetoric involved verbatim repetition; consequently, most examples from Biblical Hebrew poetry should be understood as "approximate" inclusio ("Inclusio," 45).

[158] The second line of Isa 23:1bα is problematic. A number of commentators suggest reading *māʿuzzěken* ("your fortress") for MT *mibayyit* ("without a house"), thereby making it conform to v. 14b: see Blenkinsopp, *Isa 1–39*, 342; Gray, *Isa I–XXVII*, 389; Wildberger, *Isa 13–27*, 406. While emendation seems unavoidable, the harmonization of vv. 1 and 14 is not an especially compelling solution.

[159] Blenkinsopp, *Isa 1–39*, 90; Clements, *Isaiah 1–39*, 228; Hayes and Irvine, *Isaiah*, 324–5; Christopher B. Hays, "The Covenant with Mut: A New Interpretation of Isaiah 28:1–22," *VT* 60 (2010): 233.

[160] John A. Emerton, "Some Difficult Words in Isaiah 28.10 and 13," in *Biblical Hebrews, Biblical Texts: Essays in Memory of Michael P. Weitzman* (eds. Ada Rapoport-Albert and Gillian Greenberg; JSOTSup 333/Hebrew Bible and its Versions 2; Sheffield: Sheffield Academic Press, 2001), 51–6; Baruch Halpern, "'The Excremental

"word of YHWH" to those who have rejected Isaiah's message. In this second occurrence, the sounds likely evoke the foreign speech of the invading Assyrian army, as suggested by the phrase *ûbĕlāšôn 'aḥeret* ("with another language") in v. 11.[161] In another section of the same poem, the prophet again uses repetition to subvert his opponents' claims. In v. 15, he quotes the Jerusalem leaders' boastful description of their attempts to resist Assyrian rule through political machinations. They claim to have negotiated "a covenant with Death" (*bĕrît 'et-māwet*) and "a pact with Sheol" (*wĕ'im-šĕ'ôl... ḥōzeh*) in v. 15a. In v. 15b, they further declare, "Surely, we have made lies our refuge / and in falsehood we have hidden ourselves" (*kî śamnû kāzāb maḥsēnû/ûbaššeqer nistārĕnû*); as a result of these actions, they believe that they will escape "the overwhelming flood / when it passes by" (*šôṭ šôṭēp/kî-ya'ăbōr*), almost certainly a reference to Assyria.[162] Verses 16–19 announce the divine response to these actions, using the same terms and phrases that the people themselves used to describe them. YHWH "will make" (*wĕśamtî*) justice and righteousness the measures of national well-being (v. 17a), and the people's "refuge of lies" (*maḥsēh kāzāb*) and "hiding place" (*sēter*) will be swept away by hail and water (v. 17b). According to v. 18a, their "covenant with death" (*bĕrîtĕkem 'et-māwet*) and "pact with Sheol" (*wĕḥāzûtĕkem 'et-šĕ'ôl*) will be annulled. Finally, YHWH warns them in vv. 18b–19 that, rather than escaping "the overwhelming flood, / when it passes by" (*šôṭ šôṭēp/kî-ya'ăbōr*), they will be repeatedly trampled down by it. This intricate network of repetitions not only holds these verses together as a unit but also conveys the deliberate, methodical character of God's response to the people's machinations.

The recurrence of *Leitwörter* or keywords across line groups is a related device for forming larger sections of a poem.[163] In the process,

---

Vision': The Doomed Priests of Doom in Isaiah 28," *HAR* 10 (1986): 113; Hays, "Covenant with Mut," 233–4.

[161] Emerton, "Difficult Words," 44–5.

[162] Isaiah is likely borrowing an image from Assyrian inscriptions, on which see Gordon H. Johnston, "Nahum's Rhetorical Allusions to Neo-Assyrian Conquest Metaphors," *Bibliotheca Sacra* 159 (2002): 32–4; Machinist, "Assyria and its Image," 726–8; see also Isa 8:7–8.

[163] Berlin, "Introduction to Hebrew Poetry," 309; Petersen and Richards, *Interpreting Hebrew Poetry*, 62; Watson, *CHP*, 288–9.

120   Reading the Poetry of First Isaiah

the device also highlights important themes of the poem.[164] Unlike forms of distant parallelism involving whole lines or phrases, keywords are not necessarily used to establish particular connections between the lines in which they occur, but rather to create a loose sense of coherence across lines. Isaiah 19:1–15 is an oracle against Egypt that can be divided into three units.[165] In the first section (vv. 1b–4), the proper name *miṣrayim* ("Egypt") appears seven times in thirteen lines, not counting its occurrence in the superscription in v. 1a.[166] There is at least one occurrence in every line group except v. 3b. The term does not appear at all in the second section (vv. 5–10), although v. 6 contains the biform *māṣôr*. Instead, the designation *yĕʾōr* ("Nile") occurs four times, with roughly the same effect.[167] In the final section (vv. 10–15), *miṣrayim* occurs again four more times, clustered toward the end of the poem; note also the repetition of the proper name *ṣōʿan* ("Zoan") in vv. 11, 13, and *parʿōh* ("Pharaoh") in v. 11. Taken together, these repetitions both demarcate individual units and connect them as a single work. The shifts in the keywords from section to section, which correspond to other thematic and stylistic shifts, establish the sense of the parts, while the shared associations of the different keywords with Egypt establish the sense of the whole. Other poems in First Isaiah with significant recurrence of keywords are the oracle against Moab in chapters 15–16 (√*yll*, "wail") and the "Ariel" poem in 29:1–8 (*ʾărîʾēl*, "Ariel"; √*ṣwr*, "besiege").

The poem in Isaiah 2:6–22 relies heavily on various forms of distant parallelism for its unity. Two complexes of lines recur in the poem. In vv. 10,[168] 19, and 21, the initial line contains a form of the

---

[164] Raabe, *Psalm Structures*, 189–90; Watson, *CHP*, 288.

[165] Wildberger (*Isa 13–27*, 234–9) and Kaiser (*Isa 13–39*, 99) regard these divisions as separate poems, with only the first and third attributable to Isaiah. For defenses of the unity of the poem, see Blenkinsopp, *Isa 1–39*, 314–15; Hays, "Damming Egypt," 612, 615–16; Sweeney, *Isa 1–39*, 269.

[166] See Watson, *CHP*, 365. Kaiser, who dates the poem to the Persian period, sees this repetition as evidence that the author's "poetic ability was not that of the great prophets of the eighth century" (*Isa 13–39*, 99), despite the ubiquity of *Leitwörter* in Biblical Hebrew poetry.

[167] The term is actually repeated five times in MT, but one of the two occurrences in v. 7a is missing in LXX and is usually regarded as the result of dittography: Duhm, *Jesaja*, 142; Gray, *Isa I–XXVII*, 327; Wildberger, *Isa 13–27*, 231; etc.

[168] 1QIsa[a] lacks vv. 9b–10, but the verses are attested in all of the versions and in the fragments of 4QIsa[a] and 4QIsa[b].

verb *bô'* ("enter") and the noun *ṣûr* ("rock"), along with the noun *'āpār* ("dust") in vv. 10 and 19, followed by the repeated line *mippĕnê-paḥad yhwh ûmēhădar gĕ'ônô* ("from before the terror of Yhwh and from his exalted splendor"); in vv. 19 and 21, the additional line *bĕqûmô la'ărōṣ hā'āreṣ* ("when he rises to terrify the earth") creates a triplet.[169] Similarly, the line *wĕniśgab yhwh lĕbaddô bayyôm hahû'* ("and Yhwh alone will be exalted on that day") is repeated in vv. 11 and 17; in both cases, the preceding lines contain the parallel pairs *šāḥaḥ/šāpēl* ("bowed down"/"brought low") and *'ādām/'îš* ("humankind"/"human"), which also occur in the internally parallel v. 9a (see Isa 5:15). These repeated lines do not function as refrains, since they do not occur at regular intervals or mark structural divisions in the text.[170] They simply sustain a loose sense of coherence across the poem. The repetition of the keywords *nāśā'* ("lift up"; vv. 9, 12, 14)[171] and *'ĕlîl* ("idol"; vv. 8, 18, 20) further heightens the sense of connectedness. Most commentators analyze this pericope as a redactional pastiche with a small Isaianic core.[172] Even so, the various repetitions create a strong impression of a unified whole.[173]

---

[169] LXX includes this third line in v. 10 as well. On this evidence, Duhm suggests that it has dropped out from MT (*Jesaia*, 41). It seems more likely, however, that LXX has harmonized vv. 10, 19, 21 (see Williamson, *Isa 1–5*, 197). Gray completely harmonizes vv. 10 and 19, supposing that "it is improbable that the rhythmical dissimilarity of the two occurrences of the refrain is original" (*Isa I–XXVII*, 59). Such variation, however, is common among repeated lines in Biblical Hebrew poetry, including refrains: see John Goldingay, "Repetition and Variation in the Psalms," *JQR* 68 (1978): 146–51. Both Duhm and Gray regard v. 21 as an intrusive variant of v. 19.

[170] *Contra* Gray, *Isa I–XXVII*, 48–60.

[171] The occurrence in v. 13 is probably a gloss: see Blenkinsopp, *Isa 1–39*, 193; Wildberger, *Isa 1–12*, 101; Williamson, *Isa 1–5*, 198–9. For arguments in favor of retaining it, see Michael L. Barré, "A Rhetorical-Critical Study of Isaiah 2:12–17," *CBQ* 65 (2003): 526–7.

[172] For proposals concerning its redaction history, see Barth, *Jesaja-Worte*, 222–3; Joseph Blenkinsopp, "Fragments of Ancient Exegesis in an Isaian Poem," *ZAW* 93 (1981): 51–62; Clements, *Isa 1–39*, 43; Kaiser, *Isa 1–12*, 63–6; Sweeney, *Isa 1–39*, 87–96; Wildberger, *Isa 1–12*, 81–122; Williamson, *Isa 1–5*, 206–13. For arguments for its compositional unity, see R. Davidson, "The Interpretation of Isaiah II 6ff.," *VT* 16 (1966): 1–7; Gray, *Isa I–XXVII*, 48–52; J. J. M. Roberts, "Isaiah 2 and the Prophet's Message to the North," *JQR* 75 (1985): 290–308.

[173] Williamson, *Isa 1–5*, 205.

Catalogues

Poetic lists are a literary technique attested in many poetries from different historical periods, ranging from the famous catalogue of ships in the *Iliad* (2.494–759) to the poetry of Walt Whitman.[174] Its common occurrence in Near Eastern literature should probably be understood against the larger context of ancient Near Eastern *Listwissenschaft* ("list science"), exemplified by the many lexical and onomastic lists from Egypt and Mesopotamia.[175] In light of its frequency in First Isaiah, enumerative style appears to be a characteristic of the style of this corpus, where it takes two basic forms. In texts such as Isa 3:1–3 and 18–23, whole lines are comprised almost entirely of uninterrupted series of related nouns. In other poems, members of a set are distributed one per line to bind together a longer sequence. This technique, as Watson notes, can be understood as the expansion of a word pair, connecting lines or line units that are not otherwise parallel.[176] It carries an inherent risk of predictability or monotony.[177] The examples in First Isaiah, however, are not excessively long, with the most expansive one spanning sixteen lines (Isa 10:27b–32), and the poet often varies how the listed items are used and couples the technique with other devices.

In Isa 30:6–7, a catalogue of animal names, both mundane and mythical, holds together a brief but evocative poetic sequence. Although the lines could constitute a discrete poem in their own right, linguistic and thematic similarities suggest that they are part of a larger poem including at least vv. 1–5 and perhaps the verses that follow.

---

[174] See Roger A. Hornsby and T. V. F. Brogan, "Catalog," in *TNPEPP*, 174–5.

[175] For other examples of catalogues in ancient Near Eastern poetry, see Watson, *CHP*, 349–56. On the relationship between enumerative style and *Listwissenschaft*, see Peter W. Coxon, "The 'List' Genre and Narrative Style in the Court Tales of Daniel," *JSOT* 35 (1986): 95–121. This does not necessarily mean that particular literary lists are dependent on actual lists available to the poet, although the possibility should not be ruled out in some cases. The list of state officials in Isa 3:2–3 may be compared to the Assyrian Eponym Canon or the Egyptian Onomasticon of Amenope (see Coxon, "'List' Genre," 99), while the jewelry list in Isa 3:18–23 also has ancient Near Eastern parallels: see, for example, Ronald H. Sack, "Some Remarks on Jewelry Inventories from Sixth Century B.C. Erech," *Zeitschrift für Assyriologie* 69 (1979): 41–6.

[176] Watson, *CHP*, 350.

[177] Alonso Schökel, "Isaiah," 170.

Structure and Movement 123

[6] *maśśā' bahămôt negeb*
bĕ'ereṣ ṣārâ wĕṣûqâ
lābî' wālayiš nōhēm[178]
'ep'eh wĕśārāp mĕ'ôpēp
yiś'û 'al-ketep 'ăyārîm ḥêlēhem
wĕ'al-dabbešet gĕmallîm 'ôṣĕrōtām
'al-'am lō' yô'îlû
[7] *ûmiṣrayim*[179] *hebel wārîq ya'zōrû*
lākēn qārā'tî lāzō't
rahab hammošbāt[180]

[6] The "burden" of the beasts of the Negev:
Through a land of dire distress,[181]
Lion and roaring lion,
Adder and flying serpent,
They lift their bounty on the shoulders of donkeys,
and their treasures upon the humps of camels,
Toward a people who will not help—
[7] Namely Egypt, whose help is empty and futile.
Therefore I have called this one,
"Rahab Silenced."

---

[178] MT *mēhem* ("from them") lacks an antecedent and makes little sense. Based on the parallel line, some adjective describing a lion is expected. Without changing the consonants, it would be possible to read a *hip'il* participle of *hāmâ* or *hāmam*, "roar" (Blenkinsopp, *Isa 1-39*, 413) or a *qal* participle of *hôm* (Irwin, *Isa 28-33*, 77). None of these verbs, however, ever refer to the roaring of lions. Given the possibility of *m/n* confusion, the emendation *nōhēm*, the *qal* participle of *nāham* ("roar"), is more persuasive and followed by most commentators, including Kaiser, *Isa 13-39*, 287; Wildberger, *Isa 28-39*, 131. For the use of this verb with reference to lions, see Isa 5:29-30; Prov 28:15.

[179] Many commentators delete *ûmiṣrayim* ("namely, Egypt") as an extrametrical gloss: Blenkinsopp, *Isa 1-39*, 413; Duhm, *Jesaia*, 217; Wildberger, *Isa 28-39*, 132. There is no solid reason to do so, and the term does not disrupt the poetry (*contra* Wildberger). Instead, the parallelism of *'am* ("people")/*miṣrayim* is a case of delayed identification: Irwin, *Isa 28-33*, 77; Watson, *CHP*, 336-7.

[180] MT *hēm šābet* ("they are cessation"?) is difficult, and the versions offer little help. Irwin analyzes *hēm* as a noun meaning "roar," translating the pair as "Roar-Inaction": *Isa 28-33*, 77; see also Hayes and Irvine, *Isaiah*, 340. While this solution is attractive, there is little evidence for the existence of such a noun in Bibl. Heb. A more likely solution is *hammošbāt* ("who is silenced"), a *hop'al* participle of *šābat*, which requires no change to the consonants of MT: see Blenkinsopp, *Isa 1-39*, 413; Clements, *Isa 1-39*, 245; Wildberger, *Isa 28-39*, 132.

[181] "Dire distress" is Blenkinsopp's translation (*Isa 1-39*, 413), which effectively captures the soundplay of the hendiad *ṣārâ wĕṣûqâ*.

124   *Reading the Poetry of First Isaiah*

The poetic sequence is tightly structured. Following the first line, which stands alone, a triplet and two couplets are held together by unmarked syntactic dependency, or mixing, and the logical connector *lākēn* ("therefore") joins the final couplet to the preceding lines. Coupled with the cohesive force of the catalogue, these devices create a highly concentrated piece of poetry. The first line functions as a sort of title, with a play on the term *maśśā'*, literally "burden"—the Judahite tribute carried by animals through the Negev to Egypt—but also a type of prophetic oracle (see Isa 15:1; 17:1; etc.).[182] The word "beasts" (*bahămôt*) anticipates the zoological catalogue and, as such, might be compared to a heading or final total in a non-poetic list.[183] The list includes creatures supposedly native to the Negev (lion, roaring lion, adder, flying serpent) as well as domestic animals passing through the region (donkeys, camels). One final animal appears in the last line, the mythical sea creature Rahab, here as in other biblical texts an epithet for Egypt (Isa 51:9; Ps 87:4). Ironically, though, it is not a ferocious sea monster but rather "Rahab Silenced," a creature whose unexpected impotence stands in stark contrast to the truly dangerous animals in v. 6.

Isaiah 10:27b–32 depicts the advance of an unidentified enemy army against Jerusalem from the north, offering a specific itinerary of its movement.[184] If one emends v. 27b to include a reference to Samaria, as most commentators suggest,[185] then a total of fifteen

---

[182] Blenkinsopp, *Isa 1–39*, 413; Wildberger, *Isa 28–39*, 130–1. It is perhaps surprising that such an oracle would be directed to the "beasts of the Negev," but other titles of oracles in First Isaiah are similarly enigmatic, such as the "oracle of the wilderness of the sea" (*maśśā' midbar-yām*) in 21:1.

[183] See Watson, *CHP*, 352–3.

[184] Although the identity of the invaders is uncertain, their route best fits the march of the combined Aramaean–Israelite forces against Jerusalem during the Syro-Ephraimite War; see Hayes and Irvine, *Isaiah*, 209–10; J. J. M. Roberts, "Isaiah and his Children," in *Biblical and Related Studies Presented to Samuel Iwry* (eds. A. Kort and S. Morschauser; Winona Lake, Ind.: Eisenbrauns, 1985), 201–3. To be sure, the larger context of chapter 10 points to the Assyrian army as the invaders; Roberts, however, argues that the material in Isa 10:17–34 was composed during the Syro-Ephraimite war and subsequently reincorporated into a later oracle against Assyria. For other proposed historical settings, see Marvin A. Sweeney, "Sargon's Threat Against Jerusalem in Isaiah 10,27–32," *Bib* 75 (1994): 457–70.

[185] MT *'ōl mippĕnê-šāmen* ("a yoke because of fat") makes little sense; LXX "his shoulder" (Heb. *šikmô*), for MT *šāmen*, probably represents an early emendation, influenced by Isa 9:3 (Eng. 9:4); 14:25. Among proposed modern emendations, *'ālâ mippĕnê šōmĕrôn* ("he has gone up from Samaria") requires the least change to the consonantal text and seems most probable: Hayes and Irvine, *Isaiah*, 208–9;

geographic names occur in these verses; each line of the poetic segment features the name of a city, with the single exception of v. 29aα (*'āběrû ma'bārâ*, "they crossed the ravine"). This catalogue holds the lines together as a section of the larger poem, but it also creates a sense of movement from one line to the next, pulling the reader or hearer along with the advancing army.[186] Its level of detail powerfully builds suspense, as Isaiah's audience would have quickly recognized Jerusalem as the goal of the invaders. Underscoring this sense of inevitability, the poet shifts from describing the actions of the army in vv. 27b–29a to describing the distressed reactions in the respective cities as the army passes through in vv. 29b–32a.[187] Each successive line in the sequence depicts a different point on the route until v. 32b, where the parallel pair Zion/Jerusalem emphasizes the fact that this city is the army's destination. In this way, the catalogue creates a poetic structure that compellingly engages the audience's emotions.

A list of body parts holds together a sequence of lines in Isa 30:27–30, a description of YHWH's theophanic march against the Assyrians:[188]

Wildberger, *Isa 1–12*, 447. Other geographic names have been proposed, most notably Rimmon: Duhm, *Jesaia*, 103; Gray, *Isa I–XXVII*, 208; NRSV, but these seem less likely. For a defense of MT, see Sweeney, "Sargon's Threat," 457, n. 1.

[186] Micah 1:10–15, another eighth-century prophetic poem, similarly uses a catalogue of city names to evoke an advancing army. Both poems contain a number of puns on the various city names, although these are less extensive in Isa 10.27–32 (see vv. 29b, 30b). Note also the wordplays on the names of the Philistine cities in the brief catalogue in Zeph 2:4.

[187] Gray and Wildberger suggest that the movement of the army in fact ends in v. 29a when they lodge for the night at Geba, with vv. 29b–31 describing the subsequent movement of the news of their arrival and reactions to it (Gray, *Isa I–XXVII*, 208–9; Wildberger, *Isa 1–12*, 455). The actions in v. 32, however, are clearly those of the army, which suggests that vv. 29b–31 also detail its advance, even if the poet is no longer focusing on the army itself.

[188] The authorship of Isa 30:27–33 is much debated. For Isaianic composition, see Brevard S. Childs, *Isaiah and the Assyrian Crisis* (Studies in Biblical Theology 2:3; London: SCM, 1967), 47–50; Wildberger, *Isa 28–39*, 189–94. Commentators who propose an extensive Josianic redaction of First Isaiah all assign the text to that period: Barth, *Jesaja-Worte*, 102–3; Clements, *Isa 1–39*, 252; Sweeney, *Isa 1–39*, 395–7. For dates in the Persian or Hellenistic periods, see Willem A. M. Beuken, "Isaiah 30: A Prophetic Oracle Transmitted in Two Successive Paradigms," in vol. 1 of *Writing and Reading the Scroll of Isaiah: Studies of an Interpretive Tradition* (2 vols.; eds. C. C. Boyles and C. A. Evans; VTSup 70; Formation and Interpretation of Old Testament Literature 1–2; Leiden: Brill, 1997), 369–97; Blenkinsopp, *Isa 1–39*, 423; Kaiser, *Isa 13–39*, 305–6.

[27] hinnēh šēm-yhwh
 bā' mimmerḥāq
 bō'ēr 'appô
 ûkābēd maśśā'â[189]
 śĕpātāyw mālĕ'û za'am
 ûlĕšônô kĕ'ēš 'ōkālet
[28] wĕrûḥô kĕnaḥal šôṭēp
 'ad-ṣawwā'r yeḥĕṣeh
 lahănāpâ gôyīm bĕnāpat šāw'[190]
 wĕresen mat'eh 'al lĕḥāyê 'ammîm . . .
[30] wĕhišmîa' yhwh 'et-hôd qôlô
 wĕnaḥat zĕrô'ô yar'eh

[27] Behold, the name of YHWH
 comes from afar!
 His nose is burning
 and heavy with smoke;
 His lips are full of fury;
 and his tongue is like a consuming fire.

---

[189] MT wĕkōbed maśśā'â is difficult. Some commentators read kābēd ("liver") for kōbed (Hummel, "Enclitic mem," 100; Irwin, Isa 28–33, 97–8). The other anatomical items in vv. 27–28 are parts of the face and head, however, making the inclusion of "liver" unlikely. A more likely reading is the adjective kĕbād or the participle kābēd ("is heavy"), parallel to the participle bō'ēr ("is burning"); see Sym.; Syr.; Tg.; Theod. All of the versions and many commentators take maśśā'â as a form of maśśā', "burden" (Blenkinsopp, Isa 1–39, 422; Wildberger, Isa 28–39, 186; etc.; see also NJPS; REB). Alternatively, one could take it as a different noun from √nś', referring either to the "rising" of divine anger (so Paul A. Krueger, "The Obscure Combination kbd mś'h in Isaiah 30:27: Another Description for Anger?" JNSL 26, no. 2 [2000]: 155–62) or, more likely, smoke: Barth, Jesaja-Worte, 93; Donner, Israel, 163; Victor Sasson, "An Unrecognized 'Smoke-Signal' in Isaiah XXX 27," VT 33 (1983): 90–5; NIV; NRSV. Most likely, it is a biform or pausal form of maś'ēt, "smoke signal" (Judg 20:38–40; Jer 6:1; see Lachish 4.rev.2; see also Barth; HALOT, 640; Hummel). For references to smoke from YHWH's nostrils, see 2 Sam 22:9=Ps 18:9 (Eng. 18:8); see also Job 41:12 (Eng. 41:20).

[190] MT lahănāpâ is a hip'il infinitive construct of nôp, typically "to wave, shake" (see Isa 10:32); the form reflects Aram. influence (Bauer–Leander 486jε), which increases the phonological similarity between the verb and its cognate object nāpat (Wildberger, Isa 28–39, 186–7). Traditionally, *nāpâ has been understood to mean "sieve" (BDB, 631; Duhm, Jesaia, 226; HALOT, 708). H. L. Ginsberg first proposed the meaning "yoke" (see Arb. nāf), which he connects to the geographic name nāpat/ôt dôr/dō'r in Josh 11:2; 12:23; 1 Kgs 4:11, with a denominative verb ("An Obscure Hebrew Word," JQR 22 [1931–32]: 143–5). This suggestion best fits the context, in light of the parallelism with resen ("bridle") and the gapping of the verb, and is adopted by Barth, Jesaja-Worte, 93–4; Blenkinsopp, Isa 1–39, 422; Irwin, Isa 28–33, 99; NEB; NJPS.

[28] And his breath is like an overflowing wadi
   that reaches up to the neck—
to yoke the nations with a yoke of deception,
   and a bridle that leads astray on the jaw of the peoples. . . .
[30] And Yhwh will cause the majesty of his voice to be heard,
   and the descent of his arm he will cause to be seen.

Many interpreters have called attention to the cohesive effects of this anatomical list.[191] The body parts in v. 27 (nose, lips, tongue, breath) belong to Yhwh, resulting in an extraordinarily anthropomorphic depiction of divine judgment.[192] In v. 28, by contrast, the destructive effects of the theophany are described in terms of the bodies of those who experience the theophany (neck, jaw). Despite the shift in referents, the catalogue retains coherence because all of the body parts are located on the neck and head, and they occur in roughly descending order, as is typical of such catalogues.[193] Following a brief interlude in v. 29, the catalogue resumes and concludes in v. 30 with references to the "voice" (*qôl*) and "arm" (*zĕrôa'*) of Yhwh.

READING OF ISAIAH 3:1-15

It should be clear from the preceding discussion that poetic structure takes a variety of forms in the Isaianic corpus. Whatever generalizations

---

[191] Beuken, "Isa 30," 390; Irwin, *Isa 28-33*, 97; Sasson, "Smoke Signal," 93-4; Watson, *CHP*, 355. Lists of body parts appear frequently in poetic descriptions in the Bible, in a variety of genres such as love poetry (Song 4:1-5; 5:11-16), wisdom texts (Prov 4:20-7; 6:12-17), and idol polemics (Pss 115:5-7; 135:16-17). For a more detailed discussion of the *topos*, see Michael Patrick O'Connor, "The Body in the Bible: Anatomy and Morphology," in *In Service of the Church: Essays on Theology and Ministry Honoring the Rev. Charles L. Froehle* (eds. V. J. Klimoski and M. C. Athans; St. Paul, Minn.: University of St. Thomas, 1993), 143-53; Watson, *CHP*, 353-5.

[192] While references to divine body parts are common in the HB, the number of anatomical features in these lines is remarkable. Ultimately, the point is not to describe Yhwh per se but to lend concreteness to the depiction of divine wrath. Depictions of physical characteristics in the HB are seldom meant to help the audience visualize the character in question (see Jeremy Schipper, "Body. II. Hebrew Bible/Old Testament," in *EBR* 4:270). Other descriptions of deities in ancient Near Eastern texts that include catalogues of body parts seem to be describing the cult statue: Wolfram Herrman, "Gedanken zur Geschicte des Altorientalischen Beschreibungsliedes," *ZAW* 75 (1963): 176-97; Marvin H. Pope and Jeffrey H. Tigay, "A Description of Baal," *UF* 3 (1971): 117-30.

[193] Beuken, "Isa 30," 390; Watson, *CHP*, 355.

128   Reading the Poetry of First Isaiah

one might make about poetic movement, there is no substitute for attentive readings of particular poems. In what follows, I provide such a reading of Isa 3:1-15, with special consideration of the poem's structure and movement.

[1] kî hinnēh hā'ādôn yhwh ṣĕbā'ôt
mēsîr mîrûšālaim ûmîhûdâ maš'ēn ûmaš'ēnâ[194]
kōl miš'an-leḥem wĕkōl miš'an-māyim[195]
[2] gibbôr wĕ'îš milḥāmâ
šôpēṭ wĕnābî' wĕqōsēm wĕzāqēn
[3] śar-ḥămiššîm ûnĕśû' pānîm
wĕyô'ēṣ waḥăkam ḥărāšîm ûnĕbôn lāḥaš
[4] wĕnātattî nĕ'ārîm śārêhem
wĕta'ălûlîm yimšĕlû-bām
[5] wĕniggaś hā'ām 'îš bĕ'îš
wĕ'îš bĕrē'ēhû
yirhăbû hanna'ar bazzāqēn
wĕhanniqleh bannikbād
[6] kî-yitpōś 'îš bĕ'āḥîw
bêt 'ābîw
śimlâ lĕkâ
qāṣîn tihyeh-lānû[196]
wĕhammakšēlâ hazzō't taḥat yādekā
[7] yiśśā' bayyôm hahû' lē'mōr
lō'-'ehyeh ḥōbēš
ûbĕbêtî 'ên leḥem wĕ'ên śimlâ
lō' tĕśîmūnî qĕṣîn 'ām
[8] kî kāšĕlâ yĕrûšālaim
wîhûdâ nāpāl

---

[194] The alliteration of m groups these words as a single line, contra BHS and BH³.
[195] Although attested in all the versions, kōl miš'an-leḥem wĕkōl miš'an māyim ("every support of food and every support of water") is largely regarded as a gloss: Clements, Isa 1-39, 47; Wildberger, Isa 1-12, 124; Williamson, Isa 1-5, 243; etc. The concern for physical sustenance seems out of place, and Clements and Williamson think that it reflects the siege of Jerusalem in 587 BCE. Nonetheless, the suggestion is too hypothetical to accept without reservation, especially since v. 7 suggests that food shortages could be a consequence of the leadership vacuum: Childs, Isaiah, 33; Jonathan Magonet, "Isaiah 2:1-4:6: Some Poetic Structures and Tactics," ACEBT 3 (1982): 76.
[196] This line division follows the punctuation in MT, and it is supported by the morphological and phonological matching of lĕkâ ("you have") and lānû ("our") at the ends of the resulting lines. For an older, alternative proposal, see Gray, Isa I-XXVII, 65; NJPS.

Structure and Movement 129

kî-lĕšônām ûma'allêhem 'el[197]-yhwh
   lamrôt 'ēnê kĕbôdô
[9] hakkārat pĕnêhem 'ānĕtâ bām
   wĕḥaṭṭā'tām kisdōm
   higgîdû lō' kiḥēdû[198]
   'ôy lĕnapšām
   kî-gāmĕlû lāhem rā'â
[10] 'ašrê[199] ṣaddîq kî-ṭôb
   kî-pĕrî ma'allêhem yō'kēlû
[11] 'ôy lĕrāšā'[200] rā'
   ki-gĕmûl yādāyw yē'āśeh lô
[12] 'ammî nōgĕśāyw mĕ'ôlēl
   wĕnōšîm[201] māšĕlû bô
   'ammî mĕ'aššĕrêkā mat'îm
   wĕderek 'ōrĕḥōtêkā billē'û
[13] niṣṣāb lārîb yhwh

---

[197] For MT 'el ("to"), 1QIsaᵃ has 'al ("against"). The meanings of the prepositions overlap considerably (IBHS, 216). The logic of the verse requires the meaning "against," more commonly associated with 'al, but see Gen 4:8; Isa 2:4; Qoh 9:14; etc. for this sense with 'el.

[198] BHS, followed by some commentators (for example, Williamson, Isa 1–5, 231), takes v. 9aβ as a single line: wĕḥaṭṭā'tām kisdōm higgîdû lō' kiḥēdû, "and their sin, like Sodom, they announce and do not hide." Although uncommon, the structure falls within allowable limits (two clauses, four constituents, four words; see O'Connor, HVS, 355). No other biblical tradition, however, highlights the blatancy of Sodom's sin in this way (contra Williamson, Isa 1–5, 253). I have divided it into two shorter lines, treating v. 9a in its entirety as a triplet; see also Bartelt, Book Around Immanuel, 206–7, 212; Bertil Wiklander, Prophecy as Literature: A Text-Linguistic and Rhetorical Approach to Isa 2–4 (ConBOT 22; Malmö: CWK Gleerup, 1984), 67. The middle line is a verbless clause comparing Judah's partiality to the sin of Sodom; the final line condemns the people for shamelessly flaunting this sin.

[199] The relationship between MT 'imrû ("say") and the following noun is unclear; for a creative but unconvincing proposal, see Holladay, "Isa. III 10–11," 484–6. LXX has eipontes ("say") followed by dēsōmen ("let us bind"), which has no equivalent in MT. Many commentators think that it preserves a variant from √'sr ("bind"), itself the corruption of an original 'ašrê ("happy is"), which better matches 'ôy ("woe") in the following couplet: Wildberger, Isa 1–12, 125; see also Blenkinsopp, Isa 1–39, 198; Duhm, Jesaia, 47; Williamson, Isa 1–5, 255–7.

[200] Based on v. 10a, one expects kî ("because") before rā' ("it goes badly"). Holladay ("Isa. III 10–11," 483) and Williamson (Isa 1–5, 258) think that the previous kî does "double duty"; for gapping of particles, see O'Connor, HVS, 405–6. The absence of an intervening word amplifies the phonological similarity of rāšā' ("wicked") and rā'.

[201] Reading nōšîm for MT nāšîm ("women") with LXX; Tg.; Theod.; see Blenkinsopp, Isa 1–39, 197–8; Gray, Isa I–XXVII, 68; Wildberger, Isa 1–12, 137; Williamson, Isa 1–5, 262; etc. MT is not impossible, though, and double entendre is likely.

wĕʿōmēd lādîn ʿammô-m²⁰²
[14] yhwh bĕmišpāṭ yābôʾ
ʿim-ziqnê ʿammô wĕśārāyw
wĕʾattem biʿartem hakkerem
gĕzēlat heʿānî bĕbāttêkem
[15] mallākem tĕdakkĕʾû ʿammî
ûpĕnê ʿăniyîm tiṭḥānû
nĕʾum-ʾădōnāy yhwh ṣĕbāʾôt

[1] Surely the Lord, YHWH of hosts,
will soon remove from Jerusalem and Judah staff and stay,²⁰³
every support of bread and every support of water:
[2] hero and warrior,
judge and prophet and diviner and elder,
[3] chief of fifty and dignitary,
and advisor and skilled magician and expert charmer.
[4] And I will make juveniles their chiefs,
and they will rule them with immaturity.²⁰⁴
[5] And the people will oppress themselves, one against another,
and one against a neighbor;
The lad will rise against the elder,
and the scorned against the honored.

---

²⁰² Reading ʿammō-m ("his people"), with enclitic -m, for MT ʿammîm ("peoples"), as first suggested by Hummel, "Enclitic Mem," 100. LXX and Syr. read "his people," while 1QIsaᵃ and Tg. support MT. Many commentators explain MT simply as scribal error (Wildberger, Isa 1–12, 140) or deliberate editorial change: J. A. Emerton, "Are There Examples of Enclitic Mem in the Hebrew Bible?" in Texts, Temples, and Traditions: A Tribute to Menahem Haran (eds. M. V. Fox et al.; Winona Lake, Ind.: Eisenbrauns, 1996), 335; Gray, Isa I–XXVII, 69; Kaiser, Isa 1–12, 75; Williamson, Isa 1–5, 264–5. Duhm (Jesaia, 48) and de Waard (Handbook, 20), among others, prefer MT. For traditional interpretations of MT, see David A. Baer, "'It's All About Us!' Nationalistic Exegesis in the Greek Isaiah," in As Those who are Taught: Interpretation of Isaiah from the LXX to the SBL (eds. Claire Matthews McGinnis and Patricia K. Tull; SBLSymS 27; Atlanta: Society of Biblical Literature, 2006), 34–6.

²⁰³ Many Eng. translations reflect the alliteration of mašʿēn ûmašʿēnâ, for example KJV "stay and staff" (followed here; see also Gray, Isa I–XXVII, 62–3; Williamson, Isa 1–5, 232); NIV "supply and support"; NRSV "support and staff."

²⁰⁴ Taʿălûlîm is apparently related to the hitpaʿel of √ʿll, which refers to vicious treatment or humiliation in Exod 10:2; Judg 19:25; Jer 38:19 (Gray, Isa I–XXVII, 64; Wildberger, Isa 1–12, 131–2). The parallel with nĕʿārîm also suggests a play on ʿôlēl/ʿôlāl, "child" (Williamson, Isa 1–5, 233–4). If Williamson is right in taking the term as an adverbial accusative (contra Wildberger, as translated here), then this pair is an example of terms that are morphologically and lexically parallel but not syntactically parallel (see Berlin, Dynamics, 80–3).

[6] For one will seize a relative
   in their ancestral home:[205]
"You have a cloak—
   you will be our ruler,
   and this ruin under your authority."
[7] He will answer on that day, saying,
   "I will not be a healer,
   and in my house there is neither bread nor cloak;
   do not make me the ruler of the people!"
[8] Surely, Jerusalem will stumble,
   and Judah will fall,[206]
For their speech and deeds are against Yhwh,
   to rebel against his glorious eyes.
[9] Their partiality[207] testifies against them,
   and their sin is like Sodom's—
   they declare it; they don't hide it!
Woe to their person,
   for they have brought evil upon themselves.
[10] Blessed are the righteous, for it goes well;
   for the fruit of their deeds they will eat.
[11] Woe to the wicked—it goes badly;
   for the work of their hands will be done to them.
[12] My poor people! Its taskmasters do it harm,
   and usurers rule over it.
My poor people! Your rulers lead astray,
   and the way of your paths they destroy.
[13] Yhwh rises for a lawsuit,
   and stands to judge for his people.

---

[205] Following Blenkinsopp (*Isa 1–39*, 197) and Williamson (*Isaiah 1–5*, 234), I take *bêt 'ābîw* ("his ancestral home") as an accusative of location. Note the nearly exact parallel *bêt 'ābîk* ("[in] your father's house") in Gen 24:23; see further Joüon §126h.

[206] Most commentators take the perfect verbs in this line as past actions: for example, Kaiser, *Isa 1–12*, 107; Williamson, *Isa 1–5*, 231. Alternatively, one could take them as future actions, examples of the so-called "prophetic perfect" (Bartelt, *Book Around Immanuel*, 212; Gray, *Isa I–XXVII*, 65); on this use of the perfect more generally, see GKC §106m–o; *IBHS*, 491; Joüon §112g–h. Because I read this line as the continuation of the action of v. 1, I prefer the second option.

[207] MT *hakkārat pěnêhem* could be translated "the look on their faces" (NIV; NRSV; see also Hayes and Irvine, *Isaiah*, 90), and the reference to guilty expressions is consistent with the subsequent statement that the people do not hide their sins. The idiom √*nkr pānîm*, however, means "to show partiality" in Deut 1:17; 16:19; Prov 24:23; 28:21. Targum understands the phrase in this way, which almost all commentators prefer (Gray, *Isa I–XXVII*, 55–6; Wildberger, *Isa 1–12*, 125; Williamson, *Isa 1–5*, 237–8; etc.).

[14] YHWH will come in judgment
with the elders of his people and its princes;
And you have destroyed the vineyard,
and the loot of the poor is in your houses.
[15] What have you done, that you crush my people,
and grind the face of the poor?
Oracle of my Lord, YHWH of Hosts.

In its present form, Isa 3:1–15 appears as a single poem. Its boundaries are marked by the inclusio *hā'ădôn/'ădōnāy yhwh ṣĕbā'ôt* ("the/my Lord YHWH of hosts") in vv. 1 and 15, and the repeated denouncements of Judahite leadership give it broad thematic consistency.[208] At the same time, abrupt thematic shifts and tensions within the poem have led practically all critics to treat it as a composite text, even as they acknowledge its present coherence.[209] There is nearly complete consensus that vv. 9b or 10–11 are a later addition, likely influenced by the wisdom tradition.[210] Gray and Clements further identify vv. 1–9a and 13–15 as originally separate units, both by Isaiah of Jerusalem, based on perceived differences in their condemnation of the leaders.[211] Most critics, including Blenkinsopp, Beuken, Wildberger, and Williamson, divide the text more extensively into several smaller components, both Isaianic oracles and later additions.[212] The specific historical context of the original Isaianic oracles is debated, although recent interpreters connect them to Sennacherib's invasion

---

[208] Beuken, *Jesaja 1-12*, 109; Sweeney, *Isa 1-39*, 110.

[209] For a convenient summary of proposals through 1988, see Sweeney, *Isa 1-4*, 147–8.

[210] William L. Holladay, "Isa. III 10-11: An Archaic Wisdom Passage," *VT* 18 (1968): 481–7; Wildberger, *Isa 1-12*, 134–5; Williamson, *Isa 1-5*, 258–9; etc. For arguments for their originality, see Blenkinsopp, *Isa 1-39*, 199; Hayes and Irvine, *Isaiah*, 90; Magonet, "Isa 2:1-4:6," 77–8.

[211] Gray notes that vv. 1–5 are concerned with the detrimental effects of their removal, while v. 14 emphasizes their misconduct (*Isa I-XXVII*, 60). According to Clements, vv. 1–11 criticize the leaders' international policies, whereas vv. 13–15 focus on their oppression of the lower classes (*Isa 1-39*, 49). On the latter point, Clements rightly points to v. 14, but the basis for his reading of vv. 1–11 is unclear.

[212] Beuken, *Jesaja 1-12*, 109–10; Blenkinsopp, *Isa 1-39*, 198–200; Wildberger, *Isa 1-12*, 126–7; Williamson, *Isa 1-5*, 239–43, 258–9, 263, 267–9. Becker and Kaiser similarly divide the passage into several original units but do not accept Isaianic authorship for any of them (Becker, *Jesaja*, 162–9; Kaiser, *Isa 1-12*, 68–76).

Structure and Movement   133

in 701 BCE.[213] The few interpreters who argue for the poem's original unity acknowledge the same tensions but explain them on stylistic grounds. Hayes and Irvine, for instance, argue that the poem moves from a description of a hypothetical situation (vv. 1–7), to a critique of the prophet's contemporary political situation (vv. 8–12), to an announcement of future judgment (vv. 13–15).[214] Sweeney follows Gray and Clements to some degree in taking vv. 1–11 and 13–15 as separate poems from different points in the prophet's career, but he maintains that Isaiah himself later added v. 12 to join them into a single composition.[215]

As these proposals indicate, the text exhibits loose overall coherence but also considerable fragmentation. Whatever it might finally mean for the text's composition history, this state of affairs is precisely what we have come to expect for biblical poetry. The text almost perfectly fits Gray's description of minimally structured poems: "a succession of very loosely connected lines or distichs; now and again one or two distichs may be more closely connected than the rest, but for the most part we cannot speak of greater sense divisions in such poems at all."[216] Parallelism at the level of the couplet connects a few contiguous line groups (vv. 2–3, 5, 9b–11, 12). Beyond these units, only distant repetition (for example, *śār*, "chief" in vv. 3–4, 14; *zāqēn*, "elder" in vv. 3, 14; *makšēlâ/kāšēlâ*, "heap of ruins" / "stumble" in vv. 6, 8) provides stability.[217] Thematically, the poem consists of unfolding variations on the related ideas of corrupt leadership and social disorder. The development is aggregative, not neatly temporal or logical, as the poet repeatedly returns to the same thematic material and elaborates it in new ways. The shared themes hold together the different parts of the poem, even as the repetitions provide a loose sense of structure.

---

[213] Beuken, *Jesaja 1–12*, 110; Blenkinsopp, *Isa 1–39*, 199; Williamson, *Isa 1–5*, 242; etc. For a date during the reign of Ahaz, see Clements, *Isa 1–39*, 46–7, 49; Wildberger, *Isa 1–12*, 128, 138.
[214] Hayes and Irvine, *Isaiah*, 87–92.
[215] Sweeney, *Isa 1–39*, 110. One should also note Bartelt's argument that Isa 3:1–4.1 comprises a single poem, largely on the basis of syllable counts, although this proposal has found no additional adherents (*Book around Immanuel*, 220–2).
[216] Gray, *Forms*, 190.
[217] Magonet proposes a chiastic structure encompassing the entire poem, but many parts of the proposal seem forced ("Isa 2:1–4:6," 73–6).

The prophet introduces the theme of social disorder in v. 1 by declaring the impending removal of the nation's "staff and stay" (*mašʿēn ûmašʿēnâ*), a phrase that expresses totality by pairing cognate masculine and feminine nouns.[218] Almost immediately, the poem's movement is slowed by the lengthy, bordering on tedious, list of eleven types of officials and social elites in vv. 2–3, which clarifies the meaning of "staff and stay." The prosaic effects of the list are striking; Watson suggests that it "could almost belong to an economic text."[219] Following the soundplay in v. 1aβ, the poet could have achieved euphony by grouping similar sounding words together, but these remain distributed haphazardly throughout the lines, as if the poetry itself has broken down in mimicry of the social upheaval it depicts. The list develops the sense of comprehensiveness established in v. 1 by the mixed-gender pair *mašʿēn ûmašʿēnâ* and the repetition of *kōl* ("every"). Following the lineation in *BHS*, the lines become successively longer, heightening this impression. Lacking an obvious terminal device, the list simply breaks off, giving way to Yhwh's speech in v. 4, as if even the deity has grown tired of the prophet's rambling and interrupts him.[220] In contrast to the long, detailed list of officials that will be removed from power, only one group of replacements is named in v. 4, in which "juveniles" (*nĕʿārîm*), obviously unfit for leadership, arise to fill the power vacuum. The jarring contrast underscores the suddenness of the political collapse.

Verse 5 further develops the theme of social disorder in a pair of parallel couplets, but it shifts from the question of leadership to a description of anarchic social relations. Beyond this shared theme, the relationship between vv. 1–4 and v. 5 remains vague. Does the disrespect for authority in v. 5b cause the leaders' overthrow in the earlier verses, or vice versa? The most prominent feature of v. 5 is the juxtaposition of categories of people whose interactions are normally peaceful but who are now pitted "against" (*b-*) each other (see also Isa 19:2). The first line of v. 6 is syntactically similar to the first lines of vv. 5a and 5b (verb + subject + *b-*), and the noun *ʾîš* ("one") is repeated from v. 5a. These similarities lead the audience to expect

---

[218] Blenkinsopp, *Isa 1–39*, 198; *IBHS*, 106; Lowth, *Isaiah*, 156.
[219] Watson, *CHP*, 351; see also Blenkinsopp, *Isa 1–39*, 198; Gray, *Isa I–XXVII*, 63.
[220] In Williamson's alternative lineation, the last line of the series contains three items following four lines with only two items, thus displaying terminal modification (*Isa 1–5*, 244).

further social breakdown in v. 6a, now at the level of the family, as suggested by the term 'āḥîw ("his relative"). Instead of a parallel line, however, an enjambed locative phrase (bêt 'ābîw, "in his ancestral home") follows. This couplet opens a vignette in vv. 6b–7 that vividly depicts the desperation for any form of authority amidst the social chaos.[221] The situation is so dire that merely having a cloak qualifies someone for clan leadership, but the nominee declines the honor in no uncertain terms, recognizing the true nature of the situation. The people need more than the restoration of conventional power structures—they need a "healer" (ḥōbēš). Like the list at the beginning of the poem, the vignette also slows down the movement of the poetry, first with a triplet and then with a quatrain. The exchange poignantly dramatizes the disintegration of Judahite society by focusing on the experience of a few individuals. The term makšēlâ in v. 6 anticipates the verb kāšal at the beginning of v. 8, and it may also be a sarcastic pun on the term memšālâ ("rule, authority"), as suggested by Jonathan Magonet.[222]

Verse 8a picks up the initial metaphor of "staff" from v. 1.[223] Despite the distance that separates these verses, two shared features secure the relationship between them. First, the names "Jerusalem" and "Judah" appear in both verses in the same order, which is the reverse of their order in Isa 1:1 and 2:1. Second, as indicated by the verbs, Jerusalem is grammatically feminine and Judah masculine in v. 8, recalling the contrasting genders of the pair maš'ēn ûmaš'ēnâ.[224] In light of these connections, v. 8 may be seen as the completion of the action of v. 1, forming a sort of thematic inclusio that frames the intervening material. Following the removal of the leaders who

---

[221] For similar vignettes, see Isa 4:1; Amos 4:7–8; 5:19; 6:9–10. Blenkinsopp refers to them as "cameos" (Isa 1–39, 198–9).

[222] Magonet, "Isa 2:1–4:6," 72.

[223] Admittedly, this claim runs counter to the identification of a sharp divide between Isa 3:1–7 and 8 in recent interpretation (for example, Becker, Jesaja, 164–5; Williamson, Isa 1–5, 240).

[224] Noting that yĕhûdâ may be feminine (for example, Lam 1:3) or masculine (for example, Hos 5:5) in Bibl. Heb., Berlin suggests that Isaiah has construed the term as masculine for the purposes of distant parallelism, noting Cassuto's observation that the respective genders of maš'ēn/maš'ēnâ in 3:1 correspond to those of yĕhûdâ/yĕrûšāluim (Dynamics, 41, 44; see also Williamson, Isaiah 1–5, 234). 1QIsa[a] has the feminine verb nplh following yhwdh. This could suggest that the Qumran scribe regarded Judah as feminine, or it could be simply from harmonization with the preceding feminine verb kšlh.

function as their "staff and stay"—that is, their support for standing upright and walking—Jerusalem and Judah predictably "stumble" and "fall."[225] In this way, vv. 1 and 8 metaphorically depict the nation as a disabled person, who needs assistance to walk.[226] Verses 8b–9a further attribute the demise of Judah and Jerusalem to the nation's willful defiance of Yhwh, with an ominous reference to the city of Sodom in v. 9. The identification of the people's sin as "partiality" sets the stage for the more pointed charges of corruption against the nation's leaders in vv. 14b–15. The broader general focus on good and evil in vv. 9b–11, a triad of parallel couplets, departs noticeably from the more focused denouncements in the preceding lines. Most interpreters take at least vv. 10–11 as later additions, reflecting the wisdom tradition in their perspective and perhaps origin; note the similarities between these verses and Prov 12:14.

The poem returns to its earlier themes in v. 12, a pair of parallel couplets lamenting the oppression of the people by its corrupt leaders. It is not clear whether the speaker in these lines is the prophet or Yhwh.[227] In either case, the first-person possessive suffix on ʿammî ("my people") suggests a sense of attachment and identification with the people's plight, and the shift from third-person forms in v. 12a to second-person forms in 12b heightens this personal touch. The characterization of the leaders is heavy-handed. They are called "slave-drivers" (nōgĕśāyw) and "usurers" (nōšîm), and charged with "doing harm to" (mĕʿôlēl) and "misleading" (matʿîm) the people. The verb mĕʿôlēl likely comes from the same root as taʿălûlîm ("immaturity") in v. 4 and maʿallêhem ("their deeds") in vv. 8 and 10, and, as in v. 4, there may be a play on ʿôlēl/ʿôlāl ("child"). If so, then the variant readings nōšîm ("usurers")/nāšîm ("women") in the next line may point to a double entendre suggesting that Judah's leaders are not only corrupt but also incompetent, as unfit for leadership as children or women in Isaiah's cultural context.[228] The recurrence of māšal

---

[225] Mašʿēn and mašʿēnâ are hapax legomena, but the related term mišʿenet ("staff") may refer to a crutch or cane (Exod 21:19; 2 Kgs 18:21=Isa 36:6; Zech 8:4).

[226] J. Blake Couey, "The Disabled Body Politic in Isaiah 3:1, 8," JBL 133 (2014): 95–109.

[227] Most commentators assume that the speaker is Yhwh (Gray, Isa I–XXVII, 66; Wildberger, Isa 1–12, 138), but Williamson notes both possibilities (Isa 1–5, 263).

[228] See Ward, Handbook, 20. Although Roberts does not discuss this text, he observes that differences among textual witnesses generally raise the possibility of wordplay ("Double Entendre," 44–8). For the insulting connotations of comparing

("to rule") also connects vv. 4 and 12. Clements takes these connections to mean that v. 12 describes the new, unqualified leaders described as "juveniles" in v. 4, who have now taken power.[229] It seems more likely, however, that the verse indicts Judah's longstanding leaders, whose removal was threatened at the beginning of the poem but still has not taken place.

As indicated by the third-person references to the deity, we return in v. 13 to the unmistakable voice of the prophet, who announces that YHWH has initiated a lawsuit. Many interpreters assume that it is a lawsuit against YHWH's "people" (*ammô-m*), but Williamson argues convincingly that the verbs *dîn* and *rîb* both denote judgment on behalf of the object in First Isaiah (Isa 1:17, 23; see also Isa 10:2).[230] The purpose of the suit, then, is to offer the beleaguered nation relief from its oppressive mismanagement. Verse 14a identifies the defendants as "the elders of his people and its princes" (*ziqnê 'ammô wĕśārāyw*), both terms that occurred in the list of officials in vv. 2-3. The final lines (vv. 14b-15) detail the charges against them as extortion and oppression of the poor, which had been introduced already in v. 12. The poet uses especially violent verbs to describe their actions: *bā'ar* ("to burn, destroy"); *dākā'* ("to crush"); *ṭāḥan* ("to grind"). These damning accusations leave no conclusion except that these officials must be removed—a removal that was already announced in v. 1. In this way, the poem comes full circle, with its final verse announcing the charge for which its first verse declares the punishment.[231] The inclusio reinforces this sense of return.

The structure of the poem in Isa 3:1-15 cannot be neatly plotted in a single, straight line. Instead, it proceeds almost haphazardly from one part to the next, frequently circling back to develop earlier motifs. It is difficult to discern specific information about the actions or identities of the leaders indicted in the poem, nor can one reconstruct a specific sequence of events pertaining to their removal from power and its aftermath. The unclear temporal reference of the verbs in v. 8 further contributes to this uncertainty. It is not at all clear whether the

---

soldiers to women, see Isa 19:17; Jer 51:30; Cynthia R. Chapman, *The Gendered Language of Warfare in the Israelite-Assyrian Encounter* (HSM 62; Winona Lake, Ind.: Eisenbrauns, 2004), 12-14.

[229] Clements, *Isa 1-12*, 47.
[230] Williamson, *Isa 1-5*, 265; see also Kaiser, *Isa 1-12*, 75; *contra* Wildberger, *Isa 1-12*, 141-2.
[231] Magonet, "Isa 2:1-4:6," 78.

prophet envisions Assyrian deportation or internal overthrow as the cause of the national upheaval. For these reasons, as noted earlier, interpreters have difficulty matching the poem to a specific historical crisis in the late eighth century BCE. What the poem does provide is a series of striking sketches of oppressive leadership and social disorder, creating an impression that becomes cumulatively stronger with each successive elaboration of these themes. This development leaves the audience with a profound new awareness of the rotten state to which the nation has been reduced by its current leaders and the inevitable bedlam that will result from their impending downfall, even as it remains tantalizingly vague about how that will happen.

3

Imagery and Metaphor

In his glowing characterization of Isaiah's poetry, as discussed in the Introduction to this volume, Robert Lowth attributes to the imagery in this corpus "the utmost propriety, elegance, dignity, and diversity."[1] The language of his praise now sounds dated, and it is difficult to square his highbrow assessment with, for instance, an image of tables covered in vomit and feces following a drunken orgy by Judah's priests (Isa 28:7).[2] Still, Lowth's palpable delight in Isaiah's imagery remains instructive, and the richly imagaic quality of this poetry continues to attract interpreters' attention, perhaps more than any of its other features.[3] This chapter explores the form and function of imagery in Isa 1–39, with special attention to its distinctively poetic character. Following a brief methodological discussion, I offer a survey of agricultural and animal images in this corpus. These conceptual domains are the most common sources of imagery in Isaiah's poetry, yet they encompass a wide array of images used for different—sometimes even conflicting—purposes. This survey provides the basis for more general observations about imagery as an aspect of Isaiah's poetic style. The chapter concludes with a reading of Isa 1:2–20, a richly sensual poem that deftly employs a variety of images.

---

[1] Lowth, *Lectures*, 176.
[2] For an excellent discussion of the coarse and grotesque imagery of the Prophets, see Yvonne Sherwood, "'Darke Texts Need Notes': Prophetic Poetry, John Donne and the Baroque," *JSOT* 27 (2002): 47–74.
[3] See, for example, Darr, *Isaiah's Vision*; Everson and Kim (eds.), *The Desert Will Bloom*; Exum, "Broken Pots"; Miscall, "Labyrinth"; Nielsen, *Hope for a Tree;* Quinn-Miscall, *Reading Isaiah*.

Reading the Poetry of First Isaiah

THEORY AND METHOD

In this discussion, the term "imagery" is used to designate poetic language that engages a reader or hearer's imagination by evoking the experience of sensory perceptions.[4] As the term suggests, it appeals in large measure to sight, although not to the exclusion of other senses.[5] Imagery imparts to poetry an illusion of substantive physicality—an illusion because poetic language finally remains a verbal medium, not a visual one.[6] Especially confusing is the use of the term to designate both figurative and non-figurative language, as a result of an awkward amalgamation of different uses of the term from different periods of literary criticism.[7] At first glance, these multiple uses seem untenable. Figurative language employs images not for their own sake but for particular qualities that may be creatively attributed to another subject. Even when images are not used figuratively, however, their occurrence in a poem still maps their features onto the poem itself, even if not onto a particular subject as with metaphor. W. J. T. Mitchell explains, "Since literary representation does not represent by likeness the way pictorial images do, literary representation is itself only and always metaphorical, whether or not it employs particular figures."[8] Moreover, many images have figurative overtones even when their function within poems is primarily descriptive.[9] For these reasons, it seems appropriate to discuss

---

[4] On the relationship between imagery and imagination, see Alonso Schökel, *Manual*, 95, 104–5; William P. Brown, *Seeing the Psalms: A Theology of Metaphor* (Louisville: Westminster John Knox, 2002), 8–9; W. J. T. Mitchell, "Image," in *TNPEPP*, 558.

[5] Eagleton, *Poem*, 139–40; Norman Friedman, "Imagery," in *TNPEPP*, 560. Alonso Schökel notes, however, that "sense images of taste, smell and touch are rare in biblical poetry," with the exception of Song of Songs (*Manual*, 121). The majority of images in First Isaiah are primarily visual or aural; see further Hector Avalos, "Introducing Sensory Criticism in Biblical Studies: Audiocentricity and Visiocentricity," in *This Abled Body: Rethinking Disabilities in Biblical Studies* (eds. Hector Avalos, Sarah J. Melcher, and Jeremy Schipper; SBLSemeiaSt 55; Atlanta: Society of Biblical Literature, 2007), 47–60.

[6] Eagleton, *Poem*, 142; Mitchell, "Image," 557.

[7] According to Eagleton, the use of the term to designate figurative language is largely a twentieth-century development (*Poem*, 140).

[8] Mitchell, "Image," 557; see further Brent A. Strawn, "Imagery," in *Dictionary of the Old Testament: Wisdom, Poetry & Writings* (eds. Tremper Longman III and Peter Enns; Downers Grove, Ill.: InterVarsity Press, 2008), 307.

[9] Friedman, "Imagery," 564; see further Kinzie's discussion of "literal symbols" in *Poet's Guide*, 143–4, 434–5.

figurative and non-figurative images in tandem, despite their important differences.

Nevertheless, the majority of Isaianic images have explicitly metaphorical functions. Since several recent treatments of biblical imagery include surveys of current trends in metaphor theory, there is no need to reinvent the wheel—to use a popular metaphor—beyond a brief sketch of my approach.[10] I have found the work of George Lakoff and Mark Turner particularly useful for thinking about how metaphors operate in poetry. Lakoff and Turner define metaphor as "a set of correspondences... [or] 'mapping' between two conceptual domains," which they respectively designate the "source" and "target" of the metaphor.[11] In the metaphor "life is a journey"—an example that they discuss at great length—the source is "journey" and the target is "life." As this metaphor is developed, any number of characteristics of journeys may be transferred conceptually to the more abstract category of life. For instance, individuals become travelers; death or the afterlife becomes the final destination; significant life decisions become choices between different routes; and so on.[12] Complex metaphors may be constituted by a web of associations between the source and target. Even if a particular expression of a metaphor only articulates one point of relation at the surface, any number of suggested associations may be included in the underlying conceptual transfer, although some connections are logically ruled out.[13] The power of metaphor comes in no small part from this evocative potential.

Metaphors are not merely ornamental or rhetorical flourishes, however. For Lakoff and Turner, they are cognitive devices, and common ones at that. Many deeply ingrained, seemingly obvious ways of thinking about important ideas such as life, death, or time

---

[10] See, for example, Brown, *Seeing the Psalms*, 4–8; Darr, *Isaiah's Vision*, 35–41; Brent A. Strawn, *What is Stronger than a Lion? Leonine Image and Metaphor in the Hebrew Bible and the Ancient Near East* (OBO 212; Göttingen: Vandenhoeck & Ruprecht, 2005), 5–16.

[11] Lakoff and Turner, *More Than Cool Reason*, 4, 38–9. The terms "source" and "target" are roughly equivalent to "vehicle" and "tenor," respectively, which are used by many biblicists (for example, Petersen and Richards, *Interpreting Hebrew Poetry*).

[12] Lakoff and Turner, *More Than Cool Reason*, 3–4, 9–10, 60–5. For the use of this metaphor in the HB, see Brown, *Seeing the Psalms*, 31–54.

[13] Brown, *Seeing the Psalms*, 8; Lakoff and Turner, *More Than Cool Reason*, 39, 61–4.

are inescapably metaphorical.[14] Their view of metaphor has several important implications. It explains why attempts to retrovert metaphors into supposedly literal language do not adequately account for their meanings.[15] Metaphors are sensible on their own terms. Like poetry itself, they resist paraphrase. It also means that metaphors are not linguistically deviant or perverse ways of saying one thing but meaning another. Rather, they are a legitimate function of human cognition. Ultimately, metaphors do not belong solely to the world of literature; they are ideas that are given specific form in both literary and everyday language. Thus, different poetic figures may be expressions of the same underlying metaphor, which need not even be stated explicitly. For example, the common metaphorical association between humans and animals may be evoked simply by using an adjective or verb typically associated with a particular animal without ever naming it. Poets occasionally manufacture original metaphors, but more often they use conventional metaphors in novel or interesting ways. They might find new features of the source to map onto the target, or construct unexpected combinations of different metaphors with the same target, or even destabilize conventional metaphors in order to demonstrate the limits of metaphorical discourse. Such elaborations generally demand greater cognitive effort on the part of readers or hearers and thus increase their interest in the metaphor.[16] This account of the relationship between metaphor and poetry seems generally consistent with the view that poetry uses the same components as all other kinds of language, such as rhythm and syntax, but does so more intentionally, more extravagantly, more demandingly.

Because metaphors move from source to target, they necessarily presume familiarity with the source domain, sometimes in considerable

---

[14] Lakoff and Turner, *More Than Cool Reason*, 1-9, 49-56, 136-9, 214-15; see further George Lakoff and Mark Johnson, *Metaphors We Live By* (Chicago: University of Chicago Press, 1980).

[15] Lakoff and Turner, *More Than Cool Reason*, 111-28, 215; see further Alonso Schökel, *Manual*, 100-1; Mark Johnson, "Metaphor in the Philosophical Tradition," in *Philosophical Perspectives on Metaphor* (ed. Mark Johnson; Minneapolis: University of Minnesota Press, 1981), 35-42. One might object that the kind of analysis undertaken here is an exercise in precisely this kind of literal paraphrase, but Lakoff and Turner argue that description of metaphors is a valid critical enterprise, so long as it never becomes a substitute for the metaphors themselves (*More Than Cool Reason*, 122).

[16] Lakoff and Turner, *More Than Cool Reason*, 51-4, 67-70.

detail.[17] According to Lakoff and Turner, this familiarity comes both from shared cultural understanding and individual experience.[18] Metaphors engage one's emotions in part because they draw on the memories of such experiences and their emotional resonances. The transfer of associations between source and target opens up new understandings of the target. In particular, metaphors impose structure on otherwise abstract concepts, making it possible to recognize connections and create coherences that would not otherwise be apparent. As Lakoff and Turner explain:

> Complex metaphors grip us partly because they awake in us the experience and knowledge that form the grounding of those metaphors, partly because they make the coherence of that experience and knowledge resonate, and partly because they lead us to form new coherences in what we know and experience.[19]

This new knowledge about the target enables one to evaluate it differently and even make decisions accordingly.[20] For these reasons, metaphors prove virtually indispensable for describing divine activity, which accounts for their frequent occurrence in prophetic poetry such as Isa 1–39.

This understanding of metaphor makes it possible to discuss the complexity of figurative language in First Isaiah with greater insight and clarity. Consider, for instance, an image from Isa 17:12 that is, at least in its presentation, deceptively simple:

> hôy hămôn ʿammîm rabbîm
> kahămôt yammîm yehĕmāyûn
> ûšĕʾôn lĕʾummîm
> kišʾôn mayim kabbîrîm yiššāʾûn

> Hey, the roar of many nations—
>   like the roaring of the seas they roar—
> and the clamor of the peoples—
>   like the clamor of powerful waters they clamor.

---

[17] Although some discussions of metaphor allow for reverse mapping from target to source, Lakoff and Turner insist that metaphors only move in one direction (*More Than Cool Reason*, 131–2).
[18] Lakoff and Turner, *More Than Cool Reason*, 60–6, 83–4.
[19] Lakoff and Turner, *More Than Cool Reason*, 89.
[20] Lakoff and Turner, *More Than Cool Reason*, 63–5.

Here, the sea is the source of the metaphor, and the nations are the target. While the explicit point of comparison is the volume of their respective sounds, reinforced by the repetition of the *m* phoneme, the simile readily suggests other shared features.[21] Like the sea, the nations are a vast and powerful force, which is not a comforting implication when these nations are one's enemies. For Isaiah's audience, the sea would have represented even more—a terrifying, chaotic entity, often personified as a monster, that endangers the very fabric of the cosmos.[22] Many biblical texts explicitly compare Israel or Judah's geopolitical enemies to the chaotic sea or its creatures (for example, Pss 46:3–4 [Eng. 46:2–3]; 89:10–11, 26 [Eng. 89:9–10, 25]).[23] By evoking the cosmic enemy of God to depict the armies arrayed against Jerusalem, the poet amplifies their threat and transforms this conflict into an even grander drama. At the same time, while its danger remains real, the sea is frequently depicted in ancient literature as a vanquished foe (for example, *KTU*² 1.2 iv.18–30; 1.3 iii.38–42; Ps 74:13–14). Thus, even as the simile magnifies the menace of these nations, it hints already at their ultimate defeat, as described explicitly in the next couplet. Even so, the reader or hearer does not forget their comparability to the powerful and dangerous sea, which makes their subsequent characterization as "chaff" (*mōṣ*) and "tumbleweeds" (*gilgal*)[24] before YHWH's rebuke even more striking (v. 13). Through this image, then, Isaiah offers his audience a meaningful way to conceptualize the complexity of their national crisis, at which they could not have arrived by other means.

It has become axiomatic in recent work to minimize the traditional distinction between similes such as those in Isa 17:12, which are marked by comparative terms (for example, "like" or "as" in English), and metaphors, which are not so marked.[25] To be sure, the conceptual processes necessary to make sense of these devices are nearly

---

[21] On the soundplay in this verse, see Alonso Schökel, "Isaiah," 171.

[22] See Bernard F. Batto, *Slaying the Dragon: Mythmaking in the Biblical Tradition* (Louisville: Westminster John Knox, 1992); John Day, *God's Conflict with the Dragon and the Sea: Echoes of a Canaanite Myth in the Old Testament* (University of Cambridge Oriental Publications 35; New York: Cambridge University Press, 1985).

[23] See Brown, *Seeing the Psalms*, 113–18.

[24] See Wildberger, *Isa 13–27*, 200–1; the precise nuance of *gilgal* here and in Ps 83:14 (Eng. 83:13) is uncertain.

[25] For example, Berlin, *Dynamics*, 101; Brown, *Seeing the Psalms*, 7–8; Lakoff and Turner, *More Than Cool Reason*, 111–28, 133.

identical, so it makes sense not to distinguish them at the cognitive-linguistic level. One may appropriately speak of "metaphor" as a broad category that includes both types. The formal difference should not simply be ignored, however, especially since First Isaiah displays a strong preference for similes—typically marked by k- or ka'ăšer ("like, even as")—over metaphors.[26] At the same time, it is difficult to reach any firm conclusions about the poetic effects of this difference. Typically, although not always, similes directly identify both the source and the target and demarcate explicit connections between them, whereas a metaphor may be implicitly evoked without naming the source. Lakoff and Turner suggest that similes "make a weaker claim" than metaphors, but even that is not always apparent.[27] Isaiah sometimes juxtaposes similes and metaphors with no discernible rationale (for example, Isa 18:4–6). In light of these considerations, I generally note whether a particular text involves a simile or a metaphor in my discussion of figurative language, but I make no further claims based on this distinction.[28]

This discussion of Isa 17:12 has highlighted two additional features of my approach, which distinguish this treatment from much other work on Isaianic imagery. First, it is explicitly historicist in orientation. Throughout this study, my position has been that reading an ancient poetic corpus such as First Isaiah necessarily demands attention to historical matters, and that necessity is perhaps nowhere more the case than with poetic imagery.[29] As noted earlier, the success of an image—that is, its capacity to evoke the desired imaginative response on the part of a reader or hearer—depends on its audience's possession of certain shared knowledge or experience. Darr refers to such knowledge or experience as an audience's "associated commonplaces," which she understands to be "culturally conditioned" and thus a matter for historical reconstruction.[30] In Isa 17:12, for instance,

---

[26] Alonso Schökel, "Isaiah," 171. On the grammatical structure of similes in prophetic poetry, see Terry L. Brensinger, *Simile and Prophetic Language in the Old Testament* (Mellen Biblical Press 43; Lewiston, NY: Edwin Mellen, 1996), 152–74; Petersen and Richards, *Interpreting Hebrew Poetry*, 51.
[27] Lakoff and Turner, *More Than Cool Reason*, 133.
[28] Brensinger (*Simile*, 3–4) and Petersen and Richards (*Interpreting Hebrew Poetry*, 50) take a similar approach.
[29] Friedman, "Imagery," 563.
[30] Darr, *Isaiah's Vision*, 41–2; see further Brown, *Seeing the Psalms*, 14; Lowth, *Lectures*, 47–8; Strawn, "Imagery," 308.

the prophet assumes that his audience associates the sea with chaos and threat—a safe assumption with regard to the ancient Near East in the first millennium BCE, but less so for other cultural contexts. In many cases, we have access to considerable textual, archaeological, and iconographic evidence for reconstructing the associated commonplaces of the first readers or hearers of biblical poetry.[31]

Secondly, my approach takes seriously the fact that the images in question are *poetic* images.[32] While the point may seem obvious, many recent treatments of biblical images pay surprisingly little attention to it. Instead, they focus almost exclusively on the symbolic import of the imagery in its own right or the relationships among images from different poems.[33] Such matters are an integral part of how images mean, but so too are the construction and context of images within the poems in which they occur. Poetic images live, move, and have their being within the lined discourse of verse, and the way that an image unfolds across or is contained within these lines greatly impacts the reader or hearer's reception of the image. The concurrence of an image with other features of poetic style, such as soundplay, may further enhance its effectiveness. However inherently interesting and delightful a particular image might be on its own terms, its *raison d'être* is finally its structural, stylistic, and rhetorical functions within the larger poem.[34]

On surveying the poetry of Isaiah, one is truly impressed by the "diversity" of its imagery, to use Lowth's term. The source domains include, among others, architecture (Isa 2:15; 28:16–17; 30:13); alcoholic beverages (Isa 1:22; 19:14; 28:7–8); fire (Isa 5:24; 9:19 [Eng. 9:18]; 10:16–17); the human body (Isa 1:5–6; 29:10; 30:27–28); pottery (Isa 29:16; 30:14); ships (Isa 2:16; 18:1; 23:1–2, 14); and water (Isa 8:6–7; 17:12; 28:2, 17).[35] Instead of focusing on this

---

[31] Several recent works serve as judicious models for the creative use of such data; see, for example, Brown, *Seeing the Psalms*; F. W. Dobbs-Allsopp, "Psalm 133: A (Close) Reading," *Journal of Hebrew Scriptures* 8 (2008): DOI:10.5508/jhs.2008. v8.a20, <http://www.jhsonline.org/Articles/article_97.pdf> (accessed 10 November 2014); Strawn, *Lion*.

[32] On poetic metaphor as a species of cognitive metaphor, see Lakoff and Turner, *More Than Cool Reason*, 67–80.

[33] This is especially true of many essays in Everson and Kim (eds.), *The Desert Will Bloom*.

[34] Friedman, "Imagery," 564.

[35] Note the surveys of Quinn-Miscall, *Reading Isaiah*, 66–7; Wildberger, *Isa 28–39*, 675–9; for the larger prophetic corpus, see Brensinger, *Simile*, 27–53.

diversity, however, the following discussion concentrates on two especially prominent sets of Isaianic images, drawn from the domains of agriculture and the animal world. The variety within these groups sufficiently illustrates the complexity with which this poet crafts and uses images. This approach also makes it possible to discuss with greater clarity the nuances of particular images, by comparison to similar ones in other contexts, and to identify recurring underlying metaphors. A number of intertextual connections become apparent from a survey of these domains; indeed, it may be that some examples are specifically developed with reference to others, although one should not assume that these links reflect some kind of organized lexicon of images in the poet's mind.[36] Finally, by virtue of their frequent occurrence, the use of these kinds of images becomes a characteristic feature of Isaiah's poetic style that merits attention.

AGRICULTURAL IMAGERY

Ancient Judah was an agrarian society. Philip J. King and Lawrence E. Stager note that

> Agriculture, the basis of the economy in ancient Israel, influenced practically every facet of daily life, especially the religious economic, legal, and social spheres. To describe the various aspects of daily life, biblical texts refer constantly to agriculture in the literal sense, and almost as often to agriculture in the figurative, allegorical, or symbolic sense.[37]

As indicated by the Gezer calendar, agricultural activity was ongoing throughout the year.[38] Isaiah exploits both the variety of crops cultivated in the Levant and the different stages of their production in crafting his images, as best suits the particular context. In the following section, I first discuss localized agricultural images within poems, including images drawing on the joy that accompanied successful crop production (Isa 9:2 [Eng. 9:3]; 16:8–10) and those associating

---

[36] For the limits of this approach to images, which he terms "cluster criticism," see Friedman, "Imagery," 561–3.
[37] King and Stager, *Life in Biblical Israel*, 85.
[38] Oded Borowski, *Agriculture in Iron Age Israel* (Winona Lake, Ind.: Eisenbrauns, 1987; repr., Boston: American Schools of Oriental Research, 2002), 31–44.

148   Reading the Poetry of First Isaiah

agriculture with divine judgment (Isa 5:10; 17:4–6; 18:4–6). The discussion then turns to two short poems that consist entirely of extended agricultural images (Isa 5:1–7; 28:23–29).[39]

The Joy of the Harvest

In an agricultural economy, the quality of life—if not survival itself—depends on plentiful harvests. As a result, successful harvests in ancient Israel were occasions for great joy and festivity, accompanied by dancing, shouting, and wine drinking (Judg 9:27; 21:19–21; Ps 4:8 [Eng. 4:7]; Ruth 3:7). In fact, two of the three major religious festivals of ancient Israel—the Feasts of Weeks and Booths—were originally harvest celebrations.[40] In Isa 9:2 (Eng. 9:3), the prophet appeals to this characteristic joyousness to represent the nation's reaction to the coronation of a new king:

> hirbîtā haggîlâ[41]
> higdaltā haśśimḥâ
> śāmĕḥû lĕpānêkā kĕśimḥat baqqāṣîr
> ka'ăšer yāgîlû bĕhallĕqām šālāl
>
> You have multiplied gladness;
>   you have increased joy.
> They rejoice before you as with joy at the harvest,
>   even as they are glad when they divide plunder.

---

[39] Although this section focuses on imagery that involves the intentional cultivation of fruits and vegetables, one should also note the number of plant images more generally in First Isaiah (for example, Isa 6:13; 10:33–11:1; 15:6); see Nielsen, *Hope for a Tree*; Patricia K. Tull, "Persistent Vegetative States: People as Plants and Plants as People in Isaiah," in *The Desert Will Bloom: Poetic Visions in Isaiah* (eds. A. Joseph Everson and Hyun Chul Paul Kim; Atlanta: Society of Biblical Literature, 2009), 17–34.

[40] Patrick D. Miller, *The Religion of Ancient Israel* (Library of Ancient Israel; Louisville: Westminster John Knox, 2000), 80, 83–5.

[41] MT has haggôy ("the nation") followed by lō' (K, "not") or lô (Q, "to him"). Q makes some sense, and lō'/lô interchange is well attested (for example, Exod 21:8; Ps 100:3; see BDB, 520). Most commentators, however, read haggîlâ, "gladness" (Gray, *Isa I–XXVII*, 175; Wildberger, *Isa 1–12*, 386). Although not without detractors (for example, de Waard, *Handbook*, 43), the proposal requires little change to the consonantal text. It enhances the euphony of the couplet—note the repetition of initial h-, medial -i-, and final -ā sounds—and echoes the parallelism of śāmaḥ and gîl in the following lines.

Imagery and Metaphor 149

In a common technique in this corpus (for example, Isa 1:8; 18:4; 30:17), Isaiah uses parallelism to join multiple discrete similes.[42] The joy accompanying the harvest is paired with the exuberance of dividing spoils from battle (see also Judg 5:7; 1 Sam 30:16; Ps 119:162). To borrow a phrase from Lakoff and Turner, the combination of different metaphors with the same target achieves a "relentlessness of... characterization," forcing the audience to maintain focus on the target concept and explore it from multiple angles.[43] In this case, the similes occur near the beginning of the poem, before the reason for this joy is identified, and the advance comparison to multiple, incredibly happy occasions arouses anticipation on the part of the audience. At the same time, the military background of the second image foreshadows the announcement in the following verses of the end to Judah's oppression by Assyria, portrayed metonymically with a pair of references to military gear in v. 4 (Eng. 9:5).

Conversely, the sorrow over a failed harvest is exacerbated by the memory of the joy that typically accompanies the harvest, as seen in Isa 16:8–10. In this text, the prophet describes the ruin of Moab's vineyards, contrasting their former fecundity with their present desiccation (see also Isa 32:10–13). By evoking the festivity that normally accompanies the vintage, he heightens the tone of lamentation in this section of the poem; similarly, he underscores the loss of grape production through the ironic use of terms with generally positive connotations in agricultural contexts. Like the rest of this difficult oracle, these verses flaunt ambiguity and wordplay, as the poet resists providing any information about the nature of the Moabite catastrophe beyond suggestive hints.[44]

[8] *kî šadmôt ḥešbôn 'umlāl*[45]
 gepen śibmâ

---

[42] On this technique in the prophets more generally, see Brensinger, *Simile*, 84–98.
[43] Lakoff and Turner, *More than Cool Reason*, 33.
[44] J. Blake Couey, "Evoking and Evading: The Poetic Presentation of the Moabite Catastrophe in Isaiah 15–16," in *Concerning the Nations: Essays on the Oracles Against the Nations in Isaiah, Jeremiah, and Ezekiel* (eds. Andrew Mein, Else K. Holt, and Hyun Chul Paul Kim; LHBOTS 612; New York: Bloomsbury T&T Clark, 2015), 19–31.
[45] The masculine singular verb *'umlāl* ("wither") does not agree with the feminine plural *šadmôt* ("shoots"); 1QIsa^a has a feminine singular verb (*'mllh*). On the basis of Tg., several commentators restore a form of *šādad* (*pu'al*, "to be destroyed") in the first line and take *'umlāl* with the next, including Clements, *Isa 1–39*, 155; Wilhelm Rudolph, "Jesaja xv–xvi," in *Hebrew and Semitic Studies Presented to Godfrey Rolles*

baʿălê gôyīm
hālĕmû śĕrûqqêhā
ʿad-yaʿzēr nāgāʿû
tāʿû midbār
šĕlūḥôtêhā niṭṭĕšû
ʿābĕrû yām
[9] ʿal-kēn ʾebkeh bibkî yaʿzēr
gepen śibmâ
ʾărawwāyek[46] dimʿātî
ḥešbôn wĕʾelʿālēh
kî ʿal-qêṣēk wĕʿal-qĕṣîrēk
hêdād nāpal
[10] wĕneʾĕsap śimḥâ wāgîl min-hakkarmel
ûbakkĕrāmîm lōʾ yĕrunnān lōʾ yĕrōʿāʿ
yayin bayqābîm lōʾ-yidrōk haddōrēk[47]
hêdād hišbattî[48]

[8] Surely, the shoots[49] of Heshbon wither,
the vines of Sibmah;

Driver (eds. D. Winton Thomas and W. D. McHardy; Oxford: Clarendon, 1964), 137; Wildberger, *Isa 13-27*, 112. It is conceivable that such a verb could have dropped through parablepsis, given the similar consonants of *šadmôt*. On the other hand, *šĕdēmôt* also occurs with a masculine singular verb in Hab 3:17 (see GKC §145u). This similar case suggests that one might best follow MT, which has the advantage of preserving the unbalanced lines, a common feature throughout the poem.

[46] For MT ʾărayyāwek, most critics read ʾărawwāyek ("I will drench you") from √rwh (Clements, *Isa 1-39*, 156; Gray, *Isa I-XXVII*, 294; Wildberger, *Isa 13-27*, 112). 1QIsaᵃ reads ʾrzyk ("your cedars"), with w/z interchange.

[47] LXX has no match for MT's *haddōrēk* ("the treader"), which leads some commentators to delete it as a dittograph (Gray, *Isa I-XXVII*, 295; Wildberger, *Isa 13-27*, 112). It seems more likely that LXX simply offers a smoother rendering of the cognate construction (Jones, *Howling over Moab*, 213; see also Isa 28:4 LXX).

[48] For MT hišbattî ("I have ended"), LXX has a third-person verb (*pepautai*, "has ceased"), possibly reflecting an underlying *hošbat* ("has been made to cease"). Many commentators prefer this reading, such as Gray, *Isa I-XXVII*, 294-5; Rudolph, "Jesaja xv-xvi," 137; Wildberger, *Isa 13-27*, 112. Although the shift to first-person speech is sudden, it is not uncommon in prophetic literature, and a similar shift occurs earlier in the poem in 15:9. In support of MT, see Childs, *Isaiah*, 130; Jones, *Howling over Moab*, 213.

[49] Traditionally, *šadmôt* has been taken to denote the land on which vineyards are planted (so already LXX; Syr.) or, more recently, agricultural terraces: Borowski, *Agriculture*, 17-18; Carey Ellen Walsh, *The Fruit of the Vine: Viticulture in Ancient Israel* (HSM 60; Winona Lake, Ind.: Eisenbrauns, 2000), 95-6; Wildberger, *Isa 13-27*, 149. Nicholas Wyatt has argued that it refers to part of the vine—likely the shoots that produce grapes—which better fits the Ug. and most biblical occurrences of the term:

> rulers of the nations
> > its choice vines hammered.
>
> They reached as far as Jazer,
> > wandered the desert.
>
> Its tendrils spread out,
> > crossed the sea.
>
> [9] Therefore I weep with the weeping of Jazer
> > for the vines of Sibmah.
>
> I will water you with my tears,
> > Heshbon and Elealeh,
>
> for over your ripe fruit and your harvest,
> > the shout has fallen.
>
> [10] And joy and gladness have been harvested from the orchard,
> > and in their vineyards one does not exult nor shout.
>
> The treader does not tread wine in the vats;
> > the shout I have ended.

Several commentators take these verses as "an allegorical description of the demise of the people as a ruined vineyard," in Sweeney's words.[50] While not impossible, this reading seems forced, influenced no doubt by Isa 5:1-7. The destruction of agricultural industries, including vineyards, was standard military practice in the ancient Near East.[51] There is little reason not to take literally the references to crop destruction.

"A New Look at Ugaritic *šdmt*," *JSS* 37 (1992): 149-53; see *KTU*² 1.2 i.43; 1.23 9-11; Deut 32:32; 2 Kgs 23:4; Isa 37:27; and other texts. I have followed his lead, in light of the parallelism with *gepen*, "vines." See also Jones, *Howling over Moab*, 210-11; Thomas G. Smothers, "Isaiah 15-16," in *Forming Prophetic Literature: Essays on Isaiah and the Twelve in Honor of John D. W. Watts* (eds. James W. Watts and Paul R. House; JSOTSup 235; Sheffield: Sheffield Academic, 1996), 72-3.

[50] Sweeney, *Isa 1-39*, 244; see also Clements, *Isa 1-39*, 155; Kaiser, *Isa 13-39*, 73; Miscall, *Isaiah*, 54.

[51] Steven W. Cole, "The Destruction of Orchards in Assyrian Warfare," in *Assyria 1995: Proceedings of the 10th Anniversary Symposium of the Neo-Assyrian Text Corpus Project, Helsinki, September 7-11, 1995* (eds. S. Parpola and R. M. Whiting; Helsinki: Neo-Assyrian Text Corpus Project, 1997), 29-40; Jeremy D. Smoak, "Building Houses and Planting Vineyards: The Early Inner-Biblical Discourse on an Ancient Israelite Wartime Curse," *JBL* 127 (2008): 21-3; Walsh, *Fruit*, 123-6; Jacob L. Wright, "Warfare and Wanton Destruction: A Reexamination of Deuteronomy 20:19-20 in Relation to Ancient Siegecraft," *JBL* 127 (2008): 423-58. Jones even suggests—albeit unconvincingly—that the event to which Isa 15-16 responds was a targeted raid on Moab's fields and vineyards, not a full-scale invasion (*Howling over Moab*, 247-53).

Verse 8 opens with an unbalanced couplet, followed by three short couplets with two-word lines. The verb ʾāmal ("to wither") suggests that lack of water has caused the demise of the vineyards, which calls into question the earlier impression that Moab has experienced military defeat in Isa 15:1 and 16:4 and thereby maintains the poem's ambiguity about the cause of Moab's suffering.[52] The second couplet sustains the uncertainty by allowing multiple readings, depending on whether one takes baʿălê gôyīm ("rulers of nations") as the subject and śĕrûqqêhā ("its choice vines") as the object or vice versa. If the former, the lines describe the destruction of the Moabite vineyards by the rulers of unidentified nations.[53] If the latter, they suggest that these rulers used to get drunk on wine from Moabite grapes, a nod to their popularity as an international export.[54] In support of this reading, note the use of the verb hālam ("to hammer") with reference to drunkenness in Isa 28:1; Prov 23:35.[55] Although most commentators insist on one reading over the other, intentional polysemy seems likely.[56] A reference to the vines' intoxicating quality is more contextually appropriate, while the attribution of their demise to baʿălê gôyīm is a possibility at which the couplet hints but leaves in the background. The final two couplets hyperbolically chart the once-extensive spread of the vines, locating them in such barren locales as the Arabian Desert (midbār) and the Dead Sea (yām). The verbs impart a degree of agency to the vines that borders on personification, and tāʿâ ("to wander") may be another instance of double entendre in light of Isa 28:7, in which it describes the staggering of drunkards.

In v. 9, a poetic voice expresses sorrow over Moab's plight.[57] The poetry cleverly depicts the failed harvest with language that recalls

---

[52] Gray, Isa I–XXVII, 292; Wildberger, Isa 13–27, 148; for the use of ʾāmal, see Isa 24:4, 7; Joel 1:10, 12; Nah 1:4.
[53] Childs, Isaiah, 130; Smothers, "Isa 15–16," 72; Sweeney, Isa 1–39, 244.
[54] Gray, Isa I–XXVII, 292; Rudolph, "Jesaja xv–xvi," 137; Wildberger, Isa 13–27, 112.
[55] Gray, Isa I–XXVII, 292; Wildberger, Isa 13–27, 112. Compare the use of "hammered" or "smashed" as idioms for drunkenness in colloquial North American and British English.
[56] Jones's suggestion that the double entendre extends through the end of v. 8 is less persuasive (Howling over Moab, 211, 266–7).
[57] Although almost all commentators assume it to be the voice of the poet/prophet (for example, Gray, Isa I–XXVII, 292; Wildberger, Isa 13–39, 149), the identity of the speaker is uncertain (Quinn-Miscall, Reading Isaiah, 161; Tull, Isa 1–39, 263). This apparent sympathy stands in some tension with the decidedly unsympathetic attitude toward Moab in vv. 6–7, raising the possibility that the lament in vv. 9–11 is sarcastic

more fruitful agricultural endeavors, heightening the sense of disappointment. With overstated grief, the speaker declares to the cities of Heshbon and Elealeh, "I will water you (*'ărawwāyek*) with my tears." Elsewhere in the Bible, the verb *rāwâ* describes the watering of fields or gardens by rain (Isa 55:10; Ps 65:11 [Eng. 65:10]). Its use here provides an ironic counterpoint to *'āmal* ("wither") in the previous verse. Much too late, the speaker's copious tears over the failed harvest offer the vineyard the water that it has lacked.[58] In the next couplet, the ambiguity of *hêdād* ("shout") creates further double entendre. Elsewhere, it denotes the joyful shout associated with the harvest (Jer 25:30; 48:33). This sense fits perfectly here and is clearly meant in the following verse. The verb *nāpal* ("fall"), then, would denote the cessation of joyful sounds because of the failed harvest, a point made unambiguously in v. 10.[59] On the other hand, *hêdād* may also refer to the shout of invaders (Jer 51:14; see also Jer 25:30) and *nāpal* to a military attack (Josh 11:7; Job 1:15).[60] Once again, the poet appears to have created a wordplay that, at the surface, deals with the ruined vintage and, below the surface, hints at a military incursion that may have destroyed Moab's vineyards.[61]

Verse 10 depicts a state of silence that stands in contrast not only to the expected jubilation but also to the lamentation described earlier.[62]

(see Blenkinsopp, *Isa 1–39*, 298–9; Hayes and Irvine, *Isaiah*, 244–5; Jones, *Howling over Moab*, 267–70).

[58] Jones thinks that the overstatement of using *rāwâ* with reference to tears indicates the poet's sarcasm (*Howling over Moab*, 267–8). Given the context, however, the agricultural associations of the term seem at least as relevant and support an ironic reading of the poem just as well.

[59] Compare the use of *nāpal* with *dābār* ("word") in Josh 21:45; 1 Kgs 8:56; 2 Kgs 10:10 or *yāmîm* ("days") in Num 6:12. For this reading, see Blenkinsopp, *Isa 1–39*, 294; Childs, *Isaiah*, 130; NIV; NRSV.

[60] See Shemaryahu Talmon, "Prophetic Rhetoric and Agricultural Metaphora," in *Storia e tradizioni di Israele: Scritti in onore di J. Alberto Soggin* (eds. Daniele Garrone and Felice Israel; Brescia, Italy: Paideia, 1991), 277; Wildberger, *Isa 13–27*, 148–9.

[61] Wildberger woodenly insists that "v. 9b can *only* mean that enemies have broken into the Moabite domain" (*Isa 13–27*, 148–9, emphasis added). Other interpreters allow for greater ambiguity (Gray, *Isa I–XXVII*, 293; Jones, *Howling over Moab*, 213). Jeremiah 48:33, part of an extensive reworking of Isa 15–16, expands Isa 16:10 by adding the line *hêdād lō' hêdād* ("the shout is not a shout"), presumably meaning that the shouts heard in the vineyard are not the expected shouts of joy. The use of *gîl* ("scream") in Job 3:22 is a similar case of polysemy; see C. L. Seow, *Job 1–21: Interpretation and Commentary* (Illuminations; Grand Rapids: Eerdmans, 2013), 367–8.

[62] Jones, *Howling over Moab*, 269; Kaiser, *Isa 13–39*, 74.

The lines of the first couplet are noticeably longer than the preceding ones, at least in part because of the use of word-pairs within lines (*śimḥâ wāgîl*, "joy and gladness" in v. 10aα; *lōʾ yĕrunnān lōʾ yĕrōʿāʿ*, "does not exult, does not shout" in v. 10aβ); in both cases, the pair accentuates the total absence of the emotions or sounds in question. The verb *ʾāsap* ("to gather") often refers to the act of harvest in biblical literature (Exod 23:10, 16; Deut 11:14; Isa 17:5; see also Gezer Calendar, line 1). Like other instances of agricultural terminology in these verses, it ironically calls attention to the lack of grapes to harvest.[63] The theme of absence also pervades the second couplet. Here, the absent object is no longer the celebration of the harvest but the product of the harvest, wine—itself a source of considerable joy in the ancient world (Judg 9:13; Ps 104:15; Qoh 9:7). The cognate construction *lōʾ-yidrōk haddōrēk* ("the treader does not tread") yields another long line, which opens a strikingly unbalanced couplet, even for a poem with a high concentration of such couplets. The jarring imbalance amplifies the sense of the final verb *hišbattî* ("I have ended"), as the couplet, like the expected festivities, seems to end prematurely. In various ways, then, the poet explicitly and suggestively conjures the memory of successful grape harvests to heighten the sense of loss in describing Moab's failed vineyards in Isa 16:8–10.

Agriculture and Judgment

Reflecting the centrality of agriculture to ancient life, many prophetic texts in the Hebrew Bible represent divine judgment in terms of its effects on crop production, as in the example just discussed. Another case is Isa 5:10, which threatens that huge tracts of arable land will produce miniscule yields. This threat is a variation on a common biblical futility curse, the basic statement of which can be found in Deut 28:30: "A vineyard you will plant, but you will not partake of it" (see also Lev 26:16; Deut 28:39). Variations on the curse, including its reversal, appear frequently in prophetic literature (for example, Isa 65:21; Jer 29:5; Amos 5:11).[64] Isaiah augments the vague language of the curse with specific measurements to concretize

---

[63] Wildberger, *Isa 13–27*, 150.
[64] Hillers, *Treaty Curses*, 28–9; Smoak, "Building Houses," 19–35.

Imagery and Metaphor 155

the disproportionality between labor and production (see also Hag 2:16).[65] In both lines of the couplet, these measurements suggest a ten-to-one reduction. The first line explicitly uses the numbers "ten" (*'ăśeret*) and "one" (*'eḥāt*), while the second line contrasts the units of measure *homer* and *ephah*, the former of which contained ten of the latter according to Ezek 45:11. Elsewhere in the Bible, this ratio stereotypically represents an irrecoverable loss (Isa 6:13; Amos 5:3). Such diminished productivity seems a fitting punishment for the rapacious acquisition of land by a few powerful citizens to augment their wealth, as detailed in previous verses in the oracle (Isa 5:8–9).

Perhaps related to portrayals of failed harvests as the results of divine punishment, several texts in First Isaiah depict judgment or destruction—usually of a military nature—with imagery from the realm of agriculture.[66] To use Lakoff and Turner's terms, they are different expressions of a basic underlying metaphor, which one might call "divine judgments are harvests." Several of these texts extend the metaphor by including other stages of the agricultural process that either precede or follow the harvest. In Isa 17:4–6, the prophet compares the decimation of Israel following its conquest by Assyria to the near emptiness of a harvested field or olive tree:

[4] *wĕhāyâ bayyôm hahû'*
yiddal kĕbôd ya'ăqōb
ûmišman bĕśārô yērāzeh
[5] *wĕhāyâ ke'ĕsōp qōṣēr*[67] *qāmâ*
ûzĕrō'ô šibbŏlîm yiqṣôr
wĕhāyâ kimlaqqēṭ šibbŏlîm

---

[65] "Ten yoke of a vineyard" designates the amount of land that ten pairs of oxen could plow in one day, generally taken to equal about ten acres; similarly, "a *homer* of seed" refers to the amount of land that could be sown with that amount (100–200 liters). A *bath* is variously valued between 24 and 32.5 liters, while an *ephah* equals 15–20 liters. There is some disagreement about the precise numbers; see King and Stager, *Life in Biblical Israel*, 200; Marvin A. Powell, "Weights and Measures," in *ABD* 6, 901–2; Williamson, *Isa 1–5*, 355–6.

[66] Tull, "Persistent Vegetative States," 24–6. Similar metaphors are common throughout prophetic literature, for example, Jer 51:2; Mic 3:12; see John F. Healy, "Ancient Agriculture and the Hebrew Bible: with Special Reference to Isaiah XXVIII 23–29," in *Prophets, Worship, and Theodicy* (ed. A. S. van der Woude, OTS 23, Leiden: Brill, 1984), 113.

[67] MT *ke'ĕsōp qāṣîr qāmâ* ("as when gathering a harvest, standing grain") is awkward, since the verb has two redundant objects but no subject. As a result, many commentators repoint *qāṣîr* as a participle *qōṣēr*, "harvester," including Blenkinsopp, *Isa 1–39*, 302; Gray, *Isa I–XXVII*, 309; Kaiser, *Isa 13–39*, 78.

bĕ'ēmeq rĕpā'îm
[6] wĕniš'ar-bô 'ôlēlōt
kĕnōqep zayit
šnayim šĕlōšâ gargĕrîm bĕrō'š 'āmîr
'arbā'â ḥămiššâ bis'îpê happōrîyâ[68]
nĕ'ūm yhwh 'ĕlōhê yiśrā'ēl

[4] And it will happen on that day:
The weight of Jacob will be diminished,
and the fat of his flesh will come to nothing.
[5] And it will be as when a harvester gathers standing grain,
and with his arm harvests the ears.
And it will be as when one gleans ears of corn
in the Valley of Rephaim.
[6] And there will remain in it only gleanings,
as when one strikes an olive tree:
two or three ripe olives at the head of a high limb,
four or five on the branches of the fruit tree.
An oracle of YHWH, God of Israel.

The domain or details of the imagery shift four times in these verses, but the frame wĕhāyâ (k-) ("and it will be [as]")/wĕniš'ar... k- ("and there will remain, even as") holds the complex together. The initial metaphor (v. 4), which has no agricultural connections, compares the northern kingdom's loss of territory and population to the emaciation of an obese person.[69] In v. 5a, the imagery switches to the realm of cereal production, depicting a field of standing grain in the process of being reduced to stubble. References to gleaning in the next couplet evoke the aftermath of the harvest, when the field contains at most a few scattered clusters of grain to be claimed by the socially destitute (see also Lev 19:9–10; 23:22; Ruth 2:16). The agricultural product changes to olives in v. 6, possibly triggered by the fact that šibbŏlîm ("ears") in v. 5 can also refer to branches of an olive tree (Zech 4:12). The poet imagines an olive tree that has been struck—perhaps a hint

[68] The pronominal suffix on MT bis'îpêhā ("in its branches") interrupts the construct chain, and the antecedent of the feminine pronoun is unclear. The simplest solution is to redivide the phrase as bis'îpê happōrîyâ, "the branches of the fruit tree" (see BHS; Gray, Isa I–XXVII, 309; Kaiser, Isa 13–39, 78).

[69] Although weight loss is generally regarded positively in contemporary Western culture, thinness often has negative connotations in the HB (for example, Gen 41:1–7). One finds striking visual depictions of malnourished persons, with emaciated bodies and visible ribs, in ancient Near Eastern art (ANEP, 30, fig. 102).

at the violence of Israel's conquest—to knock down its fruit (see also Deut 24:20). The number of olives left in its branches is insignificant, as suggested by the numerical sequences "two or three" and "four or five."[70] As in Isa 5:10, the numbers serve a concretizing function, although the equivocation here suggests that a precise count is unimportant. In Isa 5:10, the numbers indicated agriculture failure, whereas now they suggest a successful harvest, in which only a small amount of fruit remains uncollected; in both cases, the image conveys the effectiveness of Yhwh's judgment.

In Isa 18:4-6, Isaiah uses yet another agricultural activity and commodity, the pruning of grapevines, as a metaphor for divine judgment. These verses also contain a complex cluster of figures, as the prophet shifts images with each new verse.[71] The successive images become progressively longer—a single line each in v. 4, a couplet in v. 5, and a pair of couplets of v. 6—although none is elaborately developed:

[4] *kî kōh ʾāmar yhwh ʾēlay*
ʾešqŏṭâ wěʾabbîṭâ bimkônî
kěḥōm ṣaḥ ʿălê-ʾôr
kěʿāb ṭal běyôm[72] *qāṣîr*
[5] *kî-lipnê qāṣîr kětām-peraḥ*
ûbōser gōmēl yihyeh niṣṣâ
wěkārat hazzalzallîm bammazmērôt
wěʾet-hanněṭîšôt hēsîr hētaz
[6] *yēʿāzěbû yaḥdāw lěʿêṭ hārîm*
ûlěbehěmat hāʾāreṣ
wěqāṣ ʿālāyw hāʿayiṭ
wěkol-behěmat hāʾāreṣ ʿālāyw teḥěrāp

---

[70] On numerical sequences in biblical and ancient Near Eastern poetry, see Wolfgang M. W. Roth, "The Numerical Sequence x/x + 1 in the Old Testament," *VT* 12 (1962): 300–11; Watson, *CHP*, 144–9.
[71] Wildberger, *Isa 13–27*, 221.
[72] 1QIsa^a, MT^A, MT^L, and Tg. read *ḥōm* ("heat") here; other Heb. mss., LXX, Syr., and Vulg. read *yôm* ("day"). Wildberger prefers *yôm* because he thinks the repetition of *ḥōm* is unlikely (*Isa 13–27*, 208). His stylistic argument is not persuasive; however, a scenario in which a scribe mistakenly read *ḥōm* under the influence of the preceding line—especially if the *y* and *w* of *yôm* were written closely together—does seems more likely than a scenario in which a scribe mistook a word that had just occurred for a different one (Lowth, *Isaiah*, 239).

158   Reading the Poetry of First Isaiah

[4] For thus YHWH said to me:
I will passively watch in my abode,
like shimmering⁷³ heat above the light,
like a dew cloud on the day of the harvest.
[5] For before the harvest, when flowering is complete,
and blossoms become ripening grapes,
one will cut the shoots⁷⁴ with pruning knives,
and the sprouts one will remove, tear away.
[6] And they will be abandoned together for the vultures of the mountain,
and for the beasts of the field.
And the vultures will pass the winter upon it,
and all the beasts of the field will pass the summer upon it.

Within the context of the Isa 18, these verses apparently comprise a message delivered to the Cushites by unnamed messengers (Isa 18:2), but the real audience suggested by the poem is the Judahite officials who "overhear" the message. Isaiah wishes to discourage them from forming an alliance with the Cushites in resistance to Assyrian authority, in the days leading up to the political crisis of either 711 (see Isa 20) or 701 BCE.⁷⁵

In v. 4a, the prophet announces that YHWH will "passively watch" (ʾešqŏṭâ wĕʾabbîṭâ) the political machinations of the Cushites and Judahites. Verse 4b contains two similes that feature the images of "shimmering heat" (ḥōm ṣaḥ) and a "dew cloud" (ʿāb ṭal). Both

---

⁷³ Kaiser and Talmon, among others, read the supposed name of a summer month ṣḥ, on the basis of Arad 20.2 (Kaiser, *Isa 13–39*, 95; Talmon, "Prophetic Rhetoric," 273–4). None of the versions reads the name of a month here, however, and this name is not attested elsewhere, whereas the adjective ṣaḥ ("shimmering") occurs in Jer 4:11; Song 5:10 (Wildberger, *Isa 13–27*, 208). Further, the reading in Arad 20.2 has been widely challenged: see André Lemaire, "Note epigraphique sur la pseudo-attestation du mois 'ṣḥ,'" *VT* 23 (1973): 243–5; F. W. Dobbs-Allsopp et al., *Hebrew Inscriptions: Texts from the Biblical Period of the Monarchy with Concordance* (New Haven: Yale University Press, 2005), 43.

⁷⁴ MT zalzallîm is a *hapax*; for proposed derivations, see *HALOT*, 272; James E. Hoch, *Semitic Words in Egyptian Texts of the New Kingdom and Third Intermediate Period* (Princeton: Princeton University Press, 1994), 391; Lavik, *Tall and Smooth-Skinned*, 151; Wildberger, *Isa 13–27*, 221. Perhaps the most that one can say is that the term designates some part of a grapevine. Lavik and Wildberger assume that zalzallîm are not capable of bearing fruit, but the possibly related word salsillâ in Jer 6:9 seems to refer to a fruit-bearing vine. The term is one of several reduplicated words in the poem (ṣilṣal, v. 1; qawqāw, v. 2), and several interpreters note its phonological resonance with ṣilṣal (Clements, *Isa 1–39*, 165; Hayes and Irvine, *Isaiah*, 256; Lavik, *Tall and Smooth-Skinned*, 172).

⁷⁵ See the detailed discussion in Wildberger, *Isa 13–27*, 213, 216.

phenomena occur during summer, the former specifically during harvest (*qāṣîr*) according to Gen 8:22, which creates a link to the next line; this connection is even more explicit in textual witnesses that repeat *ḥōm* in both lines. Most likely, these images characterize the divine inactivity of v. 4a, in contrast to the bustle of human activity depicted in previous lines.[76] Shimmering heat and hovering mist both appear stationary, making them apt figures for the stillness with which God views world events. At the same time, they have powerful environmental effects.[77] This would be a novel use of these images in biblical literature, but the comparison is plausible. Alternatively, the similes may illustrate the transience of the world events that YHWH witnesses, which would resonate well with the Isaianic emphasis on the futility of human plans against the divine plan (Isa 8:10; 14:27; 30:1).[78] Imagery of dew in Hos 6:4 and 13:3 similarly exploits its ephemeral quality.[79] Different interpreters call attention to other salient qualities of heat or dew that might inform the comparison, such as height or constancy.[80] In short, these are rich images that resist narrow explanations.

The repetition of *qāṣîr* ("harvest) connects vv. 4–5, mitigating the abrupt shift of similes. The new image is one of pruning grapevines, likely the summer pruning (*zmr*) described in the Gezer Calendar.[81]

---

[76] See Brensinger, *Simile*, 142; Clements, *Isa 1–39*, 165; Kaiser, *Isa 13–39*, 95; Lavik, *Tall and Smooth-Skinned*, 136.

[77] Gray, *Isa I–XXVII*, 314–15; Tull, *Isa 1–39*, 316; Wildberger, *Isa 13–27*, 220–1.

[78] See Hayes and Irvine, *Isaiah*, 256; Lavik, *Tall and Smooth-Skinned*, 139–40.

[79] More often, dew imagery has positive connotations in the HB (for example, Deut 32:2; Hos 14:6 [Eng. 14:5]; Ps 133:3; see Dobbs-Allsopp, "Psalm 133," 14–15). In fact, Hos 6:4 and 13:3 are among the only biblical texts that use the image negatively; see Bernhard Oestreich, *Metaphors and Similes for Yahweh in Hosea 14:2–9: A Study of Hoseanic Pictorial Imagery* (Friedensauer Schriftenreihe: Reihe A, Theologie, 1; Frankfurt am Mang: Peter Lang, 1996), 160–82.

[80] Gray, *Isa I–XXVII*, 314–15; Kaiser, *Isa 13–39*, 95.

[81] See Kaiser, *Isa 13–39*, 95; Talmon, "Prophetic Rhetoric," 273; Walsh, *Fruit*, 37–8, 172–3; Wildberger, *Isa 13–27*, 221; see further Dobbs-Allsopp et al., *Hebrew Inscriptions*, 162–3. The Gezer Calendar places this pruning prior to the harvest of summer fruit, which suggests that *qāṣîr* refers to the grape harvest in v. 5a (Blenkinsopp, *Isa 1–39*, 318; Gray, *Isa I–XXVII*, 315). The more common Bibl. Heb. term for "vintage" is *bāṣîr* (Lev 26:5; Isa 32:10), but see Isa 16:9; Micah 7:1 for this sense with *qāṣîr*. Despite the reference to "pruning knives" (*mazmērôt*) in the verse, a number of interpreters insist that it refers to the total destruction of the vineyard (Gray, *Isa I–XXVII*, 315; Lavik, *Tall and Smooth-Skinned*, 167–9, 176–7; Quinn-Miscall, *Reading Isaiah*, 78). While it is possible that a pruning-knife would have been used for clearing vines, a more straightforward reading takes the reference to this instrument to mean that the verse depicts the act of pruning.

Although pruning ultimately serves a productive function, its inherently violent character, which the poem highlights, makes it an appropriate metaphor for military action. The detail that pruning takes place just as the vines yield "ripening grapes" (*bōser gōmēl*) suggests that Judah's political machinations will not come to fruition. The identity of the pruned vines has been a matter of some disagreement. Despite the popularity of alternative proposals, the Cushites are the most obvious referent.[82] Far from proving an effective ally, they will fall in battle, and their comparison to a defenseless plant indicates the ease with which they will be defeated. This reading suggests another possible connotation of the image: if the defeat of the Cushites is the pruning of the vineyard, then its harvest—likely Judah's own defeat—will follow.[83] The identity of the pruner is not immediately clear, as the verbs in v. 5 have an indefinite subject, and it may well not be a concern of the poet. Many commentators assume that Yhwh is the implied agent.[84] Instead, Assyria seems a more likely option, while Yhwh continues to observe quietly as described in v. 4.

Because *hanněṭîšôt* ("the sprouts") in v. 5 is the most likely subject of *yēʿāzĕbû* ("will be abandoned") in v. 6, the next couplet initially appears to extend the image, suggesting that the pruned vines will be thrown away and consumed by wild animals and birds. Several details immediately call this reading into question. Other biblical texts suggest that the prunings of grapevines were not simply discarded but burnt (Ezek 15:2–4; John 15:6). The term *ʿayiṭ* ("vulture"), moreover, usually refers to birds of prey (Gen 15:11; Jer 12:9), which would not normally eat foliage.[85] In a number of biblical texts, the pair "beasts of the earth/field" (*běhēmat hāʾāreṣ/haśśādeh*) and "birds of the sky" (*ʿôp haššāmayim*) refers to scavengers that devour corpses (Deut 28:26; 1 Sam 17:44, 46; Jer 15:3; 19:7).[86] Without warning, then, the

---

[82] See Seitz, *Isa 1–39*, 148 (although he thinks the text refers to events in the sixth century BCE); Wildberger, *Isa 13–27*, 218–19. Other suggestions include Assyria (Blenkinsopp, *Isa 1–39*, 311; Gray, *Isa I–XXVII*, 315); Judah (Childs, *Isaiah*, 138; Childs, *Isaiah and the Assyrian Crisis*, 45; Lavik, *Tall and Smooth-Skinned*, 182–5); and, presupposing an earlier date, Israel (Sweeney, *Isa 1–39*, 257).

[83] Suggested by J. J. M. Roberts (private communication).

[84] For example, Gray, *Isa I–XXVII*, 315; Wildberger, *Isa 13–27*, 222. If v. 5 continues the divine speech of v. 4, however, one would expect first-person verbs.

[85] Wildberger, *Isa 13–27*, 221–2.

[86] The *Stela of the Vultures*—a fragment from a third-millennium BCE limestone stele from Mesopotamia—graphically depicts vultures flying away from a battlefield with human heads and arms in their beaks and talons (*ANEP*, 95, fig. 301).

target of the metaphor has given way to its source, as the discarded vines become the bodies of Cushite soldiers killed in battle. The detail that the animals will spend two full seasons consuming the remains points to the enormity of their losses—a clear warning to Judah's leaders that the alliance under consideration will not protect them. Shemaryahu Talmon also notes that the references to "summer" (√$qyṣ$) and "winter" (√$ḥrp$), along with previous terms in vv. 4–5, evokes the fixed order of the annual cycle, suggesting that divine actions will unfold just as reliably, bringing the audience back to the images of divine constancy in v. 4.[87]

Extended Agricultural Images

The examples discussed to this point have all been relatively undeveloped images with primarily localized effects. While each plays a crucial role in its respective poem, it is finally only one among other literary features that contribute to the creation of poetic meaning. By contrast, short poems in Isa 5:1–7 and 28:23–29 are comprised entirely of extended agricultural metaphors. Whereas other such images in Isaiah focus, for the most part, on a single stage of the agricultural process, these poems impart figurative significance to the entire scope of the process, from the preparation of land to the processing of the crop. As a result, they contain a considerable amount of precise detail, including much rare, technical vocabulary, which may have contributed to their persuasiveness for an audience acquainted with agricultural techniques.[88]

The so-called "song of the vineyard" in Isa 5:1–7, an extended comparison between Israel and Judah and an unproductive vineyard, is one of the more highly regarded poems in Isaiah. It layers, in a complex fashion, agricultural imagery with courtroom language (v. 3), while also evoking the genre of the love song by using language such as *dôd* ("beloved") in v. 1. Gary Roye Williams argues that the successive twists of this poem continually thwart the interpretative expectations of the audience, thereby mimicking the "frustrated expectations" of Yʜᴡʜ, whose devotion and ultimate disappointment

---

[87] Talmon, "Prophetic Rhetoric," 274; note the successive terms *qāṣîr*, *hôm*, *qayiṣ*, and *ḥōrep* ("harvest," "heat," "summer," "winter") in Gen 8:22.
[88] Talmon, "Prophetic Rhetoric," 270–1; Walsh, *Fruit*, 91.

as the figurative vintner are central to the poem, despite the somewhat misleading title popularly given it.[89] The very choice of metaphors already suggests the degree of Yʜᴡʜ's investment in the people, as grapevines require up to three or four years of care before bearing fruit.[90] Along with the obvious tasks required for cultivation, such as hoeing and the removal of stones, three details indicate that the vintner spares no expense in providing for the vineyard. First, its site is a superior location, "a very fertile hill" (v. 1).[91] The pleasing effects of the consonance and rhyme in the phrase *běqeren ben-šāmen* (literally, "in a horn, the son of fatness") underscore the salutary quality of this location. Secondly, "choice vines" (*śōrēq*) are planted in v. 2a; the term occurs only two other times in the Hebrew Bible (Isa 16:8; Jer 2:21), in contrast to the more common *gepen*, and may be taken to refer to an expensive variety of grape.[92] Finally, the vintner constructs a tower (*migdāl*) within the vineyard, which would have provided protection as well as a cool place where workers and harvesters could rest.[93] In many vineyards in ancient Israel, temporary structures served these functions more economically (Isa 1:8); by contrast, the effort and expense involved in the construction of a tower reveal a strong commitment to the flourishing of the vineyard.

The vintner undertakes all of these preparations in anticipation of a great harvest that never arrives (v. 2). In a bizarre twist to the metaphor, he now mounts a legal case against the vineyard. He presents his devoted work on behalf of it as evidence against it, absolving him of responsibility for its poor production and justifying its destruction (vv. 3–4), which the poem describes with as much enthusiasm as it had the tending of the vineyard (vv. 5–6). Disappointment over a failed crop seems an inadequate explanation for the transformation of the vintner's concern for the vineyard's well-being

---

[89] Williams, "Frustrated Expectations," 459–65; see also Williamson, *Isa 1–5*, 328. Williams's unpersuasive attempt to read the poem as a detailed allegory of God's prior care for Israel ("Frustrated Expectations," 463–5) is not essential to his thesis.
[90] Borowski, *Agriculture*, 110; Walsh, *Fruit*, 99.
[91] For *šemen* in reference to agricultural fertility, see Deut 32:13; Ezek 34:14; Neh 9:25 (Walsh, *Fruit*, 93).
[92] Walsh, *Fruit*, 106–10.
[93] For textual and archaeological evidence concerning such structures, see Walsh, *Fruit*, 128–36; for images from early twentieth-century ᴄᴇ Palestine, see Gustaf Dalman, *Der Ackerbau* (vol. 2 of *Arbeit und Sitte in Palästina*; Gütersloh: C. Bertelsmann, 1932), fig. 16; Gustaf Dalman, *Brot, Öl und Wein* (vol. 4 of *Arbeit und Sitte in Palästina*; Gütersloh: C. Bertelsmann, 1934), fig. 94.

Imagery and Metaphor 163

into his resolve for its demolition; Carey Ellen Walsh attributes it to "the costly rashness of a spurned lover."[94] This discrepancy points beyond the metaphor's source to its target, as revealed in v. 7: the vineyard is Israel and Judah, which have failed to produce the just society expected of them. A pair of wordplays (*mišpāṭ*/*mišpāḥ*, "justice"/"bloodshed," and *ṣĕdāqâ*/*ṣĕʿāqâ*, "righteousness"/"cry for help") captures the gulf between the anticipated and actual outcomes of YHWH's work.[95] Once again, the flexibility of harvest imagery in First Isaiah is striking. Elsewhere, as already discussed, a poor harvest may literally constitute divine punishment for underhanded measures used to gain farmland (Isa 5:10), while a bountiful harvest may figuratively symbolize the totality of judgment (Isa 17:5). Now, the metaphorical poor harvest becomes the grounds for judgment, as the legal language of the poem makes clear, and the judgment itself is depicted in part as a suspension of agricultural activity (*lōʾ yizzāmēr wĕlōʾ yēʿādēr*, "it will not be pruned or hoed," v. 6).

Agricultural proficiency also plays a central role in Isa 28:23–29, although in this case the results are a bountiful harvest. The poem depicts a seasoned farmer, who carefully prepares the field (v. 24) and knows the appropriate methods for planting various crops (v. 25) and the proper techniques for harvesting and processing different grains (vv. 27–28). For example, cumin can only be threshed by hand because its small seeds would be damaged by more rigorous techniques.[96] The threshing of cereal grains, on the other hand, requires greater force, but even then the farmer precisely manages the threshing process so that the grains are not destroyed. Ultimately, the prophet attributes this skillfulness, pregnantly described in this poem as *mišpāṭ* ("proper manner"), to the divine instruction of the farmer (v. 26). God has taught the farmer well, and as a result agricultural skill becomes a reflection of and testimony to divine wisdom; indeed, the poem ends by praising YHWH's "marvelous counsel" (*hiplîʾ ʿēṣâ*) and "exalted prudence" (*higdîl tûšîyâ*) in v. 29.

---

[94] Carey Ellen Walsh, "God's Vineyard: Isaiah's Prophecy as Vintner's Textbook," *BRev* 14, no. 4 (Aug. 1998): 52.

[95] A few Eng. translations attempt to recreate the wordplay; perhaps the most successful is NJPS, "justice"/"injustice" and "equity"/"iniquity."

[96] Borowski, *Agriculture*, 63; Healy, "Ancient Agriculture," 110, 115. Biblical texts depict two additional situations in which a flail would have been used in favor of other means of threshing: when a small quantity of grain is involved (Ruth 2:17) and when military threats have made the threshing floor inaccessible (Judg 6:11).

These verses work effectively as a self-contained unit, and the strong closural force of the final verse in the previous unit (Isa 28:22) further suggests that they comprise a separate poem. Nonetheless, the repeated notes of judgment in the surrounding chapters point to an additional layer of meaning for this agricultural metaphor beyond the interpretation given within the poem itself, namely that the farmer's carefully measured actions symbolize God's judgment of Judah.[97] Similar language appears in Isa 21:10—a text that may be later than the eighth century BCE—in which the speaker addresses the audience as "my threshed one" (*mĕdūšātî*). The violent verbs in Isa 28 are well suited for depicting judgment (for example, *yēḥābeṭ*, "is beaten"; *yûdāq*, "is crushed"). Exploiting the metaphor at a cosmic level, with similar language, Second Isaiah declares that YHWH will make the returning exiles like "a threshing sledge" (*môrag ḥārûṣ*), and they will "thresh" (*tādûš*) and "crush" (*tādōq*) mountains (Isa 41:15).[98] In Isaiah's parable, by contrast, the violence is controlled and productive. Plowing and threshing do not go on forever, and the thresher carefully avoids the use of excessive force on grains that cannot withstand it. In this way, the metaphor maps on divine judgment the same sense of proportion that underlies the farmer's actions.[99] In the preceding poem, Isaiah had proclaimed the "strange" (*zār*) and "alien" (*nokrîyâ*) character of God's judgment, in that it is directed against God's own people (Isa 28:21)—a point taken up again in the next poem (Isa 29:1-3). As it turns out, Judah's judgment is not so strange to those who recognize the larger picture of divine wisdom, just as the actions of the farmer are hardly unusual to those who understand agriculture. The inherently violent act of harvesting is necessary to prepare grain for human consumption. In the same way, perhaps, the judgment of Judah represents for the prophet an indispensable stage of God's work to recreate the nation as a more faithful people (see Isa 1:24-26).

---

[97] LXX makes this interpretation explicit in v. 26: "You will be disciplined with the judgment of your God, and you will rejoice."
[98] Imagery in the Ugaritic Baal cycle similarly plays on the violent connotations of agricultural imagery to describe a battle between the deities Anat and Mot, depicting the unchecked, unrestrained fury of the former (*KTU*² 1.6 ii.30-35).
[99] Tull, *Isa 1-39*, 431-2. Again, LXX makes this explicit in its translation of v. 28, which seems influenced by Isa 57:16: "For not forever will I be angry with you, nor will the voice of my anger crush you."

ANIMAL IMAGERY

Animal imagery also occurs frequently in First Isaiah. This frequency both reflects and appeals to the common interaction between humans and animals in the ancient world, to a degree that is difficult for contemporary readers from industrialized nations to appreciate. Most cases of animal imagery are overtly metaphorical, with the animal evoked for the sake of certain features that are mapped onto another reality. In other instances, the animal references do not appear to have metaphorical impact, as their zoological characteristics receive emphasis in their own right. For instance, in Isa 30:6-7, as discussed in the previous chapter, the mention of several exotic animals characterizes a trek through the Negev as a treacherous, difficult journey. Even in such cases, though, the animal imagery serves a literary function by virtue of its impact on the texture of the poem; in many instances, moreover, one cannot rule out the possibility of latent metaphorical associations.[100] As in Isa 30:6-7, animal images in First Isaiah often occur in clusters, in which several different animals may be named. The richness of the poetry's zoological lexicon enhances the sharpness of the imagery.[101] Every different Biblical Hebrew word for "snake" is attested in First Isaiah, for instance, as is every term for "lion" except for the relatively uncommon šaḥal.[102] In the following discussion, I treat three conceptual metaphors that account for much of the animal imagery in First Isaiah: the depiction of conquered cities as habitat for animals; the depiction of nations and their leaders as animals; and finally the depiction of YHWH as an animal.

Animals and Ruined Cities

In two different poems, Isaiah uses pastoral imagery to describe urban desolation. The first instance occurs in a small poetic fragment within the series of hôy-oracles in Isa 5:8-24. It begins in v. 14, which

---

[100] Brown, *Seeing the Psalms*, 152-5; Strawn, *Lion*, 27-8.
[101] Quinn-Miscall, *Reading Isaiah*, 67.
[102] A few commentators emend Isa 16:1 to include the term šaḥal, but the proposal is not convincing (see Jones, *Howling over Moab*, 195-6, n. 90; Smothers, "Isaiah 15-16," 73). For a detailed treatment of Bibl. Heb. terminology for lions, see Strawn, *Lion*, 293-326.

describes the descent of the citizens of an unspecified city, presumably Jerusalem, into Sheol. Following the loss of its populace, the city becomes a ghost town, inhabited only by small cattle:

> wĕrā'û kĕbāśîm kĕdobrām
> wĕhŏrābôt mēḥîm yō'kēlû[103]
>
> And sheep will graze as in their pasture,
> and fatlings will eat among the ruins. (Isa 5:17)

In contrast to the clamoring crowds depicted in Isa 5:14, the image of sheep typically connotes peace and serenity; Psalm 23 is the biblical example par excellence. In this case, these associations are eerily ironic. The setting is idyllic only because of the death or deportation of the humans who lived there, producing an evocative sense of disconnect. Similar imagery occurs in the oracle against Damascus in Isa 17, after the prophet announces the destruction of Damascus and its dependent cities:

> la'ădārîm tihyênâ
> wĕrābĕṣû wĕ'ên maḥărîd
>
> They (the cities) will belong to flocks,
> and they will lie down, and no one will terrify them. (Isa 17:2b)

Here, the imagery has positive ramifications for the audience, as the desolate cities in question are those of Judah's enemies in the Syro-Ephraimite War—which may lead the audience to wonder whom the flocks that take over the cities might represent, a point that will be taken up below.

---

[103] MT wĕhārbôt mēḥîm gārîm yō'kēlû ("and sojourners will eat the ruins of fatlings") is supported by 1QIsa[a] and 4QIsa[b] but makes poor sense; for defenses of MT, see Hayes and Irvine, *Isaiah*, 105; de Waard, *Handbook*, 25–6. Many interpreters read gĕdāyîm ("kids") for gārîm following LXX (for example, Duhm, *Jesaia*, 59; Gray, *Isa I–XXVII*, 93–4; NRSV; Wildberger, *Isa 1–12*, 191–2). Note the parallelism of kebeś/gĕdî in Isa 11:6. Although none of the versions take it as an animal designation, the meaning of mēḥîm ("fatlings") is confirmed by Ps 66:15. Traditionally, hŏrābôt mēḥîm ("ruins of fatlings") has been understood as a metaphor for the deserted lands of the deported nobles (for example, Lowth, *Isaiah*, 10; among modern interpreters, de Waard; NIV; REB). Alternatively, others take gārîm/gĕdāyîm as a gloss for the less common mēḥîm, in which case mēḥîm would be the subject of the line, and MT hārbôt ("ruins of") should be revocalized as the absolute hŏrābôt ("ruins"; see Wildberger; Williamson; NRSV).

The presence of livestock in a city would not itself be remarkable, as herds of small cattle were maintained in urban settlements in ancient Israel.[104] These texts, however, portray an extraordinary scene in which flocks roam freely in an otherwise empty city. They are examples of a biblical *topos*, attested primarily in the prophetic literature, that depicts animals as the inhabitants of conquered or deserted cities (Jer 50:39; Zeph 2:6–7; Lam 5:18; etc.).[105] In other examples, the animals may include a variety of wild or exotic species along with or instead of domestic ones. This larger literary tradition brings the function of the pastoral imagery in Isa 5 and 17 into greater focus. The underlying metaphor compares the ruined city to a pasture or wilderness (see Isa 27:10). Thus, in Isa 5:17, the sheep graze in the city "*as in* their pasture" (*kĕdobrām*). The rare term *dōber* fits the context of urban desolation nicely, given its phonological and etymological connections to the terms *deber* ("plague") and *midbār* ("wilderness"). In Isa 17:2b, the metaphor unfolds similarly. The destroyed cities "belong to flocks" (*lĕʿădārîm tihyênâ*), and the quality that they share with pastures is the absence of human inhabitants, as emphasized in the second line of the couplet (*wĕʾên maḥărîd*, "and there is no one to terrify them"). In this way, the sheep imagery evokes the larger metaphor of pasturage, but the animals themselves are not overtly metaphorical, as nothing associates them with a particular target.

In light of other texts, though, these animal references may take on additional symbolic overtones. Issues of poverty and wealth are central to the immediate context of Isa 5:14, 17. The *hôy*-oracle containing these verses opens with an indictment of the lavish festivals of wealthy Judahites (Isa 5:11–12; see also Amos 6:4–7), and the declaration of punishment in v. 13 threatens exile for the people and

---

[104] See Oded Borowski, *Every Living Thing: Daily Use of Animals in Ancient Israel* (Walnut Creek, Calif.: AltaMira, 1998), 40–2.

[105] Other examples from Isa 1–39 (Isa 7:23–5; 13:19–22; 27:10; 32:14; 34:10–15) occur in texts widely regarded as later than the eighth century BCE; for further discussion, see Joseph Blenkinsopp, "Cityscape to Landscape: The 'Back to Nature' Theme in Isaiah 1–35," in *"Every City Shall be Forsaken": Urbanism and Prophecy in Ancient Israel and the Near East* (eds. Lester L. Grabbe and Robert D. Haak; JSOTSup 330; Sheffield: Sheffield Academic Press, 2001), 35–44. On the relationship between this *topos* and the treaty-curse tradition, see F. Charles Fensham, "Common Trends in Curses of the Near Eastern Treaties and *Kudurru*-Inscriptions Compared with Maledictions of Amos and Isaiah," *ZAW* 75 (1963): 163–4, 166–8; Hillers, *Treaty-Curses*, 43–54.

famine for "its nobles" (*kĕbôdô*). If one reads v. 14 in light of the preceding verses, especially given the repetition of the term *hāmôn* ("multitude"), then the revelers who descend into Sheol belong to Jerusalem's upper classes.[106] The sheep and fatlings in v. 17 may then be taken as a metaphor for lower-class Judahites who are not deported and inhabit Jerusalem after the exile of its patricians.[107] One may compare Isa 14:30, which uses pastoral imagery to describe God's provision for the poor. This reading fits nicely within the development of the theme of appetite in Isa 5:11–17, heightening the contrast among the undisturbed grazing of the sheep in v. 17, the starvation of the wealthier citizens in v. 13,[108] and the ravenous appetite of Sheol in v. 14.[109] It would also mark the reversal of the situation described in the preceding *hôy*-oracle, which condemns the obsessive acquisition of land by a few wealthy citizens (Isa 5:8–10).

A different situation obtains for Isa 17:2b. Pastoral imagery occurs frequently as a metaphor for Israel and Judah throughout the Hebrew Bible, most often in the context of the people's relationship to God or their leaders as shepherds (Isa 40:11; Jer 50:19; Ps 100:3). Given this association, Isaiah may well have Judah in mind in the second line of the couplet. After the fall of Damascus, "no one will terrify" Judah as the Syro-Ephraimite coalition had done with its threatened invasion (Isa 7:2); the same phrase (*wĕʾên maḥărîd*) also occurs in Ezek 34:28 with reference to Israel as sheep. More speculatively, one might take the "flocks" in the first line of the couplet as a reference to Judah as well, implying that it will possess the territory of Damascus after the latter's defeat by the Assyrians. In support of this reading, note that Zeph 2:7 uses similar pastoral imagery to depict future Judahite

---

[106] So Williamson, *Isa 1–5*, 373; *contra* Wildberger, *Isa 1–12*, 204.

[107] Several ancient interpretations of Isa 5:17 seem to move in this direction. For MT *kĕbāśîm*, 1QIsa^a reads *kbwšym* ("the subdued ones"), a *qal* passive participle from √*kbš*; see also LXX *hoi diērpasmenoi*, "the plundered." The reading *gārîm* for an assumed *gĕdāyîm* in MT itself may be another example of this interpretive tendency.

[108] Reading *mētê rāʿāb* ("dying of hunger") for MT *mĕtê rāʿāb* ("men of hunger"), with LXX; Syr.; Tg.; and Vulg. 1QIsa^a (*mty*) supports MT (de Waard, *Handbook*, 24; Williamson, *Isa 1–5*, 360). Gray likewise follows the versions (*Isa I–XXVII*, 93), while Blenkinsopp (*Isa 1–39*, 210) and Williamson prefer MT.

[109] The term *mēḥîm* ("fatling") further suggests richness and satiety, in contrast to the limitless appetite attributed to Sheol. These associations are not explicit in the other occurrence of the term in Ps 66:15, but note the phrase *šĕmānîm mĕmuḥāyîm* ("fattened, rich food") in Isa 25:6, in which the second term is a *puʿal* participle of √*mḥḥ*.

possession of Philistine territories. After announcing in vv. 4–6 that God will destroy the Philistines, reducing their territory to pastures and sheepfolds, Zephaniah explicitly declares that this territory will "belong to the remnant of the house of Judah" and the Judahites will "graze" (*yirʿûn*) and "lie down" (*yirbāṣûn*) in the houses of Ashkelon. Admittedly, this proposal may overread the Isaianic text, as there is no evidence that Isaiah expected the kingdom of Judah to gain control over Syrian territory.

Nations and Rulers as Animals

Dealings among nations are the target of much of Isaiah's figurative discourse, as one might expect given the book's concern with international affairs, especially the rapid increase of Assyrian power. One finds in First Isaiah several elaborations of a basic metaphor that may be articulated as "Nations and their leaders are animals" (for example, Isa 5:29; 10:13–14; 11:6–9; 14:29–30). Typically, more powerful nations are depicted as strong, dangerous animals, while weaker, docile animals usually serve as metaphors for less powerful nations. The representation of nations and their rulers as animals has many reflexes in biblical and ancient Near Eastern literature, including the depiction of personal enemies or the wicked more broadly as wild animals in the Psalms;[110] the figurative representation of rulers and their enemies by a variety of animals in ancient Egyptian and Mesopotamian literature, especially Neo-Assyrian royal inscriptions;[111] and the use of animal names as designations for state and military officials in Ugaritic and biblical texts.[112] In some cases, it seems likely that Isaiah self-consciously develops his animal images in conversation with these intertexts; more generally, they bring into greater focus the qualities associated with particular animals that would have commended them as metaphors.

Isaiah 5:26–29 describes the advancing army of an unnamed nation, most likely Assyria. At first, the description is largely non-figurative, emphasizing the invaders' speed and preparedness for

---

[110] See Brown, *Seeing the Psalms*, 136–44.
[111] See David Marcus, "Animal Similes in Assyrian Royal Inscriptions," *Orientalia* NS 46 (1977): 86–106.
[112] See Patrick D. Miller, "Animal Names as Designations in Ugaritic and Hebrew," *UF* 2 (1970): 177–86; Watson, *CHP*, 268.

battle. The one exception is the hyperbole in v. 27aβ that they "neither sleep nor slumber" (*lō yānûm wĕlō' yîšān*), a phrase used to describe God in Ps 121:4.[113] A pair of similes in v. 28b marks a sustained shift to figurative discourse, while also introducing animal imagery in this unit: the hooves of the army's horses are "like flint" (*kaṣṣōr*),[114] and the wheels of its chariots are "like the storm-wind" (*kassûpâ*), a term associated elsewhere with human armies (Jer 4:13; Amos 1:14) and with YHWH as divine warrior (Isa 29:6; Nah 1:3). While these similes are constrained to a single line each, the lion metaphor in v. 29 develops across four lines:

> *šĕ'āgâ lô kallābî'*
> *yiš'ag*[115] *kakkĕpîrîm*
> *wĕyinhōm wĕyō'ḥēz ṭerep*
> *wĕyaplîṭ wĕ'ên maṣṣîl*
>
> Its roar is like a lion;
>   it roars like young lions.
> It growls and seizes prey,
>   and safeguards it, and there is none to rescue. (Isa 5:29)

The metaphor represents the rhetorical culmination of the increasingly figurative, fantastic description of the Assyrian army, whose

---

[113] Duhm thinks that the line is intrusive because of its recurrence in Ps 121 (*Jesaia*, 63). Others disagree with his logic but still regard it as a gloss, arguing that v. 26b forms an adequate parallel to v. 27aα, making v. 27aβ unnecessary; moreover, assuming that v. 30 is also secondary, deleting this line would make Isa 5:25–29 conform in length to the stanzas in Isa 9:7–20, which contain fourteen lines (Gray, *Isa I–XXVII*, 177; Wildberger, *Isa 1–12*, 222–3; Williamson, *Isa 1–5*, 406–7). Such reasons are not convincing, as one may take v. 26b either with v. 26a or v. 27a as a triplet, and a longer final stanza to the putative original poem can be explained as terminal modification.

[114] For MT *kaṣṣar*, 1QIsa^a reads *ṣwr* (*ṣōr*, "flint"; see Exod 4:25; Ezek 3:9), and the versions use different terms meaning "rock" or "flint." One should probably read *kaṣṣōr* (see Blenkinsopp, *Isa 1–39*, 220; Clements, *Isa 1–39*, 70; Wildberger, *Isa 1–12*, 223), although it is possible that MT has preserved an otherwise unattested biform (Williamson, *Isa 1–5*, 397).

[115] In light of the imperfect verbs that follow, MT Q *yiš'ag* ("it will roar") seems preferable to MT K *wĕšā'ag* ("and it roared"); see also 1QIsa^a; Syr.; Tg. Several commentators take *šĕ'āgâ lô* ("its roar") and *wĕšā'ag/yiš'ag* as variants, assuming that a noun and verb from the same root would not occur in parallel lines (Blenkinsopp, *Isa 1–39*, 220; Gray, *Isa I–XXVII*, 98; Wildberger, *Isa 1–12*, 222). As Berlin explains, however, such a pair is an acceptable form of grammatical matching (*Dynamics*, 34, 54–6). Following 1QIsa^a, Williamson suggests a different line division altogether: *š'gh [lw] klby' yš'g/wkkpyrym ynhm/wy'ḥz...* (*Isa 1–5*, 398). While plausible, his proposal is not obviously superior to that followed here.

Imagery and Metaphor 171

actions are swift, efficient, and ultimately inescapable. References to lions outnumber references to any other animal in the Hebrew Bible, and they almost invariably present the animal as a vicious predator and menace to human well-being.[116] These associations are evident in biblical texts that portray the speaker's enemies as lions: for example, Nah 2:11–12 (Eng. 2:12–13); Pss 7:3 (Eng. 7:2); 22:14 (Eng. 22:13).

Strawn argues, with reference primarily to the Psalms, that the portrayal of one's enemies as lions both demonizes them and magnifies the threat that they represent, playing on the common association of rulers and deities with lions in biblical and ancient Near Eastern sources.[117] The depiction of the Assyrian army as a lion in this text has similar effects, and Peter Machinist even raises the possibility that it is informed by the occurrence of such metaphors in Assyrian royal annals.[118]

Central to Isa 5:29 are the most commonly discussed features of the lion in biblical texts, its roar and predatory behavior.[119] In the first couplet, the "roar" (*šĕʾāgâ*) of the army is compared to that of a "lion" (*kallābîʾ*). Even before the appearance of the term *lābîʾ*, the comparison is implicit in the term *šĕʾāgâ*, which most often refers to the sound of lions (Ezek 19:7; Zech 11:3; Job 4:10). Verse 29bβ adds no discernible content to the couplet, and any sense of development is achieved grammatically by the nominal–verbal transformation.[120] The poem does not identify a specific sound of the army as the target of the metaphor. Although v. 28 may suggest the din of oncoming chariots, the battle cry that precedes combat (Josh 6:20; Ezek 21:27 [Eng. 21:22]; 2 Chr 13.12) is more likely, given the movement from the lion's roar to its attack. Whichever the case, the capacity to arouse fear is the salient feature of the simile. Fear is the instinctive response to a lion's roar, as suggested by the rhetorical question in Amos 3:8a: "The lion has roared! / Who will not be afraid?" (*ʾaryēh šāʾāg/mî lōʾ yîrāʾ*).

---

[116] Brown, *Seeing the Psalms*, 136–9; Strawn, *Lion*, 25–7.
[117] Strawn, *Lion*, 274–6; see also Brensinger, *Simile*, 123–4.
[118] Machinist, "Assyria and Its Image," 728–9. For leonine imagery applied to Assyrian rulers, see *CAD* L, 25; Marcus, "Animal Similes," 87; Strawn, *Lion*, 178–80.
[119] See Strawn, *Lion*, 34–6.
[120] Based on Jer 51:38 and Ezek 19.2–3, 5–6, *kĕpîr* ("young lion") seems to designate a lion at a stage of development between cubhood and adulthood (Strawn, *Lion*, 308–9). The term occurs frequently in parallel with other words for lion, however, and it is unclear what significance the lion's level of maturation would have in this context.

Several biblical texts attribute environmental upheaval to this sound, particularly when the lion symbolizes Yhwh (Jer 25:30; Joel 4:16 [Eng. 3:16]; Amos 1:2). Such associations provide further evidence that the imagery paints the Assyrians as superhuman. The sound of an approaching army is always cause for alarm, but the sound of this army merits comparison with one of the most terrifying sounds known to the prophet's audience.

The second couplet is formally striking because both lines contain two clauses, an infrequent line-type in Biblical Hebrew poetry.[121] The four clauses depict a series of sequential actions, while the matching syntactic structures (verb + verb + object) provide structural stability.[122] In the first line, *wĕyinhōm* ("and it growls") is lexically parallel to *yiš'ag* ("it roars") in the previous line, establishing continuity between the contiguous couplets. The action shifts in the next clause to the lion's predatory activity. Having captured its victim, the lion "safeguards" (*wĕyaplîṭ*) it, presumably to consume it without interference from other predators.[123] The verb *pālaṭ* normally has connotations of escape from danger, and several commentators seem bothered by its use here, although few propose emendations.[124] Perhaps the choice of this verb represents another example of Isaiah's penchant to establish false expectations on the part of the audience only to thwart them and create surprise. In this case, the verb might initially suggest that the prey somehow escapes from the lion, but the following clause emphatically precludes this possibility and forces the audience to abandon its initial assumption about the meaning of the line.[125] The clause *wĕ'ên maṣṣîl* ("and there is no one to rescue") occurs in other

---

[121] In O'Connor's corpus of 1,225 lines, only thirteen percent of the lines have two clauses (*HVS*, 316).

[122] I follow O'Connor in treating the negative particle *'ên* ("there is not") as the equivalent of a verb (*HVS*, 304).

[123] See Gray, *Isa I–XXVII*, 98; Strawn, *Lion*, 335; Williamson, *Isa 1–5*, 399.

[124] For example, Gray, *Isa I–XXVII*, 98. The only other occurrence of the *hip'il* of √*plṭ* is Mic 6:14, an obscure verse that offers little help in establishing the verb's meaning here. Ehrlich emends *wĕyaplîṭ* to *wĕyib'al* ("and he will swallow"), supposing '/ṭ confusion in the paleo-Heb. script (*Jesaja*, 24). The emendation has no support from the versions, and Williamson doubts that √*bl'* would have been used of a lion (*Isa 1–5*, 399).

[125] Amos 3:12 makes a similar rhetorical move. The first line of the couplet initially appears to describe a shepherd who "rescues" (*yaṣṣîl*) a sheep from a lion; however, the line is enjambed, and the object is delayed until the second line: "two thigh-bones or the lobe of an ear" (*štê kĕrā'ayim 'ô bĕdal 'ōzen*). The second line reveals that the attempted rescue was not successful, demanding reinterpretation of the first line.

Imagery and Metaphor 173

biblical texts dealing with lions (Hos 5:14; Mic 5:7; Pss 7:3 [Eng. 7:2]; 50:22), highlighting the pervasive respect for the animal's predatory prowess among ancient Israelites.[126] This claim of inescapability heightens the impression of the Assyrian attack as inevitable, which helps establish it as the decisive final event in the series of divine punishments recounted in Isa 9:7–20 + 5:25–29, the putative original poem to which these lines likely formed the conclusion.

A cluster of zoological images occurs in Isaiah 10:13–14, part of a speech by the poetically rendered king of Assyria that demonstrates his blasphemous hubris. In these lines, the ruler proudly takes credit for his military successes, contradicting the prophet's earlier claim that Assyria is only "the staff of [God's] anger" (Isa 10:5). The use of animal imagery intensifies the braggadocio of the rhetoric:

[13] *kî ʾāmar bĕkōaḥ yādî ʿāśîtî*
    ûbĕḥokmātî kî nĕbûnôtî
    wĕʾāsîr[127] *gĕbûlōt ʿammîm*
    waʿătûdōtêhem[128] *šôśētî*
    wĕʾôrîd kĕʾabbîr[129] *yôšĕbîm*

---

[126] See Strawn, *Lion*, 340.

[127] Given the surrounding perfect and *waw*-consecutive verbs, most commentators think that the imperfect verbs in v. 13b should be repointed as *waw*-consecutives: Blenkinsopp, *Isa 1–39*, 252; Gray, *Isa I–XXVII*, 202; Stuart A. Irvine, "Problems of Text and Translation in Isaiah 10.13bb," in *History and Interpretation: Essays in Honour of John H. Hayes* (eds. M. P. Graham et al.; JSOTSup 173: Sheffield: JSOT Press, 1993) 140–1; Wildberger, *Isa 1–12*, 413. The full spellings support MT's vocalization, since *hipʿil waw*-consecutive verbs would typically be written defectively. The sequence *yqṭl-qṭl-yqṭl* in the triplet is a form of morphological variation, which is further supported by the alternation in position of the verbs.

[128] MT Q *ʿătûdōtêhem* ("their 'goats'") uses an animal name as a metaphor for leaders. MT K *ʿătîdōtêhem* means "their supplies"; elsewhere, the adjective *ʿātîd* means "ready, prepared" (Job 15:24; Esth 3:14). Sym. and Vulg. support the Q, while other versions and 1QIsa[a] support the K. Among the few commentators who discuss it, Wildberger (*Isa 1–12*, 413) prefers the K, while Gray admits the plausibility of both readings (*Isa I–XXVII*, 202). Siegfried Mittmann has argued strongly for the Q: "'Wehe! Assur, Stab meines Zorns' (Jes 10,5–9.13aβ–15)," in *Prophet und Prophetenbuch: Festschrift für Otto Kaiser zum 65. Geburstag* (eds. Volkmar Fritz et al.; BZAW 185; Berlin: de Gruyter, 1989), 120–1. The use of *ʿătûdîm* as a term for rulers in Isa 14:9 increases the plausibility of its occurrence here, especially if one accepts Isaianic authorship of that text.

[129] MT K *kĕʾabbîr* ("like a bull") and Q *kabbîr* ("mighty") appear to preserve genuine variants. For the evidence from the versions, see Irvine, "Isa 10.13bb," 137–9. Many commentators assume the whole line is corrupt and propose considerable changes, seeking to recover a "missing" parallel line (see, among others, Clements, *Isa 1–39*, 113; Duhm, *Jesaia*, 100; Kaiser, *Isa 1–12*, 229; Wildberger, *Isa 1–12*,

[14] *wattimṣā' kaqqēn yādî*
lĕḥêl hā'ammîm
wĕke'ĕsōp bêṣîm 'ăzūbôt
kol-hā'āreṣ 'ănî 'āsāptî
wĕlō' hāyâ nōdēd kānāp
ûpōṣeh peh ûmĕṣapṣēp

[13] For he says, "By the strength of my hand I have acted,
and by my wisdom, for I am insightful.
And I have removed the borders of peoples,
and their 'goats' I have plundered,
and like a bull I have brought down their enthroned ones.[130]
[14] And my hand has reached out, as if into a nest,
to the treasure of the peoples.
And like gathering abandoned eggs,
the whole world I have gathered.
And there was none who fluttered a wing,
or opened a beak, or even chirped." (Isa 10:13–14)

While the speech is a creation of the prophet, put into the mouth of the unnamed king, its overall tone and several particular expressions—including the use of animal similes—echo the language of Assyrian royal inscriptions, although at times in novel ways.[131] Given the likelihood that Isaiah and his audience were acquainted with Assyrian propaganda, these resonances impart a degree of realism to this portrayal of the king's haughtiness.

Following the consonants of the Masoretic Text in v. 13bß, the Assyrian king compares himself to a bull (*'abbîr*). The metaphor has precedent in Mesopotamian literature, including royal inscriptions in which kings compare themselves to wild bulls (Akk. *rīmu*).[132] Similar

---

413). MT makes acceptable sense, however, and the line as it stands is part of a tightly constructed triplet.

[130] My translation assumes that the third-person plural suffix on *'ātûdōtêhem* ("their 'goats'") is operative for *yōšĕbîm* ("enthroned ones") as well. For *yāšab* ("sit") as a circumlocution for "ruler" (i.e., one who sits on a throne) or "reign," see 1 Sam 4:4; Pss 2:4; 9:8 (Eng. 9:7); Lam 5:19.

[131] Gallagher, *Sennacherib's Campaign*, 78–83; Machinist, "Assyria and Its Image," 725, 734–5.

[132] *CAD* R, 361–2; Gallagher, *Sennacherib's Campaign*, 81–2; Marcus, "Animal Similes," 87–8.

royal imagery is attested in Egypt.[133] In the Bible, the terms *šôr* ("bull") and *'abbîr* also occur as designations for officials or warriors and as metaphors for Israel's enemies.[134] In all of these cases, brute force seems to be the primary characteristic mapped onto the human target; indeed, *'abbîr* has etymological associations with power and strength.[135] This is certainly the case in Isa 10:13, as the king calls attention to the incredible power demonstrated by his ability to depose the rulers of other nations. In Assyrian inscriptions, references to bulls also emphasize the animal's ability to move across mountainous terrain.[136] The connotation of agility also fits the Assyrian's boast, which assumes that he occupies a high vantage point from which to "bring down ... rulers" (*wĕ'ôrîd ... yôšĕbîm*). The image may have blasphemous connotations, as the same term appears in a divine epithet in Isa 1:24 (*'ăbîr yiśrā'ēl*, "the Bull of Israel").[137] Assuming from this occurrence that Isaiah's audience is familiar with this epithet, they might understand the king here to be usurping the position of YHWH, whom he had in fact earlier dismissed as an idol (Isa 10:10–11).[138]

In addition to comparing himself to an animal, the Assyrian may also use animal imagery to characterize the objects of his conquest.

---

[133] Patrick D. Miller, "El the Warrior," *HTR* 60 (1967): 423–4; Emily Teeter, "Animals in Egyptian Literature," in *A History of the Animal World in the Ancient Near East* (ed. Billie Jean Collins; HO 64; Leiden: Brill, 2002), 266–7. Miller notes the artistic portrayal of the Egyptian king Narmer "as a bull trampling the enemy or knocking down a fortified city" ("El the Warrior," 424); see *ANEP*, 90–1, figs. 291–292; 93, fig. 297.

[134] For *'abbîr*, see Isa 34:7; Ps 22:13 (Eng. 22:12); Job 24:22; for *šôr*, see Gen 49:6. See further Miller, "El the Warrior," 421; Miller, "Animal Names," 180–1, 185.

[135] Compare Akk. *abāru* ("strength"). Both *BDB* (7) and *HALOT* (6) treat the term as an adjective meaning "strong, powerful"; so also Nahum M. Sarna, "The Divine Title *'abhîr ya'ăqôbh*," in *Essays on the Occasion of the Seventieth Anniversary of the Dropsie University (1909–1979)* (eds. A. I. Katsh and L. Nemoy; Philadelphia: Dropsie University, 1979), 389–96. As Miller notes, however, almost every biblical usage of the term may be taken as a reference to bulls or horses, and the Ug. cognate *ibr* ("bull, buffalo") suggests that the Heb. term is a noun designating an animal ("Animal Names," 180).

[136] Marcus, "Animal Similes," 87–8.

[137] Compare *'ăbîr ya'ăqōb* ("Bull of Jacob") in Gen 49:24; Isa 49:26; 60:16; Ps 132:2, 5; on this epithet, see Miller, "El the Warrior," 421; Niditch, *Oral World*, 15–17. The distinction between *'ăbîr* as a divine title and *'abbîr* as a term for animals is most likely a Masoretic innovation, but see Sarna, "Divine Title." For bull imagery for other ancient Near Eastern deities, see *CAD* R, 361–2; Marjo C. A. Korpel, *A Rift in the Clouds: Ugaritic and Hebrew Descriptions of the Divine* (Ugaritisch-biblische Literatur 8; Münster: Ugarit-Verlag, 1990), 524–8; Miller, "El the Warrior," 418–20, 423.

[138] See Irvine, "Isa 10.13bb," 143–4; Miscall, *Isaiah*, 43.

Following the Masoretic vocalization of v. 13bα, the king refers to the rulers whom he has despoiled as "goats" (ʿātûdôt), a term that appears as a designation for rulers in Isa 14:9; Ezek 39:18; Zech 10:3.[139] Jeremiah 50:8 depicts goats as the leaders of their flocks, suggesting a possible rationale for this metaphor. The term ʿātûd appears most frequently in the context of slaughter or sacrifice (Num 7:17–88; Jer 51:40; Ps 50:13; etc.), which could inform its use here as a metaphor for conquered rulers. More generally, however, the use of animal terms as designations for leaders draws on positive qualities of these animals such as strength or leadership, so it seems likely that the designation further highlights the prowess of the Assyrian by portraying his opponents as powerful in their own right. One should be careful, though, not to overread the image, given both the uncertainty over the text and the possibility that such animal designations may have been largely unreflexive or even dead metaphors.

By contrast, the avian imagery of v. 14, which develops over three couplets, clearly emphasizes the weakness of the Assyrian's victims. The first two couplets compare his acts of plunder and conquest to reaching into "a nest" (qēn) and "gathering abandoned eggs" (ʾēsōp bêṣîm ʿăzūbôt).[140] The third couplet portrays the expected but absent resistance to these aggressions as "fluttering a wing" (nōdēd kānāp), "opening a beak" (ûpōṣeh peh), and "chirping" (mĕṣapṣēp). The progressively weaker character of these actions underscores the lack of even the slightest opposition. Egg imagery is apparently unattested as a conquest metaphor in ancient Near Eastern texts, but several of the Mari letters refer to the practice of egg collection to obtain food for the royal table.[141] Bowls or baskets of large birds' eggs also appear in ancient Egyptian art.[142] Among biblical texts, Deut 22:6–7 prohibits egg gatherers from harming a mother bird that is sitting on its nest.

---

[139] See Miller, "Animal Names," 184.

[140] Gallagher (*Sennacherib's Campaign*, 82) tentatively connects the nest imagery in this verse to the motif of inaccessible enemy cities as nests in Neo-Assyrian royal annals; in that case, however, the metaphor emphasizes the difficulty of conquest, whereas here it emphasizes its ease.

[141] ARM 14, 86 25–30; see Jack M. Sasson, "The King's Table: Food and Fealty in Old Babylonian Mari," in *Food and Identity in the Ancient World* (eds. Cristiano Grottanelli and Lucio Milano; History of the Ancient Near East, Studies 9; Padova: SARGON Editrice e Libreria, 2004), 187.

[142] Borowski, *Every Living Thing*, 152; Patrick F. Houlihan, "Animals in Egyptian Art and Hieroglyphs," in *A History of the Animal World in the Ancient Near East* (ed. Billie Jean Collins; HO 64; Leiden: Brill, 2002), 109, fig. 3.2; 125, fig. 3.10.

Job 39:14–15 notes that an ostrich "abandons" (ta'ă'zōb) its eggs due to its stupidity; here, however, the mother seems to have fled the nest out of fear of the oncoming assault. The language of abandonment may implicitly suggest divine absence, in conjunction with the Assyrian's earlier boast in vv. 10–11 that the deities of conquered nations could not thwart his advances. Assyrian inscriptions sometimes cite the abandonment of enemy cities by their deities as a factor in Assyrian conquests.[143] If so, the claim that "there was none who fluttered a wing" is especially suggestive in light of biblical references to YHWH's wings as an image of divine protection, such as Deut 32:11; Pss 36:8 (Eng. 36:7); 91:4; and Ruth 2:12.[144]

An unusual juxtaposition of animal images occurs in the opening couplets of an oracle against the Philistines in Isa 14:28–32:

> 'al-tiśměḥî pělešet kullēk
> kî nišbar šēbeṭ makkēk
> kî-miššōreš nāḥāš yēṣē' ṣepa'
> ûpiryô śārāp mĕ'ôpēp
>
> Do not rejoice, Philistia, any of you,
>   that the rod that struck you is shattered;
> for from the root of the snake will come forth an adder,
>   and its fruit will be a flying serpent. (Isa 14:29)

Initially, the poet depicts the unnamed ruler who had oppressed the Philistines as a "rod" (šebeṭ), a common figure in First Isaiah for the subjugation of one nation by another or by YHWH (Isa 9:3; 10:5, 15; 30:31). The term may also denote a royal scepter (Gen 49:10; Judg 5:14; Ps 45:7 [Eng. 45:6]), further suggesting its suitability as a metaphor for a ruler. This rod has now been shattered (nišbar), presumably a reference to the death of the ruler. In Isa 9:2–3 (Eng. 9:3–4) the breaking (√ḥtt) of the rod on Judah signals an end to

---

[143] Sennacherib, for instance, claims that the gods of several enemy cities—which he had earlier compared to "the nest of the eagle" (qin-ni našri)—"deserted them and left them empty" (i-zi-bu-šu-nu-ti-ma ú-šab-šu-u) in advance of his attack: Daniel David Luckenbill, *The Annals of Sennacherib* (University of Chicago Oriental Publications 2; Chicago: University of Chicago Press, 1924), 64; see further Mordechai Cogan, *Imperialism and Religion: Assyria, Judah, and Israel in the Eighth and Seventh Centuries B.C.E.* (SBLMS 19; Missoula, Mont.: Scholars Press, 1974), 9–21.

[144] See the discussion in Brown, *Seeing the Psalms*, 20–3; Joel M. LeMon, *Yahweh's Winged Form in the Psalms: Exploring Congruent Iconography and Texts* (OBO 242; Fribourg: Academic Press; Göttingen: Vandenhoeck & Ruprecht, 2010).

oppression and thus a cause for joy. Here, however, the Philistines are commanded not to rejoice, despite the apparent good news. In the next couplet, the words *šōreš* ("root") and *piryô* ("its fruit") introduce the image of a tree. This image marks the transition from the deceased ruler to his successor, portrayed respectively as the root and fruit of a single tree, and suggests continuity between their Philistine policies—hence the warning against premature celebration. The shift in metaphors is not incongruous. A rod is a wooden object (Isa 10:15), and, in Num 17:23 (Eng. 17:8), Aaron's "staff" (*maṭṭeh*)— a term that often occurs in parallel with *šebeṭ* in Isaiah (Isa 10:5, 15; 14:5; 28:27)—sprouts and bears fruit.[145]

By an unexpected twist, however, the root turns out not to be that of a tree, but that of a "snake" (*nāḥāš*). The mixed metaphor is jarring and, on the surface, nonsensical; snakes, after all, do not have roots. Nonetheless, the image succeeds associatively, if not logically, in light of the common connection of serpents and trees in the ancient Near East, as seen for instance in Gen 3 and the Mesopotamian myth of Etana.[146] Further, a rod and a serpent may be associated by their similar shapes.[147] The shift from the benign tree imagery to the more sinister serpentine imagery heightens the degree of threat posed to the Philistines by the unnamed ruler and his successor. Elsewhere in the Bible, references to snakes typically portray the animals as wild and dangerous, focusing especially on their sharp teeth and venomous bite (Num 21:6–8; Amos 5:19; Pss 58:5 [Eng. 58:4]; 140:4 [Eng. 140:3]).[148] The portrayal of the new ruler as a "flying serpent" (*śārāp mĕ'ôpēp*), a fantastic and exotic creature (see Isa 6:2, 6; 30:6), suggests that he will be an even greater menace to the Philistines than his predecessor, a more mundane, if hardly innocuous, snake.[149]

---

[145] Note also Ezek 19:11–12, in which *maṭṭeh* refers to branches from a grapevine, later to become "scepters of rulers" (*šibṭê mōšĕlîm*).

[146] See Lowell K. Handy, "Serpent, Religious Symbol," *ABD* 5:1113–16; Francis Landy, "Seraphim and Poetic Process," in *The Labour of Reading: Desire, Alienation, and Biblical Interpretation* (ed. Fiona C. Black et al.; SemSt; Atlanta: Society of Biblical Literature, 1999), 21–2.

[147] Note the transformation of Moses' rod into a serpent in Exod 4:1–5; 7:9–12. Hayes and Irvine suggest that "the snake terminology may play on the fact that rods/walking sticks were carved and shaped to produce a snake appearance," although they cite no evidence for this practice (*Isaiah*, 237).

[148] See Brown, *Seeing the Psalms*, 139–40.

[149] For a rich discussion of the recurrent term *śārāp* in Isaiah, see Landy, "Seraphim and Poetic Process." Some interpreters take the three terms for snakes in this

As one might imagine, the identity of this ruler has been a subject of considerable interest, with most interpreters opting for one Neo-Assyrian king or another. The superscription dating this oracle to "the year of the death of King Ahaz" (Isa 14:28) has been taken to suggest that the deceased king is Tiglath-Pileser III.[150] This identification, however, requires dating Ahaz's death to 727 BCE, the year in which Tiglath-Pileser died, whereas many scholars prefer the date 715 BCE.[151] Assuming the credibility of the superscription, it seems more natural to identify the deceased ruler in the poem with Ahaz himself. No extant sources indicate that he engaged in military activity against the Philistines, but Sweeney plausibly suggests that his appeal to Assyria during the Syro-Ephraimite War and subsequent "responsibility for maintaining Assyrian interests in the region," which negatively impacted the Philistines, justifies his portrayal as their oppressor.[152] To be sure, the image of the rod occurs most often in First Isaiah with reference to Assyria. In Isa 11:4, however, a Judahite king strikes the nations with "the rod of his mouth" (šebeṭ pîw). The tree images in Isa 11:1 and 14:29 are remarkably similar, and Isa 11 also contains references to snakes in v. 8, further connecting it to this oracle. These connections would be even more significant if, as is certainly plausible, Isa 11:1–10 was written with the reign of Hezekiah, and thus with the death of Ahaz, in mind.

verse as references to different animals and thus three successive rulers (Blenkinsopp, *Isa 1–39*, 292–3; Clements, *Isa 1–39*, 149; Landy, "Seraphim and Poetic Process," 21). More likely, however, ṣepaʿ ("adder") and śārāp ("serpent") are parallel terms referring to the same person, as the focus of the oracle is the deceased ruler's immediate successor (see Gray, *Isa I–XXVII*, 268; Kaiser, *Isa 13–39*, 53; Wildberger, *Isa 13–27*, 96).

[150] For example, Hayes and Irvine, *Isaiah*, 236–7; Seitz, *Isa 1–39*, 139; Wildberger, *Isa 13–27*, 92–4. Other interpreters, not wanting to place too much weight on a possibly secondary superscription, note that any number of eighth-century Assyrian kings or even Nebuchadnezzar II of Babylon conducted campaigns against the Philistines (Blenkinsopp, *Isa 1–39*, 292–3; Childs, *Isaiah*, 127–8; Clements, *Isa 1–39*, 149). Kaiser, as usual, dates this text very late and so identifies the ruler as Alexander the Great (*Isa 13–39*, 53).

[151] On the chronological difficulties associated with Ahaz's reign, see J. Blake Couey, "Ahaz," *NIDB* 1:83–4. For arguments for the later date for his death, see Nadav Na'aman, "Hezekiah and the Kings of Assyria," *Tel Aviv* 21 (1994): 235–54; repr. in *Ancient Israel and Its Neighbors: Interaction and Counteraction* (Winona Lake, Ind.: Eisenbrauns, 2005).

[152] Sweeney, *Isa 1–39*, 234.

The poem's imagery shifts yet again in Isa 14:30, although it remains within the domain of the animal world:

> wĕrā'û bĕkôrê dallîm
> wĕ'ebyônîm lābeṭaḥ yirbāṣû
> wĕhēmattî bārā'āb šoršēk
> ûšĕ'ērîtēk yahărōg[153]
> And the firstborn of the poor will graze,
> and the needy will lie down securely;
> but I will kill your root with hunger,
> and your remnant will be slain.

In biblical texts, the verbs rā'â ("graze") and rābaṣ ("lie down") are often used of domestic livestock, both literally and metaphorically (for example, Gen 41:2, 18; Num 22:27; Isa 30:23). By using these verbs, then, the first couplet of this verse depicts the most vulnerable inhabitants of Judah as small cattle, evoking the sense of tranquility associated with such animals. Their untroubled rumination and rest differ from the harsh repercussions that the Philistines can expect from the new king, which were hinted in the previous verse and are now described in the next couplet. The term "root" (šoršēk) recalls v. 29 and thereby helps to stabilize the highly variable complex of images. In contrast to the fecund root of the serpent, the root of the Philistines will not survive, nor will their "remnant" (šĕ'ērîtēk; note the soundplay with šoršēk). Within the logic of the shifting imagery, as Landy explains, "The flying seraph presides over, and permits the existence of, a zone of immunity, where the poor and needy peacefully graze."[154] This combination of figures is surprising, as a poisonous snake would normally represent a threat to livestock. In this detail, Isa 14:28–32 again echoes Isa 11:1–10, especially 11:8.

---

[153] Commentators generally harmonize the two verbs to eliminate the discrepancy between first- and third-person forms in MT (for example, Blenkinsopp, *Isa 1–39*, 291; Clements, *Isa 1–39*, 149; Duhm, *Jesaia*, 124–5; Wildberger, *Isa 13–27*, 88). Most of the versions employ a similar strategy. The first-person verb assumes YHWH as the subject, while the subject of the third-person verb could be either rā'āb ("hunger") in the previous line or śārāp mĕ'ôpēp ("flying serpent") in the previous verse (Kaiser, *Isa 13–39*, 56; de Waard, *Handbook*, 68). Alternatively, the verb could be impersonal and thus the functional equivalent of a passive (so Syr.), as suggested by C. L. Seow (private communication).

[154] Landy, "Seraphim," 22–3.

Imagery and Metaphor 181

Indeed, the description of the peaceable kingdom in Isa 11:6–9 is perhaps the most celebrated instance of animal imagery in Isaiah. In one of the corpus's more lengthily developed images, these verses depict the disruption of the food chain that lies at the heart of animal activity. The comprehensiveness of this transformation is underscored by the number of species named in the poem, including many of the most dangerous and feared carnivores of the ancient world: wolf (*zĕ'ēb*, v. 6), leopard (*nāmēr*, v. 6), two kinds of lions (*kĕpîr*, v. 6; *'aryēh*, v. 8), bear (*dōb*, v. 7), and two varieties of poisonous snakes (*pāten*; *ṣip'ônî*, v. 8).[155] Denuded of their ferocity, these animals not only cease to prey on other creatures but now live in harmonious community with defenseless herbivores, who forswear their instinctive fear of their former adversaries. Repeated references to young animals and children at play (*'ēgel* ["calf"], v. 6; *na'ar qāṭōn* ["a small child"], v. 6; *yaldêhen* ["their young"], v. 7; *yônēq* ["nursling"], v. 8; *gāmûl* ["weaned child"], v. 8) suggest that even the most vulnerable creatures need not fear harm. Further, the threatening waters of the sea no longer appear as a figure of dangerous chaos but now function as a simile for the universal knowledge of YHWH, which ultimately accounts for this radically reconfigured world (v. 9).

These verses powerfully represent the transformed character of life under the righteous Davidic king whose reign the poem celebrates. Although it seems unlikely that Isaiah means it straightforwardly as a depiction of the future, the description of the animal kingdom at the very least symbolizes drastic changes in the world order that may be expected under the new royal administration.[156] Given the frequency with which Isaiah portrays nations as animals in his poetry, it may serve more specifically as a broadly conceived metaphor for international peace, in which powerful nations no longer conquer weaker ones—most notably Judah.[157] (Sadly, in the war-torn worlds of the eighth century BCE and twenty-first century CE alike, this metaphorical reading seems almost as far-fetched as a literal one.) It is tempting to identify different animals in the poem with specific nations, taking

---

[155] For other biblical lists of dangerous animals, which overlap considerably with Isa 11:6–8, see Hos 13:7–8; Dan 7:3–6.

[156] By contrast, Isa 65:25 alludes to this text in an eschatological context as an actual description of a future, new earth (see v. 17).

[157] See William L. Holladay, *Isaiah: Scroll of a Prophetic Heritage* (Grand Rapids: Eerdmans, 1978), 111–12; Seitz, *Isa 1–39*, 106–7. Along with examples from Isa 1–39, Seitz also appeals to the vision of the beasts in Dan 7 in support of this interpretation.

the lion, for instance, to represent Assyria on the basis of Isa 5:29, but the text does not bear the weight of this sustained allegorical reading.[158] Rather, the image is more evocative than precise. As observed at the beginning of this discussion, the dynamics of relations between weaker and more powerful animals are what commends the zoological realm as a source of metaphors for dealings among nations. The imagery in Isa 11:6–9 both presupposes and subverts these dynamics, making this text in many ways the culmination of this line of discourse in Isaiah's poetry.

God as Animal

As this discussion has shown, Isaiah frequently imagines humans as animals. By contrast, he seldom imagines God in zoological terms, a striking reticence in light of the common occurrence of such metaphors in other biblical texts.[159] An exception to this reticence is a suggestive combination of animal images that portrays conflicting expectations for Judah's future during the Assyrian crisis of 701 BCE:

[4] kî kōh ʾāmar-yhwh ʾēlay
ka ʾăšer yehgeh hāʾaryēh
wĕhakkĕpîr ʿal-ṭarpô
ʾăšer yiqqārēʾ ʿālāyw
mĕlōʾ rōʿîm
miqqōlām lōʾ yēḥāt
ûmēhămônām lōʾ yaʿăneh
kēn yērēd yhwh ṣĕbāʾôt liṣbōʾ
ʿal-har-ṣîyôn wĕʿal-gibʿātāh
[5] kĕṣippŏrîm ʿāpôt
kēn yāgēn yhwh ṣĕbāʾôt ʿal-yĕrûšālāim
gānôn wĕhaṣṣēl
pāsōaḥ wĕhamlēṭ[160]

---

[158] For this reason, Sweeney's identification of the "small child" of v. 6 as the juvenile king Josiah is unconvincing (*Isa 1–39*, 204). Even Clements, who accepts the premise of a Josianic redaction, dismisses the possibility of a reference to a child king here (*Isa 1–39*, 124).

[159] See Brown, *Seeing the Psalms*, 144–52; Strawn, *Lion*, 58–65, 250–71.

[160] In MT, the second and fourth verbs in this series are pointed as *hipʿil* perfects (*wĕhiṣṣîl*, "and he will deliver"; *wĕhimlîṭ*, "and he will rescue"), but it seems preferable to point all four verbs as infinitives absolute (see Joüon §123n; Wildberger, *Isa 28–39*, 217).

[4] For thus says Yhwh to me:
　　Even as the lion growls,
　　　and the young lion over its prey,
　　when summoned against it
　　　is a full band of shepherds;
　　at their voice it does not tremble,
　　　and at their noise it does not cringe—
　　thus will Yhwh of hosts descend to fight
　　　against the mountain of Zion and its hill.
[5] As flying birds,
　　　thus will Yhwh of hosts be a shield over Jerusalem,
　　shielding and delivering,
　　　sparing and rescuing. (Isa 31:4–5)

The first simile (v. 4) depicts a lion guarding its prey from a group of shepherds, but its relationship to its target, the descent of the divine warrior on Jerusalem, remains vague. In the first place, it is unclear what action of the lion comprises the point of comparison. Is the divine combat somehow like the lion's growling—an ominous sound, to be sure, although less ferocious than a roar—or its fearlessness in the face of human opposition, or its consumption of the prey, which is not explicitly described but certainly implied in the verse? Second, Yhwh's intentions toward Jerusalem are difficult to discern, due largely to the multivalence of the preposition ʽal. Does Yhwh descend for battle "upon" Zion, against Jerusalem's enemies, or "against" Zion, through the agency of Jerusalem's enemies?

A few commentators take this verse as a positive portrayal of the deity's protection of Jerusalem from its invaders, represented by the shepherds.[161] Although the next verse may well require such a reinterpretation of the simile, it seems unlikely for a variety of reasons that this would be the reader or hearer's initial interpretation. First, as indicated by the repetition of the preposition ʽal, the simile links Zion with the lion's prey. As Exum observes, this connection does not seem promising: "A lion may defend its prey, but with the intention of devouring it, not protecting it."[162] Second, lion imagery typically has negative connotations when applied to God in the Hebrew Bible (for

---

[161] Blenkinsopp, *Isa 1–39*, 427; Hayes and Irvine, *Isaiah*, 349; Wildberger, *Isa 28–39*, 221–2.

[162] Exum, "Broken Pots," 338; so also Strawn, *Lion*, 61.

example, Hos 13:7–8; Job 10:16).[163] Third, the rescue of a sheep from a lion by a shepherd is portrayed as a valiant and heroic event in the Hebrew Bible, even when unsuccessful (for example, 1 Sam 17:34–37; Amos 3:12).[164] Finally, and perhaps most decisively, the expression *ṣābā' 'al* means "fight *against*" in other texts, most notably Isa 29:7–8 (see also Num 31:7; Zech 14:12).[165] For these reasons, a negative interpretation of the lion imagery, in which the deity attacks Jerusalem, seems more contextually likely. This effect depends not so much on specific similarities between the actions of the lion and Yhwh as the sense of terror and inescapable harm evoked by the animal figure. Isaiah portrays the advancing Assyrian army as a roaring lion in Isa 5:29; now, he seems to depict Jerusalem in the clutches of an even more fearsome lion, one that regards attempted human opposition as a trifle barely worth acknowledging.

The next simile in Isa 31:5 has many similarities to v. 4, including the nearly identical frames *ka'ăšer/kĕ-... kēn* ("even as... thus") and the repetition of the divine title *yhwh ṣĕbā'ôt* ("Yhwh of hosts") and the preposition *'al*, as well as the common animal imagery. These similarities condition the audience to expect another simile depicting a divine threat against Jerusalem. That possibility remains open even after the first line of v. 5, since the birds in question could be birds of prey. As clearly indicated by the opening verb, however, the next line describes the deity's protection of Jerusalem: "thus will Yhwh of hosts be a shield over Jerusalem."[166] As noted in the discussion of Isa 10:14, a mother bird is a common

---

[163] Even passages in which the imagery seems to have a positive sense, such as Hos 11:10 and Joel 4:16 (Eng. 3:16), are ambiguous at best; see Strawn, *Lion*, 60–4.

[164] In the context of Sennacherib's invasion, the shepherds may be a figure of the Egyptian support for which Judah hopes (Clements, *Isa 1–39*, 257; Sommer, "Ambiguity," 332). This interpretation seems even more likely if one views Isa 31:4–5 as the continuation of 31:1–3, which warns against reliance on Egypt (see Sweeney, *Isa 1–39*, 402–6).

[165] Wildberger argues that the verb *yērēd* ("will descend"), not *liṣbō'* ("to fight"), in fact governs *'al* (*Isa 28–39*, 219). While not impossible, the placement of the preposition argues against this view, although word order in Biblical Hebrew poetry admittedly displays greater variability than in prose.

[166] Sweeney still insists on a negative interpretation (*Isa 1–39*, 407). As Isa 5:29 demonstrates, Isaiah is certainly capable of reversing the usual senses of terms for rescue or protection, but it would seem perverse to do so with four consecutive verbs; see Yael Shemesh, "Isaiah 31,5: The Lord's Protecting Lameness," *ZAW* 115 (2003): 256–7. Blenkinsopp (*Isa 1–39*, 427) also points out that the verse contains the generic term *ṣippōrîm* ("birds"), rather than *'ayit* ("birds of prey").

biblical figure for divine protection. Indeed, Isa 31:5 may be taken as a response to Isa 10:14; instead of an abandoned nest, the Assyrian armies find a very present mother defending her young.[167] Still, the shift from threat to deliverance in Isa 31:4–5 is incredibly jarring, as even the poet seems to recognize. The second couplet of v. 5 contains four verbs denoting protection, as if to reassure the audience that they correctly understood the second simile.

The task remains to reconcile the earlier, negative interpretation of v. 4 with this new development. Exum suggests that the positive simile in v. 5 "limits and controls" the reading of v. 4, forcing the reader or hearer to reinterpret it.[168] The lion's fierce defense of its prey must be positive after all, and the phrase $ṣābā'$ $'al$ must uncharacteristically mean "fight over" instead of "fight against."[169] Such retrospective patterning occurs elsewhere in First Isaiah (for example, Isa 1:10; 5:11). In this case, as Tull observes, the poetic reversal may mimic the real-world experience of a military threat that is ultimately neutralized.[170] The choice of image seems counterintuitive, but no more so than the use of the verb $pālaṭ$ to describe a lion's removal of its prey in Isa 5:29. This resolution does not feel entirely satisfying, however. Exum herself convincingly argues against Wildberger's positive reading of v. 4, and Sommer and Strawn contend that the menacing image of the lion is too powerfully and extensively elaborated to be so easily forgotten.[171] Even if v. 5 secures a positive interpretation for the pair of similes, one still has to wonder what YHWH intends to do with Jerusalem after delivering the city from the Assyrians. Any sense of resolution thus remains ambiguous and uneasy, and one questions whether an attempt to reconcile the conflicting images is even the best approach. Given the similar inconsistency in other Isaianic oracles from this period (for example, Isa 29:1–8), it may simply be that Isaiah expected Judah to experience divine action in such inconsistent, if not outrightly contradictory, ways over the course of the crisis of 701 BCE.[172]

---

[167] See Clements, *Isa 1–39*, 257–8, although it need not follow that Isa 31:5 is a redactional addition inspired by Isa 10:14, as he concludes.
[168] Exum, "Broken Pot," 338; see also Sommer, "Ambiguity," 334.
[169] Sommer, "Ambiguity," 333.   [170] Tull, *Isa 1–39*, 463.
[171] Sommer, "Ambiguity," 334; Strawn, *Lion*, 62–3.
[172] Along these lines, J. J. M. Roberts connects Isa 31:4–5 to the "strange work" and "alien deed" of YHWH in Isa 28:21 (cited in Strawn, *Lion*, 62, n. 165).

READING OF ISAIAH 1:2-20

The foregoing discussion has isolated a number of tendencies in Isaiah's use of imagery in his poems. In the majority of cases, images have primarily local effects. They serve the rhetorical needs of a particular moment of the poem, and their impact is largely contained within the lines in which they occur, occasionally extending to contiguous line groups but seldom beyond. This localization is consistent with the generally centrifugal character of Biblical Hebrew poetry, in which the development of the parts outweighs the sense of the whole.[173] Few Isaianic poems are sustained meditations on single images. Isaiah 5:1-7 and 28:23-29 are exceptions to this rule, but they are also—perhaps as a result—relatively short poems. Images may be developed across several lines, which increases the force of their effect by slowing the movement of the poem and forcing the reader or hearer to savor the image more fully. For figurative images, this extension may impart greater complexity to the relationship between the source and target by incorporating more points of contact between the two. Such development, however, does not mitigate the more limited scope of their effects. Isaiah also displays a penchant for shifting images, sometimes in rapid succession. These shifts may involve images from related domains, in which case the impression of movement is less pronounced, or they may juxtapose completely different images, as sometimes happens with paired similes. Especially sudden or seemingly premature shifts catch the audience off guard, and they relativize the force of any individual image, suggesting that it is inadequate on its own to capture the desired quality of its target.

To explore how a variety of images may unfold within a single poem, I offer the following reading of Isa 1:2-20. Consistent with the tendencies noted earlier, individual images in this poem are restricted in scope. At the same time, certain recurring images have more extensive effects by virtue of their accumulation, which allows them to serve more significant structural and communicative functions within the poem.

---

[173] Grossberg, *Centripetal and Centrifugal*, 5-13.

[2] šimʿû šāmayim
   wěhaʾăzînî ʾereṣ
      kî yhwh dibbēr[174]
   bānîm giddaltî wěrômamtî
   wěhēm pāšěʿû bî
[3] yādaʿ šôr qōnēhû
   waḥămôr ʾēbûs běʿālāyw
   yiśrāʾēl lōʾ yādaʿ
      ʿammî lōʾ hitbônān
[4] hôy gôy ḥōṭēʾ
      ʿam kebed ʿāwōn
         zeraʿ měrēʿîm
            bānîm mašḥîtîm
   ʿāzěbû ʾet-yhwh
      niʾăṣû ʾet-qědôš yiśrāʾēl
         nāzōrû ʾāḥôr
[5] ʿal meh tukkû ʿôd
      tôsîpû sārâ
   kol-rōʾš loḥŏlî
      wěkol-lēbāb dawwāy
[6] mikkap-regel wěʿad-rōʾš
      ʾên-bô mětōm
   peṣaʿ wěḥabbûrâ
      ûmakkâ ṭěrîyâ
   lōʾ-zōrû wělōʾ ḥubbāšû
      wělōʾ rukkěkâ baššāmen
[7] ʾarṣěkem šěmāmâ
      ʿārêkem śěrūpôt ʾēš
   ʾadmatkem lěnegděkem
      zārîm ʾōkělîm ʾōtāh
         ûšěmāmâ kěmahpēkat zārîm[175]

---

[174] It is tempting to take v. 2a as an "A- A- // A—" couplet, with an internally parallel first line (see *BHS*). In such couplets, however, the second line is typically longer than either half of the first line, which is not the case here. The division of v. 2a as a triplet seems more likely given the closing triplet, with a nearly identical final line, in v. 20.

[175] Most commentators emend MT *zārîm* ("strangers") to *sědôm* ("Sodom"), with which *mahpēkâ* always occurs ("overthrown") elsewhere (Deut 29:22 [Eng. 29:23]; Isa 13:19; Jer 49:18; 50:40; Amos 4:11; see Gray, *Isa I–XXVII*, 13; Wildberger, *Isa 1–12*, 18; Williamson, *Isa 1–5*, 50). Although the emendation is plausible, the versions support MT, and the apparently redundant comparisons in both vv. 7 and 8 may be explained as examples of the so-called *k- veritas* (see GKC §118x; Joüon §133g; *IBHS*, 203), despite Williamson's objections. The variation on the stereotyped phrase anticipates the occurrences of *sědôm* in vv. 9–10 (Tull, *Isa 1–39*, 57).

188   Reading the Poetry of First Isaiah

[8] wĕnôtĕrâ bat-ṣîyôn
    kĕsukkâ bĕkārem
    kimlûnâ bĕmiqšâ
    kĕʿîr nĕṣôrâ[176]
[9] lûlê yhwh ṣĕbāʾôt
    hôtîr lānû śārîd
    kimʿat[177] kisdōm hāyînû
    laʿămōrâ dāmînû
[10] šimʿû dĕbar-yhwh
     qĕṣînê sĕdōm
     haʾăzînû tôrat ʾĕlōhênû
     ʿam ʿămōrâ
[11] lāmâ-lî rōb-zibḥêkem
     yōʾmar yhwh
     śābaʿtî ʿōlôt ʾêlîm wĕḥēleb mĕrîʾîm
     wĕdam pārîm ûkĕbāśîm wĕʿattûdim lōʾ ḥāpāṣtî[178]
[12] kî tābōʾû lirʾōt[179] pānāy
     mî-biqqēš zōʾt miyyedkem
     rĕmōs ḥăṣērāy [13] lōʾ tôsîpû
     hābîʾ minḥōt šāwʾ[180]

---

[176] For MT nĕṣûrâ ("guarded," √nṣr), LXX, Syr., and Tg. apparently read a nipʿal participle of √ṣwr ("besiege"). While the verb is not otherwise attested in the nipʿal, the change requires no consonantal emendation and makes nice sense. For alternative interpretations or emendations, see Gray, Isa I–XXVII, 14; Wildberger, Isa 1–12, 20; Williamson, Isa 1–5, 51–2.

[177] MT includes kimʿat with the preceding clause, modifying śārîd (thus, "a few survivors"), followed by most interpreters (for example, Gray, Isa I–XXVII, 14; Wildberger, Isa 1–12, 20). Williamson (Isa 1–5, 53–4) reads the term with the next line, based on comparable texts such as Pss 81:15 (Eng. 81:14); 94:17 (see also Kaiser, Isa 1–12, 17). I have followed his proposal, which appropriately suggests a narrow escape from Sodom's fate.

[178] Although these lines are significantly longer than surrounding ones, further division does not seem possible. The first two words of the second line are a construct chain, and the predicate lōʾ ḥāpāṣtî ("I do not delight") is too short to stand alone. The only alternative would be a line break between ûkĕbāśîm ("and lambs") and wĕʿattûdim ("and goats"), which would diminish the cumulative effect of the list of animals.

[179] MT has as a nipʿal infinitive (lērāʾōt, "to appear"), which LXX supports. Syr., however, has an active verb, and most commentators think an original qal infinitive has been altered to avoid the suggestion that humans can see God (Wildberger, Isa 1–12, 34; Williamson, Isa 1–5, 75; etc.); see also Exod 34:24; Deut 31:11; Ps 42:3 (Eng. 42:2).

[180] MT, followed by BHS, isolates rĕmōs ḥăṣērāy ("trampling my courts") as its own line. The phrase hābîʾ minḥat-šāwʾ ("bringing a meaningless gift") then becomes the object of lōʾ tôsîpû ("do not continue"). By contrast, LXX has rĕmōs ḥăṣērāy as the object of lōʾ tôsîpû, and it reads minḥōt ("gifts") for MT minḥat ("gift"), taking that phrase as a verbless clause. This division, which is followed by NRSV and REB, achieves more balanced lines and offers a more pointed critique of the Judahite cult, which MT may have intentionally softened (Gray, Isa I–XXVII, 19, 24–5; Williamson, Isa 1–5, 76–7).

qĕṭōret tô'ēbâ hî' lî
ḥōdeš wĕšabbāt qĕrō' miqrā'
lō'-'ûkal 'āwen wa'ăṣārâ
[14] *ḥodšêkem ûmô'ădêkem*
śānĕ'â napšî
hāyû 'ālay lāṭōraḥ
nil'êtî nĕśō'
[15] *ûbĕpāriśkem kappêkem*
'a'lîm 'ênay mikkem
gam kî-tarbû tĕpillâ
'ênennî šōmēa'
yĕdêkem dāmîm mālē'û
[16] *raḥăṣû hizzakkû*
hāsîrû rōa' ma'allêkem
minneged 'ênāy
ḥidlû hārēa' [17] *limdû hêṭēb*
diršû mišpāṭ 'aššĕrû ḥāmôṣ[181]
šipṭû yātôm rîbû 'almānâ
[18] *lĕkû-nā' wĕniwwākĕḥâ*
yō'mar yhwh
'im-yihyû ḥăṭā'êkem kaššānî-m[182]
kaššeleg yalbînû
'im-ya'dîmû kattôlā'
kaṣṣemer yihyû
[19] *'im-tō'bû ûšĕma'tem*
ṭûb hā'āreṣ tō'kēlû
[20] *wĕ'im-tĕmā'ănû ûmĕrîtem*
ḥereb[183] *te'ukkēlû*
kî pî yhwh dibbēr

---

[181] MT *ḥāmôṣ* is a *nomen agentis* from √*ḥmṣ*, "treat violently" (Bauer-Leander, 470kα), which may also occur in Isa 16:4 (1QIsa[a] *ḥmwṣ*, but compare MT *hammēṣ*, "the extortioner"). The versions unanimously read a passive form, and many interpreters follow suit (Blenkinsopp, *Isa 1–39*, 180; Kaiser, *Isa 1–12*, 24; Wildberger, *Isa 1–12*, 36). The meaning of the verb *'aššĕrû* is likewise complicated. It may be derived from √ *'šr* I ("lead, direct"; so Tg.; Sym.), √ *'šr* II ("declare happy"; so Syr.; Aq.; Theod.), or perhaps √*yšr* ("be straight, upright"); LXX *hrusasthe* ("rescue") is a free translation. Based on Isa 3:12 and 9:15 (Eng. 9:16), a derivation from √ *'šr* I seems most likely (Gray, *Isa I–XXVII*, 25–6; Williamson, *Isa 1–5*, 80–1).

[182] MT *šānîm* ("scarlet") is difficult, as the term is singular (*šānî*) everywhere except here and Prov 31:21; 1QIsa[a] reads *šny*. Cohen, following Dahood, suggests that the plural in MT results from a misread enclitic *–m* ("Enclitic-*mem*," 245–8).

[183] On the basis of 1QIsa[a], Syr., and Tg., Blenkinsopp (*Isa 1–39*, 180) and Wildberger (*Isa 1–12*, 54) emend MT *ḥereb* ("sword") to *baḥereb* ("by the sword"), the more typical construction for expressing instrumentality with passive verbs (*IBHS*, 385),

[2] Hear, O heavens,
and give ear, O earth,
For Y<small>HWH</small> has spoken.
"Children I have raised and reared,
but they have rebelled against me.
[3] The ox knows its owner,
and the ass its master's trough;
Israel does not know;
my people do not understand."
[4] Hey, sinful nation,
people weighty with iniquity,
offspring who commit evil,
children who act wickedly,
who have abandoned Y<small>HWH</small>,
who have scorned the Holy One of Israel,
who have turned away.[184]
[5] Why are you still being beaten,
do you continue insubordination?
The whole head is sick,
and the whole heart faint.
[6] From the sole of the foot up to the head,
there is no soundness in it,
only bruises and stripes
and oozing wounds;
they are not pressed or bandaged
or softened with oil.
[7] Your land is a desolation,

especially with the noun *ḥereb* (Num 14:3; Isa 3:25; Lam 2:21; see GKC §119o). MT is preferable on stylistic grounds. The omission of the preposition in poetry is not surprising (see Ps 17:13), and its absence strengthens the parallelism between vv. 19b and 20b, which heightens the wordplay in these verses. Gray, followed by van der Kooij, reads the otherwise biblically unattested *ḥārūb* ("carob husks"), on the basis of Akk., Aram., and Mid. Heb.: Gray, *Isa I–XXVII*, 30; Arie van der Kooij, "Textual Criticism of the Hebrew Bible: Its Aim and Method," in *Emanuel: Studies in the Hebrew Bible, Septuagint, and Dead Sea Scrolls in Honor of Emanuel Tov* (eds. Shalom M. Paul et al.; VTSup 94; Leiden: Brill, 2003), 733–4.

[184] Despite the third-person verbs, the final lines of this verse continue the direct address initiated by the vocative *hôy* and resumed explicitly in v. 5; see Hayes and Irvine, *Isaiah*, 71–2; J. J. M. Roberts, "Form, Syntax, and Redaction in Isaiah 1:2–20," *Princeton Seminary Bulletin* NS 3 (1982): 300–1; see further Delbert R. Hillers, "*Hôy* and *Hôy*-Oracles: A Neglected Syntactic Aspect," in *The Word of the Lord Shall Go Forth: Essays in Honor of David Noel Freedman* (eds. Carol Meyers and Michael O'Connor; Winona Lake, Ind.: Eisenbrauns, 1983), 185–8.

your cities burned with fire;
your countryside—in your presence,
   foreigners eat it,
      and the desolation is as if overthrown by foreigners.
[8] And daughter Zion is left
   like a booth in a vineyard,
      like a shelter in a cucumber field,
      like a besieged city.
[9] "Had not Yhwh of hosts
   left for us a few survivors,
like Sodom we would have soon become,
   to Gomorrah we would have been likened."
[10] Hear the word of Yhwh,
   O rulers of Sodom!
Give ear to the instruction of our God,
   O people of Gomorrah!
[11] "What to me is the multitude of your sacrifices?"
   says Yhwh.
"I am gorged on burnt offerings of rams and fat of cattle,
   and in the blood of cows, lambs, and goats I take no delight!
[12] When you come to see my face,
   who sought this from your hand?
Trampling my courts [13] do not continue!
   Bringing offerings is meaningless;
      incense is an abomination to me!
New moons and sabbaths, the convoking of convocations—[185]
   I cannot endure iniquitous assemblies!
[14] Your new moons and your appointed festivals,
   my very self hates.
They have become a burden upon me
   that I am tired of bearing.
[15] And when you spread your hands,
   I will avert my eyes from you;
even when you increase prayers,
   I will not listen.
Your hands are full of blood:
   [16] wash up, clean yourselves!
Remove the evil of your deeds
   from before my eyes!
Stop doing evil; [17] learn to do good;

---

[185] For this translation of *qĕrō' miqrā'*, see Gray, *Isa I–XXVII*, 21.

       seek justice; lead the oppressor aright;
          advocate for the orphan; stand up for the widow!
[18] Come, let us dispute together,"
    says YHWH.
"Though your sins be like scarlet,
    like snow they may yet be white;
though they be red like crimson,
    like wool they may yet become.
[19] If you are willing and obey,
    the good of the land you will eat;
[20] but if you refuse and rebel,
    by the sword you will be eaten."
    For the mouth of YHWH has spoken.

The identification of Isa 1:2–20 as a single poem is more contested than was the case for the texts considered at the end of the previous chapters.[186] As indicated by the separate superscriptions in Isa 1:1 and 2:1, the entire first chapter functions on some level as a single unit within the Book of Isaiah. Most commentators do not find a more pronounced break between vv. 20 and 21 than between any of the other compositional units that they identify in the chapter, at least some of which are attributable to the eighth-century prophet.[187] This tendency is reinforced by the growing consensus that Isa 1 was deliberately assembled to function as an introduction to the book as a whole. On the other hand, much like Isa 3:1–15, the boundaries of Isa 1:2–20 are marked by an inclusio (*kî* [*pî*] *yhwh dibbēr*, "for [the mouth of] YHWH has spoken," vv. 2, 20), and recurring keywords and images hold these verses together.[188] At the very least, as Sweeney and Williamson maintain, they constitute a distinct subunit within Isa 1, which can be attributed to the careful design of a sensitive editor.[189] A minority of interpreters, including Yehoshua Gitay, J. J. M. Roberts,

---

[186] For an overview of proposed boundaries for the opening unit of the book through the early 1980s, see John T. Willis, "The First Pericope in the Book of Isaiah," *VT* 34 (1984): 63–77.

[187] For example, Blenkinsopp, *Isa 1–39*, 180–1; Childs, *Isaiah*, 16–17; Clements, *Isa 1–39*, 28–9; Tull, *Isa 1–39*, 50–1; Wildberger, *Isa 1–12*, 9.

[188] Sweeney, *Isa 1–39*, 64–5; Williamson, *Isa 1–5*, 29–30, 81–2; Willis, "First Pericope," 69–70.

[189] Sweeney, *Isa 1–39*, 64; Williamson, *Isa 1–5*, 81; see also Gray, *Isa I–XXVII*, 3. Both Sweeney and Williamson take vv. 1–18 as a collage of originally separate Isaianic prophecies and vv. 19–20 as a later addition.

and John T. Willis, argue for the compositional unity of the passage on the basis of genre or rhetoric.[190] Although I remain sympathetic to this view, my reading of the poem would be largely unaffected if it had a more complicated compositional history. Interpreters generally take Isa 1:7–8 as a reference to Sennacherib's invasion of Judah in 701 BCE,[191] and vv. 10–17 can be read against this background as well.[192] The poem is divided into two sections of roughly equal length (vv. 2–9 and 10–20). Each begins with the pair of imperative verbs *šim'û* ("listen") and *ha'ăzînî/û* ("give ear," vv. 2, 10) and closes with a conditional statement or statements (vv. 9, 18b–20). The first section denounces the people of Judah for their faithlessness and senselessness, demonstrated by their continued rebellion against YHWH despite suffering a catastrophic military invasion. In the second section, the deity lambasts their endless piety but offers to restore their fortunes if they adhere to traditional expectations for social justice.

The poem opens in v. 2a by summoning "heaven" and "earth" to listen to the divine speech. This summons evokes the atmosphere of legal proceedings (see also Deut 32:1; Mic 6:1–2; Ps 50:4) and suggests that the people of Judah have wronged YHWH.[193] Calling "earth" (*'āreṣ*) as a witness anticipates v. 8, in which the "earth" (*'arṣĕkem*) has been laid waste because of Judah's transgression, making it an

---

[190] Yehoshua Gitay, "Reflections on the Study of the Prophetic Discourse: The Question of Isaiah I 2–20," *VT* 33 (1983): 216; Roberts, "Form, Syntax, and Redaction," 301; Willis, "First Pericope," 68–72.

[191] For example, Sweeney, *Isa 1–39*, 77; Wildberger, *Isa 1–12*, 21–2; Williamson, *Isa 1–5*, 63. Alternatively, Hayes and Irvine connect these verses to an earthquake during the reign of King Uzziah (see Amos 1:1; Zech 14:5) and thus locate Isa 1:2–20 early in the prophet's career (*Isaiah*, 70, 73). Other interpreters reject claims of Isaianic authorship and date them to the aftermath of the Babylonian invasion in 587 BCE: Ehud Ben Zvi "Isaiah 1,4–9, Isaiah, and the Events of 701 BCE in Judah. A Question of Premise and Evidence," *SJOT* 5 (1991): 95–111; Kaiser, *Isa 1–12*, 20–1; de Jong, *Isaiah among the Ancient Near Eastern Prophets*, 158–60.

[192] Blenkinsopp, *Isa 1–39*, 184; Roberts, "Form, Syntax, and Redaction," 294; Willis, "First Pericope," 75–6. Sweeney argues strongly against this position (*Isa 1–39*, 80).

[193] Based on this detail, many commentators identify the poem as a "covenant lawsuit" (for example, Roberts, "Form, Syntax, and Redaction"; Wildberger, *Isa 1–12*, 9–11; Tull, *Isa 1–39*, 52–3; Willis, "First Pericope," 73–4). This identification has recently been challenged; see Dwight R. Daniels, "Is There a 'Prophetic Lawsuit' Genre?" *ZAW* 99 (1987): 347–50, 354–60; Williamson *Isa 1–5*, 26–7; Williamson, "Isaiah 1 and the Covenant Lawsuit," in *Covenant as Context: Essays in Honour of E. W. Nicholson* (eds. A. D. H. Mayes and R. B. Salters; Oxford: Oxford University Press, 2003), 393–406.

aggrieved party to the indictment.[194] YHWH speaks in v. 2b, characterizing the people as defiant children. The compound predicate *giddaltî wĕrômamtî* ("I have raised and reared") denotes the extent of the deity's paternal care, despite which the nation has "rebelled," although the precise character of that rebellion is not specified. The language implies that they are ungrateful for their care, but v. 3 portrays them as woefully ignorant of it, in contrast to livestock who recognize their owner and food source. The charge is especially insulting because the capacity to "know" (√*yd*ʿ) is a characteristic difference between humans and animals in the Hebrew Bible (Pss 32:9; 73:22; Job 35:11). The negative progression in v. 3 was discussed in the previous chapter. One may note further that these couplets develop a negated metaphor, establishing a comparison that ought to prove valid but does not.[195] This verse also introduces two prominent image clusters that will recur throughout the poem—animal imagery and food imagery.[196] Throughout vv. 2-3, the first-person speech reveals deep divine pathos, as YHWH complains to the cosmos that common livestock show more loyalty than the deity's own children/nation.

Until this point, the people have only overheard the accusations against them. In v. 4, the prophet addresses them for the first time with four disparaging vocative phrases, the last one of which resumes the parent–child metaphor.[197] The portrayal of the people's foolishness continues in v. 5a, as the speaker expresses shock that they persist in their rebellion despite devastating consequences. The consequences are depicted as being "beaten" (√*nkh*), a common biblical image for divine punishment that reflects the domain of parental discipline (for example, 2 Sam 7:14).[198] Within First Isaiah, this

---

[194] Daniels, "Prophetic Lawsuit," 358.
[195] See Alonso Schökel, *Manual*, 107, who compares Job 14:7-10.
[196] On the recurrence of food imagery in Isa 1:2-20, see Roy F. Melugin, "Figurative Speech and the Reading of Isaiah 1 as Scripture," in *New Visions of Isaiah* (eds. Roy F. Melugin and Marvin A. Sweeney; JSOTSup 214; Sheffield: Sheffield Academic Press, 1996), 291.
[197] Tull, *Isa 1-39*, 53-5.
[198] The description of child abuse and the apparent victim-blaming in Isa 1:5 are highly disturbing (Blenkinsopp, *Isa 1-39*, 183). On the one hand, this text reflects the historical reality that striking a child was an accepted disciplinary practice in the ancient world; on the other hand, the unrestrained abuse is a metaphor for an extreme situation, which suggests that the poem's audience would have regarded it as unusual. For a thoughtful critique of the child/parent metaphor in prophetic literature, see Julia

image resonates with the repeated depiction of Assyria as the rod with which YHWH will strike Judah. The question in v. 5a contains a horrific double entendre, as the interrogative *'al meh* ("why?"; see Num 22:32; Jer 8:14; etc.) can literally be rendered "upon what" (Job 38:6; 2 Chr 32:10), suggesting that Judah is so severely wounded that no part of the body remains untouched for further blows.[199] Indeed, the next four couplets graphically describe the imagined body of the beaten child. The repetition of *kol-* ("the whole") and the phrase *mikkap-regel wĕ'ad rō'š* ("from the sole of the foot up to the head"; see also Lev 13:12; Deut 28:35; Job 2:7) chart the extent and severity of the punishment. Verse 6 sharpens this impression with a mini-catalogue of nouns denoting injuries (*peṣa'*, "bruise"; *ḥabbûrâ*, "stripe"; *makkâ*, "wound"). The description is grotesque to the point of absurdity, reflecting the speaker's perception that Judah absurdly refuses to change its actions.

The target of the metaphor is revealed in v. 7, where the endless wounds on the child's body become locations devastated by an invading army. To secure this connection, three geographical terms (*'arṣĕkem*, "your land"; *'ārêkem*, "your cities"; *'admatkem*, "your countryside") match the three nouns denoting injuries in v. 6. The statement that "foreigners eat" (*'ōkĕlîm*) Judah's land picks up the food imagery from v. 3. There, the ass had recognized its food provider, unlike Judah; now, Judah's food stores are plundered in their sight. Initially, the opening line of v. 8 appears to celebrate Jerusalem's narrow survival, but then a pair of similes compare the city to "a booth" (*sukkâ*) and "a lodge" (*mĕlûnâ*), highlighting its vulnerability following the destruction of the surrounding countryside.[200] Such structures provided shelter for agricultural laborers, but

---

M. O'Brien, *Challenging Prophetic Metaphor: Theology and Ideology in the Prophets* (Louisville: Westminster John Knox, 2008), 77–100.

[199] Gray rightly notes the absurdity of such a question (*Isa I–XXVII*, 11). Rather than an argument against this rendering, however, the absurdity seems to be the very point.

[200] Gray, *Isa I–XXVII*, 13–14; *contra* Williamson, *Isa 1–5*, 71. For a discussion of *sukkâ* in a similar context in Lam 2:6, see Dobbs-Allsopp, *Weep*, 69–71. It need not follow, as he argues, that this parallel means that Isa 1:8 "depicts Jerusalem's destruction" (*Weep*, 146). Rather, the evocation of the city lament genre indicates how close the city has come to destruction, much as the use of *qînâ*-rhythm in Amos 5:1–2 suggests the imminent destruction of Israel before it has taken place.

they were temporary edifices meant only to last a season.[201] The unfolding similes invite the audience to imagine a uniform expanse of cultivated land, punctuated only by a forlorn, unimpressive hut, which appears all the more fragile in its isolation. They also portray the land of Judah as a "vineyard" or "cucumber field," which fits well with the image of foreigners devouring the land—ironically, one of the outcomes that agricultural shelters were intended to prevent. The final line of the quatrain also begins with the preposition k-, suggesting a third simile. Instead, it literally describes Jerusalem as "a besieged city," as if the prophet, unable to find another apt image, gives up and simply acknowledges the harsh reality of the situation.[202]

Verse 9 quotes the people of Judah—their only response in the poem.[203] Initially, their assessment of the situation appears correct. They acknowledge their precarious state, using the same verb ($\sqrt{ntr}$, "to leave") that the speaker had used in v. 8, and they attribute their survival to YHWH.[204] The second couplet, however, reveals their ongoing lack of perception. Although they would have indeed turned out like Sodom and Gomorrah had YHWH not delivered them, they contend that they have nothing in common with the proverbial cities because they were not destroyed. This conclusion arrogantly presumes the certainty of their survival, even though v. 5 had warned of future blows and v. 8 had emphasized Jerusalem's ongoing vulnerability. More problematically, their attempt to distance themselves from Sodom and Gomorrah reveals their refusal to take responsibility for their actions. Because they were spared the proverbial fate of these cities, they imply that they must not share their proverbial sinfulness,

---

[201] For images of agricultural shelters in early twentieth-century CE Palestine, see Dalman, *Der Ackerbau*, figs. 12–15; note the flimsiness of the structure that appears in fig. 12. Permanent stone towers were also constructed for the same purpose, as depicted in Isa 5:2.

[202] Compare the seemingly redundant characterization of an army as "like warriors" (*kĕgibbôrîm*) and "like fighters" (*kĕ'anšê milḥāmâ*) in Joel 2:7, which Alter describes as "literal designations rhetorically masquerading as similes" (*Art of Biblical Poetry*, 42).

[203] The first-person plural language in v. 9, which does not occur otherwise in the poem save for v. 18, suggests the presence of speech; see, for example, Isa 28:15; 29:11. For pronominal shifts as an indicator of direct discourse, see Rolf A. Jacobson, *"Many are Saying": The Function of Direct Discourse in the Hebrew Psalter* (JSOTSup 397; London: T&T Clark, 2004), 21–2; Cynthia L. Miller, *The Representation of Speech in Biblical Hebrew Narrative: A Linguistic Analysis* (HSM 55; Atlanta: Scholars Press, 1996), 62–9.

[204] Tull, *Isa 1–39*, 60.

either. In this way, the first section of the poem ends by allowing the people to demonstrate directly the ignorance that the poet has repeatedly attributed to them.

To open the second section of the poem, the prophet addresses the people as "rulers of Sodom" and "people of Gomorrah" in v. 10. These monikers, which are emphasized by the vocative enjambment, categorically overturn the people's logic from v. 9. Their wickedness does merit comparison with that of those two cities, and the phonic similarity of ʿam ("people") and ʿămōrâ ("Gomorrah") further accentuates the similarity.[205] The allusion hints at the hitherto unspecified nature of Judah's sin, as Sodom is associated with social and legal injustice in other prophetic texts (Isa 3:9; Ezek 16:49). The prophet's voice now gives way to that of Yhwh, who speaks exclusively for the remainder of the poem, and explicit indications of divine speech in vv. 11, 18, and 20 reinforce this shift. It is as if the people's obduracy has become so impenetrable that the deity must take over for the prophet and address them directly. Elaborating earlier charges that the nation is faithless and stupid, vv. 11–15 attack their cultic practices. A sequence of caustic rhetorical questions (vv. 11–12) and sharp denunciations (vv. 13–15a) verbally enact the blows dealt to Judah in the first section of the poem, and the diatribe seems as excessive as the endless sacrifices that it denounces. Throughout, the imagery imparts striking concreteness to these verses.

The central claim of this diatribe is that Yhwh rejects the worship of the people, which has become preposterously excessive. Corroborating this criticism, the poet lists *ad nauseam* different kinds of sacrificial animals (v. 11), religious festivals (vv. 13–14), and cultic observances (vv. 13–14). Verse 14 calls the people's festivals a "burden" (*tôrāḥ*) on the deity, possibly an ironic pun on the word *tôrâ* ("Torah"). The highly anthropomorphic depiction of Yhwh—note the references to "face" (v. 12), "throat" (*napšî*; v. 14), and "eyes" (v. 15)—reflects the underlying assumption that sacrifices are a meal for the deity.[206] This concurrence of animal and food imagery recalls the same combination in v. 3, where the people failed to recognize the source of their sustenance, in contrast to the dumb ass. Now, Yhwh refuses their offered sustenance of "rams . . . cattle . . . cows, lambs, and goats" (vv. 12–13). Indeed, the deity claims to be "gorged"

---

[205] Alonso Schökel, "Isaiah," 167.
[206] See Gray, *Isa I–XXVII*, 21; Melugin, "Figurative Speech," 290–1.

(śābaʿtî) on their sacrifices in v. 11,[207] and the phrase śānĕʾâ napšî ("my very self hates") in v. 14 possibly connotes nausea.[208] In the final line of v. 15, Yhwh justifies this rejection. The people's hands, which had presented the offerings and made gestures of prayer, "are full of blood (dāmîm)." The plural of dām usually denotes violent bloodshed (for example, Gen 4:10–11; 1 Sam 26:20; 1 Kgs 2:5), so it does not refer directly to the sacrificial blood mentioned in v. 11.[209] Nevertheless, the repetition is not accidental. The mixture of different kinds of blood in the poem powerfully figures an unseemly combination of piety and injustice.[210] This statement is the most specific accusation of wrongdoing against Judah in the poem.

Verses 16–17 contain a series of imperatives explaining how the people may regain Yhwh's favor. The short clauses of the internally parallel lines quicken the pace of the poem, especially in contrast to the long, often multi-line clauses in the preceding verses. This change in pace lends a sense of urgency to the commands in these verses. The short clauses also suggest that the divine expectations of Judah are relatively simple, which makes the people's prior refusal to obey them seem all the more ridiculous. The first two verbs in v. 16, "wash up" (raḥăṣû) and "make yourselves clean" (hizzakkû), extend the image of bloody hands from the previous verse. The repeated reference to the divine eyes equates "the evil of [their] doings" with the ritual activities listed in v. 15. Verse 17 urges the people to enact social justice. Although the verse contains some novel locutions, such as the enigmatic ʾaššĕrû ḥāmôṣ ("lead the oppressor aright"), it also uses stereotypical language such as "widow" (yātôm) and "orphan" (ʾalmānâ), which occurs frequently in similar contexts in First Isaiah and other biblical texts (Isa 1:23; 10:2; see also Deut 10:18; Jer 7:6; Zech 7:10). This familiar diction reinforces the sense that that these demands are neither new nor unreasonable. Although the verse does not directly accuse the people of failing to act justly, the repeated commands to do so assume such failure, confirming the earlier hint in the allusion

---

[207] The verb √śbʿ ("to be satisfied") occurs frequently with reference to food (Deut 8:10; Isa 9:19 [Eng. 9:20]; Ps 59:16 [Eng. 59:15]).
[208] So Alonso Schökel, taking nepeš to refer to the throat (Manual, 103). The embodied language in this part of the poem make this proposal attractive, although other biblical texts that use the verb √śnʾ with nepeš do not have this sense (2 Sam 5:8; Ps 11:5).
[209] Gray, Isa I–XXVII, 23; Tull, Isa 1–39, 62; Williamson, Isa 1–5, 98.
[210] Wildberger, Isa 1–12, 48.

to Sodom that injustice has been the underlying problem throughout the poem.[211]

These demands form the basis for possible reconciliation between the deity and the people in the final verses of the poem. YHWH invites them to arbitration in v. 18, with the verb *niwwakkĕḥâ* ("let us dispute together") returning the poem to the arena of legal proceedings.[212] Two pairs of conditional statements follow, each introduced by *'im* ("although, if"). The first pair (v. 18) raises the possibility that the nation's guilt, for which the poem has made an overwhelming case, might be taken away. In an evocative use of color imagery—unusual for First Isaiah—red depicts the people's continued sinfulness, extending the blood imagery of v. 15; likewise, white raises the possibility of restored innocence through images of snow and wool. The second pair of conditional statements (vv. 19–20) presents the people with a choice, reprising the imagery of food one last time. Obedience to the deity will make it possible for them to "eat the good of the land" (*ṭûb hā'āreṣ tō'kēlû*), reversing the earlier "eating" (*'ōkĕlîm*) of their land by foreigners (v. 7). The consequences of continued rebellion are likewise couched in terms of eating, only now Judah "will be eaten by the sword" (*ḥereb tĕ'ukkĕlû*). Just as a personified heaven and earth appeared as witnesses at the beginning of the poem, the personified sword emerges at the end as the potential executioner. The metaphor of the devouring sword (see 2 Sam 2:26; Isa 31:8) conveys the weapon's capacity to slice, while ascribing to it a frightening degree of agency and appetite.[213] In light of this metaphor, the phrase "mouth of YHWH" (*pî yhwh*) in the final line may play on the expression "mouth of the sword" (*pî ḥereb*; for example, Deut 13:16 [Eng. 13:15]; Judg 1:8; 1 Sam 22:19). This line forms an inclusio with v. 2a, bracketing the poem with an emphasis on the divine origin of its content.

Although this discussion has hardly captured the depth of the poem's images, it provides some grounds for an account of their structural significance. In most cases, as one expects in this corpus,

---

[211] Tull, *Isa 1–39*, 61.
[212] *Contra* Daniels, "'Prophetic Lawsuit,'" 348–9.
[213] The metaphor finds visual expression in the construction of some ancient Near Eastern swords in the third to second millennia BCE, in which the blade extends from the open mouth of a lion's head carved into the hilt; see Joshua Berman, "The 'Sword of Mouths' (Jud. III 16; Ps. CXLIX 6; Prov. V.4): A Metaphor and its Ancient Near Eastern Context," *VT* 52 (2002): 299–300, 303, figs. 1–2.

they are tightly contained with largely local effects. The metaphors of the beaten body (vv. 5–6) and agricultural structures (v. 8), for instance, powerfully figure the historical circumstances of the poem, which are not explicitly in view elsewhere. Familial language in vv. 2, 4 is less developed and more diffuse but still restricted largely to those verses, as is true for the variegated cultic language of vv. 11–15. Other images have wider effects. Allusions to Sodom and Gomorrah in vv. 9–10, which is anticipated by *mahpēkat* ("overthrown") in v. 7, bridge the two sections of the poem. Food imagery, which typically occurs in conjunction with animal imagery, enjoys the greatest frequency and most consistent distribution (vv. 3, 7–8, 11, 19–20). It is associated with many of the important themes of the poem, including the people's rebellion against Yhwh, their punishment, the inadequacy of their acts of devotion, and the possibility of future restoration. In short, the richly assorted images in Isa 1:2–20 have powerful evocative effects within the lines in which they occur, and a few have more extensive impact across the poem as a whole. Taken together, they provide this sophisticated piece of ancient literature with substantial rhetorical punch.

Conclusion

"More or Less Happy Misunderstandings"

This is an exciting time for the study of Isaiah, as demonstrated by the current explosion of scholarly work and impassioned debate about almost every aspect of the book. For all of the attempts over the past thirty years to read the Book of Isaiah as a unified whole, however, little work has focused on poetry *qua* poetry in the book. As a result, much of its literary richness has been underappreciated, especially in chapters 1–39. This study is an attempt to fill that gap. Proceeding from the presupposition that poetic style and textual meaning are inseparable, it has explored in some depth three central features of the style of First Isaiah, which contains one of the most remarkable and provocative poetic voices in the Hebrew Bible.

Chapter 1 deals with lineation, the *sine qua non* of verse. Lineation remains a contested matter for the Isaianic corpus because no ancient biblical manuscripts of prophetic books consistently mark line breaks in visible fashion, although units delimited by punctuation within these manuscripts sometimes correspond to poetic lines. This fact does not mean that Isaiah contains no poetry, because lineation is primarily an aural phenomenon that exists independently of textual representation. It does mean that interpreters must actively identify the line breaks in Isaianic poetry and provide compelling arguments to support proposed divisions. Several factors may assist in this process. Parallelism is the most reliable marker because it creates identifiable frames for poetic lines, in which major syntactic junctures generally correspond to line endings. In the case of enjambed, non-parallel lines, attention to syntax and soundplay provides useful clues. Because Biblical Hebrew poetry is non-metrical, line lengths cannot be predicted on the basis of recurring, quantifiable patterns. At the same time, poetic lines typically fall within a range of two to six words, with three- and four-word lines appearing most frequently in First Isaiah. Awareness of this range can narrow the possibilities for line breaks in uncertain cases. Finally, an awareness of the syntactic constraints that typically restrict the shapes of lines offers another set of controls. With minor modifications, O'Connor's *Hebrew Verse Structure* provides the most helpful description of these constraints. Lineation reinforces and even creates poetic meaning in a variety of ways. As a result, decisions about lineation should be made in conjunction with other stages of the interpretive process, and readings of biblical poems should include arguments for these decisions.

Chapter 2 discusses poetic structure, understood as the means by which poems move from beginning to end, albeit seldom in a neatly linear fashion. This movement unfolds at two levels. The most concentrated movement happens within pairs of lines—that is, couplets. Larger groups are also attested but occur less frequently. Parallelism and enjambment are the major options for joining lines in Isaiah's poetry, as in Biblical Hebrew poetry more generally. The former creates a sense of progression or development in a multitude of ways; even when it does not, the simple expectation of a parallel line, established in most poems by the consistency of the phenomenon, drives the movement of the poem. Isaiah skillfully exploits the grammatical, semantic, and phonological aspects of parallel lines, to use Berlin's categories. In some lines, the conjunction of semantic contrast and syntactic or phonological equivalence creates a sense of narrative development. In other lines, subtle semantic differences between matching words or syntactic transformations establish a more restrained sense of progression. Enjambment moves poetry forward by means of syntactic dependency, as a single enjambed line is incomplete without its partner. The presence of enjambed lines within a poem provides structural relief from the dominance of parallelism. Triplets, quatrains, and even larger line groups frequently combine parallelism and enjambment. Because they occur less commonly than couplets, these line groups effectively mark the beginning or end of poems, or they give added rhetorical emphasis to the content of their lines. Single lines, which occur even less frequently in First Isaiah, serve similar functions.

While parallelism and enjambment consistently establish tight relationships within line groups, structural connections between line

Conclusion: "More or Less Happy Misunderstandings" 203

groups across poems are more loosely articulated in Biblical Hebrew poetry and in First Isaiah. Multiple line groups may combine to form larger sections of poems—frequently if inaptly called "strophes" or "stanzas"—but these sections seldom appear in predictable patterns. The impression of movement throughout a poem depends largely on thematic connections. Formal devices play some role in this process as well, frequently holding together individual sections of the poem or bridging multiple such sections. Although there is great variation in the deployment of such devices, Isaiah uses three of these regularly: parallelism and enjambment at the level of the couplet; distant parallelism and repetition; and catalogues. Within a poem, multiple thematic connections and formal devices work in tandem, and sometimes at cross purposes, to secure a tentative sense of structural unity. The larger structures of Isaianic poems unfold differently, and they only become apparent over the course of the reader or hearer's experience of any given poem.

Finally, poetic images are the topic of Chapter 3. Both non-figurative and figurative images verbally replicate sensory experiences and thereby appeal to an audience's imagination. Figurative images or metaphors project selected features from one conceptual domain onto another, lending insight into unappreciated aspects of their target. In order to grasp their richness, one must use relevant textual and iconographic evidence to reconstruct an ancient audience's possible range of associations with particular images in biblical poems. Images play an important role in the rhetoric of Isaiah's poetry because of their capacity to elicit a variety of emotional reactions. The prophet crafts a striking assortment of images from a number of different sources. Agriculture and the animal world are evoked with significant frequency, but even within these complexes there is great variety. In his agricultural images, Isaiah alludes in both positive and negative contexts to the joy that accompanies successful harvests in an agrarian economy, and he creatively associates different aspects of crop production with divine judgment. The animal images, which draw on a wide range of common tropes attested in ancient Near Eastern literature, include the portrayal of conquered cities as pasturage for livestock, the association of nations and their leaders with various domestic and wild species, and an especially multivalent depiction of God as both lion and bird. Isaiah likes to group multiple images together within poems, sometimes shifting dramatically from one domain to another; paired similes are an especially common example of this tendency. Even when developed across several lines, images have mostly local effects in their respective poems, although short poems may occasionally unfold a single, elaborate image.

In addition to exploring these three topics, this study has the broader aim of demonstrating that poetic language in Isa 1–39 constitutes a distinctive form of discourse that must be appreciated on its own terms. The poetic vignette of the unwilling ruler in Isa 3:6–7, for instance, captures a feeling of tense desperation amidst social anarchy in distinctively poetic fashion through its use of short, often verbless lines, unexpected and incongruous images, and elliptical dialogue. Comparable content could certainly appear in various prose genres, but the effects would be very different. In Isa 31:4–5, the stark juxtaposition of two animal similes with opposite meanings hauntingly portrays the prophet's conflicting expectations for Yhwh's involvement in the Assyrian crisis. It is difficult to imagine the achievement of such an effortless paradox in another medium. As a result of this close relationship between form and content, attention to the style of Isaiah 1–39 makes a significant difference for the interpretation of these texts, from relatively minor text-critical decisions to broad theological and ideological questions. Even if all of the examples offered in this book are not equally convincing, the cumulative number should make the point sufficiently that form and content cannot be neatly separated in this corpus.

Amidst the detailed analyses of selections from Isaiah's poetry, the discussion has at times no doubt lost sight of the proverbial forest for the trees. I trust that this is not a shortcoming, but rather an unavoidable and even welcome concession to the particularity of poetic discourse, especially in such a diverse and diffuse corpus. Given the objectives of this study, though, a more general description of the characteristics of the poetry of First Isaiah is in order. Many of these features characterize Biblical Hebrew poetry in general, but some distinctive tendencies can be isolated in this corpus. Isaiah's poems are written in free verse. The typical line contains three or four words, with longer or shorter lines often used for particular effects. The poet's bag of tricks for line formation includes chiasm, anaphora, and sound patterning, but not to a significantly greater degree than in other biblical poems. More characteristic of his style is internal parallelism, including the "A- A- // A—" couplets identified by Watson. These poems contain noticeably more enjambed lines than many other collections of biblical poetry, approaching in some poems

Conclusion: "More or Less Happy Misunderstandings" 205

the high percentages that obtain for Lamentations. They also contain a high occurrence of parallelism and enjambment encompassing whole line groups and not simply lines. These features, along with the intricacy of the clausal structures in general, are all examples of a syntactic complexity that is typical of Isaianic style. Structurally, the poems tend to be loosely organized, with limited centralizing features that may not fully overcome the sense of disconnect among the parts. This loose organization allows for greater elaboration of individual images or motifs. Other noteworthy characteristics include the use of catalogues as a structural device; frequent wordplay, especially double entendre; the careful shaping and subsequent frustration of the audience's expectations through retrospective patterning; and a high incidence of imagery, usually localized and moderately developed, and regularly grouped in diverse clusters.

This constellation of recurrent features affects the tone and texture of the poetry in significant ways, often resonating with important themes in Isa 1–39. Isaiah's characteristic complexity requires considerable attention on the part of the audience, even as it rewards that attention by sustaining their interest. The demanding character of the poetry perhaps unwittingly plays some role in accomplishing the prophet's divine commission to "make sluggish the mind of this people... lest they perceive with their mind" (Isa 6:10).[1] Constant surprises prove both delightful and devastating, and the persistent thwarting of the audience's expectations mimics the anticipated thwarting of all human enterprises that oppose YHWH (Isa 8:10). Through the effective use of parallelism, thematic development, and rapid shifts in imagery, the prophet elaborates with apparently endless enthusiasm on his denouncements of sinful behavior or threats of divine judgment, leaving the object of his critique no excuse or escape. The poetry is often quite dark, with frequent evocations of lament, likely reflecting the historical context of increased Assyrian military activity and uncertainty over Judah's future. Against this backdrop, however, the notes of comfort and reassurance, if muted by comparison, shine all the more brightly. Natural imagery, including but not limited to the agricultural and animal images examined in Chapter 3, imparts an air of earthiness to many poems. Ironically, given Isaiah's largely negative

---

[1] For more on this connection, see Stephen A. Geller, *Sacred Enigmas: Literary Religion in the Hebrew Bible* (London: Routledge, 1996), 108–41; Sommer, "Ambiguity," 342–5.

view of human wisdom (for example, Isa 5:21; 29:14), the syntactic complexity, clever puns, and use of catalogues establish an almost scholastic tone. The speaking voice that emerges from these poems is by turns sarcastic, antagonistic, erudite, heartbroken, confident, hopeful—in short, as complexly constructed as the poems themselves. Even in a treatment of this length, it has not been possible to account adequately for many important aspects of Isaiah's poetic style, as a result of both the size of the corpus and the richness of its contents. Several topics deserve further study, and I would like to highlight three of these here, some of which have been mentioned already in passing. Many scholars have recognized and discussed various aspects of Isaiah's penchant for soundplay.[2] Nonetheless, certain features of his sonic repertoire merit additional consideration, including the frequent use of reduplicated words, especially *pilpel* and related verbal forms (for example, *yĕsaksēk* in Isa 9:10 [Eng. 9:11]; *mĕṣapṣēp* in Isa 10:14; *mĕṭalṭelkā* in Isa 22:17). Second, the effects of Isaiah's diction would be a fruitful avenue for exploration. Like other Biblical Hebrew poems, texts in Isaiah 1–39 use a striking number of rare or unusual words. Of particular interest is the predilection for loanwords in this corpus (for example, *šalmōnîm*, "gifts," in Isa 1:23; *šĕkîyôt*, "armadas," in Isa 2:17; *sĕʾôn*, "sandal," in Isa 9:3 [Eng. 9:4]). This seems to be part of a larger strategy of imitating foreign speech, especially in poems depicting other nations, which has been discussed by Gary A. Rendsburg.[3] Finally, these poems frequently call attention to their status as speech. As prophecy, of course, much of Isaiah 1–39 presents itself as the direct speech of a prophetic intermediary who speaks on behalf of the deity, but other voices appear in this corpus as well. Wildberger has briefly sketched Isaiah's extensive use of citations in his poetry, noting especially his purported quotations of his detractors (for example, Isa 5:19; 29:15; 30:10–11).[4] One could build

---

[2] In addition to observations on individual examples in commentaries, especially those of Gray, Wildberger, and Williamson, note Alonso Schökel's comments on consonance, rhyme, and onomatopoeia ("Isaiah," 167–8, 170–1) and Roberts's study of double entendre ("Double Entendre").

[3] Gary A. Rendsburg, "Linguistic Variation and the 'Foreign' Factor in the Hebrew Bible," in *Language and Culture in the Near East* (eds. Shlomo Izre'el and Rina Drory; Israel Oriental Studies 15; Leiden: Brill, 1996), 181–2, 184–5; on similar phenomena in the Book of Job, see Edward L. Greenstein, "The Language of Job and its Poetic Function," *JBL* 122 (2003): 651–66.

[4] Wildberger, *Isa 28–39*, 679–81.

on these observations in a number of ways, including a study of the creation of poetic personas through speech, such as the Assyrian king in Isa 10:5–15 or Y<small>HWH</small> throughout the corpus. Much work, obviously, remains to be done.

In a 1903 letter to an admirer and would-be writer, the German poet Rainer Maria Rilke warned, "With nothing can one approach a work of art so little as with critical words: they always come down to more or less happy misunderstandings."[5] Over the course of this exploration of the poetry of First Isaiah, the truth of Rilke's estimation of literary criticism has become painfully apparent. Despite its misunderstandings, which one at least trusts are more happy than less, this study has grown out of repeated experiences of being delighted, horrified, and moved by its subject. I hope that my critical words have, however imperfectly, suggested something of the virtuosity of these poems and, above all, that they will encourage and serve future readings of them. Should that prove to be the case, this project will have been a success.

---

[5] Rilke, *Letters to a Young Poet* (trans. M. D. Herter Norton; New York: W. W. Norton, 1993), 17.

Bibliography

Alonso Schökel, Luis. "Isaiah." Pages 165–83 in *The Literary Guide to the Bible*. Edited by Robert Alter and Frank Kermode. Cambridge, MA: Belknap Press of Harvard University Press, 1987.

Alonso Schökel, Luis. *A Manual of Hebrew Poetics. Subsidia Biblica* 11. Rome: Pontifical Biblical Institute, 1988.

Alter, Robert. *The Art of Biblical Poetry*. New York: Basic Books, 1985.

Alter, Robert. *The Book of Psalms: A Translation with Commentary*. New York: Norton, 2009.

Andersen, Francis I. and A. Dean Forbes. "Prose Particle Counts of the Hebrew Bible." Pages 165–83 in *The Word of the Lord Shall Go Forth: Essays in Honor of David Noel Freedman in Celebration of his Sixtieth Birthday*. Edited by Carol Meyers and Michael O'Connor. Winona Lake, IN: Eisenbrauns, 1983.

Andersen, Francis I. and David Noel Freedman. *Amos: A New Translation with Introduction and Commentary*. Anchor Bible 24A. New York: Doubleday, 1989.

Auld, A. Graeme. "Poetry, Prophecy, Hermeneutic: Recent Studies in Isaiah." *Scottish Journal of Theology* 33 (1980): 577–81.

Avalos, Hector. "Introducing Sensory Criticism in Biblical Studies: Audiocentricity and Visiocentricity." Pages 47–60 in *This Abled Body: Rethinking Disabilities in Biblical Studies*. Edited by Hector Avalos, Sarah J. Melcher, and Jeremy Schipper. Society of Biblical Literature Semeia Studies 55. Atlanta: Society of Biblical Literature, 2007.

Avigad, Nahman. "The Epitaph of a Royal Steward from Siloam Village." *Israel Exploration Journal* 3 (1953): 137–52.

Baer, David A. "'It's All About Us!' Nationalistic Exegesis in the Greek Isaiah." Pages 29–48 in *As Those who are Taught: Interpretation of Isaiah from the LXX to the SBL*. Edited by Claire Mathews McGinnis and Patricia K. Tull. Society of Biblical Literature Symposium Series 27. Atlanta: Society of Biblical Literature, 2006.

Barré, Michael L. "A Rhetorical-Critical Study of Isaiah 2:12–17." *Catholic Biblical Quarterly* 65 (2003): 522–34.

Barry, Peter. *Beginning Theory: An Introduction to Literary and Cultural Theory*. 2nd ed. Manchester: Manchester University Press, 2002.

Bartelt, Andrew H. *The Book around Immanuel: Style and Structure*. Biblical and Judaic Studies 4. Winona Lake, IN: Eisenbrauns, 1996.

Bartelt, Andrew H. "Isaiah 5 and 9: In- or Interdependence?" Pages 157–74 in *Fortunate the Eyes that See: Essays in Honor of David Noel Freedman in Celebration of his Seventieth Birthday*. Edited by A. B. Beck et al. Grand Rapids: Eerdmans, 1995.

Barth, Hermann. *Die Jesaja-Worte in der Josiazeit*. Wissenschafliche Untersuchungen zum Alten und Neuen Testament 48. Neukirchen-Vluyn: Neukirchener Verlag, 1977.

Barton, John. "Historical Criticism and Literary Interpretation: Is There Any Common Ground?" Pages 3–15 in *Crossing the Boundaries: Essays in Biblical Interpretation in Honour of Michael D. Goulder*. Edited by Stanley E. Porter et al. Biblical Interpretation Series 8. Leiden: Brill, 1994.

Batto, Bernard F. *Slaying the Dragon: Mythmaking in the Biblical Tradition*. Louisville: Westminster John Knox, 1992.

Becker, Uwe. *Jesaja, von der Botschaft zum Buch*. Forschungen zur Religion und Literatur des Alten und Neuen Testaments 178. Göttingen: Vandenhoeck & Ruprecht, 1997.

Ben Zvi, Ehud. "Isaiah 1,4–9, Isaiah, and the events of 701 BCE in Judah. A Question of Premise and Evidence." *Scandinavian Journal for the Study of the Old Testament* 5 (1991): 95–111.

Ben Zvi, Ehud and Michael H. Floyd (eds.). *Writings and Speech in Israelite and Ancient Near Eastern Prophecy*. Society of Biblical Literature Symposium Series 10. Atlanta: Society of Biblical Literature, 2000.

Berlin, Adele. *The Dynamics of Biblical Parallelism*. Bloomington, IN: Indiana University Press, 1985.

Berlin, Adele. *Biblical Poetry through Medieval Jewish Eyes*. Bloomington, IN: Indiana University Press, 1991.

Berlin, Adele. "Introduction to Hebrew Poetry." Pages 301–15 in vol. 4 of *The New Interpreter's Bible*. Edited by Leander E. Keck. 12 vols. Nashville: Abingdon, 1994.

Berman, Joshua. "The 'Sword of Mouths' (Jud. III 16; Ps. CXLIX 6; Prov. V.4): A Metaphor and its Ancient Near Eastern Context." *Vetus Testamentum* 52 (2002): 291–303.

Beuken, Willem A. M. "Isaiah 30: A Prophetic Oracle Transmitted in Two Successive Paradigms." Pages 369–97 in vol. 1 of *Writing and Reading the Scroll of Isaiah: Studies of an Interpretive Tradition*. Edited by Craig C. Broyles and Craig A. Evans. 2 vols. Supplements to *Vetus Testamentum* 70. Formation and Interpretation of Old Testament Literature 1–2. Leiden: Brill, 1997.

Beuken, Willem A. M. *Jesaja 1–12*. Translated by Ulrich Berges. Herders Theologischer Kommentar zum Alten Testament. Freiburg: Herder, 2003.

Beuken, Willem A. M. "Obdurate Short-Sightedness in the Valley of Vision: How Atonement of Iniquity is Forfeited (Isa 22:1–14)." Pages 45–63 in *One Text, A Thousand Methods: Studies in Memory of Sjef van Tilborg*.

Edited by Patrick Chatelion Counet and Ulrich Berges. Biblical Interpretation Series 71. Leiden: Brill, 2005.
Beuken, Willem A. M. *Jesaja 13-23*. Translated by Ulrich Berges. Herders Theologischer Kommentar zum Alten Testament. Freiburg: Herder, 2007.
Black, Jeremy A. *Reading Sumerian Poetry*. London: Athlone Press, 1998.
Blenkinsopp, Joseph. "Fragments of Ancient Exegesis in an Isaian Poem." *Zeitschrift für die alttestamentliche Wissenschaft* 93 (1981): 51-62.
Blenkinsopp, Joseph. *Isaiah 1-39: A New Translation with Introduction and Commentary*. Anchor Bible 19. New York: Doubleday, 2000.
Blenkinsopp, Joseph. "Judah's Covenant with Death (Isaiah XXVIII 14-22)." *Vetus Testamentum* 50 (2000): 472-83.
Blenkinsopp, Joseph. "Cityscape to Landscape: The 'Back to Nature' Theme in Isaiah 1-35." Pages 35-44 in *"Every City Shall be Forsaken": Urbanism and Prophecy in Ancient Israel and the Near East*. Edited by Lester L. Grabbe and Robert D. Haak. *Journal for the Study of the Old Testament*: Supplement Series 330. Sheffield: Sheffield Academic Press, 2001.
Borowski, Oded. *Agriculture in Iron Age Israel*. Winona Lake, IN: Eisenbrauns, 1987. Repr., Boston: American Schools of Oriental Research, 2002.
Borowski, Oded. *Every Living Thing: Daily Use of Animals in Ancient Israel*. Walnut Creek, CA: AltaMira, 1998.
Brensinger, Terry L. *Simile and Prophetic Language in the Old Testament*. Mellen Biblical Press 43. Lewiston, NY: Edwin Mellen, 1996.
Brogan, T. V. F. "Meter." Pages 768-83 in *The New Princeton Encyclopedia of Poetry and Poetics*. Edited by Alex Preminger and T. V. F. Brogan. Princeton: Princeton University Press, 1993.
Brogan, T. V. F. "Poetry." Pages 938-42 in *The New Princeton Encyclopedia of Poetry and Poetics*. Edited by Alex Preminger and T. V. F. Brogan. Princeton: Princeton University Press, 1993.
Brogan, T. V. F. "Stanza." Pages 1211-13 in *The New Princeton Encyclopedia of Poetry and Poetics*. Edited by Alex Preminger and T. V. F. Brogan. Princeton: Princeton University Press, 1993.
Brogan, T. V. F. "Verse and Prose." Pages 1346-51 in *The New Princeton Encyclopedia of Poetry and Poetics*. Edited by Alex Preminger and T. V. F. Brogan. Princeton: Princeton University Press, 1993.
Brogan, T. V. F., Alex Preminger, and Edward R. Weismiller. "Verse Paragraph." Page 1352 in *The New Princeton Encyclopedia of Poetry and Poetics*. Edited by Alex Preminger and T. V. F. Brogan. Princeton: Princeton University Press, 1993.
Brooks, Cleanth. "The Heresy of Paraphrase." Pages 67-79 in *The Well-Wrought Urn: Studies in the Structure of Poetry*. New York: Harcourt, Brace, Jovanovich, 1975.

Brown, Francis, Samuel R. Driver, and Charles A. Briggs (eds.). *A Hebrew and English Lexicon of the Old Testament, with an Appendix Containing the Biblical Aramaic.* Oxford: Clarendon, 1907.
Brown, William P. "The So-Called Refrain in Isaiah 5:25–30 and 9:7–10:4." *Catholic Biblical Quarterly* 52 (1990): 432–43.
Brown, William P. *The Ethos of the Cosmos: The Genesis of Moral Imagination in the Bible.* Grand Rapids: Eerdmans, 1999.
Brown, William P. *Seeing the Psalms: A Theology of Metaphor.* Louisville: Westminster John Knox, 2002.
Carr, David M. "Reaching for Unity in Isaiah." *Journal for the Study of the Old Testament* 57 (1993): 61–80.
Carr, David M. *Writing on the Tablet of the Heart: Origins of Scripture and Literature.* Oxford: Oxford University Press, 2005.
Chapman, Cynthia R. *The Gendered Language of Warfare in the Israelite-Assyrian Encounter.* Harvard Semitic Monographs 62. Winona Lake, IN: Eisenbrauns, 2004.
Childs, Brevard S. *Isaiah and the Assyrian Crisis.* Studies in Biblical Theology 2:3. London: SCM, 1967.
Childs, Brevard S. *Isaiah: A Commentary.* Old Testament Library. Louisville: Westminster John Knox, 2001.
Clements, Ronald E. *Isaiah 1–39.* New Century Bible. Grand Rapids: Eerdmans, 1980.
Clements, Ronald E. "The Prophecies of Isaiah and the Fall of Jerusalem in 587 B.C." *Vetus Testamentum* 30 (1980): 421–36.
Cloete, Walter Theophilus Woldemar. *Versification and Syntax in Jeremiah 2–25: Syntactical Constraints in Hebrew Colometry.* Society of Biblical Literature Dissertation Series 117. Atlanta: Scholars Press, 1989.
Cogan, Mordechai. *Imperialism and Religion: Assyria, Judah, and Israel in the Eighth and Seventh Centuries B.C.E.* Society of Biblical Literature Monograph Series 19. Missoula, MT: Scholars Press, 1974.
Cohen, Harold R. (Chaim). *Biblical Hapax Legomena in the Light of Akkadian and Ugaritic.* Society of Biblical Literature Dissertation Series 37. Missoula, MT: Scholars Press, 1978.
Cohen, Harold R. (Chaim). "The Enclitic-mem in Biblical Hebrew: Its Existence and Initial Discovery." Pages 231–60 in *Sefer Moshe: The Moshe Weinfeld Jubilee Volume: Studies in the Bible and the Ancient Near East, Qumran, and Post-Biblical Judaism.* Edited by Chaim Cohen et al. Winona Lake, IN: Eisenbrauns, 2004.
Cole, Steven W. "The Destruction of Orchards in Assyrian Warfare." Pages 29–40 in *Assyria 1995: Proceedings of the 10th Anniversary Symposium of the Neo-Assyrian Text Corpus Project, Helsinki, September 7–11, 1995.* Edited by S. Parpola and R. M. Whiting. Helsinki: Neo-Assyrian Text Corpus Project, 1997.

Collins, Terrence. *Line-Forms in Hebrew Poetry: A Grammatical Approach to the Stylistic Study of the Hebrew Prophets*. Studia Pohl: Series Maior 7. Rome: Pontifical Biblical Institute, 1978.

Collins, Terrence. "Line Forms in Hebrew Poetry." *Journal of Semitic Studies* 23 (1978): 228–44.

Conrad, Edgar W. *Reading Isaiah*. Overtures to Biblical Theology. Minneapolis: Fortress, 1991.

Conrad, Edgar W. "Prophet, Redactor and Audience: Reforming the Notion of Isaiah's Formation." Pages 306–26 in *New Visions of Isaiah*. Edited by Roy F. Melugin and Marvin A. Sweeney. *Journal for the Study of the Old Testament*: Supplement Series 214. Sheffield: Sheffield Academic Press, 1996.

Cooper, Alan M. *Biblical Poetics: A Linguistic Approach*. Ann Arbor, MI: University Microfilms, 1977.

Corley, Jeremy. "Rhyme in the Hebrew Prophets and Wisdom Poetry." *Biblische Notizen* 132 (2007): 55–67.

Couey, J. Blake. "Ahaz." Pages 83–4 in vol. 1 of *The New Interpreter's Dictionary of the Bible*. Edited by Katharine Doob Sakenfeld. 5 vols. Nashville: Abingdon, 2006.

Couey, J. Blake. "The Disabled Body Politic in Isaiah 3:1, 8." *Journal of Biblical Literature* 133 (2014): 95–109.

Couey, J. Blake. "Evoking and Evading: The Poetic Presentation of the Moabie Catastrophe in Isaiah 15–16." Pages 19–31 in *Concerning the Nations: Essays on the Oracles Against the Nations in Isaiah, Jeremiah, and Ezekiel*. Edited by Andrew Mein, Else K. Holt, and Hyun Chul Paul Kim. Library of Hebrew Bible/Old Testament Studies 612. New York: Bloomsbury T&T Clark, 2015.

Coxon, Peter W. "The 'List' Genre and Narrative Style in the Court Tales of Daniel." *Journal for the Study of the Old Testament* 35 (1986): 95–121.

Cross, Frank Moore, Jr. "Studies in the Structure of Hebrew Verse: The Prosody of Lamentations 1:1–22." Pages 129–55 in *The Word of the Lord Shall Go Forth: Essays in Honor of David Noel Freedman in Celebration of His Sixtieth Birthday*. Edited by Carol L. Meyers and M. O'Connor. American Schools of Oriental Research Special Volume Series 1. Winona Lake, IN: Eisenbrauns, 1983.

Cross, Frank Moore Jr. and David Noel Freedman. *Studies in Ancient Yahwistic Poetry*. Society of Biblical Literature Dissertation Series 21. Missoula, MT: Scholars Press, 1975. Repr., The Biblical Resource Series. Grand Rapids: Eerdmans, 1997.

Cullhed, Anna, "Original Poetry: Robert Lowth and Eighteenth-Century Poetics," Pages 25–47 in *Sacred Conjectures: The Context and Legacy of Robert Lowth and Jean Astruc*. Edited by John Jarick. Library of Hebrew Bible/Old Testament Studies 457. New York: T&T Clark, 2007.

Dahood, Mitchell. *Psalms III, 100–150*. Anchor Bible 17A. Garden City: Doubleday, 1968.

Dalman, Gustaf. *Der Ackerbau*. Vol. 2 of *Arbeit und Sitte in Palästina*. Gütersloh: C. Bertelsmann, 1932.

Dalman, Gustaf. *Brot, Öl und Wein*. Vol. 4 of *Arbeit und Sitte in Palästina*. Gütersloh: C. Bertelsmann, 1934.

Daniels, Dwight R. "Is There a 'Prophetic Lawsuit' Genre?" *Zeitschrift für die alttestamentliche Wissenschaft* 99 (1987): 339–60.

Darr, Katheryn Pfisterer. *Isaiah's Vision and the Family of God*. Literary Currents in Biblical Interpretation. Louisville: Westminster John Knox, 1994.

Darr, Katheryn Pfisterer. "Literary Perspectives on Prophetic Literature." Pages 127–43 in *Old Testament Interpretation: Past, Present, and Future: Essays in Honor of Gene M. Tucker*. Edited by James L. Mays et al. Nashville: Abingdon, 1995.

Davidson, R. "The Interpretation of Isaiah II 6ff." *Vetus Testamentum* 16 (1966): 1–7.

Day, John. *God's Conflict with the Dragon and the Sea: Echoes of a Canaanite Myth in the Old Testament*. University of Cambridge Oriental Publications 35. New York: Cambridge University Press, 1985.

Dietrich, Manfried, Oswald Loretz, and Joaquín Sanmartín (eds.). *The Cuneiform Alphabetic Texts from Ugarit, Ras Ibn Hani, and Other Places*. 2nd ed. Abhandlungen zur Literatur Alt-Syren-Palästinas und Mesopotamiens 8. Münster: Ugarit Verlag, 1995.

Dobbs-Allsopp, F. W. *Weep, O Daughter of Zion: A Study of the City-Lament Genre in the Hebrew Bible*. Biblica et Orientalia 44. Rome; Pontifical Biblical Institute, 1993.

Dobbs-Allsopp, F. W. "Rethinking Historical Criticism." *Biblical Interpretation* 7 (1999): 235–71.

Dobbs-Allsopp, F. W. "The Psalms and Lyric Verse." Pages 346–79 in *The Evolution of Rationality: Interdisciplinary Essays in Honor of J. Wentzel van Huyssteen*. Edited by F. LeRon Shults. Grand Rapids: Eerdmans, 2006.

Dobbs-Allsopp, F. W. "Psalm 133: A (Close) Reading," *Journal of Hebrew Scriptures* 8 (2008): doi:10.5508/jhs.2008.v8.a20. <http://www.jhsonline.org/Articles/article_97.pdf> (accessed 13 January 2015).

Dobbs-Allsopp, F. W. "Poetry, Hebrew." Pages 550–8 in vol. 4 of *The New Interpreter's Dictionary of the Bible*. Edited by Katharine Doob Sakenfeld. 5 vols. Nashville: Abingdon, 2009.

Dobbs-Allsopp, F. W. "The Effects of Enjambment in Lamentations (Part 2)." *Zeitschrift für die alttestamentliche Wissenschaft* 113 (2001): 370–85.

Dobbs-Allsopp, F. W. "The Enjambing Line in Lamentations: A Taxonomy (Part I)." *Zeitschrift für die alttestamentliche Wissenschaft* 113 (2001): 219–39.

Dobbs-Allsopp, F. W. "Space, Line, and the Written Biblical Poem in Texts from the Judean Desert." Pages 19–61 in *Puzzling Out the Past: Studies in Northwest Semitic Languages and Literatures in Honor of Bruce Zuckerman.* Edited by Marilyn J. Lundberg, Steven Fine, and Wayne T. Pitard. Culture and History of the Ancient Near East 55. Leiden: Brill, 2012.

Dobbs-Allsopp, F. W., J. J. M. Roberts, C. L. Seow, and R. S. Whitaker (eds.). *Hebrew Inscriptions: Texts from the Biblical Period of the Monarchy with Concordance.* New Haven: Yale University Press, 2005.

Donner, Herbert. *Israel unter den Völkern; die Stellung der klassischen Propheten des 8. Jahrhunderts v. Chr. zur Aussenpolitik der Könige von Israel und Juda.* Supplements to *Vetus Testamentum* 11. Leiden: Brill, 1964.

Driver, G. R. "Linguistic and Textual Problems: Isaiah I–XXXIX." *Journal of Theological Studies* 38 (1937): 36–49.

Driver, G. R. "Isaiah I–XXXIX: Textual and Linguistic Problems." *Journal of Semitic Studies* 13 (1968): 36–57.

Duhm, Bernard. *Das Buch Jesaia übersetzt und erklärt.* 5th ed. Göttingen: Vandenhoeck & Ruprecht, 1968.

Eagleton, Terry. *How to Read a Poem.* Oxford: Blackwell, 2007.

Ehrlich, Arnold B. *Jesaja, Jeremia.* Vol. 4 of *Randglossen zur Hebräischen Bibel: textcritisches, sprachliches und sachliches.* Leipzig: J. C. Hinrichs, 1912.

Emerton, J. A. "Are There Examples of Enclitic *Mem* in the Hebrew Bible?" Pages 321–38 in *Texts, Temples, and Traditions: A Tribute to Menahem Haran.* Edited by Michael V. Fox et al. Winona Lake, IN: Eisenbrauns, 1996.

Emerton, J. A. "Notes on the Text and Translation of Isaiah XXII 8–11 and LXV 5." *Vetus Testamentum* 30 (1980): 437–51.

Emerton, J. A. "Some Difficult Words in Isaiah 28.10, 13." Pages 39–76 in *Biblical Hebrews, Biblical Texts: Essays in Memory of Michael P. Weitzman.* Edited by Ada Rapoport-Albert and Gillian Greenberg. *Journal for the Study of the Old Testament*: Supplement Series 333/Hebrew Bible and its Versions 2. Sheffield: Sheffield Academic Press, 2001.

Everson, A. Joseph, and Hyun Chul Paul Kim (eds.). *The Desert Will Bloom: Poetic Visions in Isaiah.* Society of Biblical Literature: Ancient Israel and its Literature 4. Atlanta: Society of Biblical Literature, 2009.

Exum, J. Cheryl. "Of Broken Pots, Fluttering Birds, and Visions of the Night: Extended Simile and Poetic Technique in Isaiah." *Catholic Biblical Quarterly* 43 (1981): 331–52.

Exum, J. Cheryl. *Song of Songs: A Commentary.* Old Testament Library. Louisville: Westminster John Knox, 2005.

Fensham, F. Charles. "Common Trends in Curses of the Near Eastern Treaties and *Kudurru*-Inscriptions Compared with Maledictions of

Amos and Isaiah." *Zeitschrift für die alttestamentliche Wissenschaft* 75 (1963): 155-75.

Finnegan, Ruth. *Oral Poetry: Its Nature, Significance, and Social Context.* Cambridge: Cambridge University Press, 1977. Repr., Bloomington, IN: Indiana University Press, 1992.

Fogle, Stephen F., and T. V. F. Brogan. "Envelope." Pages 360-1 in *The New Princeton Encyclopedia of Poetry and Poetics.* Edited by Alex Preminger and T. V. F. Brogan. Princeton: Princeton University Press, 1993.

Fokkelman, J. P. *Reading Biblical Poetry: An Introductory Guide.* Translated by Ineke Smit. Louisville: Westminster John Knox, 2001.

Franke, Chris. *Isaiah 46, 47, and 48: A New Literary Critical Reading.* Biblical and Judaic Studies 3. Winona Lake, IN: Eisenbrauns, 1994.

Freedman, David Noel. "Acrostics and Metrics in Hebrew Poetry." Pages 51-76 in *Poetry, Pottery, and Prophecy: Studies in Early Hebrew Poetry.* Winona Lake, IN: Eisenbrauns, 1980. Repr. from *Harvard Theological Review* 65 (1972): 367-92.

Freedman, David Noel. "What the Ass and the Ox Know—But the Scholars Don't." *Bible Review* 1 (February 1985): 42-4.

Freedman, David Noel. "Another Look at Biblical Hebrew Poetry." Pages 11-28 in *Directions in Biblical Hebrew Poetry.* Edited by Elaine R. Follis. *Journal for the Study of the Old Testament*: Supplement Series 40. Sheffield: Sheffield Academic Press, 1987.

Freedman, David Noel. "Pottery, Poetry, and Prophecy: An Essay on Biblical Poetry." Pages 51-76 in *Poetry, Pottery, and Prophecy: Studies in Early Hebrew Poetry.* Winona Lake, IN: Eisenbrauns, 1980. Repr. from *Journal of Biblical Literature* 96 (1977): 5-26.

Friedman, Norman. "Imagery." Pages 559-66 in *The New Princeton Encyclopedia of Poetry and Poetics.* Edited by Alex Preminger and T. V. F. Brogan. Princeton: Princeton University Press, 1993.

Fullerton, Kemper. "The Book of Isaiah: Critical Problems and a New Commentary." *Harvard Theological Review* 6 (1913): 478-50.

Gallagher, William R. *Sennacherib's Campaign to Judah: New Studies.* Studies in the History and Culture of the Ancient Near East 18. Leiden: Brill, 1999.

Garr, W. Randall. "The *Qinah*: A Study of Poetic Meter, Syntax, and Style." *Zeitschrift für die alttestamentliche Wissenschaft* 95 (1983): 54-75.

Geller, Stephen A. *Parallelism in Early Biblical Poetry.* Harvard Semitic Monographs 20. Missoula, MT: Scholars Press, 1979.

Geller, Stephen A. "The Dynamics of Parallel Verse: A Poetic Analysis of Deut 32:6-12." *Harvard Theological Review* 75 (1982): 35-56.

Geller, Stephen A. "Hebrew Prosody and Poetics: I. Biblical." Pages 509-11 in *The New Princeton Encyclopedia of Poetry and Poetics.* Edited by Alex Preminger and T. V. F. Brogan. Princeton: Princeton University Press, 1993.

Geller, Stephen A. *Sacred Enigmas: Literary Religion in the Hebrew Bible*. London: Routledge, 1996.
Giese, Ronald L. "Strophic Hebrew Verse as Free Verse." *Journal for the Study of the Old Testament* 61 (1994): 29-38.
Ginsberg, H. L. "An Obscure Hebrew Word." *Jewish Quarterly Review* 22 (1931-32): 143-5.
Gitay, Yehoshua. "Deutero-Isaiah: Oral or Written?" *Journal of Biblical Literature* 99 (1980): 185-97.
Gitay, Yehoshua. "Reflections on the Study of the Prophetic Discourse: The Question of Isaiah I 2-20." *Vetus Testamentum* 33 (1983): 207-21.
Gitay, Yehoshua. "The Effectiveness of Isaiah's Speech." *Jewish Quarterly Review* 75 (1984): 162-72.
Gitay, Yehoshua. "Oratorical Rhetoric: The Question of Prophetic Language with Special Attention to Isaiah." *Amsterdamse Chaiers voor Exegese en bijbelse Theologie* 10 (1989): 72-83.
Gitay, Yehoshua. *Isaiah and His Audience: The Structure and Meaning of Isaiah 1-12*. Studia Semitica Neerlandica. Assen: Van Gorcum, 1991.
Goldingay, John. "Repetition and Variation in the Psalms." *Jewish Quarterly Review* 68 (1978): 146-51.
Good, Robert. "Zechariah 14:13 and Related Texts: Brother Against Brother in War." *Maarav* 8 (1992): 39-47.
Gordon, Cyrus H. *Ugaritic Textbook: Grammar*. Analecta orientalia 38:1. Rev. ed. Rome: Pontifical Biblical Institute, 1998.
Gordon, Robert P. "The Legacy of Lowth: Robert Lowth and the Book of Isaiah in Particular," Pages 57-76 in *Biblical Hebrews, Biblical Texts: Essays in Memory of Michael P. Weitzman*. Edited by Ada Rapoport-Albert and Gillian Greenberg. *Journal for the Study of the Old Testament*: Supplement Series 333/Hebrew Bible and its Versions 2. Sheffield: Sheffield Academic Press, 2001.
Gottwald, Norman K. "Poetry, Hebrew." Pages 829-38 in vol. 3 of *The Interpreter's Dictionary of the Bible*. Edited by George A. Buttrick. 4 vols. Nashville: Abingdon Press, 1962.
Gray, George Buchanan. *A Critical and Exegetical Commentary on the Book of Isaiah I-XXVII*. International Critical Commentary. Edinburgh: T. & T. Clark, 1912.
Gray, George Buchanan. *The Forms of Hebrew Poetry*. London: Hodder & Stoughton, 1915. Repr. New York: Ktav Publishing House, 1972.
Greenstein, Edward L. "How Does Parallelism Mean?" Pages 4-70 in *A Sense of Text: The Art of Language in the Study of Biblical Literature*. Edited by L. Nemoy. *Jewish Quarterly Review Supplement*. Winona Lake, IN: Eisenbrauns, 1983.
Greenstein, Edward L. "The Language of Job and its Poetic Function." *Journal of Biblical Literature* 122 (2003): 651-66.

Grossberg, Daniel. *Centripetal and Centrifugal Structures in Biblical Poetry.* Society of Biblical Literature Monograph Series 39. Atlanta: Scholars Press, 1989.

Gruber, Mayer I. "The Meaning of Biblical Parallelism: A Biblical Perspective." *Prooftexts: A Journal of Jewish Literary History* 13 (1993): 289–93.

Guillaume, A. "A Note on the Meaning of Isaiah XXII.5" *Journal of Theological Studies* NS 14 (1963): 383–5.

Halpern, Baruch. "'The Excremental Vision': The Doomed Priests of Doom in Isaiah 28." *Hebrew Annual Review* 10 (1986): 109–21.

Handy, Lowell K. "Serpent, Religious Symbol." Pages 1113–16 in vol. 5 of *The Anchor Bible Dictionary.* Edited by David Noel Freedman. New York: Doubleday, 1992.

Harris, Robert Allen. *Discerning Parallelism: A Study in Northern French Medieval Jewish Exegesis.* Brown Judaic Studies 341. Providence: Brown University Press, 2004.

Hartman, Charles O. *Free Verse: An Essay on Prosody.* Princeton: Princeton University Press, 1980. Repr. Evanston, IL: Northwestern University Press, 1996.

Haüblein, Ernst and T. V. F. Brogan. "Strophe." Page 1215 in *The New Princeton Encyclopedia of Poetry and Poetics.* Edited by Alex Preminger and T. V. F. Brogan. Princeton: Princeton University Press, 1993.

Hayes, John H. and Stuart A. Irvine. *Isaiah the Eighth Century Prophet: His Times and his Preaching.* Nashville: Abingdon, 1987.

Hays, Christopher B. "Damming Egypt/Damning Egypt: The Paranomasia of *skr* and the Unity of Isa 19,1–10." *Zeitschrift für die Alttestementliche Wissenschaft* 120 (2008): 612–17.

Hays, Christopher B. "The Covenant with Mut: A New Interpretation of Isaiah 28:1–22." *Vetus Testamentum* 60 (2010): 212–40.

Healy, John F. "Ancient Agriculture and the Hebrew Bible: with Special Reference to Isaiah XXVIII 23–29." Pages 108–19 in *Prophets, Worship, and Theodicy.* Edited by A. S. van der Woude. *Oudtestamentische Studiën* 23. Leiden: Brill, 1984.

Heffelfinger, Katie M. *I am Large, I Contain Multitudes: Lyric Cohesion and Conflict in Second Isaiah.* Biblical Interpretation Series 105. Leiden: Brill, 2011.

Hens-Piazza, Gina. *New Historicism.* Guides to Biblical Scholarship. Minneapolis: Fortress, 2002.

Herrman, Wolfram. "Gedanken zur Geschicte des Altorientalischen Beschreibungsliedes." *Zeitschrift für die Alttestementliche Wissenschaft* 75 (1963): 176–97.

Hillers, Delbert R. *Treaty-Curses and the Old Testament Prophets.* Biblica et Orientalia 16. Rome: Pontifical Biblical Institute, 1964.

Hillers, Delbert R. "*Hôy* and *Hôy*-Oracles: A Neglected Syntactic Aspect." Pages 185–8 in *The Word of the Lord Shall Go Forth: Essays in Honor of David Noel Freedman.* Edited by Carol Meyers and Michael O'Connor. Winona Lake, IN: Eisenbrauns, 1983.

Hillers, Delbert R. *Lamentations: A New Translation with Introduction and Commentary*. 2nd ed. Anchor Bible 7A. New York: Doubleday, 1992.
Hoch, James C. *Semitic Words in Egyptian Texts of the New Kingdom and Third Intermediate Period*. Princeton: Princeton University Press, 1994.
Holladay, William L. "Isa. III 10–11: An Archaic Wisdom Passage." *Vetus Testamentum* 18 (1968): 481–7.
Holladay, William L. *Isaiah: Scroll of a Prophetic Heritage*. Grand Rapids: Eerdmans, 1978.
Holladay, William L. "*Hebrew Verse Structure* Revisited (I): Which Words 'Count'?" *Journal of Biblical Literature* 118 (1999): 19–32.
Holladay, William L. "*Hebrew Verse Structure* Revisited (II): Conjoint Cola and Further Suggestions." *Journal of Biblical Literature* 118 (1999): 401–16.
Hollander, John. *Rhyme's Reason*. 3rd ed. New Haven: Yale University Press, 2000.
Hoop, Raymond de. "The Colometry of Hebrew Verse and the Masoretic Accents: A Recent Approach." Pts. 1 and 2. *Journal of Northwest Semitic Languages* 26, no. 1 (2000): 47–73; 26, no. 2 (2000): 61–100.
Hornsby, Roger A. and T. V. F. Brogan. "Catalog." Pages 174–5 in *The New Princeton Encyclopedia of Poetry and Poetics*. Edited by Alex Preminger and T. V. F. Brogan. Princeton: Princeton University Press, 1993.
Houlihan, Patrick F. "Animals in Egyptian Art and Hieroglyphs." Pages 97–143 in *A History of the Animal World in the Ancient Near East*. Edited by Billie Jean Collins. Handbuch der Orientalistik 64. Leiden: Brill, 2002.
Hrushovski, Benjamin. "On Free Rhythms in Modern Poetry." Pages 173–90 in *Style in Language*. Edited by Thomas A. Sebeok. Cambridge, MA: Technology Press of the Massachusetts Institute of Technology; New York: John Wiley & Sons, 1960.
Hrushovski, Benjamin. "Prosody, Hebrew." Cols. 1196–1240 in vol. 13 of *Encyclopedia Judaica*. 16 vols. Jerusalem: Keter, 1971.
Hummel, Horace D. "Enclitic *Mem* in Early Northwest Semitic, Especially Hebrew." *Journal of Biblical Literature* 76 (1957): 85–104.
Hurvitz, Avi. "*BYT-QBRWT* and *BYT-ʿLM*: Two Funerary Terms in Biblical Literature and their Linguistic Background." *Maarav* 8 (1992): 59–68.
Irvine, Stuart A. "Problems of Text and Translation in Isaiah 10.13bb." Pages 133–44 in *History and Interpretation: Essays in Honour of John H. Hayes*. Edited by M. Patrick Graham, William P. Brown, and Jeffrey K. Kuan. *Journal for the Study of the Old Testament*: Supplement Series 173. Sheffield: JSOT Press, 1993.
Irwin, William H. *Isaiah 28–33: Translation with Philological Notes*. Biblica et Orientalia 30. Rome: Pontifical Biblical Institute, 1977.

Jacobson, Rolf A. *"Many are Saying": The Function of Direct Discourse in the Hebrew Psalter*. Journal for the Study of the Old Testament: Supplement Series 397. London: T&T Clark, 2004.

Johnson, Mark. "Metaphor in the Philosophical Tradition." Pages 3–47 in *Philosophical Perspectives on Metaphor*. Edited by Mark Johnson. Minneapolis: University of Minnesota Press, 1981.

Johnston, Gordon H. "Nahum's Rhetorical Allusions to Neo-Assyrian Conquest Metaphors." *Bibliotheca Sacra* 159 (2002): 21–45.

Jones, Brian C. *Howling Over Moab: Irony and Rhetoric in Isaiah 15–16*. Society of Biblical Literature Dissertation Series 157. Atlanta: Scholars Press, 1996.

Jong, Matthijs J. de. *Isaiah Among the Ancient Near Eastern Prophets: A Comparative Study of the Earliest Stages of the Isaiah Tradition and the Neo-Assyrian Prophecies*. Supplements to *Vetus Testamentum* 117. Leiden: Brill, 2007.

Joüon, Paul. *A Grammar of Biblical Hebrew*. Translated and revised by Takamitsu Muraoka. 2 vols. Subsidia biblica 14/1–2. Rome, 1991.

Kaiser, Otto. *Isaiah 13–39: A Commentary*. Translated by R. A. Wilson. Old Testament Library. Philadelphia: Westminster, 1974.

Kaiser, Otto. *Isaiah 1–12: A Commentary*. Translated by John Bowden. 2nd ed. Old Testament Library. Philadelphia: Westminster, 1983.

Kautsch, Emil (ed.). *Gesenius' Hebrew Grammar*. Translated by A. E. Cowley. 2nd ed. Oxford: Clarendon, 1910.

Kawashima, Robert S. *Biblical Narrative and the Death of the Rhapsode*. Indiana Studies in Biblical Literature. Bloomington: Indiana University Press, 2004.

Kessler, Martin. "Inclusio in the Hebrew Bible." *Semitics* 6 (1978): 44–9.

King, Philip J. and Lawrence E. Stager. *Life in Biblical Israel*. Library of Ancient Israel. Louisville, KY: Westminster John Knox, 2001.

Kinzie, Mary. *A Poet's Guide to Poetry*. Chicago Guides to Writing, Editing, and Publishing. Chicago: University of Chicago Press, 1999.

Kissane, Edward J. *The Book of Isaiah: Translated from a Critically Revised Hebrew Text with Commentary*. 2 vols. Rev. ed. Dublin: Browne and Nolan, 1960.

Koehler, L., W. Baumgartner, and J. J. Stamm. *The Hebrew and Aramaic Lexicon of the Old Testament*. Translated and edited under the supervision of M. E. J. Richardson. 4 vols. Leiden: Brill, 1994–1999.

Kooij, Arie van der. "Textual Criticism of the Hebrew Bible: Its Aim and Method." Pages 729–39 in *Emanuel: Studies in the Hebrew Bible, Septuagint, and Dead Sea Scrolls in Honor of Emanuel Tov*. Edited by Shalom M. Paul, Robert A. Kraft, Lawrence H. Schiffman, and Weston W. Fields. Supplements to *Vetus Testamentum* 94. Leiden: Brill, 2003.

Korpel, Marjo C. A. *A Rift in the Clouds: Ugaritic and Hebrew Descriptions of the Divine*. Ugaritisch-biblische Lietratur 8. Münster: Ugarit-Verlag, 1990.

Korpel, Marjo C. A. and Josef M. Oesch (eds.). *Delimitation Criticism: A New Tool in Biblical Scholarship*. Pericope: Scripture as Written and Read in Antiquity 4. Assen: Koninklijke Van Gorcum, 2000.

Krueger, Paul A. "The Obscure Combination *kbd mś'h* in Isaiah 30:27: Another Description for Anger?" *Journal of Northwest Semitic Languages* 26, no. 2 (2000): 155–62.

Kugel, James L. *The Idea of Biblical Poetry*. New Haven: Yale University Press, 1981. Repr., Baltimore: Johns Hopkins University Press, 1998.

Kuntz, J. Kenneth. "Biblical Hebrew Poetry in Recent Research, Part I." *Currents in Research: Biblical Studies* 6 (1998): 31–64.

Kuntz, J. Kenneth. "Biblical Hebrew Poetry in Recent Research, Part II." *Currents in Research: Biblical Studies* 7 (1999): 35–79.

Lakoff, George and Mark Turner. *More than Cool Reason: A Field Guide to Poetic Metaphor*. Chicago: University of Chicago Press, 1989.

Landy, Francis. "Poetics and Parallelism: Some Comments on James Kugel's *The Idea of Biblical Poetry*." *Journal for the Study of the Old Testament* 28 (1984): 68–87.

Landy, Francis. "Seraphim and Poetic Process." Pages 15–34 in *The Labour of Reading: Desire, Alienation, and Biblical Interpretation*. Edited by Fiona C. Black, Roland Boer, and Erin Runions. Semeia Studies. Atlanta: Society of Biblical Literature, 1999.

Lavik, Marta Høyland. *A People Tall and Smooth-Skinned: The Rhetoric of Isaiah 18*. Supplements to *Vetus Testamentum* 112. Leiden: Brill, 2007.

Lemaire, André. "Note epigraphique sur la pseudo-attestation du mois 'ṣḥ.'" *Vetus Testamentum* 23 (1973): 243–5.

LeMon, Joel M. *Yahweh's Winged Form in the Psalms: Exploring Congruent Iconography and Texts*. Orbis Biblicus et Orientalis 242. Fribourg: Academic Press; Göttingen: Vandenhoeck & Ruprecht, 2010.

LeMon, Joel M. and Brent A. Strawn. "Parallelism." Pages 502–15 in *Dictionary of the Old Testament: Wisdom, Poetry & Writings*. Edited by Tremper Longman III and Peter Enns. Downers Grove, IL: InterVarsity Press, 2008.

Lessing, R. Reed. "Satire in Isaiah's Tyre Oracle." *Journal for the Study of the Old Testament* 28 (2003): 89–112.

Lessing, R. Reed. *Interpreting Discontinuity: Isaiah's Tyre Oracle*. Winona Lake, IN: Eisenbrauns, 2004.

Linafelt, Tod and F. W. Dobbs-Allsopp. "Poetic Line Structure in Qohelth 3:1." *Vetus Testamentum* 60 (2010): 249–59.

Longman, Tremper III. "A Critique of Two Recent Metrical Systems." *Biblica* 63 (1982): 230–54.

Lowth, Robert. *Lectures on the Sacred Poetry of the Hebrews*. Edited by Calvin E. Stowe. Translated by G. Gregory. New ed. Boston: Crocker & Brewster, 1829.

Lowth, Robert. *Isaiah: A New Translation; With a Preliminary Dissertation, and Notes, Critical, Philological, and Explanatory.* 10th ed. Cambridge, MA: James Munroe and Company, 1834.

Lubetski, Meir and Claire Gottlieb. "Isaiah 18: The Egyptian Nexus." Pages 364–84 in *Boundaries of the Ancient Near Eastern World: A Tribute to Cyrus H. Gordon.* Edited by Meir Lubetski et al. *Journal for the Study of the Old Testament*: Supplement Series 273. Sheffield: Sheffield Academic Press, 1998.

Luckenbill, Daniel David. *The Annals of Sennacherib.* University of Chicago Oriental Institute Publications 2. Chicago: University of Chicago Press, 1924.

Lugt, Pieter van der. *Cantos and Strophes in Biblical Hebrew Poetry, with Special Reference to the First book of the Psalter.* Oudtestamentische Studiën 53. Leiden: Brill, 2006.

Machinist, Peter. "Assyria and its Image in the First Isaiah." *Journal of the American Oriental Society* 103 (1983): 719–37.

Magonet, Jonathan. "Isaiah 2:1–4:6: Some Poetic Structures and Tactics." *Amsterdamse Chaiers voor Exegese en bijbelse Theologie* 3 (1982): 71–85.

Mankowski, Paul V. *Akkadian Loanwords in Biblical Hebrew.* Harvard Semitic Studies 47. Winona Lake, IN: Eisenbrauns, 2000.

Marcus, David. "Animal Similes in Assyrian Royal Inscriptions." *Orientalia* NS 46 (1977): 86–106.

Meer, Willem van der and Johannes C. de Moor (eds.). *The Structural Analysis of Biblical and Canaanite Poetry. Journal for the Study of the Old Testament*: Supplement Series 74. Sheffield: JSOT Press, 1988.

Melugin, Roy F. "The Book of Isaiah and the Construction of Meaning." Pages 39–55 in vol. 1 of *Writing and Reading the Scroll of Isaiah: Studies of an Interpretive Tradition.* Edited by Craig C. Broyles and Craig A. Evans. 2 vols. Supplements to *Vetus Testamentum* 70. Formation and Interpretation of Old Testament Literature 1–2. Leiden: Brill, 1997.

Melugin, Roy F. "Figurative Speech and the Reading of Isaiah 1 as Scripture." Pages 282–305 in *New Visions of Isaiah.* Edited by Roy F. Melugin and Marvin A. Sweeney. *Journal for the Study of the Old Testament*: Supplement Series 214. Sheffield: Sheffield Academic Press, 1996.

Miller, Cynthia L. *The Representation of Speech in Biblical Hebrew Narrative: A Linguistic Analysis.* Harvard Semitic Monographs 55. Atlanta: Scholars Press, 1996.

Miller, Cynthia L. "A Lingusitc Approach to Ellipsis in Biblical Poetry (Or, What to Do When Exegesis of What is There Depends on What Isn't)." *Bulletin for Biblical Research* 13 (2003): 251–70.

Miller, Cynthia L. "The Relation of Coordination to Verb Gapping in Biblical Poetry." *Journal for the Study of the Old Testament* 32 (2007): 41–60.

Miller, Patrick D. "El the Warrior." *Harvard Theological Review* 60 (1967): 411–31.

Miller, Patrick D. "Animal Names as Designations in Ugaritic and Hebrew." *Ugarit-Forschungen* 2 (1970): 177–86.
Miller, Patrick D. "The Theological Significance of Biblical Poetry." Pages 214–30 in *Language, Theology, and the Bible: Essays in Honour of James Barr*. Edited by Samuel E. Balantine and John Barton. Oxford: Clarendon, 1994.
Miller, Patrick D. *The Religion of Ancient Israel*. Library of Ancient Israel. Louisville: Westminster John Knox, 2000.
Miscall, Peter D. "Isaiah: The Labyrinth of Images." *Semeia* 54 (1992): 103–21.
Miscall, Peter D. *Isaiah*. Readings. Sheffield: JSOT Press, 1993.
Mitchell, W. J. T. "Image." Pages 556–9 in *The New Princeton Encyclopedia of Poetry and Poetics*. Edited by Alex Preminger and T. V. F. Brogan. Princeton: Princeton University Press, 1993.
Mittmann, Siegfried. "'Wehe! Assur, Stab meines Zorns' (Jes 10,5–9.13aβ–15)." Pages 111–34 in *Prophet und Prophetenbuch: Festschrift für Otto Kaiser zum 65. Geburstag*. Edited by Volkmar Fritz, Karl-Friedrich Pohlmann, and Hans-Christoph Schmitt. Beihefte zur Zeitschrift für die alttestamentliche Wissenschaft 185. Berlin: Walter de Gruyter, 1989.
Moor, Johannes C. de. "The Art of Versification in Ugarit and Israel. I: The Rhythmical Structure." Pages 119–39 in *Studies in Bible and the Ancient Near East Presented to Samuel E. Loewenstamm on His Seventieth Birthday*. Edited by Y. Avishur and J. Blau. Jerusalem: E. Rubenstein's Publishing House, 1978.
Moorey, P. R. S. *Ancient Mesopotamian Materials and Industries: The Archaeological Evidence*. Oxford: Clarendon, 1994.
Morris, Gerald. *Prophecy, Poetry and Hosea*. Journal for the Study of the Old Testament: Supplement Series 219. Sheffield: Sheffield Academic Press, 1996.
Mosca, Paul G. "Isaiah 28:12e: A Response to J. J. M. Roberts." *Harvard Theological Review* 77 (1984): 113–17.
Muchiki, Yoshiyuki. *Egyptian Proper Names and Loanwords in North-West Semitic*. Society of Biblical Literature Dissertation Series 173. Atlanta: Society of Biblical Literature, 1999.
Muilenburg, James. "Form Criticism and Beyond." *Journal of Biblical Literature* 88 (1969): 1–18.
Na'aman, Nadav. "Hezekiah and the Kings of Assyria." *Tel Aviv* 21 (1994): 235–54. Repr. pages 97–118 in *Ancient Israel and Its Neighbors: Interaction and Counteraction*. Winona Lake, IN: Eisenbrauns, 2005.
Nathan, Leonard. "Narrative Poetry." Pages 814–18 in *The New Princeton Encyclopedia of Poetry and Poetics*. Edited by Alex Preminger and T. V. F. Brogan. Princeton: Princeton University Press, 1993.
Niditch, Susan. *Oral World and Written Word: Ancient Israelite Literature*. Library of Ancient Israel. Louisville: Westminster John Knox, 1996.

Nielsen, Kirsten. *There is Hope for a Tree: The Tree as Metaphor in First Isaiah*. Journal for the Study of the Old Testament: Supplement Series 65. Sheffield: JSOT Press, 1989.

Nissinen, Martti. "How Prophecy Became Literature." *Scandinavian Journal of the Old Testament* 19 (2005): 153–72.

O'Brien, Julia M. *Challenging Prophetic Metaphor: Theology and Ideology in the Prophets*. Louisville: Westminster John Knox, 2008.

O'Connell, Robert H. *Concentricity and Continuity: The Literary Structure of Isaiah*. Journal for the Study of the Old Testament: Supplement Series 188. Sheffield: Sheffield Academic Press, 1994.

O'Connor, Michael Patrick. "The Body in the Bible: Anatomy and Morphology." Pages 143–53 in *In Service of the Church: Essays on Theology and Ministry Honoring the Rev. Charles L. Froehle*. Edited by V. J. Klimoski and M. C. Athans. St. Paul, MN: University of St. Thomas, 1993.

O'Connor, Michael Patrick. *Hebrew Verse Structure*. 2nd ed. Winona Lake, IN: Eisenbrauns, 1997.

Oestreich, Bernhard. *Metaphors and Similes for Yahweh in Hosea 14:2–9: A Study of Hoseanic Pictorial Imagery*. Friedensauer Schriftenreihe: Reihe A, Theologie, 1. Frankfurt am Main: Peter Lang, 1996.

Pardee, Dennis. "Ugaritic and Hebrew Metrics." Pages 113–30 in *Ugarit in Retrospect: Fifty Years of Ugarit and Ugaritic*. Edited by George Douglas Young. Winona Lake, IN: Eisenbrauns, 1981.

Pardee, Dennis. *Ugaritic and Hebrew Poetic Parallelism: A Trial Cut ('nt I and Proverbs 2)*. Supplements to *Vetus Testamentum* 39. Leiden: Brill, 1988.

Parker, Simon B. "Parallelism and Prosody in Ugaritic Narrative Verse." *Ugarit-Forschungen* 6 (1974): 283–94.

Pattie, Thomas S. "The Creation of the Great Codices." Pages 61–72 in *The Bible as Book: The Manuscript Tradition*. Edited by John L. Sharpe III and Kimberly van Kampen. London/New Castle, DE: British Library/Oak Knoll Press, 1998.

Petersen, David L. and Kent Harold Richards. *Interpreting Hebrew Poetry*. Guides to Biblical Scholarship. Minneapolis: Fortress, 1992.

Pinsky, Robert. *The Sounds of Poetry: A Brief Guide*. New York: Farrar, Straus & Giroux, 1998.

Pope, Marvin H. and Jeffrey H. Tigay. "A Description of Baal." *Ugarit-Forschungen* 3 (1971): 117–30.

Powell, Marvin A. "Weights and Measures." Pages 897–908 in vol. 6 of *The Anchor Bible Dictionary*. Edited by David Noel Freedman. 6 vols. New York: Doubleday, 1992.

Pritchard, James. *The Ancient Near East in Pictures Relating to the Old Testament*. 2nd ed. Princeton: Princeton University Press, 1969.

Quinn-Miscall, Peter D. *Reading Isaiah: Poetry and Vision*. Louisville: Westminster John Knox, 2001.

Raabe, Paul R. *Psalm Structures: A Study of Psalms with Refrains*. Journal for the Study of the Old Testament: Supplement Series 104. Sheffield: Sheffield Academic Press, 1990.

Raffel, Burton. *How to Read a Poem*. New York: Meridian, 1984.

Raphael, Rebecca. "That's No Literature, That's My Bible: On James Kugel's Objections to the Idea of Biblical Poetry." *Journal for the Study of the Old Testament* 27 (2002): 37–45.

Rendsburg, Gary A. "Linguistic Variation and the 'Foreign' Factor in the Hebrew Bible." Pages 177–90 in *Language and Culture in the Near East*. Edited by Shlomo Izre'el and Rina Drory. Israel Oriental Studies 15. Leiden: Brill, 1996.

Reventlow, Henning Graf. *From the Enlightenment to the Twentieth Century*. Vol. 4 of *History of Biblical Interpretation*. Translated by Leo G. Perdue. Society of Biblical Literature Resources for Biblical Studies 63. Atlanta: Society of Biblical Literature, 2010.

Rilke, Rainer Maria. *Letters to a Young Poet*. Translated by M. D. Herter Norton. New York: W. W. Norton, 1993.

Roberts, J. J. M. "A Note on Isaiah 28:12." *Harvard Theological Review* 73 (1980): 48–51.

Roberts, J. J. M. "Form, Syntax, and Redaction in Isaiah 1:2–20." *Princeton Seminary Bulletin* NS 3 (1982): 293–306.

Roberts, J. J. M. "Isaiah 2 and the Prophet's Message to the North." *Jewish Quarterly Review* 75 (1985): 290–308.

Roberts, J. J. M. "Isaiah and his Children." Pages 193–203 in *Biblical and Related Studies Presented to Samuel Iwry*. Edited by A. Kort and S. Morschauser. Winona Lake, IN: Eisenbrauns, 1985.

Roberts, J. J. M. "Yahweh's Foundation in Zion (Isa 28:16)." Pages 292–310 in *The Bible and the Ancient Near East: Collected Essays*. Winona Lake, IN: Eisenbrauns, 2002. Repr. from *JBL* 106 (1987): 27–45.

Roberts, J. J. M. "Double Entendre in First Isaiah." *Catholic Biblical Quarterly* 54 (1992): 39–48.

Roberts, J. J. M. "Historical-Critical Method, Theology, and Contemporary Exegesis." Pages 393–405 in *The Bible and the Ancient Near East*. Winona Lake, IN: Eisenbrauns, 2002. Repr. from pages 131–41 in *Biblical Theology: Problems and Perspectives in Honor of J. Christian Beker*. Edited by S. J. Kraftchick et al. Nashville, Abingdon: 1995.

Roth, Wolfgang M. W. "The Numerical Sequence x/x + 1 in the Old Testament." *Vetus Testamentum* 12 (1962): 300–11.

Rowlands, E. R. "The Targum and the Peshitta Version of the Book of Isaiah." *Vetus Testamentum* 9 (1959): 178–91.

Rudolph, Wilhelm. "Jesaja xv–xvi." Pages 130–43 in *Hebrew and Semitic Studies Presented to Godfrey Rolles Driver*. Edited by D. Winton Thomas and W. D. McHardy. Oxford: Clarendon, 1964.

Sack, Ronald H. "Some Remarks on Jewelry Inventories from Sixth Century B.C. Erech." *Zeitschrift für Assyriologie* 69 (1979): 41–6.

Sæbø, Magne. "Traditio-Historical Perspectives on Isaiah 8:9–10: An Attempt to Clarify an Old *Crux Interpretum.*" Pages 108–21 in *On the Way to Canon: Creative Tradition History in the Old Testament. Journal for the Study of the Old Testament*: Supplement Series 191. Sheffield: Sheffield Academic Press, 1998. Trans. and repr. of "Zur Traditionsgeschicte von Jesaia 8,9–10," *Zeitschrift für die alttestamentliche Wissenschaft* 76 (1964): 132–44. Translated by Birgit Mänz-Davies.

Sarna, Nahum M. "The Divine Title ʾabhîr yaʿăqôbh." Pages 389–96 in *Essays on the Occasion of the Seventieth Anniversary of the Dropsie University (1909–1979).* Edited by A. I. Katsh and L. Nemoy. Philadelphia: Dropsie University, 1979.

Sasson, Jack M. "The King's Table: Food and Fealty in Old Babylonian Mari." Pages 179–215 in *Food and Identity in the Ancient World.* Edited by Cristiano Grottanelli and Lucio Milano. History of the Ancient Near East, Studies 9. Padova: SARGON Editrice e Libreria, 2004.

Sasson, Victor. "An Unrecognized 'Smoke-Signal' in Isaiah XXX 27." *Vetus Testamentum* 33 (1983): 90–5.

Schipper, Jeremy. "Body. II. Hebrew Bible/Old Testament." Pages 270–4 in vol. 4 of *The Encyclopedia of the Bible and its Reception.* Edited by Hans-Josef Klauck et al. 30 vols. Berlin: Walter de Gruyter, 2012.

Schmitt, John J. *Isaiah and his Interpreters.* New York: Paulist, 1986.

Schniedewind, William M. *How the Bible Became a Book: The Textualization of Ancient Israel.* Cambridge: Cambridge University Press, 2004.

Schoors, Antoon. "Historical Information in Isaiah 1–39." Pages 75–93 in *Studies in the Book of Isaiah: Festschrift Willem A. M. Beuken.* Edited by J. van Reuiten and M. Vervenne. Bibliotheca Ephemeridum theologicarum Lovaniensium 132. Leuven: Leuven University Press/Uitgeverïj Peeters, 1997.

Scott, R. B. Y. "The Literary Structure of Isaiah's Oracles." Pages 175–86 in *Studies in Old Testament Prophecy Presented to Theodore H. Robinson on his Sixty-fifth Birthday, August 9th, 1946.* Edited by H. H. Rowley. Edinburgh: T&T Clark, 1957.

Seitz, Christopher R. "Isaiah 1–66: Making Sense of the Whole." Pages 105–26 in *Reading and Preaching the Book of Isaiah.* Edited by Christopher R. Seitz. Philadelphia: Fortress, 1988.

Seitz, Christopher R. *Isaiah 1–39. Interpretation: A Bible Commentary for Teaching and Preaching.* Louisville: Westminster John Knox, 1993.

Seow, C. L. *Ecclesiastes: A New Translation with Introduction and Commentary.* Anchor Bible 18C. New York: Doubleday, 1997.

Seow, C. L. *Job 1–21: Interpretation and Commentary.* Illuminations. Grand Rapids: Eerdmans, 2013.

Shea, William. "The Qinah Structure of the Book of Lamentations." *Biblica* 60 (1979): 103–7.
Shemesh, Yael. "Isaiah 31,5: The Lord's Protecting Lameness." *Zeitschrift für die Alttestamentiche Wissenschaft* 115 (2003): 256–60.
Sherwood, Yvonne. "'Darke Texts Need Notes': Prophetic Poetry, John Donne and the Baroque." *Journal for the Study of the Old Testament* 27 (2002): 47–74.
Sloane, Thomas A. "Rhetoric and Poetry." Pages 1045–52 in *The New Princeton Encyclopedia of Poetry and Poetics*. Edited by Alex Preminger and T. V. F. Brogan. Princeton: Princeton University Press, 1993.
Smith, Barbara Herrnstein. *Poetic Closure: A Study of How Poems End*. Chicago: University of Chicago Press, 1968.
Smith, Mark S. *Untold Stories: The Bible and Ugaritic Studies in the Twentieth Century*. Peabody, MA: Hendrickson, 2001.
Smoak, Jeremy D. "Building Houses and Planting Vineyards: The Early Inner-Biblical Discourse on an Ancient Israelite Wartime Curse." *Journal of Biblical Literature* 127 (2008): 19–35.
Smothers, Thomas G. "Isaiah 15–16." Pages 70–85 in *Forming Prophetic Literature: Essays on Isaiah and the Twelve in Honor of John D. W. Watts*. Edited by James W. Watts and Paul R. House. *Journal for the Study of the Old Testament*: Supplement Series 235. Sheffield: Sheffield Academic Press, 1996.
Sommer, Benjamin D. "The Scroll of Isaiah as Jewish Scripture, or, Why Jews Don't Read Books." Pages 225–42 in *SBL Seminar Papers, 1996*. Society of Biblical Literature Seminar Papers 35. Chico, CA: Scholars Press, 1996.
Sommer, Benjamin D. "Is it Good for the Jews? Ambiguity and the Rhetoric of Turning in Isaiah." Pages 321–45 in vol. 1 of *Birkat Shalom: Studies in the Bible, Ancient Near Eastern Literature, and Postbiblical Judaism Presented to Shalom M. Paul on the Occasion of his Seventieth Birthday*. Edited by Chaim Cohen, Victor Avigdor Hurowitz, Avi Hurvitz, Yochanan Muffs, Baruch J. Schwartz, and Jeffrey H. Tigay. 2 vols. Winona Lake, IN: Eisenbrauns, 2008.
Stansell, Gary. "Lowth's Isaiah Commentary and Romanticism." Pages 148–82 in *SBL Seminar Papers, 2000*. Society of Biblical Literature Seminar Papers 39. Atlanta: Society of Biblical Literature, 2000.
Stansell, Gary. "The Poet's Prophet: Bishop Robert Lowth's Eighteenth-Century Commentary on Isaiah." Pages 223–42 in *"As Those who are Taught": The Interpretation of Isaiah from the LXX to the SBL*. Edited by Claire Mathews McGinnis and Patricia K. Tull. Society of Biblical Literature Symposium Series 27. Atlanta: Society of Biblical Literature, 2006.
Steinberg, Theodore L. "Isaiah the Poet." Pages 299–310 in *Mappings of the Biblical Terrain: The Bible as Text*. Edited by Vincent L. Tollers and John R. Maier. Bucknell Review 33:2. Lewisburg, PA/London: Bucknell University Press/Associated University Presses, 1990.

Strawn, Brent A. *What is Stronger than a Lion? Leonine Image and Metaphor in the Hebrew Bible and the Ancient Near East.* Orbis Biblicus et Orientalis 212. Göttingen: Vandenhoeck & Ruprecht, 2005.

Strawn, Brent A. "Imagery." Pages 306–15 in *Dictionary of the Old Testament: Wisdom, Poetry & Writings.* Edited by Tremper Longman III and Peter Enns. Downers Grove, IL: InterVarsity Press, 2008.

Strawn, Brent A. "Lyric Poetry." Pages 437–46 in *Dictionary of the Old Testament: Wisdom, Poetry & Writings.* Edited by Tremper Longman III and Peter Enns. Downers Grove, IL: InterVarsity Press, 2008.

Sweeney, Marvin A. *Isaiah 1–4 and the Post-Exilic Understanding of the Isaianic Tradition.* Beihefte zur Zeitschrift für die alttestamentliche Wissenchaft 171. Berlin: Walter de Gruyter, 1988.

Sweeney, Marvin A. "The Book of Isaiah in Recent Research." *Currents in Research: Biblical Studies* 1 (1993): 141–62.

Sweeney, Marvin A. "Sargon's Threat Against Jerusalem in Isaiah 10,27–32." *Biblica* 75 (1994): 457–70.

Sweeney, Marvin A. *Isaiah 1–39, with an Introduction to Prophetic Literature.* Forms of the Old Testament Literature 16. Grand Rapids: Eerdmans, 1996.

Sweeney, Marvin A. "Reevaluating Isaiah 1–39 in Recent Critical Research." *Currents in Research: Biblical Studies* 4 (1996): 79–114.

Talmon, Shemaryahu. "Prophetic Rhetoric and Agricultural Metaphora." Pages 267–79 in *Storia e tradizioni di Israele: Scritti in onore di J. Alberto Soggin.* Edited by Daniele Garrone and Felice Israel. Brescia, Italy: Paideia, 1991.

Tate, Marvin E. "The Book of Isaiah in Recent Study." Pages 22–56 in *Forming Prophetic Literature: Essays on Isaiah and the Twelve in Honor of John D. W. Watts.* Edited by James W. Watts and Paul R. House. Journal for the Study of the Old Testament: Supplement Series 235. Sheffield: Sheffield Academic Press, 1996.

Teeter, Emily. "Animals in Egyptian Literature." Pages 251–70 in *A History of the Animal World in the Ancient Near East.* Edited by Billie Jean Collins. Handbuch der Orientalistik 64. Leiden: Brill, 2002.

Thiel, Winfried. "Duhm, Bernhard Lauardus (1847–1928)." Pages 310–11 in vol. 1 of *Dictioinary of Biblical Interpretation.* Edited by John H. Hayes. 2 vols. Nashville: Abingdon, 1999.

Tov, Emmanuel. *Textual Criticism of the Hebrew Bible.* 2nd ed. Minneapolis: Fortress, 2001.

Tov, Emmanuel. *Scribal Practices and Approaches Reflected in the Texts Found in the Judean Desert.* Studies on the Texts of the Desert of Judah 54. Leiden: Brill, 2004.

Toorn, Karel van der. *Scribal Culture and the Making of the Hebrew Bible.* Cambridge, MA: Harvard University Press, 2007.

Tull, Patricia K. "What's New in Lowth? Synchronic Reading in the Eighteenth and Twenty-First Centuries." Pages 183–217 in *SBL Seminar Papers, 2000*. Society of Biblical Literature Seminar Papers 39. Atlanta: Society of Biblical Literature, 2000.

Tull, Patricia K. "One Book, Many Voices: Conceiving of Isaiah's Polyphonic Message." Pages 279–314 in *"As Those who are Taught": The Interpretation of Isaiah from the LXX to the SBL*. Edited by Claire Mathews McGinnis and Patricia K. Tull. Society of Biblical Literature Symposium Series 27. Atlanta: Society of Biblical Literature, 2006.

Tull, Patricia K. "Persistent Vegetative States: People as Plants and Plants as People in Isaiah." Pages 17–34 in *The Desert Will Bloom: Poetic Visions in Isaiah*. Edited by A. Joseph Everson and Hyun Chul Paul Kim. Atlanta: Society of Biblical Literature, 2009.

Tull, Patricia K. *Isaiah 1–39*. Smyth & Helwys Bible Commentary 14A. Macon, GA: Smyth & Helwys, 2010.

Uchelen, N. A. van. "Isaiah I 9—Text and Context." Pages 155–63 in *Remembering All the Way: A Collection of Old Testament Studies Published on the Occasion of the Fortieth Anniversary of the Oudtestamentisch Werkgezelschap in Nederland*. Edited by A. S. van der Woude. Oudtestamentische Studiën 21. Leiden: Brill, 1981.

Ulrich, Eugene. "Sense Divisions in Ancient Manuscripts of Isaiah." Pages 297–301 in *Unit Delimitation in Biblical Hebrew and Northwest Semitic Literature*. Edited by Marjo C. A. Korpel and Josef M. Oesch. Pericope: Scripture as Written and Read in Antiquity 4. Assen: Koninklijke Van Gorcum, 2003.

Ulrich, Eugene and Peter W. Flint. *Introductions, Commentary, and Textual Variants*. Vol. 2 of *Qumran Cave 1 II: The Isaiah Scrolls*. Discoveries in the Judaean Desert 32. Oxford: Clarendon Press, 2010.

Ussishkin, David. "The Necropolis from the Time of the Kingdom of Judah at Silwan, Jerusalem." *Biblical Archaeologist* 33 (1970): 34–46.

Vermeylen, Jacques. *Du prophète Isaïe à l'apocalyptique*. 2 vols. Etudes bibliques. Paris: Gabalda, 1977–78.

Waard, Jan de. *A Handbook on Isaiah*. Textual Criticism and the Translator 1. Winona Lake, IN: Eisenbrauns, 1997.

Walsh, Carey Ellen. "God's Vineyard: Isaiah's Prophecy as Vintner's Textbook." *Bible Review* 14, no. 4 (Aug. 1998): 42–9, 52–3.

Walsh, Carey Ellen. *The Fruit of the Vine: Viticulture in Ancient Israel*. Harvard Semitic Monographs 60. Winona Lake, IN: Eisenbrauns, 2000.

Waltke, Bruce K., and Michael P. O'Connor. *An Introduction to Biblical Hebrew Syntax*. Winona Lake, IN: Eisenbrauns, 1990.

Watson, Wilfred G. E. *Traditional Techniques in Classical Hebrew Verse*. Journal for the Study of the Old Testament: Supplement Series 170. Sheffield: Sheffield Academic Press, 1994.

Watson, Wilfred G. E. *Classical Hebrew Poetry: A Guide to its Techniques*. Journal for the Study of the Old Testament: Supplement Series 26. Sheffield: JSOT Press, 1986. Repr., London, T&T Clark, 2005.

Watson, Wilfred G. E. "The Study of Biblical Hebrew Poetry: Past—Present—Future." Pages 124–54 in *Sacred Conjectures: The Context and Legacy of Robert Lowth and Jean Astruc*. Edited by John Jarick. Library of Hebrew Bible/Old Testament Studies 457. New York: T&T Clark, 2007.

Watts, John D. W. *Isaiah*. 2 vols. Rev. ed. Word Biblical Commentary 24–25. Waco, TX: Word Books, 2005.

Weinfeld, Moshe. "Covenant Terminology in the Ancient Near East and its Influence on the West." *Journal of the American Oriental Society* 93 (1973): 182–96.

Weippert, Manfred. "Mitteilungen zum Text von Ps 19 5 und Jes 22 5." *Zeitschrift für die alttestamentliche Wissenschaft* 73 (1961): 97–9.

Wesling, Donald, and Enriko Bollobaś. "Free Verse." Pages 425–7 in *The New Princeton Encyclopedia of Poetry and Poetics*. Edited by Alex Preminger and T. V. F. Brogan. Princeton: Princeton University Press, 1993.

Westermann, Claus. *Basic Forms of Prophetic Speech*. Translated by H. C. White. Louisville, KY: Westminster John Knox, 1991.

Wiklander, Bertil. *Prophecy as Literature: A Text-Linguistic and Rhetorical Approach to Isa 2–4*. Coniectanea biblica: Old Testament Series 22. Malmö: CWK Gleerup, 1984.

Wildberger, Hans. *Isaiah 1–12*. Translated by Thomas H. Trapp. Continental Commentary. Minneapolis: Fortress, 1991.

Wildberger, Hans. *Isaiah 13–27*. Translated by Thomas H. Trapp. Continental Commentary. Minneapolis: Fortress, 1997.

Wildberger, Hans. *Isaiah 28–39*. Translated by Thomas H. Trapp. Continental Commentary. Minneapolis: Fortress, 2002.

Williams, Gary Roye. "Frustrated Expectations in Isaiah v 1–7: A Literary Interpretation." *Vetus Testamentum* 35 (1985): 459–65.

Williamson, H. G. M. *The Book Called Isaiah: Deutero-Isaiah's Role in Composition and Redaction*. Oxford: Oxford University Press, 1994.

Williamson, H. G. M. "The Messianic Texts in Isaiah 1–39." Pages 238–70 in *King and Messiah in Israel and the Ancient Near East: Proceedings of the Oxford Old Testament Seminar*. Edited by John Day. Journal for the Study of the Old Testament: Supplement Series 270. Sheffield: Sheffield Academic Press, 1998.

Williamson, H. G. M. "Isaiah 1 and the Covenant Lawsuit." Pages 393–406 in *Covenant as Context: Essays in Honour of E. W. Nicholson*. Edited by A. D. H. Mayes and R. B. Salters. Oxford: Oxford University Press, 2003.

Williamson, H. G. M. "In Search of The Pre-exilic Isaiah." Pages 181–206 in *In Search of Pre-Exilic Israel: Proceedings of the Oxford Old Testament*

Seminar. Edited by John Day. *Journal for the Study of the Old Testament*: Supplement Series 406. London: T&T Clark, 2004.

Williamson, H. G. M. *A Critical and Exegetical Commentary on Isaiah 1–5*. International Critical Commentary. London: T&T Clark, 2006.

Willis, John T. "The First Pericope in the Book of Isaiah." *Vetus Testamentum* 34 (1984): 63–77.

Willis, John T. "Alternating (ABA'B') Parallelism in the Old Testament Psalms and Prophetic Literature." Pages 49–76 in *Directions in Biblical Hebrew Poetry*. Edited by Elaine R. Follis. *Journal for the Study of the Old Testament*: Supplement Series 40. Sheffield: Sheffield Academic Press, 1987.

Willis, John T. "Textual and Linguistic Issues in Isaiah 22, 15–25." *Zeitschrift für die alttestamentliche Wissenchaft* 105 (1993): 377–99.

Wimsatt, W. K. and Monroe C. Beardsley. "The Intentional Fallacy." Pages 3–19 in *The Verbal Icon: Studies in the Meaning of Poetry*. Lexington, KY: University Press of Kentucky, 1954.

Wolff, Hans Walter. *Joel and Amos*. Translated by Waldemar Janzen et al. Hermeneia. Philadelphia: Fortress, 1977.

Worgul, John E. "The Quatrain in Isaianic Poetry." *Grace Theological Journal* 11 (1990): 189–90.

Wright, Jacob L. "Warfare and Wanton Destruction: A Reexamination of Deuteronomy 20:19–20 in Relation to Ancient Siegecraft." *Journal of Biblical Literature* 127 (2008): 423–58.

Wyatt, Nicholas. "A New Look at Ugaritic šdmt." *Journal of Semitic Studies* 37 (1992): 149–53.

Yee, Gale A. "The Anatomy of Biblical Parody: The Dirge Form in 2 Samuel 1 and Isaiah 14." *Catholic Biblical Quarterly* 50 (1988): 565–86.

Yeivin, Israel. *Introduction to the Tiberian Masorah*. Translated by E. J. Revell. Masoretic Studies 5. Atlanta: Scholars Press, 1980.

Young, G. Douglas. "Ugaritic Prosody." *Journal of Near Eastern Studies* 9 (1950): 124–33.

Index of Selected Authors

Alonso Schökel, Luis 3, 29, 37, 40, 44, 46, 48, 73, 81, 91, 106, 110–11, 117, 122, 140, 142, 144–5, 194, 197–8, 206
Alter, Robert 3, 11, 20, 30, 37, 42, 63, 67, 72–5, 78, 81, 83–6, 100, 112, 159, 196
Andersen, Francis I. 64, 77
Auld, A. Graeme 11

Baer, David A. 130
Barré, Michael L. 121
Bartelt, Andrew H. 11, 41, 64, 106, 109–10, 129, 131, 133
Barth, Hermann 2, 121, 125–6
Barton, John 12–13
Becker, Uwe 59, 132, 135
Ben Zvi, Ehud 193
Berlin, Adele 3, 14, 33, 36, 43–4, 49, 64, 71–5, 85, 87–8, 91, 93, 108, 116–17, 119, 130, 135, 144, 170, 173, 202
Beuken, Willem A. M. 3, 17, 58–61, 125, 127, 132–3
Black, Jeremy A. 15, 17
Blenkinsopp, Joseph 9–11, 25, 30, 34–5, 51, 57–9, 61–2, 64–5, 77–9, 88, 96, 98, 102, 105, 118, 120–1, 123–6, 129, 131–5, 153, 159–60, 167–8, 170, 173, 179–80, 183–4, 189, 192–4
Borowski, Oded 147, 150, 162–3, 167, 176
Brensinger, Terry L. 145–6, 149, 159, 171
Brogan, T. V. F. 1–2, 21, 24, 42, 109, 117, 122
Brooks, Cleanth 2
Brown, William P. 79, 110, 140–1, 144–6, 165, 169, 171, 177–8, 182

Carr, David M. 13, 17
Childs, Brevard S. 59, 110, 115, 125, 128, 150, 152–3, 160, 179, 192
Clements, Ronald E. 2, 9, 57, 59, 78, 98, 102, 104–5, 118, 121, 123, 125, 128, 132–3, 137, 149–51, 158–9, 170, 179–80, 182, 184–5, 192

Cloete, Walter Theophilus Woldemar 22, 25–6, 29–30, 34, 40–2, 46–8, 50–1
Cohen, Harold R. (Chaim) 83, 113, 115, 189
Collins, Terrence 29, 38, 49–50
Conrad, Edgar W. 11, 16
Cooper, Alan M. 40, 44, 46
Corley, Jeremy 61
Cross, Frank Moore, Jr. 31, 47

Dahood, Mitchell 76, 189
Daniels, Dwight R. 193–4, 199
Darr, Katheryn Pfisterer 11–12, 16, 139, 141, 145
Davidson, R. 121
Dobbs-Allsopp, F. W. 14–17, 22–3, 26, 29–30, 32, 38–9, 42–3, 47, 53–4, 61, 70–1, 90–1, 93–4, 98–9, 111, 146, 158–9, 195
Donner, Herbert 104, 126
Driver, G. R. 58, 88, 104
Duhm, Bernard 7–9, 34, 51, 57–8, 62–5, 77, 88, 90, 110, 120–1, 123, 125–6, 129–30, 166, 170, 173, 180

Eagleton, Terry 1–2, 14, 49, 140
Ehrlich, Arnold B. 76, 79, 88, 96, 102, 172
Emerton, J. A. 64–5, 106, 118–19, 130
Everson, A. Joseph 11–12, 146
Exum, J. Cheryl 11–12, 14, 87, 139, 183, 185

Finnegan, Ruth 25, 27, 33
Flint, Peter W. 17
Fokkelman, J. P. 30, 41, 109
Forbes, A. Dean 64
Franke, Chris 109
Freedman, David Noel 27, 31, 41, 44, 47, 64, 77, 106, 109–10, 190
Friedman, Norman 140, 145–7

Gallagher, William R. 59–60, 62, 64, 174, 176

Geller, Stephen A. 21-2, 34, 37, 40, 44-6, 48, 69, 71, 96, 98, 205
Giese, Ronald L. 43
Ginsberg, H. L. 126
Gitay, Yehoshua 15-16, 25, 106, 192
Goldingay, John 121
Gordon, Robert P. 4, 6, 71
Gottlieb, Claire 104
Gottwald, Norman K. 37
Gray, George Buchanan 3-4, 7, 8, 10, 22, 25, 29-30, 32, 34-6, 46-8, 51, 56-9, 61-2, 64-5, 77-80, 88, 96, 98, 100, 104-5, 109-10, 118, 120-1, 125, 128-34, 136, 148, 150, 152-3, 155-6, 159-60, 166, 168, 170, 172-3, 179, 187-92, 195, 197-8, 206
Greenstein, Edward L. 21, 29, 32, 65, 67, 70, 74, 87, 90, 100, 206
Grossberg, Daniel 72, 111, 117, 186
Guillaume, A. 58

Halpern, Baruch 118-19
Hartman, Charles O. 21, 39, 42-3
Hayes, John H. 7, 9, 59, 78-9, 82, 104, 106, 118, 123-4, 131-3, 153, 158-9, 166, 178-9, 183, 190, 193
Hays, Christopher B. 89, 118-20
Healy, John F. 155, 163
Heffelfinger, Katie M. 5
Hillers, Delbert R. 38, 47, 83, 154, 167, 190
Hoch, James C. 158
Holladay, William L. 45, 51, 53-4, 92, 129, 132, 181
Hollander, John 21, 41
Hoop, Raymond de 28
Hummel, Horace D. 89, 126, 130
Hrushovski, Benjamin 42-4, 48

Irvine, Stuart A. 7, 9, 59, 78-9, 82, 104, 106, 118, 123-4, 131-3, 153, 158-9, 166, 173, 175, 178-9, 183, 190, 193
Irwin, William H. 76, 86-8, 101-2, 114, 123, 126-7

Jacobson, Rolf A. 203
Johnson, Mark 82, 141-6, 149, 155
Johnston, Gordon H. 119
Jones, Brian C. 9, 11, 15, 25, 150-3, 165
Jong, Matthijs J. de 2, 17, 59, 62, 193

Kaiser, Otto 9, 35, 59, 61, 98, 102, 120-1, 123, 125, 130-2, 137, 151, 153, 155-6, 158-9, 173, 179-80, 188-9, 193
Kessler, Martin 117-18
Kim, Hyun Chul Paul 11-12, 146
King, Philip J. 96, 147, 155
Kinzie, Mary 21, 33, 38, 93, 140
Kissane, Edward J. 41
Kooij, Arie van der 190
Krueger, Paul A. 126
Kugel, James L. 10, 23, 29, 33, 43, 46, 69, 71-5, 81, 84, 98-9, 108
Kuntz, J. Kenneth 10, 51, 72

Lakoff, George 82, 141-6, 149, 155
Landy, Francis 72, 178-80
Lavik, Marta Høyland 104, 158-60
Lemaire, André 158
LeMon, Joel M. 72, 91, 177
Lessing, R. Reed 11, 95, 99
Linafelt, Tod 54
Longman, Tremper III 41, 44
Lowth, Robert 3-8, 10, 13-14, 22-9, 36-7, 43, 71, 88, 112, 134, 139, 145-6, 157, 166
Lubetski, Meir 104

Machinist, Peter 17, 119, 171, 174
Magonet, Jonathan 128, 132-3, 135, 137
Melugin, Roy F. 11-12, 194, 197
Miller, Cynthia L. 32, 90, 196
Miller, Patrick D. 14, 43, 148, 169, 175-6
Miscall, Peter D. 11-12, 16, 139, 151, 175
  see also Quinn-Miscall, Peter D.
Mitchell, W. J. T. 140
Mittmann, Siegfried 173
Moor, Johannes C. de 40-2, 44, 109
Muilenburg, James 5, 14

Niditch, Susan 25, 175
Nielsen, Kirsten 11, 139, 148

O'Brien, Julia M. 194-5
O'Connell, Robert H. 12
O'Connor, Michael Patrick 8, 15, 22-3, 25, 29-30, 32-3, 39, 41-2, 45, 47-54, 64, 66, 69-70, 74, 85, 91-7, 101, 109, 114-16, 127, 129, 172, 190, 202
Oestreich, Bernhard 159

Index of Selected Authors

Pardee, Dennis 33-4, 37, 42, 44, 54, 109, 117
Parker, Simon B. 83
Petersen, David L. 14, 26, 30, 40-2, 69, 72, 108-9, 111, 119, 141, 145
Pinsky, Robert 24-7, 38

Quinn-Miscall, Peter D. 11, 139, 146, 152, 159, 165
  see also Miscall, Peter D.

Raabe, Paul R. 54, 108-10, 120
Raffel, Burton 1, 111
Rendsburg, Gary A. 206
Richards, Kent Harold 14, 26, 30, 40-2, 69, 72, 108-9, 111, 119, 141, 145
Rilke, Rainer Maria 207
Roberts, J. J. M. 11, 13, 102, 106-7, 113-14, 121, 124, 136, 160, 185, 190, 192-3, 206
Rowlands, E. R. 89
Rudolph, Wilhelm 149-50, 152

Sæbø, Magne 34
Sarna, Nahum M. 175
Sasson, Victor 126-7
Schipper, Jeremy 127
Schoors, Antoon 53
Scott, R. B. Y. 151
Seitz, Christopher R. 9, 12, 59, 78, 160, 179, 181
Seow, C. L. 86, 153, 180
Shemesh, Yael 184
Sherwood, Yvonne 139
Smith, Barbara Herrnstein 21, 25, 29, 34, 39, 43, 67-71, 95, 109-10, 116-17
Smith, Mark S. 39
Smoak, Jeremy D. 151, 154
Smothers, Thomas G. 151-2, 165
Sommer, Benjamin D. 13, 115, 184-5, 205
Stager, Lawrence E. 96, 147, 155
Stansell, Gary 6-7, 13
Strawn, Brent A. 12, 72, 91, 140-1, 145-6, 165, 171-3, 182-5
Sweeney, Marvin A. 2-3, 9, 12, 16, 59, 62, 78, 98, 106, 110, 120-1, 124-5, 132-3, 151-2, 160, 179, 182, 184, 192-4

Talmon, Shemaryahu 153, 158-9, 161
Tate, Marvin E. 12
Toorn, Karel van der 13, 17, 25
Tov, Emmanuel 23, 30
Tull, Patricia K. 4, 6, 10-13, 23-4, 26-7, 57, 59, 64, 93, 130, 148, 152, 155, 159, 164, 185, 187, 192-4, 196, 198-9
Turner, Mark 82, 141-6, 149, 155

Uchelen, N. A. van 93
Ulrich, Eugene 17, 24

Vermeylen, Jacques 3, 178

Waard, Jan de 56, 114, 130, 148, 166, 168, 180
Walsh, Carey Ellen 150-1, 159, 161-3
Watson, Wilfred G. E. 10, 22, 28, 30, 32, 36-7, 39-40, 42-3, 46, 55, 61, 63, 67, 69, 90, 94, 97-100, 103, 106-9, 117, 119-20, 122-4, 127, 134, 157, 169, 204
Watts, John D. W. 12
Weippert, Manfred 58
Wiklander, Bertil 129
Wildberger, Hans 3, 8-9, 25, 30, 34, 36, 41, 51, 56-7, 59, 62-6, 77-83, 89, 96, 98-101, 104-6, 110, 115, 118, 120-1, 123-6, 128-33, 136-7, 144, 146, 148, 150, 152-4, 157-60, 166, 168, 170, 173, 179-80, 182-5, 187-9, 192-3, 198, 206
Williams, Gary Roye 11, 81, 95, 161-2
Williamson, H. G. M. 3, 10-11, 17, 36, 41, 46, 78, 80, 83, 90, 93, 96, 100, 105-6, 110, 113, 121, 128-37, 155, 162, 166, 168, 170, 172, 187-9, 192-3, 195, 198, 206
Willis, John T. 37, 52, 82, 192-3
Wolff, Hans Walter 77
Worgul, John E. 100, 114
Wyatt, Nicholas 150-1

Yee, Gale A. 95
Young, G. Douglas 82

Index of Biblical and other Ancient Texts

HEBREW BIBLE

Genesis
2:11 51
4:8 129
4:10–11 198
8:2 90
8:22 159, 161
15:11 160
17:4 77
31:36 113
41:1–7 156
41:2 180
41:18 180
49:6 175
49:10 177
49:24 175

Exodus
2:23 58
4:1–5 178
4:25 170
7:9–12 178
10:2 130
15 23
17:6 77
21:8 148
21:19 136
23:10 154
23:16 154
24:9–11 88
25:30 80
34:24 188

Leviticus
13:12 195
19:4 33
19:9–10 156
23:22 156
26:5 159
26:16 154

Numbers
6:12 153
7:17–88 176
14:3 190
17:23 (Eng. 17:8) 178

21:6–8 178
22:27 180
22:32 195
31:7 184

Deuteronomy
1:17 131
3:21 51
8:10 198
10:18 198
11:14 154
13:16 (Eng. 13:15) 199
16:19 131
20:20 86, 157
22:6–7 176
24:20 157
28:26 160
28:30 83, 154
28:35 195
28:39 154
29:22 (Eng. 29:23) 187
31:11 188
32 23
32:1 193
32:2 159
32:11 177
32:13 162
32:32 151

Joshua
6:20 171
11:2 126
11:7 153
12:23 126
21:45 153

Judges
1:8 199
4–5 63
5 23
5:7 149
5:14 177
6:11 163
9:13 154
9:27 148
18:7 56
18:28 56

Index of Biblical and other Ancient Texts

19:25 130
20:38–40 126
20:43 113
21:19–21 148

1 Samuel
2:8 86
4:4 174
14:1 86
14:4 86
14:12 86
17:34–37 184
17:44 160
17:46 160
17:53 113
22:4 86
22:19 199
26:20 198
30:16 149

2 Samuel
2:26 199
5:8 198
7:14 194
22 23
22:9 126
23:14 86

1 Kings
2:5 198
4:11 126
8:7 80
8:56 153
20:36 77

2 Kings
10:10 53
16:9 58
18:21 136
20:12–13 60
20:20 65
23:4 151

Isaiah
1:1–31 18
1:1 135, 192
1:2–20 186–200
1:2 118, 193–4, 200
1:3 45–6, 72–5, 193–5, 197, 200
1:4 194, 200
1:5 146, 194–6, 200
1:6 37, 53, 146, 195, 200
1:7 193, 195, 199–200
1:8 101, 114, 149, 162, 193, 195–6, 200
1:9 93, 193, 196–7, 200
1:10 93, 112, 185, 193, 197, 200
1:11 197–8, 200
1:12 197, 200
1:13 197
1:14 197–8
1:15 197–9
1:16 36, 198
1:17 36, 137, 198
1:18 112, 197, 199
1:19 52–3, 112, 199–200
1:20 52–3, 118, 197, 199–200
1:21–26 117–18
1:22 146
1:23 83, 137, 198, 206
1:24–26 164
1:24 175
1:25 96–7
1:29 112
2:1 135, 192
2:4 129
2:5–22 18
2:6–22 8, 120–1
2:7 33–4, 112
2:8 33–4, 99–100, 121
2:9–10 120–1
2:11 100, 121
2:12–17 82, 100
2:12 99, 121
2:13–14 121
2:15 146
2:16 83, 146
2:17 106, 121, 206
2:18 121
2:19 120–1
2:20 33, 121
2:21 120
2:22 100
3:1–3 105–6, 122
3:1–15 19, 109, 128–38, 192
3:1–4:1 18, 133
3:1 134, 137
3:2–3 122, 133–4, 137
3:2–4 10
3:3 133
3:4 88, 133–4, 136–7
3:5 37–8, 97, 112, 133–4
3:6 99, 133, 135, 204
3:7 94, 101, 135, 204
3:8 49, 116, 133, 135–6
3:9–11 39, 112, 133–6
3:9 136–7, 197

Isaiah (cont.)
3:10 136
3:12 88, 112, 133, 136–7, 189
3:13 85, 137
3:14–15 136–7
3:14 80, 133, 137
3:16–24 105
3:16 116
3:18–23 105–6, 122
3:18 39
3:19–21 106
3:24 106
3:25 90, 190
4:1 135
5 110
5:1–7 79, 95, 151, 161–3
5:1–29 18
5:1 25, 83, 162
5:2 37, 53, 82, 162, 196
5:3 116, 162
5:4 39, 162
5:5 80–1, 91–2, 162
5:6 162–3
5:7 163
5:8–10 168
5:8–24 165
5:8 86, 116, 155
5:9 85, 99, 107, 155
5:10 48, 154–5, 157, 163
5:11–17 168
5:11 46, 86, 112–14, 167, 185
5:12 64, 105, 167
5:13 116, 167–8
5:14 84–5, 116, 165–8
5:15–16 82
5:15 37, 121
5:17 166–8
5:19 206
5:20 112
5:21 206
5:22 113
5:23 86
5:24 86, 146
5:25 116
5:25–29 110, 170, 173
5:26–29 169
5:26 170
5:27 170
5:28 170
5:29–30 123
5:29 10, 169–73, 182, 184–5
6:2 178
6:6 178
6:10 205
6:13 148, 155
7:2 168
7:23–25 167
7:25 80
8:6 116, 146
8:7–8 119, 146
8:9–22 18
8:9 34–6
8:10 34–6, 88, 99, 107, 159
8:13 37
8:15 40, 52
8:23–9:20 (Eng. 9:1–21) 18
9–10 110
9:1 (Eng. 9:2) 92, 112
9:2 (Eng. 9:3) 148–9, 177–8
9:3 (Eng. 9:4) 101, 124, 177–8, 206
9:4 (Eng. 9:5) 99
9:5 (Eng. 9:6) 94, 106
9:6 (Eng. 9:7) 88, 106
9:7–20 (Eng. 9:8–21) 110, 170, 173
9:10 (Eng. 9:11) 206
9:15 (Eng. 9:16) 189
9:16 (Eng. 9:17) 116
9:18–20 (Eng. 9:19–21) 97
9:19 (Eng. 9:20) 146, 198
10:1–2 116
10:1–34 18
10:2 85–6, 137, 198
10:3 85
10:5–15 207
10:5 102–3, 173, 177–8
10:6 37, 80, 115–16
10:8–9 101
10:9 60
10:10–11 177
10:11 88, 103
10:13 169, 173–7
10:14 37, 169, 173–7, 184–5, 206
10:15 101, 103, 177–8
10:16 116
10:16–17 146
10:17–34 124
10:19 39
10:27–29 125
10:27–32 122, 124–5
10:27 124
10:29 125
10:30 125
10:32 102, 125–6
10:33–11:1 148

Index of Biblical and other Ancient Texts 239

11:1-5 30-3
11:1-10 18, 179
11:1 31-2, 78-9, 179-80
11:2 31-2, 101
11:3 31
11:4 31-2, 179
11:5 32
11:6-7 112, 166, 181
11:6-9 169, 181-2
11:8 180-2
11:9 39, 181
13-23 55
13:1 55
13:11 114
13:19-22 167
13:19 187
14:1-21 95
14:4-32 18
14:5 178
14:9 173, 176
14:13 94
14:18 82
14:24 99, 107
14:25 86
14:26 35, 49, 51
14:27 35, 51-2, 88, 112, 116, 205
14:28-32 100, 177, 180
14:28 98, 179
14:29 39, 61, 79, 169, 177-80
14:30 168-9, 180
14:31 37, 53, 61, 116
14:32 94, 97-8
15:1-16:12 18, 95, 151
15:1 25, 47, 55, 107, 112, 124, 152
15:2 39
15:5 112
15:6 37, 53, 148
15:9 150
16:1 165
16:4 37, 152, 189
16:8-10 149-54
16:8 152, 162
16:9 116, 152-3, 159
16:10 77, 153-4
17:1-14 18
17:1 55, 77-8, 107, 124
17.2 166-9
17:4-6 155-7
17:5 154-7, 163
17:10 88
17:12 112, 143-5, 146
17:13 144

18:1-6 18
18:1 39, 146
18:2 103-5, 158
18:4-6 145, 157-61
18:4 94, 101, 107, 149, 158-61
18:5 159-61
18:6 160-1
18:7 104
19:1-15 18, 120
19:1-4 120
19:1 55, 78, 120
19:2 97, 134
19:3 120
19:4 88-90, 97
19:5-10 120
19:6 120
19:8 46
19:10-15 120
19:11 94, 99, 120
19:13 120
19:14 146
19:16-25 106
19:17 137
21:1-10 48
21:1 55
21:10 164
21:11 55
21:12 77
21:13 55
22:1-14 19, 55-67, 100, 109
22:1-23 18
22:1 107
22:2 61-2
22:3-4 60-2
22:5-8 99
22:5 60, 62
22:6 59-60, 63
22:7 63
22:8-11 59, 64-5
22:8 60, 63, 65
22:9-10 65
22:11 59, 64-5
22:12 60, 62, 65-6
22:13 66
22:14 60, 66-7
22:15 55, 99
22:16 37, 81-3
22:17 206
22:18 83
22:22 89
22:23 88
23:1-14 18, 95

Isaiah (cont.)
23:1-2 146
23:1 55, 118
23:3 88
23:7-9 99-100
23:12 39
23:14 118, 146
24:4 152
24:7 152
24:9 113
24:10 89
25:5 114
25:6 168
27:10 167
28:1-29 18
28:1 152
28:2 101, 146
28:3 39
28:4 39, 106, 150
28:7 139, 146, 152
28:8 88, 146
28:9 25, 46
28:10 25, 116, 118
28:11 39, 116, 119
28:12 99, 106-7, 112, 116
28:13 39-40, 94, 104, 116, 118-19
28:14 93, 101-2
28:15 66, 119
28:16 106, 119, 146
28:17 119, 146
28:18 39, 88-9, 119
28:19 119
28:20 76-7
28:21 164
28:22 39, 164
28:23-29 163-4
28:24 163
28:25 163
28:26-9 163
28:26 88, 163
28:27 163, 178
28:28-9 163
29:1-3 164
29:1-8 185
29:1-16 18
29:3 86-7
29:4-5 114-15
29:6 170
29:7 86, 184
29:8 184
29:10 146
29:11 66

29:13 101, 116
29:14 206
29:15 206
29:16 146
30:1-5 122
30:1-17 18
30:1 35, 101
30:2 86
30:6 107, 122-4, 165, 178
30:7 94, 122-4, 165
30:9 101
30:10 85, 116, 206
30:11 37, 206
30:12 86, 116
30:13 100, 146
30:14 99-100, 146
30:16 112
30:17 149
30:18 46
30:23 180
30:27-28 146
30:27-30 125-7
30:27-33 18
30:31 177
31:1-3 184
31:1-9 18
31:1 84, 86
31:3 36, 99-100
31:4 85, 99, 101, 116, 182-5, 204
31:5 182-5, 204
31:8 199
32:9-14 48
32:10-13 149
32:10 159
32:14 167
32:15-18 79
33:4 32
33:16 86
34:7 175
34:10-15 167
36:6 136
37:22 102
37:27 151
39:1-2 60
40-66 5
40:9 102
40:11 168
41:15 164
41:19 105
45:1 86, 89
45:8 79

Index of Biblical and other Ancient Texts 241

48:10 96
49:26 175
51:9 124
55:10 153
56:12 113
57:16 164
60:16 175
61:10–62:9 23
65:21 154
65:25 181
66:2 98

Jeremiah
2:21 162
2:22 96
4:11 158
4:13 170
5:14 47
6:1 126
6:9 158
7:6 198
8:14 195
8:19 58
12:9 160
14:14 33
15:3 160
15:6 47
19:7 160
25:30 153, 172
29:5 154
38:19 130
48:33 153
49:18 187
50:8 176
50:19 168
50:39 167
50:40 187
51:2 155
51:14 153
51:30 137
51:38 171
51:40 176

Ezekiel
3:9 170
4:2 86
15:2–4 160
16:49 197
19:2–3 120
19:5–6 120
19:7 171
19:11–12 178
21:27 (Eng. 21:22) 171

22:18 96
22:22 96
23:23 58
28:7 114
31:12 114
33:32 25
34:14 162
34:19 80
34:28 168
39:18 176
45:11 155

Hosea
2:8 80
4:3 105
5:5 135
5.14 173
6:4 159
11:10 184
13:3 159
13:7–8 181, 184
14:6 (Eng. 14:5) 159

Joel
1:10 152
1:12 152
2:7 196
4:16 (Eng. 3:16) 172, 184

Amos
1:1 193
1:2 172
1:5 58
1:14 170
3:8 171
3:12 172, 184
4:7–8 135
4:11 187
5:1–2 195
5:3 155
5:11 83, 154
5:19 77, 135, 178
6:4–7 167
6:9–10 135
9:7 58

Micah
1:10–15 125
3:12 155
4:14 86
5:7 173
6:1–2 193
6:14 172
7:1 159

Micah (cont.)
  7:4 80
  7:10 80

Nahum
  1:2-8 27
  1:3 170
  1:4 152
  2:2 (Eng. 2:1) 86
  2:11-12 (Eng. 2:12-13) 171

Habakkuk
  1:13 64
  2:6 102
  2:18 33
  3:17 150

Zephaniah 94
  1:13 83
  2:4-6 169
  2:4 125
  2:6-7 167-9

Haggai
  2:16 155

Zechariah
  4:12 156
  7:10 198
  8:4 136
  9:1 56
  9:8 86
  9:9 80
  10:3 176
  11:3 171
  14:5 193
  14:12 184

Malachi
  3:2 51

Psalms 5, 20, 23, 54, 108, 117, 169
  2:4 174
  4:8 (Eng. 4:7) 148
  5:3 (Eng. 5:2) 58
  7:3 (Eng. 7:2) 171, 173
  9:8 (Eng. 9:7) 174
  10:2 113
  11:5 198
  17:13 190
  18:9 (Eng. 18:8) 126
  19:15 (Eng. 19:14) 67
  22:13 (Eng. 22:12) 32, 175
  22:14 (Eng. 22:13) 171
  23 166
  31:3-4 (Eng. 31:2-3) 86
  32:9 194
  33:13 64
  36:8 (Eng. 36:7) 177
  40:2 (Eng. 40:1) 58
  42:3 (Eng. 42:2) 188
  45:7 (Eng. 45:6) 177
  46:3-4 (Eng. 46:2-3) 144
  49:12 (Eng. 49:11) 82
  50:4 193
  50:13 176
  50:22 173
  54:5 (Eng. 54:3) 114
  58:5 (Eng. 58:4) 178
  59:16 (Eng. 59:15) 198
  63:12 (Eng. 63:11) 89
  65:11 (Eng. 65:10) 153
  66:15 166, 168
  73:22 194
  74:13-14 144
  76:4 (Eng. 76:3) 105
  76:11 (Eng. 76:10) 56
  81:15 (Eng. 81:14) 188
  83:14 (Eng. 83:13) 144
  84:10 (Eng. 84:9) 64
  86:14 114
  87:4 124
  89:10-11 (Eng. 89:9-10) 144
  89:26 (Eng. 89:25) 144
  91:4 177
  94:17 188
  96:5 33
  100:3 148, 168
  104:15 154
  111 29
  112 29
  115:5-7 127
  119:62 149
  120-34 111
  121:4 170
  125:5 67
  127:2 113
  132:2 175
  132:5 175
  133:3 67, 159
  135:16-17 127
  140:4 (Eng. 140:3) 178

Job 23, 206
  1:10 80
  1:15 153
  2:7 195
  3:6 32
  3:22 153
  4:10 171

Index of Biblical and other Ancient Texts

9:30 96
10:16 184
13:4 33
14:7-10 194
14:8 79
15:24 173
17:13 82
19:24 82
24:22 175
28:24 64
30:23 82
30:24 58
35:11 194
38:6 195
38:7 86
39:14-15 177
41:12 (Eng. 41:20) 126

Proverbs 23
1:6 102
1:27 86
4:20-7 127
6:12-17 127
7:21 32
12:14 136
15:19 80
23:29-35 114
23:35 152
24:23 131
28:15 123
28:21 131
31:4 113
31:6 113
31:21 189

Ruth
2:12 177
2:16 156
2:17 163
3:7 148

Song of Songs 111, 140
1:5-8 67
4:1-5 127
4:7 61
5:10 158
5:11-16 127

Qoheleth (Ecclesiastes)
9:7 154
9:14 86, 129
12:5 82

Lamentations 23, 38, 111, 205
1-4 94
1:3 135
2:6 195
2:13 93
2:18 93
2:21 190
4:19 113
5:18 167
5:19 174

Esther
3:14 173

Daniel
7:3-6 181

Nehemiah
9:25 162

2 Chronicles
12:4 86
13:12 171
32:5 65
32:10 195
32:31 60

APOCRYPHA AND NEW TESTAMENT

Sirach 23

Matthew
21:1-5 80

John
15:6 160

OTHER ANCIENT TEXTS

Annals of Sennacherib 177
Babylonian Talmud 23
Cyrus cylinder 62
Deir 'Alla inscriptions 82
Erra epic 97
Gezer calendar 147, 154, 159
Iliad 122
Lachish letters 126
Palmyranean tomb inscriptions 82
Sefire inscriptions (*KAI* 224) 89
Siloam tunnel inscription 65, 82
Ugaritic texts (*KTU^2*) 39, 84, 144, 151, 164
Zakkur inscription (*KAI* 202) 86

Index of Subjects

A- A- // A— lines 37, 39, 53, 55, 115, 187, 204
acrostics 27, 29, 110
agricultural imagery 147–64, 195–6, 203, 205
  gleaning 156
  harvesting 148–9, 151–63
  pruning 157–60
  threshing 163–4
  vineyard 79–81, 149–54, 160–3, 196
  see also animal imagery, imagery, metaphors
Ahaz 98, 133, 179
allegory 147, 151, 162, 182
alliteration 39–40, 58, 128, 130
  see also assonance, consonance, soundplay
anaphora 33–4, 204
animal imagery 165–85, 194–200, 203–5
  bird 160–1, 176–7, 184–5, 203
  bull 174–5
  goat 176, 197
  lion 77, 124, 165, 171–3, 181–5, 203
  livestock 45–6, 72–3, 160–1, 166–9, 172, 180, 184, 194–5, 197, 203
  sacrificial 176, 197–8
  snake 77, 122–4, 165, 178–81
  see also agricultural imagery, imagery, metaphors
assonance 61, 76
  see also alliteration, soundplay
Assyria 2, 16–17, 51–2, 59–60, 62–3, 65, 77, 84, 98, 102–4, 115, 119, 122, 124–5, 137–8, 149, 151, 155, 158, 160, 169–71, 173–7, 179, 182, 184–5, 195, 204–5, 207
  invasion of Jerusalem in 701 BCE 59, 93, 132–3, 158, 182, 184–5, 193
  royal annals/inscriptions 63, 119, 169, 171, 174–6, 177
  see also Sargon II, Sennacherib, Tiglath-Pileser III

Babylon 59, 62
  invasion of Jerusalem in 587 BCE 59, 128, 193
  see also Nebuchadnezzar II
ballast variant see deletion compensation
Battle of Kish 59–60, 62–3
  see also Sennacherib
bicolon see couplet
brevity see terseness

canto see stanza
catalogues 111, 122–7, 195, 203
  see also lists
chiasm 32, 64, 89, 133, 204
closure 52, 65, 67, 117, 164
  see also terminal modification
conditional sentences 52, 193, 199
consonance 162, 206
  see also alliteration, soundplay
construct chains 31, 38, 46, 48, 188
contrast 73–5, 91, 202
  grammatical/morphological 64, 83, 85, 87, 90, 97, 135, 173
  lexical/semantic 76–8, 81, 83–4, 86–7, 89, 97, 99, 202
  syntactic 78
  see also equivalence, parallelism
couplets
  movement within 70–95
  nomenclature 30
  structural functions 69–71, 95–6, 202
  unbalanced see qînâ rhythm
  with parallel lines 70–91, 202
  with enjambed lines 70–1, 91–5, 202
  see also enjambment, parallelism
curses 83, 154–5, 167
Cush 104, 158–61
Cyrus 62

Dead Sea Scrolls 8, 23
deletion 32, 37, 90, 97, 104, 126, 129
  compensation 46, 83–5, 206
Dickinson, Emily 82
diction 9, 206

Index of Subjects

divine judgment 66–7, 81, 106, 116, 127, 133, 148, 154–5, 157, 163–4, 203, 205
divine plan 35, 49, 51–2, 65, 159, 205
double entendre 102, 129, 136, 152–3, 195, 205
  see also puns, wordplay

Elam 59–60
ellipsis *see* deletion
emendation 7–9, 18
enclitic -*m* 89, 113, 130, 189
enjambment 29, 38–9, 49, 55, 65, 69–71, 91–101, 104, 111–12, 115–16, 135, 172, 197, 201–5
equivalence 73–5, 91, 202
  grammatical/morphological 32, 61, 76, 99, 113–14, 117, 128, 130, 170
  lexical/semantic 29, 31, 64, 72–3, 75, 78–9, 88, 92, 113–14, 117, 130, 172
  phonological 61, 66, 76–8, 87, 96–7, 99, 117, 128, 202
  syntactic 29, 31, 64, 79, 87, 96–7, 113, 130, 172, 202
  see also contrast, parallelism, synonymy, word pairs

figurative language *see* metaphor
final form readings of Isaiah 11–13, 15
five-line units 103–4, 106–7
free verse 25, 28, 42–3, 68, 109–10, 204
  see also meter

gapping *see* deletion

hapax legomena 77, 83, 86, 136, 158
Hezekiah 60, 81, 106
historical approaches to Isaiah 7, 14–18, 145–6
hôy-oracles 86, 165, 167–8, 190
hyperbole 81, 83, 152, 170

imagery 4–5, 9–12, 63, 77–9, 82, 110, 115, 119, 139–86, 195–200, 203–4
  alcohol 113–14, 146, 152, 154
  architecture 146
  body 125–7, 146, 195
  child 136, 181, 194–5
  color 199
  effects of 146, 161, 186, 200, 203–4
  fire 99, 146
  food 194–5, 197–8

pastoral 165–8, 180
plant/tree 79–80, 148, 178–9
pottery 99, 146
rod/staff 177–9, 194–5
shifts in 156–7, 159, 178–80, 186, 203–5
ship 146
water/sea 99, 119, 143–4, 146, 153, 181
  see also agricultural imagery, animal imagery, metaphors
inclusio 87, 100, 110, 117–18, 132, 135, 137, 192, 199

keywords 110, 119–21, 192

laments 47, 53, 61, 95, 152, 195, 205
Leitwörter see keywords
lexical pairs *see* word pairs
lines
  as basic unit of biblical verse 21–2, 29–30
  effects of 1–2, 21–2, 29, 35–7, 55, 61–3, 67
  end-stopped 28–9, 31, 38, 71, 92, 108
  graphic representation of 6, 22–5, 201
  identification of 25–40, 47–55, 61–7, 97, 101, 105, 107, 128, 134, 170, 201–2
  length of 35–7, 43–9, 51–2, 55, 66, 201–2, 204
  pause between 21–2, 29, 37–9, 49, 52, 63, 68–9, 91, 93, 95, 99
  syntactic structure of 49–54, 172
  see also A- A- // A— lines, enjambment, parallelism
lists 105–6, 122, 125, 127, 181, 197
  see also catalogues
loanwords 83, 206
love poetry 127, 161

manuscripts, biblical 22–3, 201
Masoretic Text
  Codex Leningrad 26
  punctuation 28, 31, 41, 46–7, 51, 61–3, 99, 105, 128, 201
Merodach-baladan 60, 63, 65
metaphors 63–4, 81–2, 84–5, 96, 135–6, 140–9, 155–7, 160–86, 194–5, 199–200
  see also agricultural imagery, animal imagery, imagery, similes

246 Index of Subjects

meter 4, 6–8, 40–4
  see also free verse
metonymy 149
mimesis, poetic 36, 49, 104–5, 134, 185, 205
mixing 115–16, 124
monocolon see single lines

narrativity, poetic 75–81, 90, 96–7, 202
  see also vignettes
Nebuchadnezzar II 179
  see also Babylon
New Criticism 14–15

onomatopoeia 118, 206

parallelism 4, 8–9, 27–38, 44, 48, 51–5, 61–8, 70–92, 96–9, 101–4, 107, 111–23, 135, 149, 170–92, 190, 198, 202–5
  as indicator of lineation 27–38, 48, 55, 201
  between couplets 37–8, 48, 52, 55, 61, 92, 100–1, 111–15, 134, 136, 203, 205
  distant 111, 117, 120, 135
  internal 29, 34–7, 39, 53–5, 62, 66, 187, 198, 204
parataxis 109, 116
particles
  as indicators of prose 64, 106
  in word counts 45–6
personification 84, 144, 152, 199
Philistines 53, 59, 97–8, 125, 169, 177–80
poetry
  and prophecy 4–5, 7–8, 25, 45, 64, 108, 116, 139, 143
  definition of 1–2
  non-metrical see free verse
  performance of 24–5, 28, 100
  prophecy and poetry 4–5, 7
  temporal experience of 68–9, 81, 110
  translation of 6, 19–20, 31, 33, 58, 102, 113, 123, 130, 163
  versus prose 1–2, 64, 66
puns 44, 53, 102, 113, 135, 197
  see also double entendre, wordplay

qînâ rhythm 47, 53, 61–3, 95, 118, 150, 152, 154, 195
quatrain 32, 69, 94, 100–3, 111, 135, 196, 202

quotations 9, 93–4, 99, 119, 196, 206
quotative frames 94, 98–9, 101, 106–7

reduplicated words 58, 158, 206
refrains 108–10, 121
repetition 30, 32–3, 40–1, 46, 58, 60, 62, 65–6, 69–70, 74, 77–8, 99, 108, 117–21, 133–4, 144, 157, 159–60, 183–4, 195, 198, 203
retrospective patterning 69, 93, 172, 183, 185
rhetorical questions 103, 172, 198
rhyme 6, 40, 61–2, 75, 106, 162, 206
  see also soundplay
rhythm 8–9, 26, 29, 41–2, 46–9, 142
Rossi, Azariah de 71

Sargon II 59
  see also Assyria
satire 95
scansion 40–1, 44–7
sections of poems 60, 100, 108–12, 117, 119–20, 125, 193, 197, 200, 203
  see also stanza, structure
Sennacherib 59–60, 62, 93, 132, 177, 184, 193
  see also Assyria, Battle of Kish
Septuagint 23–4, 62
similes 101, 114, 144–5, 149, 158–9, 170–1, 174, 181, 183–5, 195–6, 203–4
  see also metaphors
single lines 69, 99, 104, 107–8, 202
Sodom 93, 129, 131, 136, 187–8, 191, 196–7, 199–200
soundplay 9, 19, 39–40, 52, 55, 57–8, 60, 62–3, 66, 76–8, 99, 123, 129, 134, 144, 146, 148, 180, 201, 206
  see also alliteration, assonance, consonance, rhyme
stanza 8, 69, 108–10, 170, 203
  see also structure
stress 40–2, 44, 46, 48, 55
strophe see stanza
structure, poetic 2, 8, 19, 60, 68–71, 91–2, 95, 100, 108–11, 117, 121, 127–8, 133, 137, 193, 200, 202–3, 205
  see also sections of poems, stanza
syllable counts 44

synonymy 75, 79, 82, 91
syntactic dependency *see* enjambment, mixing
syntax 14, 21, 28-9, 38-9, 44, 49-55, 71, 74, 77-8, 86-91, 94, 142
  poetic constraints on 49-55
Syro-Ephraimite War 124, 168, 179

terminal modification 34, 67, 100, 108, 134, 170
  see also closure
terseness 48, 53
Tiglath-Pileser III 179
  see also Assyria
transformation, syntactic 87-8, 202
  contrast in mood 88
  nominal-verbal 88, 171
  positive-negative 88-9
  subject-object 88-90, 92, 97
tricolon *see* triplet

triplet 18, 30-1, 36, 48, 53, 63-7, 70, 97-105, 107-8, 111-12, 118, 121, 124, 129, 135, 170, 173-4, 187

Ugaritic 8, 39, 41, 46, 58, 91, 150, 169, 175

verse paragraphs 8, 109
vignettes 135, 204
  see also narrativity
Vulgate 24

Whitman, Walt 15, 29, 122
wisdom tradition 127, 132, 136, 206
word counts 44-9
word pairs 60, 64, 79, 80-1, 102, 113, 118, 121-2, 125, 130, 134-5, 154, 160, 172, 178
wordplay 53, 89, 102, 125, 136, 149, 153, 163, 190, 205
  see also double entendre, puns